THE VAULT GUIDE
TO THE TOP 25 BANKING EMPLOYERS

2009 European Edition

is made possible through the generous support of the following sponsors:

VAULT career library

J.P.Morgan

LEHMAN BROTHERS

Merrill Lynch

BARCLAYS CAPITAL

5 The North Colonnade
Canary Wharf
London, E14 4BB
United Kingdom
Tel: +44 (0) 20 7623 2323
www.barcap.com

The Stats

Employer Type: Public Company
Ticker Symbol: BARC (LSE); BCS
(NYSE); 8642 (Tokyo)
Group Chief Executive: Robert "Bob"
Diamond Jr
2007 Revenue: £23bn
2007 Profit: £5bn
2006 Revenue: £22bn
2006 Profit: £5.1bn
No. of Employees: 5,500 in Europe
No. of Offices: Locations in 29 countries

Departments

Distribution • E-commerce • Financing •
Indices • Investment Banking • Private
Equity • Research • Risk Management

European Locations

London (HQ)
France • Germany • Ireland • Italy • The
Netherlands • Portugal • Spain•
Switzerland • United Kingdom

Key Competitors

Goldman Sachs • J.P. Morgan •
Lehman Brothers • Merrill Lynch

Employment Contact

www.barcap.com/campusrecruitment

See the Vault profile on Page 104

WE LIKE TO CULTIVATE AN ENTREPRENEURIAL SPIRIT.

YOU, FOR EXAMPLE

EXPECT EXCELLENCE

In just 11 years, here at Barclays Capital, we've grown from a new operation into one of the world's leading investment banks.

And that's something you can't do by committee. Instead, we encourage our people to have ideas and run with them. To exercise their autonomy. To follow their commercial instincts. You could say that entrepreneurialism is our watchword. (You see, even with our watchword we like to think big.) To find out more, visit barcap.com/expectexcellence

barcap.com/expectexcellence   EARN SUCCESS EVERY DAY

BARCLAYS WEALTH

Interesting Fact :

" Barclays Wealth's global footprint means that graduates have 16 locations worldwide to choose from. "

THE FUTURE OF PRIVATE BANKING.
WORK. WHAT'S IT TO YOU?

As one of the leading international wealth management businesses, we serve high net worth, affluent and corporate clients on a global basis. Our Private Banking businesses, which span Europe, the Middle East, Africa and Asia with a growing presence in the Americas, are the core of our long-term growth.

We are looking for graduates keen to build a long-term career in the field of Private Banking, and who have the passion to build the investment, banking and client facing skills required to be successful in this challenging arena. If you have what it takes, our three year structured training programme offers you the opportunity to obtain the CFA™, gain valuable international experience through overseas placements, and to be stretched by our highly experienced team. Regardless of your nationality and place of study, we have opportunities available in the UK, Switzerland, Monaco, Spain, Italy, UAE, India, Singapore and Hong Kong.

For more information about our analyst and associate opportunities, and to apply online, please visit barclayswealth.com/think

Barclays Wealth is the wealth management division of Barclays and operates through Barclays Bank PLC and its subsidiaries. Barclays Bank PLC is registered in England and authorised and regulated by the Financial Services Authority. Registered No: 1026167. Registered office: 1 Churchill Place, London E14 5HP.

AGE AWARE We are. Are you?

We'll judge you on your ability and nothing else.

BARCLAYS WEALTH

BBVA S.A.

Plaza de San Nicolás, 4
48005 Bilbao (Vizcaya),
Spain
Tel: +34 91 374 60 00
www.bbva.com

The Stats

Employer Type: Public Company
Ticker Symbol: BBVA (Madrid); BBV (NYSE)
Chairman: Francisco González
2007 Revenue: €18.1bn
2007 Profit: €6.0bn
2006 Revenue: €15.7bn
2006 Profit: €4.7bn
No. of Employees: 111,913
No. of Offices: 8,028 in 31 countries

Divisions

Asset Management • Corporate Banking • Finance • Global Markets • Human Resources • Investment Banking • Marketing and Communication • Private Banking • Retail Banking • Technology and Computing Systems • Wholesale Banking

Locations in Europe

Bilbao (HQ)
Belgium • France • Germany • Italy • Portugal • Russia • Spain • Switzerland • United Kingdom

Key Competitors

Banco Sabadell • Banco Santander

Employment Contact

www.bbva.com
(Click on "Employment")

See the Vault profile on Page 200

BBVA, one of the Top Companies for Leaders developing talent worldwide.

Fortune, October 2007.

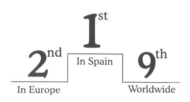

2nd
In Europe

1st
In Spain

9th
Worldwide

Being committed to people has led us to the top.

These awards acknowledges BBVA's international role as one of the world's best companies, with a commitment to talent, and of which you can be part.

Join us at www.bbva.com

adelante.

BNP PARIBAS GROUP

16, Boulevard des Italiens
Paris, 75009
France
Tel: +33 1 40 14 45 46
www.bnpparibas.com

The Stats

Employer Type: Public Company
Ticker Symbol: BNP (Euronext Paris);
8664 (Tokyo)
Chairman: Baudouin Prot
2007 Revenue: €12.2bn
2007 Profit: €7.8bn
2006 Revenue: €10.8bn
2006 Profit: €7.3bn
2007 No. of Employees: 162,700
2006 No. of Employees: 140,000
No. of Offices: 2,200 branches

Departments

Asset Management and Services •
BNP Paribas Capital (Private Equity) •
Corporate and Investment Banking •
Retail Banking

European Locations

Paris (HQ)
Austria • Belgium • Bulgaria • Cyprus •
Czech Republic • France • Germany •
Greece • Hungary • Ireland • Italy •
Jersey • Luxembourg • Monaco •
Norway • The Netherlands • Poland •
Portugal • Romania • Russia • Serbia
and Montenegro • Slovakia • Spain •
Sweden • Switzerland • Turkey •
Ukraine • United Kingdom

Key Competitors

Crédit Agricole • Lazard • Société
Générale

Employment Contact

careers.bnpparibas.com
www.recrutement.bnpparibas.com

See the Vault profile on Page 126

LOVE MODELS

WHEN YOU HEAR SOPHISTICATED MODELS, DO YOU THINK OF ADVANCED MATHEMATICAL STRATEGIES FOR IMPROVING TRADING PERFORMANCE?

We do. Our focus on providing our clients with technically sophisticated, bespoke banking solutions has helped us grow into one of the world's leading investment banks. And our strong balance sheet and rigorous risk management* has us well placed for the future – but what will drive our ongoing success and define our appeal to clients in new and expanding markets?

The answer is simple – ideas. Having the vision and confidence to invest in ideas, and the patience to let them flourish is what will make a great firm even better. That's why, even in the face of difficult market conditions, we're still growing, still innovating and still looking for people like you to make us even better. If you are looking for a career that truly values creative thinking, quantitative ability and entrepreneurial spirit, then invest in a career with BNP Paribas.

*One of only four banks worldwide to be rated AA+ by Standard & Poor's

Investing in ideas
graduates.bnpparibas.com

BNP PARIBAS
CORPORATE & INVESTMENT BANKING

CITI

Citigroup Centre
33 Canada Square
Canary Wharf
London, E14 5LB
United Kingdom
Tel: +44 (0) 20 7986 4000
www.citigroup.com

The Stats

Employer Type: Public Company
Ticker Symbol: C (NYSE)
Chief Executive: Vikram Pandit
2007 Revenue: $81.6bn
2007 Profit: $3.61bn
2006 Revenue: $89.6bn
2006 Profit: $21.5bn
No. of Employees: 320,000
No. of Offices: 7,500 offices in 104 countries on six continents

Departments

Consumer Banking • Global Cards •
Global Wealth Management •
Institutional Clients Group

European Locations

London (European HQ)
Belgium • Bulgaria • Czech Republic •
France • Germany • Hungary • Ireland •
Italy • Luxembourg • Poland • Romania •
Slovakia • Spain • Sweden • Switzerland •
Ukraine • United Kingdom

Key Competitors

Goldman Sachs • J.P. Morgan • Merrill Lynch • Morgan Stanley

Employment Contact

www.careers.citigroup.com

See the Vault profile on Page 94

OPPORTUNITY NEVER SLEEPS.

Dreams. **Realities.**

In California, after a hard day studying, Jen's finally ready to rest. Three time zones away, in New York, Lisa – Jen's future mentor – is shaking hands on funding for an irrigation project in Western Africa. Meanwhile, half a world away, Investment Banking Associate Rajid is returning from a meeting with government officials in Kazakhstan. At any moment, someone in our global firm is opening new markets. Someone's closing deals. Someone's gaining skills to pass on to the next generation. A career with us is full of variety and challenge. Because Jen isn't working for us yet, but we've already been working for her. That's why, at Citi, opportunity never sleeps. oncampus.citi.com

Citi never sleeps‚

CREDIT SUISSE

Interesting Fact :

     66 Since 2007, Credit Suisse's premises in London and Frankfurt - two of the Bank's major centers in Europe - have relied exclusively on renewable, "green" power. In Switzerland, Credit Suisse is one of the principle purchasers of "green" electricity. **99**

Uetlibergstrasse 231
P.O. Box 700
CH 8070 Zurich
Switzerland
Tel: +41 1 332 6400

1 Cabot Square
London, E14 4QJ
United Kingdom
Tel: +44 (0)20 7888 8888

The Stats

Employer Type: Public Company
Ticker Symbol: CSGN (SWX); CS (NYSE)
Group Chief Executive: Brady W. Dougan
IB Chief Executive: Paul Calello
2007 Revenue: €39bn
2007 Profit: €7.7bn
2006 Revenue: CHF 38.6bn
2006 Profit: CHF 11.3bn
No. of Employees: 45,000
No. of Offices: 57

Departments

Asset Management • Investment Banking • Private Banking

European Locations*

*Not limited to IB locations

Zurich (Global HQ)
Austria • Czech Republic • Denmark • France • Germany • Gibraltar • Greece • Guernsey • Hungary • Italy • Jersey • Lichtenstein • Luxembourg • Monaco • The Netherlands • Poland • Portugal • Russia • Slovakia • Spain • Sweden • Switzerland • Ukraine • United Kingdom

Key Competitors

Lehman Brothers • Merrill Lynch • Morgan Stanley • UBS

Employment Contact

www.credit-suisse.com/careers

For Graduate programmes

graduate.recruitment@credit-suisse.com

See the Vault profile on Page 66

Some think
one point of view.

**We think
thousands
of opinions.**

There's great strength in keeping an open mind.
A great wisdom to be had from sharing personal
experience. And that's why we trust our people to
work more independently, using their best judgement
to innovate and influence our business.

Take a closer look at **www.credit-suisse.com/careers**

Thinking New Perspectives.

CREDIT SUISSE

ESADE BUSINESS SCHOOL

Interesting Fact :

" On-campus diversity is a highly enriching element of The ESADE MBA enabling our students to fine tune their multicultural leadership competencies and global outlook. Of the 150 candidates in our Class of 2009 Full Time MBA programmes, 83% are international students representing over 40 countries across all geographic regions. "

FIDELITY INTERNATIONAL

Interesting Fact :

" Did you know Fidelity International is half owned by the Johnson family and half owned by employee shareholders? "

J.P. MORGAN INVESTMENT BANK

Interesting Fact :

66 On Monday April 14, 1913, the day of J.P. Morgan's funeral, the New York Stock Exchange was closed until noon in his honor. 99

10 Aldermanbury
London, EC2V 7RF
United Kingdom
Tel: +44 (0)20 7742 4000
www.jpmorgan.com

The Stats

Employer Type: Subsidiary of
JPMorgan Chase & Co (JPM)
Ticker Symbol: JPM (NYSE)
Chief Executive: Jamie Dimon
IB co-Chief Executives:
Steve Black, Bill Winters
2007 Revenue: $71.4bn
2007 Profit: $15.4bn
2006 Revenue: $62.0bn
2006 Profit: $14.4bn
No. of Employees: 180,000
No. of IB Employees: 26,000
No. of Offices: 60+

Departments

Advisory • Debt and Equity
Underwriting • Institutional Equities •
Market Making • Prime Brokerage •
M&A • Research • Restructuring •
Trading and Investing

European Locations

London (European HQ)
Belgium • Czech Republic • France •
Germany • Greece • Italy • The
Netherlands • Portugal • Russia • Spain •
Sweden • Switzerland • Turkey • United
Kingdom

Key Competitors

Goldman Sachs • Merrill Lynch •
Morgan Stanley

Employment Contact

www.jpmorgan.com/careers

See the Vault profile on Page 28

VAULT career library

J.P.Morgan

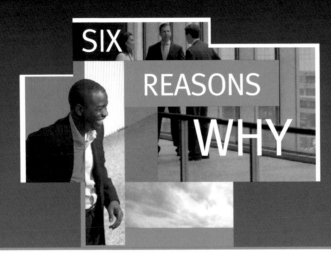

SIX REASONS WHY

Some investment banks will give you a good reason or two to join them. At J.P. Morgan, we'll give you six: Our scale, scope and prestige; our reputation as a business innovator; the quality of training and development; the chance to make a personal impact; the exceptional quality of our work and the spirit of cooperation and teamwork. Still need convincing? Visit our website and meet us on campus. **This is where you need to be.**

jpmorgan.com/careers

LEHMAN BROTHERS

25 Bank Street
London, E14 5LE
United Kingdom
Tel: +44 (0)20 7102 1000
www.lehman.com

The Stats

Employer Type: Public Company
Ticker Symbol: LEH (NYSE)
Chairman and Chief Executive:
Richard S. Fuld Jr.
2007 Revenue: $19.3bn
2007 Profit: $4.2bn
2006 Revenue: $17.6bn
2006 Profit: $4bn
No. of Employees: 25,000+
No. of Offices: 55

Departments

Capital Markets • Corporate Division •
Investment Banking • Investment
Management

European Locations

London (European HQ)
France • Germany • Italy • Luxembourg •
The Netherlands • Russia • Spain •
Sweden • Switzerland • United Kingdom

Key Competitors

Goldman Sachs • Merrill Lynch •
Morgan Stanley

Employment Contact

www.lehman.com/careers

See the Vault profile on Page 58

LEHMAN BROTHERS

Drive the growth of multinational companies. Keep worldwide commerce on the move. Advise global business leaders. At Lehman Brothers, it's all in a day's work.

With over 50 principal offices in 28 countries, Lehman Brothers serves the financial needs of corporations, governments, private equity firms, hedge funds and high net worth individuals globally. By serving them, our reach extends far beyond numbers.

Your skills can take you places at Lehman Brothers. Join us today and shape the businesses of tomorrow.

Find out more about our opportunities at www.lehman.com/careers

A Career That Moves The World

MERRILL LYNCH

Financial Centre
2 King Edward Street
London, EC1A 1HQ
United Kingdom
Tel: +44 (0)20 7743 4457
www.ml.com

European Locations

London (European HQ)
Belgium • France • Germany • Ireland • Italy • Luxembourg • Monaco • The Netherlands • Poland • Portugal • Spain • Sweden • Switzerland • Turkey • United Kingdom

The Stats

Employer Type: Public Company
Ticker Symbol: MER (NYSE)
Chief Executive: John A. Thain
2007 Revenue: $11.3bn
2007 Profit (Loss): ($8.6bn)
2006 Revenue: $33.7bn
2006 Profit: $7.09bn
No. of Employees: 60,000+
No. of Offices: 800+

Key Competitors

Goldman Sachs • J.P. Morgan • Morgan Stanley

Employment Contact

www.ml.com/careers/europe
Campus Recruitment Hotline
Tel: +44 (0)20 7 996 3528

Departments

Banking • Corporate and Enterprise Groups (including Technology and HR) • Global Markets and Investment Banking • Global Research • Global Wealth Management

See the Vault profile on Page 38

global reputation

[**limitless potential**]

growth and success

inspiring colleagues

Merrill Lynch is one of the world's leading wealth management, capital markets and advisory companies. Our iconic brand and global capabilities offer you the chance to realise your potential whilst working side-by-side with thought leaders on projects of breathtaking scope and complexity. Join us and you can also benefit from a performance-based culture of excellence, where respect for the individual, commitment to breakthrough, big-picture thinking and enduring values create an environment for your continued growth and success.

We must receive your completed application by **Friday 31st October 2008** for the Full-Time programme and **Monday 15th December 2008** for the Summer Internship programme.

For more information or to apply online, please visit **ml.com/careers/europe**

TOP 100
THE TIMES
GRADUATE EMPLOYERS

ml.com/careers/europe

Merrill Lynch is an equal opportunity employer.

Global Markets & Investment Banking | Global Research | Global Wealth Management   **Merrill Lynch**

THE ROYAL BANK OF SCOTLAND GROUP

Interesting Fact :

❝ We invest more than £1 million every week in deserving causes. ❞

RBS
36 St. Andrews Square
Edinburgh, EH2 2YB
United Kingdom
Tel: + 44 (0) 131 556 8555
www.rbs.com

The Stats

Employer Type: Public Company
Ticker Symbol: RBS (LSE)
Chairman: Sir Thomas F.W. McKillop
Group Chief Executive: Sir Frederick A. Goodwin
2007 Revenue: £31.1bn
2007 Profit: £7.7bn
2006 Revenue: £28bn
2006 Profit: £6.5bn
No. of Employees: 170,000
No. of Offices: 2,720 offices and branches

Departments

ABN AMRO • Global Markets • Group Manufacturing • Regional Markets • Group Functions • RBS Insurance

European Locations

Edinburgh (Global HQ)
Austria • Belgium • Czech Republic • Denmark • Finland • France • Germany • Gibraltar • Greece • Italy • Ireland • Luxembourg • Monaco • The Netherlands • Norway • Poland • Portugal • Romania • Russian Federation • Slovakia • Spain • Sweden • Switzerland • Turkey • United Kingdom

Key Competitors

Barclays • Citi • HSBC Holdings

Employment Contact

Graduate recruitment RBS Group:
www.makeitrbs.com

Graduate recruitment Global Markets:
www.rbs.com/gmgraduates
Careers: www.rbs.com/careers

See the Vault profile on Page 116

STEPHEN
Joined July 2007
ANALYST LEVERAGE FINANCE
New York

'**STIMULATING** work **DYNAMIC GROWTH,** and a formidable **PRESENCE** in all major financial centres – that's what drew me to **GLOBAL MARKETS.**'

Make it happen in Global Markets

We are a dynamic, fast-paced business, rich with opportunity. We have achieved our leading position in global banking by setting our sights high. We thrive thanks to people who bring new ideas and who enjoy the challenge of stretching their capabilities. People who want to grow, with us.

STANDARD CHARTERED BANK

1 Aldermanbury Square
London
EC2V 7SB
United Kingdom
Tel: +44 (0) 207 280 7500
www.standardchartered.com

The Stats

Employer Type: Public Company
Ticker Symbol: STAN (LSE)
Chairman: Mervyn Davies
2007 Revenue: $11.1bn
2007 Profit: $2.9bn
2006 Revenue: $8.62bn
2006 Profit: $2.35bn
No. of Employees: 54,000
No. of Offices: 1,299

Divisions

Consumer Banking • Corporate Real Estate Services • Finance • Human Resources • Legal and Compliance and Assurance • Technology and Operations • Wholesale Banking

European Locations

London (European HQ)
France • Jersey • Switzerland • United Kingdom

Employment Contact

careers.standardchartered.com

See the Vault profile on Page 372

You have a desire to learn we provide the opportunities

Go places with the world's best international bank.

International Graduate Programme.

At Standard Chartered Bank, we have a history of fast tracking careers to groom managers of tomorrow. As a rapidly growing bank with strong financial performance and robust foundation for growth, we provide a wealth of career opportunities.

We are looking to attract highly ambitious, intelligent, creative and achievement orientated graduates to join our International Graduate Programme. If you have a desire to build an extraordinary career in Banking, please visit us at www.standardchartered.com/graduates.

Standard Chartered

| Go Places |

www.standardchartered.com/graduates

TEACH FIRST

London
14 Heron Quay,
Canary Wharf,
London
E14 4JB
Tel: 0844 880 1800
Fax: 020 7900 3304

Midlands
Sandwell Academy,
Halfords Lane,
West Bromwich,
West Midlands
B71 4LG
Tel: 0121 5000 760
Fax: 020 7900 3304

North West
40 Princess Street,
Manchester
M1 6DE
Tel: 0161 234 0073
Fax: 0161 234 0074

CEO & Founder: Brett Wigdortz

Locations

Teach First works with schools in the following Local Authorities

London
Barking and Dagenham • Barnet • Bexley • Brent • Bromley • Croydon • Ealing • Greenwich • Hackney • Hammersmith and Fulham • Haringey • Hillingdon • Hounslow • Islington • Kensington and Chelsea • Lambeth • Lewisham • Redbridge • Southwark • Tower Hamlets • Waltham Forest • Westminster

Midlands
Birmingham • Enfield • Nottingham • Sandwell • Solihull • Walsall

North West
Bolton • Manchester • Merton • Newham • Oldham • Rochdale • Salford • Tameside • Trafford

Employment Contact

http://graduates.teachfirst.org.uk/

VAULT career library

Will you...

Do something different?
Accelerate your career?
Put something back?
Inspire a generation?
Change lives?
Take a lead?

Whatever you do,
Teach First.

Teach First
LEARNING TO LEAD

www.teachfirst.org.uk

UBS INVESTMENT BANK

UBS Global Headquarters
Bahnhofstrasse. 45
P.O. Box CH-8098
Zurich
Switzerland
Tel: +41 (0) 11 234 11 11
www.ubs.com

The Stats

Employer Type: Public Company
Ticker Symbol: UBS (NYSE, VTX)
Chief Executive: Marcel Rohner
IB Chairman and Chief Executive:
Jerker Johansson
2007 Revenue: CHF 31.9bn
2007 Profit (Loss): (CHF 3.8bn)
2006 Revenue: CHF 47.7bn
2006 Profit: CHF 12.7bn
No. of Employees: 80,000+
No. of Offices: 50+

Departments

Business Banking • Currencies and
Commodities • Global Asset
Management • Global Wealth
Management • Investment Bank
(Equities, Finance, Fixed Income and
Money Markets, Global Asset
Management, Legal and Compliance)

European Locations

Zurich (Global HQ)
London (Investment Bank HQ)
Austria • Belgium • Channel Islands •
Cyprus • Czech Republic • France •
Germany • Greece • Ireland • Italy •
Luxembourg • Monaco • The
Netherlands • Poland • Portugal • Russia •
Spain • Sweden • Switzerland • Turkey •
United Kingdom

Key Competitors

Morgan Stanley • Merrill Lynch • Credit
Suisse • Lehman Brothers

Employment Contact

www.ubs.com/careers

See the Vault profile on Page 72

Together we...

We are proud to be one of the world's premier financial institutions. And we got there by ensuring we put clients first: our success is theirs. Alongside this we place a high value on individuals with entrepreneurial spirit, enthusiasm, passion and commitment. Because at UBS, you are an integral part of a global team. You will take on unique and interesting challenges in a competitive financial marketplace. And have the opportunity to perform on the global stage, in a role that can offer high visibility and a chance to show us what you are made of. Right from the start.

It starts with you: www.ubs.com/graduates

UBS is an Equal Opportunity Employer. We respect and seek to empower each individual and the diverse cultures, perspectives, skills and experiences within our workforce.

Wealth	Global Asset	Investment
Management	Management	Bank

 You & Us ❀ UBS

It's your life story.
It's your mission statement.
It's the key to the shiny new
penthouse of your future.
But until anyone actually sees it
it's just another sheet of A4.
Isn't it time to set your CV free?

guardianjobs
.co.uk

THE MEDIA'S WATCHING VAULT! HERE'S A SAMPLING OF OUR COVERAGE:

"A rich resource of company information for prospective employees worldwide: Vault's content is credible, trustworthy and most of all, interesting."
- *The Guardian*

"[Vault tells] prospective joiners what they really want to know about the culture, the interview process, the salaries and the job prospects."
- *Financial Times*

"Thanks to Vault, the truth about work is just a tap of your keyboard away."
- *The Telegraph*

"The best place on the Web to prepare for a job search"
- *Money magazine*

"A killer app."
- *The New York Times*

"Vault has a wealth of information about major employers and job-seeking strategies as well as comments from workers about their experiences at specific companies."
- *The Washington Post*

Vault Guide to the

Top 25 Banking Employers

· 2009 European Edition ·

For information about permission to reproduce selections from this book, contact Vault.com Ltd., 6 Baden Place, London, SE1 1YW, +44(0)20 7357 8553.

ISBN 13: 978-1-58131-608-7
ISBN 10: 1-58131-608-9
Printed in the United Kingdom

ACKNOWLEDGEMENTS

Thank you to everyone at Vault for their enormous help with this guide. Special thanks to Sarah Underwood, Nicole Kai Kobilansky, Eli Lee, Thomas Nutt, Marcy Lerner, Derek Loosevelt, Sila Cameselle Vila, Soy Panday, Amanda Woolf, Rochelle Mathieson, Harmandeep Singh, Graeme Buscke, Fernando Sdrigotti, Priya Kantaria, Gavin Woods and Djo Rahmoune.

We are especially grateful to the staff at all of the firms who helped with this book, and to the banking professionals who took the time out of their busy schedules to do our survey, to be interviewed, or to answer any and all of our questions.

TABLE OF CONTENTS

The Best of the Rest

A GUIDE TO THIS GUIDE

To understand how the information in our company profiles are organised, we have created a glossary of terms for you to refer to. This "Guide to this Guide" defines the terminology and section headers we use to present all the information our profiles feature.

Firm Facts

Locations: A listing of the company's offices, with the city (or cities) of its European headquarters bolded. We have only listed cities within Europe.

Departments and Divisions: Official departments and divisions that employ a significant portion of the firm's employees. Departments are listed in alphabetical order, regardless of their size and prominence.

Employment Contact: The name of the department, correspondence address, contact telephone number and/or website that the firm has identified as the best way for job-seekers and applicants to submit their CVs and/or answer any questions about the recruitment process and opportunities at the firm.

The Stats

Employer Type: The firm's classification as a publicly traded company, privately held company or subsidiary of a public or private company.

Ticker Symbol: The stock symbol of a public company on a specific stock exchange, as well as the exchange (s) on which the company's stock is traded.

Chairman, Chief Executive: The name and title of the leader(s) of the firm or group.

Revenue: The gross income (in the relevant currency) that the firm generated in the specified fiscal year(s). Some privately owned firms do not disclose this information. Numbers included are from the most recent year the information is available. Revenue is worldwide except where otherwise stated.

Net Profit: The return minus the costs made by the firm in the stated fiscal year. As with net revenue, some firms do not disclose this information. When information is available, profits given will be worldwide unless stated otherwise.

Employees: The total number of employees at a firm across all of its offices (unless otherwise specified). Some firms do not disclose this information. Figures from the most recent year the information are included if available.

No. of Offices: Worldwide except where otherwise stated.

Pluses and Minuses: The best and worst things, respectively, about working at the firm. Pluses and minuses are taken from the opinions of insiders based on our surveys and interviews.

The Buzz: When conducting our prestige survey, we asked respondents to include comments about the firms they were rating. Survey respondents were not able to comment on their own firm. We collected a sampling of these comments in The Buzz. We tried to include quotes that represented the common external perceptions of a given firm. The quotes may not always reflect what insiders say in our surveys and interviews. We think The Buzz is a way of gauging external opinion of a company.

The Profiles

The profiles are divided into five sections: *The Scoop, Getting Hired, Our Survey Says, Pluses and Minuses* and *The Buzz*.

The Scoop: The firm's history, clients, recent developments and other points of interest.

Getting Hired: Valuable information about any available internships and graduate programmes; qualifications the firm looks for in new associates and analysts, specific tips on getting hired as well as other notable aspects of the hiring process.

Our Survey Says: Actual quotes from surveys and interviews with current employees of the firm on such topics as a firm's culture, hours, travel requirements, salaries, training and more. Profiles of some firms do not include an Our Survey Says section.

INTRODUCTION

A sk anyone who has even remotely kept an eye on the headlines through 2007 and 2008 and they'll be quick to tell you that these two years have earned their place in the history of modern banking for numerous reasons. A series of major noteworthy events kicked off in the spring of 2007, sparked by the then potential takeover of ABN Amro by Britain's Barclays Bank. The Dutch bank was eventually acquired by a truly European trio of the Royal Bank of Scotland, Dutch Fortis and Spain's Santander, but first the business world was treated to a highly publicised game of cat and mouse.

Following on from this came the Jérôme Kerviel rogue trader scandal at France's Société Générale bank. The news, which broke in January 2008, was reported as the biggest ever case of fraud in European banking.

Then there is the US subprime mortgage crisis, which is having its direct effects in Europe. The British mortgage lender and bank Northern Rock almost collapsed in September 2007, only ten years after it was first floated on the LSE. The UK government had to dive in to save the institution, by taking it under "temporary" ownership in February 2008. This was only after Sir Richard Branson of the Virgin empire (all the time chaperoned by the government) courted the idea of taking over the bank himself.

As if banking crises hadn't come thick and fast already, not long after, there was the demise of Bear Stearns in the US and its subsequent acquisition by JPMorgan Chase. The dollar hit record lows, the euro reached record highs ... and through all this, Europe's age-old banking industry has persevered.

For the third European edition of the *Vault Guide to the Top 25 Banking Employers*, we are featuring 66 of Europe's top firms and are including prestige rankings for the top-25 firms, as selected by the employees of the banks who participated in our survey. The guide features both European banks and the European operations of leading international banks.

The profiles in our guide are based on industry surveys, research and extensive feedback from employees about everything from company culture to compensation, training, management, perks and benefits. They also offer their valuable perspective about interviews, internships and diversity at their firms.

Working on the third European edition of the *Vault Guide to the Top 25 Banking Employers* has been very rewarding. The guide has grown in leaps and bounds over its three editions, and you'll find it is a fantastic resource for anyone interested in pursuing a career in European banking.

Good luck.

Saba Haider, Editor

THE STATE OF EUROPEAN BANKING

T here has been so much drama in the European banking sector between 2007 and 2008 that it has, at times, made great television. In less than a year the world has seen the spectacular fall of banking giants, queues of angry customers outside a British bank for the first time since the 19th century, a massive rogue trader scandal in France, tens of thousands of job losses and stories of malicious rumours planted to stir trouble at international banks. Oh, and a global subprime crisis.

In the spring of 2007, Europe's banking sector was comfortably (and excitedly) busy with a series of mergers and acquisitions, and several large banks were set on eating each other whole. Italy's UniCredit paid more than 29 billion dollars in May last year for its smaller rival Capitalia, creating Europe's second-largest bank after HSBC. A fierce bidding war for Dutch bank ABN Amro also held the continent's attention, with Barclays pitting itself against a pan-European consortium comprised of the Royal Bank of Scotland, the Benelux's Fortis and Spanish banking giant Santander.

Yet once the US mortgage market hit the buffers in late spring 2007 and its impact began to spread around the world, lending of all sorts began to dry up, and many of the mighty looked set to fall.

This has caused significant shifts in European banking priorities. Previously in the mature markets of North America and Europe, lending had risen to historic highs, thanks to booming property prices and a general loosening of regulations. Whereas lenders would typically be allowed to borrow perhaps three times their income in a normal market, by 2006 they were borrowing on far higher multiples and at proportions above the value of their properties, with banks presuming that future rises in value would secure these loans.

> " Italy's UniCredit paid more than $29 billion in May 2007 for smaller rival Capitalia, creating Europe's second-largest bank after HSBC "

Known in the US as "Ninja" loans ("No income, no job"), the practice of issuing loans like this had not been seen in Western markets since the late 1980s, just before the last major house price crash. Since late 2007, conditions have worsened across almost all kinds of banking in Europe. The deterioration has taken place in several stages, each accompanied by a dramatic event. Some of the most notable events in this process demonstrate the fragility of customer confidence in retail banking and the dangers of over-borrowing (Northern Rock), the lack of proper oversight (Société Générale) and the dangerous contagion of market rumours (Bear Stearns and HBOS).

On the Northern Rocks

One of the UK's largest mortgage lenders, Northern Rock's business model was to lend money to customers that it had borrowed from other financial institutions at a lower interest rate. Once the credit crunch took hold in summer 2007, it could no longer borrow at these advantageous rates and began to run out of money. This news spread across the UK and its many thousands of account holders queued to retrieve their money in case it went bankrupt. Eventually the UK government took the bank over by nationalising it and bringing security to depositors, but leaving the UK taxpayer with a very large potential liability.

The practice of lending to on-lend, as exemplified by Northern Rock, is now under close scrutiny, with other European governments watching developments with interest. If their own major financial institutions were to get into trouble, would they do something similar — especially if the UK appears to have achieved good results? Regardless, the situation has still been an embarrassment for the UK's financial regulators — who have admitted that they failed to act in time — and for the British government, which had prided itself on solid financial management.

Société Kerviel

When 31-year-old French trader Jérôme Kerviel was found to have lost Société Générale almost five billion euros, it was reported by the media as the biggest fraud in financial history, wiping out profits from France's second-largest bank for 2007 and raising fears that the bank would be acquired by a rival sometime in the coming months or years. Some felt that the heavy stock market losses that happened in the same week as the news of the fraud broke were linked to it. Certainly it did nothing to bolster confidence in banks.

The scandal was seized upon by some commentators as evidence that the banking profession had sunk to new lows. "The banking industry used to have a reputation for honesty, trust and prudence," said Roger Steare, professor of organisational studies at the Cass Business School in London. "This latest scandal, on top of the massive losses in credit markets and the ongoing incidence of mis-selling to retail customers, indicates that there is a systematic deficit in ethical values within the banking industry."

The Société Générale case, however, was more about complexity and lack of oversight rather than about an ethical gap. Financial products have become so labyrinthine and pass through so many people's hands that it can be a Herculean task for individual banks to exactly know the state of their liabilities. These gaps in oversight were further evinced when major banks began to go public on writedowns that appeared to have come out of nowhere, even for bank employees who were paid to be in the know. In many cases, these writedowns went up and up in the course of their publication, as closer scrutiny was made of the exact value lost.

Europe is undergoing a period of turbulence, as in the US, where the older generation of banking managers who grew up in a relatively slow-paced environment, with a few, relatively straight-forward products, is giving way to a generation of managers with highly specialised IT skills, dealing with very complex financial instruments, with different risk

> ❝ The [SocGen] scandal was seized upon by some commentators as evidence the banking profession had sunk to new lows ❞

and reward parameters, operating outside the traditional geographical and financial boundaries. Learning how to avoid Jérôme Kerviel-style scenarios will be crucial for the bankers of tomorrow.

No picnic for this Bear

In the first couple of weeks after the subprime situation in the US hit the international headlines, the financial pages were reporting that Bear Stearns bank in the US had been forced to close two of its large mortgage lending operations because of bad debt. It was not alone, but it was taking a bigger and faster hit than many of the other banks.

Around nine months later, the problems had not gone away and Bear Stearns was effectively bankrupt. It was acquired by J.P. Morgan for a fraction of its value just a year earlier, putting the financial community on notice that even the big boys were not immune to disaster.

A couple of weeks later, Halifax Bank of Scotland (HBOS) in the UK found itself at the centre of an unexpected storm when rumours began to circulate that it was in trouble with bad debt and might have to be sold or go out of business. Its share price plunged. HBOS managers and directors kicked up a big fuss about how outrageous it was that unfounded rumours should be flying around. In a few days, the stock market price returned to normal and it emerged that several of the top directors had quickly bought hundreds of thousands of pounds worth of shares, while they were low, "to show support for the bank," as they put it. How fortunate for them that the share price quickly rose again...

In better times, such unfounded rumours would not have been given any credence. Today, it is only too possible to imagine a large bank crashing, thanks to Northern

Rock and Bear Stearns doing the previously unthinkable. The mood of anxiety in the banking profession had turned to desperation by spring 2008, as the scale of losses across the industry, both in money and jobs, became clear. By mid-March, industry experts were warning of 15 percent job losses in US and European investment banking firms. Research agency Experian estimated that as many as 200,000 jobs would disappear across the global financial services sector during 2008, with 65,000 having gone between August 2007 and the beginning of 2008. In total, 12 million people are employed in financial services in the US and Europe.

Restructuring work is writ large among the new opportunities for graduates in European banking. Many companies in various business sectors such as real estate, retail and indeed financial services are well-run and profitable enterprises with solid customer bases. However, they have over-borrowed and are facing cashflow difficulties as interest rates rise and lending becomes tighter. Banks have a major role to play in helping companies turn themselves around and regain stability.

At the same time, opportunities in the emerging markets of China, India, Russia and throughout Central and Eastern Europe, are providing new scope for many European banks. For example, in March 2008 Barclays paid 745 million dollars for Russia's Expobank, showing its appetite to do business in a country where lending is rising at 45 percent annually. Deutsche Bank formally launched itself in China in January 2008, as many fellow European banks have done in recent years.

Salaries available in the banking sector will still be among the highest in Europe, but the mood of buoyant optimism that has permeated the sector for the past five or more years has certainly diminished.

What many will find themselves doing this year is working to prevent losses and restructure companies. Many banks have been left with bad debt, from unwisely granted mortgages or from businesses that have failed. European banks are now shoring up their defences and trying not to allow more debt to accumulate. Graduates who understand how the banking landscape is changing and show awareness of the new priorities will find there is still a great range of opportunities in the industry.

The Vault 25
PRESTIGE RANKINGS
for 2009

RANKING METHODOLOGY

T he *Vault Guide to the Top 25 Banking Employers,* 2009 European edition, features 66 banking and financial services firms either based in or with significant operations in Europe. Our editors selected the firms from previous Vault surveys that gauged opinions of industry insiders and employed various factual data, including the size of a firm in terms of its revenue or assets, to determine if the firm qualifies as a top European banking employer. The firms identified were asked to distribute our online survey to relevant employees and many banks agreed to participate. The survey consisted of questions about life at the respective firm (or former firm) and asked participants to rate all of the listed firms being featured in the guide in terms of prestige.

In the spring of 2008, banking and finance professionals from nine banks across the UK and Europe took Vault's 2009 Top European Banking Employers Survey. The following firms participated in the survey this year: Citi, Goldman Sachs, HypoVereinsBank (HVB), ING, J.P. Morgan Investment Bank, Jefferies & Co., Lehman Brothers, Merrill Lynch and The Royal Bank of Scotland (RBS). Participants were asked to rate companies with which they were familiar on a scale of one to ten, with ten being the most prestigious. They were not allowed to rate their own employer. All surveys were completed anonymously by participants throughout the UK and Europe. For those companies that did not participate, Vault contacted employees at the respective firm(s) through other proprietary sources. Those professionals took the same survey as the employees at firms that participated.

Vault averaged the prestige scores given by the professionals for each of the firms in this guide and ranked the top-25 in order, with the highest score belonging to our No. 1 firm, Goldman Sachs. Banking giant Goldman received a score of 8.903, nearly one full point higher than the No. 2 firm, Morgan Stanley (8.198). Rounding out the top-five were J.P. Morgan Investment Bank (7.902) at No. 3, Merril Lynch (7.462) at No. 4 and Deutsche Bank AG (7.453) at No. 5. □

THE VAULT 25 • 2009

RANK	Firm	Score	European HQ
1	Goldman Sachs	8.9038	London
2	Morgan Stanley	8.1980	London
3	J.P. Morgan Investment Bank	7.9021	London
4	Merrill Lynch	7.4620	London
5	Deutsche Bank AG	7.4536	Frankfurt
6	The Blackstone Group	7.2661	London
7	Lehman Brothers	7.2316	London
8	Credit Suisse	6.9398	Zurich
9	UBS Investment Bank	6.9309	Zurich
10	NM Rothschild & Sons	6.6719	London
11	Lazard	6.4409	London
12	Citi	6.4219	London
13	Barclays Capital	6.2353	London
14	HSBC Holdings	6.0182	London
15	The Royal Bank of Scotland (RBS)	6.0000	Edinburgh
16	BNP Paribas	5.6176	Paris
17	Bank of America	5.2391	London
18	Société Générale	5.1835	Paris
19	Macquarie Bank	5.0000	London
20	Greenhill & Co	4.7245	London
21	Dresdner Kleinwort	4.7000	Frankfurt
22	Lloyds TSB	4.6250	London
23	ABN AMRO*	4.6010	Amsterdam
24	Bear Stearns & Co**	4.5705	London
25	UniCredit	4.4455	Milan

*ABN AMRO was acquired by RBS, Fortis and Santander in October 2007
** Bear Stearns was acquired by J.P. Morgan Chase in May 2008

GOLDMAN SACHS

Peterborough Court
133 Fleet Street
London, EC4A 2BB
United Kingdom
Tel: +44 (0) 207 774 1000
www.gs.com

The Stats

Employer Type: Public Company
Ticker Symbol: GS (NYSE)
Chief Executive: Lloyd C. Blankfein
2007 Revenue: $45.9bn
2007 Profit: $11.5bn
2006 Revenue: $37.6bn
2006 Profit: $9.5bn
No. of Employees: 31,495 worldwide
No. of Offices: 62 worldwide

Departments

Finance • Global Compliance • Global
Investment Research • Human Capital
Management • Investment Banking •
Investment Management • Legal and
Management Controls • Merchant
Banking/Private Equity • Operations •
Securities • Services • Technology

European Locations

London (European HQ)
France • Germany • Ireland • Italy •
Russia • Spain • Sweden • Switzerland •
United Kingdom

Key Competitors

J.P. Morgan
Merrill Lynch
Morgan Stanley

Employment Contact

www.gs.com/careers

Pluses

• "Very smart but humble people"
• "Very strong culture"

Minuses

• "Work-life balance could be addressed
  further"
• "Reduce the number of hours"

THE BUZZ
WHAT EMPLOYEES AT OTHER FIRMS ARE SAYING

• "Cream of the investment banks; always
  seem to get things right"
• "The smartest firm on the street"
• "They think of people only as a
  number"
• "Good if you don't mind not having a
  life"

VAULT career
library

THE SCOOP

G oldman Sachs is an industry leader and has long been regarded by graduates as the number one destination for anyone with aspirations of a career in banking. The company's prestigious investment banking division serves clients in the industrial, consumer, natural resources, health care, financial institutions, real estate, special products, technology, media and telecommunications industries.

The world-renowned firm offers financial advisory services for Mergers & Acquisitions (M&A), divestitures and debt and equity capital. In 2007, Goldman Sachs ranked as the number one M&A advisor globally according to Thomson Financial, a ranking it has, impressively, held every year since 1997. In European M&A, the bank was ranked third in 2007, behind Morgan Stanley and UBS. However, as it is working on some of the biggest European deals announced in 2008, it is likely that the firm will chart higher in 2008 year-end European M&A rankings.

Founded in the US in 1869, Goldman Sachs (GS) opened its first European office in London in 1970. Additional European offices later opened in Frankfurt, Paris, Madrid, Geneva, Zurich, Milan, Dublin, Moscow and Stockholm. Goldman's London office is the hub of its European operations and permanently employs approximately 5,500 people. The firm's business arms include investment banking, trading and principal investments, asset management and securities services.

Escaping the crunch?

Goldman Sachs managed to avoid the drastic losses that plagued many of its rivals during the credit crunch experienced in 2007 and 2008. As *The New York Times* commented in November 2007, Goldman Sachs "got it so right when everyone else was getting it so wrong". One key strategy that helped the bank stay afloat while others drowned was that in late 2006, its executives astutely decided to reduce its stockpile of mortgages and mortgage-related securities and buy insurance against further losses. By the time the credit crisis hit in July 2007, Goldman had offloaded many of the risky mortgage products that other banks had blithely continued to sell. This allowed it to register a strong performance while other banks lost their footing.

No-one gets out alive

That said, things began to look ropey for Goldman in August 2007, when the firm revealed that its Global Opportunities Fund needed a three billion US dollar bailout after its value was dragged down from approximately five billion to three billion dollars on the back of market volatility. Along with many other qualitative funds which run on computer models, this hedge fund suffered badly. However, Goldman Sachs looked at the underlying value of the stocks in the fund and was convinced the fundamentals would bounce back. As a result, it put more of its own money into the fund which reassured co-investors and the fund traded back up.

However, with the US recession leading to a slowing in global growth in 2008, analysts predicted that Goldman's businesses would experience tougher conditions. Specifically, after its strong 2007 earnings in mortgages, private equity-related activities and securitisation, it was predicted that in 2008 the gap would narrow between Goldman and its competitors. At the end of 2007, the group's chief financial officer, David Viniar, finally announced that Goldman Sachs was becoming more "cautious" about profit forecasts.

As part of its annual performance review conducted among its staff, Goldman Sachs culled five percent of its "underperforming" 31,500-strong workforce in January 2008.

The expected profit drop finally arrived not long after, in March 2008, when Goldman announced a two billion dollar writedown. Approximately one billion dollars of this came from losses on mortgage loans and securities whilst a further billion or so dollars of loss were of non-investment grade credit.

> " Goldman Sachs 'got it right when everyone else got it so wrong' "

This drop was, however, less steep than analysts had forecast. One of the problems afflicting Goldman was the declining value of its 4.9 percent stake in the Industrial and Commercial Bank of China (ICBC), whose share price has dropped considerably since its IPO in 2006. Goldman invested 2.3 billion dollars for its minority shareholding in the Chinese bank, whose underperformance is a challenge to the group.

The Goldman touch

By mid-June 2008, Goldman had managed to beat analyst expectations of low earnings. Compared to other banks, Goldman had bounced back and showed off its ability to offset credit crisis-linked declines. The bank's securities services performed particularly strongly, with reports suggesting that Goldman was picking up market share from Bear Stearns, which collapsed in March 2008. By the middle of 2008, even the Industrial and Commercial Bank of China had rallied and was doing Goldman proud, with a gain of 214 million dollars reported on the investment.

The company had more to boast about as 2008 continued. It was announced that the tough banking giant had nabbed the top spot for Global M&A in 2007, by volume of deals, at 1.3 trillion dollars for 418 deals. The bank was placed lower, but still did well when it came to European M&A, for which it charted 700 billion US dollars worth of deals in 2007. Out of the Top 20 Global Financial Institutions, Goldman ranked 17th by market value as of March 31, 2008, at 41.6 billion euros. In May 2008, *The Financial Times* reported that Goldman Sachs had also scooped the top spot for top brokers covering stocks in the US, winning "by virtue of its impressive range of coverage and the strength of its analysts across all areas it covers". Merrill Lynch and Citigroup, however, were not far behind it.

Gold rush

In the past, Goldman's great performances have equalled big bonuses for its employees. According to a December 2006 report, company chief executive Lloyd C. Blankfein received a 53.4 million dollar bonus that year, the highest ever given to a banking executive. Blankfein smashed his own record when he took home a 68.5 million dollar bonus in 2007, as the firm passed through the credit crisis relatively unscathed. That said, windfalls have varied between Goldman's American and European employees. Like most US-based banks in Europe, Goldman pays bonuses in US dollars and many European staffers who didn't link their bonuses to average exchange rates saw their total haul slip behind their American counterparts' year-end gifts, as the dollar further weakened against the Euro and the British pound.

Sour Kraus

An internal memo from Goldman Sachs' chief executive Lloyd Blankfein revealed in March 2008 that the co-head of the firm's investment management division, Peter Kraus, was to retire at the end of that month. Among Kraus' achievements is the development of the firm's investment management business into a world leader, which manages close to one trillion dollars. The group has flourished for the past decade, seeing almost entirely organic growth of 30 percent a year and today it towers above its humble roots as a small collection of money market funds. The business has had its fingers burned a little between late 2007 and early 2008, thanks to weak performances by several in-house hedge funds. Internal sources have said that Kraus's retirement is unrelated to this. Though he retired from his chief post, Kraus stayed on with the banking giant as a senior director.

Assertive in Asia

Despite the credit squeeze of early and mid-2008, pressing on with its Asian expansion was on the cards for the bank. *The Financial Times* reported in June 2008 that Goldman Sachs was increasingly counting on Asia and its key economies of

China and India for revenue streams. To this end, the bank sent one of its top European dealmakers, Richard Campbell-Breeden, to Hong Kong to co-head its Asian M&A practice. He was hardly alone — a further 15 senior bankers relocated or were recruited to Goldman's Asian securities division.

10,000 women

Amidst all this, the bank has not forgotten its benevolent side. In one of the largest philanthropic undertakings in the history of Wall Street, Goldman Sachs announced in March 2008 the launch of its altruistic 10,000 Women initiative. The 100 million dollar scheme aims to give women in the developing world access to business and management education. Particularly targeting women already involved in small businesses in developing countries, the drive will provide training in marketing, e-commerce, accounting and accessing capital. Speaking in *The Financial Times*, Lloyd Blankfein said, "10,000 Women focuses on a critical yet often overlooked area where we believe Goldman Sachs can use its resources and convening power to help build the foundation to expand the ranks of businesswomen, managers and entrepreneurs around the world."

GETTING HIRED

Choice of beginnings

Your employment with Goldman Sachs can begin in several ways: you can start as an intern, a new analyst, a new associate, or as an experienced hire. For all of these levels you can apply online — simply click the "Apply Now" link in the top right of the company careers page at www.gs.com/careers.

If it's an internship you're after, Goldman Sachs offers ten-week summer internships in its primary locations across the world with a view to giving people an idea of what goes on at the company day-to-day. If you're currently pursuing a university degree then you're at summer analyst level, while the summer associate internship is designed for candidates working towards MBAs or advanced degrees.

Goldman Sachs also provides a selection of short Spring programmes of between three days and two weeks. These are for students either in their first year of a three-year degree or second year of a four-year degree. Alternatively, a small number of "unique" internships are also available, for three, six or even 12 months. Take a look at the "Unique Internships" link on the company website for more information.

Summer internships kick off with an orientation to the entire firm, an introduction to its culture and a look at the perks of working for Goldman Sachs. This is followed by division-specific training. Throughout the programme, you'll have a mentor and a "buddy" to lend you assistance and guidance.

The intern way in

For internships you can expect two rounds of interviews, says an intern in London. "The first round is a general 30-minute interview and an aptitude test in numerical and verbal reasoning," he notes. "The second round typically consists of up to four 30-minute interviews back to back." Often these will be with senior figures in the firm, such as vice presidents or associates.

A first year associate also based in London points out that the interview process varies hugely between departments. For the technology department, "two rounds of interviews are carried out roughly a week apart." The first round includes a "technical interview followed by a general competency interview," while the second round includes a "group 'crisis management' interview and a technical interview."

In terms of what's covered in the interviews, according to an associate in the Paris office, "the topics include one's motivation for being a banker at Goldman Sachs, technical skills and cultural fit, together with teamwork and leadership experiences."

What are you getting yourself into?

Internships are a central recruiting tool for Goldman Sachs. The firm "extends full-time offers to 75 percent of interns," we are told by insiders. Emphatically, "it is much more difficult to enter as a graduate," says one first-year analyst in London. Participation in an internship shows an "interest in and a desire to understand the industry and the company," adds a team leader in London.

Described by one second-year analyst as "a ten-week interview," the internship process makes it "much easier to get hired." Looking beyond landing the job, the experience an internship gives you "is of great help in the first period as a full-time employee — I worked on everything a full-time analyst would, including some live transactions" says a member of the investment banking team. However, the bank is keen to make it clear it also frequently hires students for full-time roles who have not taken part in its summer internship programme.

Analyst this!

If you want to jump right in as a full-time analyst, you can be reassured that your choice of degree discipline is not important — Goldman Sachs will consider economists and historians equally, provided you can prove you have an interest in financial markets. The firm's recruitment ethos says it is "built upon our belief that a candidate's understanding of the Goldman Sachs culture is as important as the skills and talent she or he can bring to the firm."

The interview process will give you an opportunity to meet many of the professionals with whom you may end up working. At the first round, you will typically talk about your past experience and achievements, while the second round will be more technical and assess how good a fit you are for the department you applied for. If you're taken on as an analyst, you'll be treated to ongoing developmental assignments throughout your years in the position, as well as exposure to multiple disciplines. All in, the firm offers very good opportunities for mobility in a plethora of different directions from the beginning.

By association

To become an associate at Goldman Sachs, you can apply directly if you have an MBA under your belt as well as two to five years of relevant work experience. Analysts can also be promoted to associates once they have achieved a certain professional standing within the firm. To apply for an associate position, you will typically have two interviews. In them, Goldman Sachs will be trying to gauge your compatibility with its particular business areas as well as testing your technical knowledge. In general, the company says that an associate's role is a mainline to leadership positions, so your opportunities to explore the career path you would like are well provided for by the firm's formal mobility process.

OUR SURVEY SAYS

Live to work, work to live

Hours worked per week can range from 50 to 80, with one investment banker in London boasting he worked "over 100 hours" one week. "Depending on the projects on which we are staffed, we can get extremely little sleep," he tells us. A first-year programming analyst says that "set hours do not really appear to be an issue," explaining "the emphasis is more on productivity and getting things done." Working at weekends is a frequent occurrence, respondents say, with one simply adding that late hours "come with the job."

"I generally think we work more hours than peers at other banks," a London-based investment banker in his second year says, "but given the relaxed team atmosphere there is some flexibility left for a social life." On the other hand, hours worked do vary strongly between departments. Certain areas of the firm, like investment banking, work long hours and "give the public the impression that everyone here works 16-hour days. This just isn't true," one analyst reveals. "I work 11–12 hours a day, and when I've finished I just go home." He sums up the hours topic succinctly, saying: "The mentality about hours is stay until the job is done, not one minute more or less."

Joining the "Global We"

There is a very positive outlook from respondents about Goldman Sachs' corporate culture. "It's very strong at this firm," a first year analyst in the investment banking division tells us. People are encouraged and rewarded for "working hard and as part of a team." Relationships both within and between teams are "very good," and all employees "have the common goal to provide the best solution for the client, and to maintain the sound reputation of the firm."

A programming analyst in his first year relates: "it's very inclusive and the emphasis is on a "global we.'" Despite limited corporate experience and being new to the team, "my input is considered equally with those more experienced around me," he informs us.

A first-year associate in the firm's Paris office reports "a very strong culture," which is "very different from other Wall Street firms." There is a great focus on teamwork and "very smart but humble people," he asserts. All senior people are "truly accessible" and juniors are "clearly involved in all steps of a transaction, rather than just being number-crunchers."

There's a mentality of "we made it through this highly selective recruitment process, so now lets get to work and prove we're meant to be here" concludes a first-year programming analyst in London.

By order of the management

When it comes to management, Goldman Sachs staff has nothing but praises to sing. "They respect your views, opinions and ideas from day one," an analyst in London tells us. "They are constantly training and educating, whilst keeping a good balance of asking my opinions on issues." One staffer in the Paris office says that all in all, the top management is "really world-class" and have "a lot of respect for the junior people." So what can a great firm do better? "Reduce the number of hours!" exclaims one investment banker.

Giving something back

All those hours in the office must be good for something right? Right. One female insider in London listed perks such as personal shopping at Selfridges [a high-end

London department store] with the Women's Network team, social events such as wine tasting, sailing and an offsite in Spain as some of the things the firm does to keep its staff happy. "Free parking!" one lucky staffer, probably outside of London, exclaimed in response to the query, "and you get free taxis home after 10pm."

The verdict on working for GS is a fusion of satisfaction and hard work. "There is good career progression and meritocracy, but you do work really hard," a female banker in London tells us. "I wish the work/life balance could be addressed further," a first-year analyst says.

It's a diverse industry

There is a great focus on diversity at GS, with the firm "entirely focused on this matter and its implementation," a Parisian worker tells us. He goes on to observe that the "'white male' majority model perception is not accurate," and insists the firm is very focused on recruiting ethnic minority staff.

The firm's attitude to women is also admirable, staff tell us. "The Women's Network is amazing and has fantastic events on a regular basis," says an investment banker in London. He adds that the firm has a "high number of female managers," and women have "an unusually high representation in the technology department." □

INVESTING

COMPANY NAME
Manor Care
Pharm Product

4.9
-2.5
25.4
-15.5
-27.5
0.9
5.3

Service
.1
2.3
7.4
$6.5
26.8
-30.4
-26.5
-35.5
30.1
14.
-3.
ge
ions
cions
rks
s
work

-8.1
-3.0
-4.4
-4.1

11.4
10.0
10.2
14.4

-11.6
-17.4

-6.9
10.5

-2.7
-6.6
9.2

for
sou
Sound
Marke
lated b

NA
20.7
NA
10.2

164.2
28.9
182.9

-6.7
-19.8
6.6
26.5

-3.4
-7.3
8.5
-0.7

1.5
-0.1
-1.4
8.8

10.2
8.7
7.4

-2.0
3.8
-1.7

7.1
12.9
7.4
9.1

15.7
59.1
12.6
29.1

-13.4
30.0
-16.6

Solutions
itney Bowes
Industry Group Average

76.0
155.8
129.5
232.8
210.4

49.7
15.9
15.8
15.7

-4.9
0.8
-13.1
-19.7

Food Products
NutriSystem
NBTY

23.2
-7.9
32.1
20.3
26.1
12.1
5.5
25.2

10.
42.8
11.6
17.4
0.6
15.6
-2.8
-17.7
19.5

-19.5
36.9
20.1
35.1
16.8
1.8

onal
ms
ta Mat.
es
rials
andard
oup Average

25 Cabot Square
Canary Wharf
London, E14 4QA
United Kingdom
Tel: +44 (0) 20 7425 8000
www.morganstanley.com

The Stats

Employer Type: Public
Ticker Symbol: MS (NYSE, Pacific
Exchange)
Chief Executive: John J. Mack
2007 Revenue: $28.02bn
2007 Profit: $3.2bn
2006 Revenue: $29.83bn
2006 Profit: $7.47bn
No. of Employees: 48,256
No. of Offices: 600+

Departments

Asset Management • Finance • Global
Capital Markets • Global Wealth
Management • Investment Banking •
Investment Management • Operations •
Sales and Trading • Technology

European Locations

London (European HQ)
France • Germany • Hungary • Italy •
The Netherlands • Russia • Spain •
Sweden • Switzerland • Turkey • United
Kingdom

Key Competitors

Citi • Credit Suisse • Deutsche Bank •
Goldman Sachs

Employment Contact

www.morganstanley.com/careers

THE BUZZ
WHAT EMPLOYEES AT OTHER FIRMS ARE SAYING

• "They know what they're doing"
• "Very good professionally"
• "Overvalued versus other top-tier
  banks"
• "Stiff culture"

THE SCOOP

ndustry giant Morgan Stanley has the world in its arms. Comprised of three main divisions: institutional securities, global wealth management and investment management, the group offers individual investors around the world brokerage, investment and financial services. The client segments covered by the bank range from affluent to high-net-worth. Morgan Stanley's retail brokerage network is one of the largest in the US and among the products it offers are mutual funds, equities, fixed income products, alternative investments, separately managed accounts, banking, mortgages, insurance and annuities.

Institutional investment management, as you might expect, comprises a suite of investment strategies to cater for the varied needs of institutional investors worldwide. Morgan Stanley's institutional securities business offers financial services to corporations, governments and institutional investors across the world. In Japan, this arm offers investment banking, research, equity and fixed income sales and trading, distressed asset trading, securitisation and real estate services.

Fast-track to success

First founded in 1935, Morgan Stanley has grown to become a powerful global investment bank. Its roots go back even further, however, to 1854, when Junius S. Morgan took a job with a London bank. The Morgans were Americans and Junius' son, J. Pierpont Morgan, became one of the world's first celebrity financiers, helping to build the American rail system and forming General Electric and US Steel. Built by former employees of J.P. Morgan, Morgan Stanley first arrived in Europe in 1967 opening an office in Paris; an office in London followed in 1975. As of summer 2008, the New York-based bank has close to 600 offices across 33 countries worldwide.

Bull in a China shop

In February 2008, news media reported Morgan Stanley was looking for someone to take its 34.3 percent stake in China International Capital Corp. (CICC) off its hands, as of mid-2008. The firm assisted in CICC's creation in the mid-1990s. As access to the lucrative (and alluring) Chinese brokerage industry is usually difficult to obtain, the CICC surely represents a fantastic opportunity for the right investor. The Chinese corporation is the top underwriter of initial public offerings in what is now the largest IPO market in the world. As of June 2008, the stake had not yet been sold.

That said, the Chinese stock market had fallen by a third since its late autumn 2007 highs, along with its trading volumes and the proposed reining-in of large secondary listings in the domestic market as a result. Adding to this are concerns over CICC's chief executive, Levin Zhu, who is said to run the firm like his own empire and opposes the sale of the stake to a foreign firm. Commentators are wondering how easily Morgan will be able to pass its stake on.

Swooping on Hawker

Looking to increase its hedge fund offering amid a sharp increase in demand for commodity funds, in April 2008 Morgan Stanley took a minority stake in London-based commodity fund Hawker Capital. Hawker manages around 300 million US dollars in assets and began trading in October 2007. It invests primarily in commodities

> " J. Pierpont Morgan, one of the world's first celebrity financiers, helped build the American rail system "

and equities in "capacity-based markets," which include shipping, airline industries, oil, gas and grain. It is thought that the unusual step of selling a stake only six months into its existence is a move by Hawker to assist its growth — the fund is already opening a research office in Beijing.

The fund will be available to customers through Morgan's investment management platform, which offers several funds via a minority stake ownership. As well as a 19 percent stake in Lansdowne Partners — one of London's largest hedge funds — the bank also holds part of Avenue Capital and Traxis Partners of the US, together with Frontpoint, which it owns entirely.

Morgan Stanley still standing

Despite suffering alongside other banks from the fallout of the subprime crisis, Morgan Stanley remained competitive on the global M&A playing field, completing 395 M&A deals in 2007. The firm came second in announced global volume of M&A deals in 2007, with nearly a trillion dollars' worth, also placing in the top-three in Europe. The bank continued to excel into 2008, thanks to its role as co-lead book runner on rights issues worth 15.9 billion euros, making it a top adviser in Europe's equity capital markets and the second-largest US securities firm after Goldman Sachs.

Despite all the league table successes, the repercussions of the credit crisis were far from over. In February 2008, the bank said it would close its British home loans business, as well as cull 1,500 jobs worldwide (five percent of its workforce) to try to compensate for its earlier 9.4 billion dollar writedown. The job cuts would come primarily in its mortgage divisions, with approximately 350 of them taking place at the firm's European headquarters in London.

By mid-2008, the trouble thickened as Morgan Stanley reported a colossal 57 percent drop in earnings as the firm's revenue from asset management and investment banking declined. It remains to be seen if the layoffs taking place across the global financial sector can outrun current market conditions to bring the books back in order.

GETTING HIRED

The world of Morgan Stanley

Morgan Stanley offers 21 graduate programmes around the world, spanning a range of business areas. Of these programmes the ones available in Europe are credit, finance, equity research, investment banking, investment management, operations, prime brokerage, private wealth management, sales and trading, the "Spring Insight Programme" and technology. Each area designs its own programme, so they are closely tailored to the real positions that they run parallel to.

Programmes can vary in length and start time considerably, so be sure to find out well in advance if the programme you select is available as a full-time, summer or industrial placement and whether it can be undertaken by those with little or no experience at analyst level. Some programmes may even be limited to the associate level, seeking applications only from those with several years of experience and an MBA or other advanced degree.

Analysts are hired from a wide range of backgrounds and after brief classroom training gain the majority of their instruction on the job, while working alongside more experienced professionals. The firm promises responsibility early on, as well as the opportunity to foster a network of colleagues and develop further through an ongoing development curriculum offered throughout their career.

Associate programmes also consist of a brief intensive training period, followed by work alongside more experienced employees and a significant level of responsibility. Flexibility in your position is offered and encouraged as a means of improving your skills.

It's all online

The application process for a job at Morgan Stanley begins either by filling out an online application or during one of the firm's many campus recruitment events. The prestigious employer is open about the fact that it is constantly seeking "very focused" employees and has a popular internship programme that often leads to full-time employment. Deadlines tend to be around November, but this does vary with the specific programme you choose, as well as your region, so make sure you double-check on the website at: www.morganstanley.com/about/careers. If Morgan Stanley wants to take your application further, you will be phoned soon after you submit your application for a technical telephone interview, when you'll be asked "technical questions about the role you applied for, and will be expected to know many things in detail."

The interview-athon

If you're one of the lucky ones that lands an interview, make sure you thoroughly express your interest in both the firm and role as the interviewers are "very perceptive to enthusiasm levels," say insiders. Staffers across all divisions say they had two rounds of interviews. One source, who first interviewed for a summer analyst position, says the first interview was on campus with "a professional" from the firm.

Questions that are "typical of an investment bank interview" were asked — "except it was very friendly and not particularly technical". The second round, a source says, was in London over what he describes as "a full day called the 'assessment centre', starting with some tests and group discussion over some imaginary problems and ending with three interviews in the afternoon with senior people." He adds, "One of these interviews was very technical, pushing me to where I could not answer correctly. The other two were more of the behavioural type, trying to see what I was interested in and whether there was good fit."

An ex-intern says both of the assessment day interviews were "quite relaxed" adding, "I didn't feel like they were trying to catch me out. I was made to feel relaxed throughout the assessment process." One analyst, who interviewed for a role in the popular investment banking division, describes the two-round interview process: "The first round is fit-based whereas the second round is organised as a one-day assessment centre which involves group exercises, one-on-one Investment Bank interviews, a numerical/reasoning test and a one-on-one case study."

The group exercise involves the discussion of a business situation where candidates simulate a board meeting. One employee explains that in the simulated board meeting there is not much room for preparation, "as the teamwork ability is what seems to matter here." Those who got the offers contributed creative ideas directed to the core issues, not those who tried to be great leaders without making effective team contributions.

Interviews in the first round are personality-based, says an employee, adding: "Nonetheless, those with previous experience got a lot of technical questions. Some also reported consulting questions, such as market sizing, where simple calculations had to be done." Our employee, rather relevantly, slips in some handy advice: "Those who have read the *Vault Guide to Finance Interviews* should not have any problems."

Quantitative elements

Maths-phobes need not fear, as "The numerical test is very easy." Our insider's advice for the test is simple: "Answer questions correctly rather than rushing through it — nobody in my group finished it! Go to the Morgan Stanley careers page to get an idea of what such tests look like. Practise your school maths — percentages, multiplying and dividing, fractions etc. That's it. The case study is very simple and involved a business disposal situation where various alternatives for the seller have to be evaluated. It is essential that you ask the interviewer loads of questions and that you prepare a good structure for your analysis, as in consulting interviews."

An ex-intern reflected on his experience of getting hired with satisfaction: "I believe that Morgan Stanley's recruitment process was very good. It was best to have most of the selection stages on one day in the form of an assessment centre. In addition, I agree with having two interviews on the day as this provides a fairer assessment of your suitability."

One first-year analyst says, "About 50 percent of equity interns make it onto the full-time payroll." Another insider and former intern explains that at the end of the internship, all interns are interviewed about their experience and have a feedback session with their manager. That information is then used to decide if an intern will be offered a graduate position. Insiders do point out that if you're interested in a role in the coveted investment banking division, the firm expects you to have incredible marks on your transcript — and if you haven't interned for the firm, you must simply be "very good."

J.P. MORGAN
INVESTMENT BANK

10 Aldermanbury
London, EC2V 7RF
United Kingdom
Tel: +44 (0)20 7742 4000
www.jpmorgan.com

The Stats

Employer Type: Subsidiary of
JPMorgan Chase & Co (JPM)
Ticker Symbol: JPM (NYSE)
Chief Executive: Jamie Dimon
IB co-Chief Executives:
Steve Black, Bill Winters
2007 Revenue: $71.4bn
2007 Profit: $15.4bn
2006 Revenue: $62.0bn
2006 Profit: $14.4bn
No. of Employees: 180,000
No. of IB Employees: 26,000
No. of Offices: 60+

Departments

Advisory • Debt and Equity Underwriting •
Institutional Equities • Market Making •
Prime Brokerage • M&A • Research •
Restructuring • Trading and Investing

European Locations

London (European HQ)
Belgium • Czech Republic • France •
Germany • Greece • Italy • The
Netherlands • Portugal • Russia • Spain •
Sweden • Switzerland • Turkey • United
Kingdom

Key Competitors

Goldman Sachs • Merrill Lynch • Morgan
Stanley

Employment Contact

www.jpmorgan.com/careers

Pluses

• "Face time does not exist"
• "Focused on training and development"

Minuses

• "Very bureaucratic"
• "Can be easy for an individual to be
  overlooked"

THE BUZZ
WHAT EMPLOYEES AT OTHER FIRMS ARE SAYING

• "Good opportunities"
• "Strong M&A house"
• "Had better days, but still very good"
• "Thoroughbred, but slow to adapt"

THE SCOOP

J PMorgan Chase & Co, based in New York, is a leading global financial services firm boasting assets of more than 1.6 trillion US dollars and more than 170,000 employees in 60 countries worldwide. The firm's investment banking division, J.P. Morgan Investment Bank, is an international investment banking powerhouse and has offices throughout Europe. In 2005, its franchise was enhanced through a joint venture with Cazenove, one of the leading corporate brokers in the UK.

More about Morgan?

J.P. Morgan's business spans six key areas: investment banking, worldwide securities services, private banking, asset management, One Equity Partners and private client services. Through this diverse range of financial services, J.P. Morgan serves the interests of clients with complex financial needs. These range from corporations, governments, private firms and financial institutions to non-profit organisations, wealthy individuals and institutional investors.

Making headlines

In 2008, the banking world stood aghast as long-established investment bank and broker Bear Stearns sailed within a hair's breadth of insolvency. It had reported a 61 percent drop in profits in the closing months of 2007 and had just announced a 1.2 billion dollar writedown on mortgage-backed securities, amongst other things. There were major fears of a market crash if it went under. And then, on March 14, 2008, financial services giants JPMorgan Chase & Co arranged emergency funding for their once competitors Bear Stearns, with the aid of the Federal Reserve as the liquidity crisis deepened.

Bear Stearns' shares dropped in value by 50 percent. Two days later, J.P. Morgan agreed to buy Bear Stearns for 236 million dollars, or two dollars a share. Soon after this initial agreement, J.P. Morgan amended the merger terms. Under the new terms, each share of Bear Stearns common stock would be exchanged for 0.21753 shares of JPMorgan Chase & Co common stock, or approximately ten dollars a share. J.P. Morgan began to tighten its grip on Bear in April, 2008, by merging the two firms' investment banking units.

Hard to Bear

The new, post-Bear Stearns acquisition structure sees investment banking, M&A and capital markets co-run by J.P. Morgan Investment Bank heads Steve Black and Bill Winters, with only five of the 26 top positions beneath them held by former Bear bankers. Bear staff staying on in the new firm include Jeff Urwin, head of investment banking in the Americas. J.P. Morgan's senior executives began turning their attention to the job cuts needed among the 14,000 employees on Bear's roster.

In May 2008, J.P. Morgan announced the axe would come down, eliminating 8,000 Bear Stearns jobs worldwide. Making the redundancies even harder to, ahem, bear, were the 4,000 lay-offs among J.P. Morgan executives, which related to the merger as well as to the fallout from the American housing crisis.

J.P. Morgan chief executive Jamie Dimon has, according to media reports, been quite thorough with the restructuring. In May 2008, news source CNBC published reports of people at the firm claiming as many as 200 executives being laid off in two days.

Oldest game in the world

Whilst the Bear Stearns events grabbed the headlines in 2008, J.P. Morgan had hardly been quiet up until then. The bank found itself involved in some of the most significant transactions and financial happenings of the 20th century. The creation of the world's first billion dollar corporation in 1901, United States Steel, and the 1915 arrangement of the then largest foreign loan in Wall Street History — 500 million dollars to the allies in World War I — are not least among them. There was also the small matter of delivering the US Government and the gold standard from economic crisis in 1895 and bailing out New York City and the NYSE from a spate of insolvency in 1907.

> ❝ The bank [was] involved in some of the most significant transactions and financial happenings of the 20th century ❞

The company, which went public in 1940, had built up a strong global practice as the 21st century kicked in. At the turn of the millennium — September 13, 2000, to be precise — Chase Manhattan Bank acquired J.P. Morgan for approximately 36 billion dollars in stock. The combined entity, which united two of the oldest and most prestigious banks in the US, was tough going initially, with profits plunging, but by 2004, the bank was recovering strongly. In a few years it bounced back stronger than ever.

New pace

By July 2007, the division reported that profits were up by 41 percent to 1.2 billion dollars, with fees jumping 39 percent to 1.9 billion dollars. This surge was, according to the company, "driven by record advisory fees, strong debt underwriting fees and record equity underwriting fees".

By January 2008, the bank felt the tremors from the US economic slowdown. The investment banking division's net income and net revenue dropped. Fixed income market revenue also slumped, by 70 percent, due to a 1.3 billion dollar writedown on subprime positions and markdowns in securitised products. The company admitted that it would be "extremely cautious" entering 2008.

Still strong

As of March 31, 2008 JPMorgan Chase & Co was still going strong despite the credit crunch. In 2007, the bank was ranked third by market value on the Thomson Reuters list of the Top 20 Global Financial Institutions, at 91.25 billion euros. The prestigious league ranking compliments the 361 M&A deals the bank completed worldwide in 2007, amounting to an announced volume of 922.3 billion dollars.

Both worldwide and in Europe, the bank ranked No.4 in the M&A league tables. In terms of global debt and equity underwriters, J.P. Morgan was ranked second on the 2007 Thomson Reuters Financial League Tables, with 554.14 billion dollars worth of business on its books.

GETTING HIRED

Learning the ropes

The best way to work out whether J.P. Morgan is for you is to apply for an internship. The summer internship programme runs for 12 weeks from June to September, although if your availability is flexible you could also enrol in the spring, autumn or winter internships. These last from three to nine months. Specific internship dates are available on the company careers page.

Survey participants emphasised the importance of undertaking an internship with the firm to improve your chances of getting a full-time position. Most successful interns do apply for a job at J.P. Morgan and receive an offer one source says, explaining that it's an "important avenue for training and recruiting talent". He adds that employees like to get to know each other in a "more relaxed and comprehensive way during an internship, compared to a two-day assessment centre."

As well as a chance to wow your potential employers-to-be, an internship can help you get your head around banking as a career. According to one source "my summer internship was superb because it enabled me to really understand which part of the bank I wanted to work in." You can also get a good sampling of the range of work on offer he observes, noting that the firm was very flexible with "allowing me to switch business areas following the internship."

The investment banking division recruits interns in four areas: country M&A teams, pan-European sector teams, country capital markets teams (debt and equity) and the securitised products team. Within any of these teams your time will be split between marketing and carrying out transactions within investment banking.

If you'd rather spend your summer months doing something other than banking, don't despair. There are always jobs available to others through the "regular channels outside of internships," one employee in London says. "They're important, but not key to gaining employment."

Join the Morgan organ

You'll learn to perform in-depth company and industry research, data analysis, and how to draw strategic conclusions from the process. You'll be expected to then present your results to your team, and clarify or debate any aspect with confidence. Early on in the internship you'll work alongside senior J.P. Morgan bankers and important clients — often the chief executives and chief financial officers of major corporations and government representatives.

Please sign here

For specific information on what each of the four investment banking division internships concentrates on, you should have a look under internships on the company careers page. To apply, you'll need fluent English and the company notes that another European language is a definite advantage. It also warns that you may have to work long hours and be subject to high stress levels, so proving that you're cut out for the banking lifestyle is an important part of the process.

If you are a graduate or in your final year of university, you can apply for J.P. Morgan's full-time analyst programme. If you're at the MBA level, the European MBA summer associate programme might be for you, as it is the main starting point for those who want to be part of the full-time associate programme. To apply visit the firm's careers page at: www.jpmorgan.com/careers. Experienced professionals looking for new opportunities can browse and apply for vacancies on the careers page under the "Experienced Employee" option.

Discerning taste

J.P. Morgan is considered very discerning and insiders maintain that the company goes out of its way to find the right candidates. One analyst said: "The best and brightest come in many shapes and forms and our recruiting strategy reflects our desire to draw from the broadest possible pool of talent with a passion to exceed and work together in a spirit of partnership."

That said, the interview process is described as "gruelling" and "rigorous," as J.P. Morgan likes to make sure it's bringing the right people on board. An associate says the firm tests "everything from analytics to teamwork" and adds that "professionalism and communication skills are crucial". Another adds, "Candidates are reviewed and tested in multiple rounds by members of different business areas. Finally, senior management judges applicants during an assessment day." A vice-president notes, "In my experience, only a fraction of the candidates in the final round assessment centres are given offers."

You've got the right stuff

An internship is almost always an ideal way to land a job but, as one source says, "Many employees cite the internship as a key advantage in getting a full-time position but it is far from a sure thing." A first-year analyst says, "It is the review processes completed by the members of the team you work with that count the most."

Former interns speak highly of the programme, explaining the internship work is quite involved, allowing interns to gain actual hands-on experience. One insider says, "We worked on marketing projects, helping to generate new ideas for clients and helped with research and valuation assignments. Interns have the opportunity to work on live deals and often meet with clients from the start, quickly earning big responsibility. You learn a tremendous amount and it is a very realistic work experience for students."

OUR SURVEY SAYS

When do you knock off?

You can expect to work an average of 50-60 hours a week under normal circumstances — if there isn't a major international credit crisis going on, for example. Hours are obviously variable and some sources report working 70 and even 80 hour weeks, while emphasising that hours are "comparable with other top tier investment banks." However, team members are encouraged to use their full holiday allowance over the year, sources went on to add.

Encouragingly, "face time does not exist," and when you are done with your work you can go home, an employee in the leveraged finance department tells us, along with a number of other respondents. Even with the long hours, "the day flies," a content banker confides.

As far as giving up your weekends goes, be reassured. Exceptional working hours are an "occasional event rather than regular or expected" says a member of the sales team, and they're always "business related, reflecting the demands of a particularly complex or urgent client project." A member of the trading division happily confesses he has "no weekend work".

It's worth noting, then, that weekend work and the number of hours worked per week vary significantly for different teams. This is another crucial reason for doing an internship in banking before choosing banking as a career as it's "the best way" to make an informed work/life balance choice, advises a junior employee.

Huge but friendly

Sources described the firm's culture as "friendly and diverse," with one respondent commenting, "I especially like the emphasis on hiring and retaining women. It's something the firm takes very seriously."

Compared to other firms, reveals one source with experience in other banks, "the excellence and drive that people often talk about with regard to other companies is actually prevalent here, but it is also a really enjoyable place to work." Senior managers are easy to approach — there is very little hierarchy, and there is a "strong focus on personal development and education", insiders reveal. Other respondents had difficulties with the sheer scale of the bank, noting that J.P. Morgan can feel "very large at times" and "it can be easy for an individual to get overlooked, especially in larger teams." It can also feel "very bureaucratic, simply because of the administrative overheads that such a large organisation requires." On the upside however, insiders at the firm tell us that J.P. Morgan's culture is "highly inclusive", "global in outlook and feel", "firmly focused on training and development", "impressively professional", "dedicated to perfect execution" and "highly international."

"Meritocracy comes to mind," summarised one source, "you are being really challenged to perform without it being an aggressive place. People have a lot of patience and are eager to help, especially when you're new."

Come one, come all

Citing initiatives such as the Corporate Diversity Council, one minority respondent observes that the diversity recruitment and retention is "clearly mandated from the very top," and has resulted in a number of programmes that aim to better recruit, retain and develop traditionally under-represented candidates within the bank. "It's not perfect yet however," one source notes, adding, "it's something the firm is very focused on, but given the nature of the industry, there is still room for improvement." The bank does appear to be working hard on the issue. An associate tells us: "J.P. Morgan is very involved in this regard." The bank runs a program called J.P. Morgan Launching Leaders, hosting an educational event at the bank for talented Afro-Caribbean undergraduates. There's also the bank's Black Leadership Forum, or IB BLF. The mission of the IB BLF is to promote black leadership at all levels of the investment bank through concentrated and continuous efforts. The BLF facilitates the creation of "networking and career development opportunities for black employees."

If you thought banking was a man's world, J.P. Morgan employees would have you think again. One female respondent tells us "I cannot recall any instances when being a woman would impact my job, relationships with management or subordinates, evaluation or compensation, or any other area of my career." A first-year analyst summarises that "respect for all of our colleagues is pivotal to J.P. Morgan's culture." The bank is deeply committed to cultivating an inclusive environment where everyone can succeed based on merit.

R.E.S.P.E.C.T.

J.P. Morgan employees were generally pleased with the accessibility and respect their managers exhibited. One notes, "I've always been treated fairly and with respect by my managers." The quality of management is becoming increasingly important for each manager, he says, explaining that the firm is actually "set apart by its quality of management." Another employee believes one of the bank's differentiating factors is "the respect with which senior bankers treat juniors as well as their openness to explain concepts and mentor staff."

"Not everyone here is perfect, sure," relates a manager, "But I am proud to be able to claim honestly that management and leadership is taken very seriously by top management." Managers are clearly evaluated by how well they function as a boss with their team.

Perhaps most importantly, "there is a real mechanism for feedback in both directions." One of the manifestations of this mechanism is the Analyst and Associate

Development Council, which "shapes the strategy for analysts and associates." Essentially the AADC is a group of senior managers, analysts and associates who actively work to improve the working environment and set the company's recruiting and training strategy.

The council ensures recruiting, training and development during the first few years are "carefully structured" so that the working population "can build a strong foundation with us, and receive fair and honest treatment," a worker notes. Significantly, employees can submit an "anonymous evaluation of managers in this respect" and the score has "direct influence on their year-end evaluation."

Meals and wheels

Work perks that staff are particularly keen on include a post-9pm meal allowance and free cabs home after 9:30pm. The flexible rotation programme for both divisions and locations was also rated highly, as was the four-week sabbatical available to analysts after promotion to associate level.

Several staff gripes centre on meritocracy, with comments such as: "Promotion policies are still not completely meritocratic". One disappointed insider says, "Too many people get promoted to VP on time-served rather than on ability." As with all meritocracies however, merit also determines the appreciation of the system by those subject to it.

"I get to make the choice every year whether to stay or go elsewhere" one zealous banker tells us. "When a headhunter calls I ask them to give me a single reason why to move from J.P. Morgan if I am continuing to do well there. They usually struggle to give a coherent answer."

Rounding the firm off, one staffer says, "There are places that pay well, places that give you free time and places that challenge you. But there are no others that do all three of the above to such a high level." □

MERRILL LYNCH

Financial Centre
2 King Edward Street
London, EC1A 1HQ
United Kingdom
Tel: +44 (0)20 7743 4457
www.ml.com

The Stats

Employer Type: Public Company
Ticker Symbol: MER (NYSE)
Chief Executive: John A. Thain
2007 Revenue: $11.3bn
2007 Profit (Loss): ($8.6bn)
2006 Revenue: $33.7bn
2006 Profit: $7.09bn
No. of Employees: 60,000+
No. of Offices: 800+

Departments

Banking • Corporate and Enterprise
Groups (including Technology and HR) •
Global Markets and Investment Banking •
Global Research • Global Wealth
Management

European Locations

London (European HQ)
Belgium • France • Germany • Ireland •
Italy • Luxembourg • Monaco • The
Netherlands • Poland • Portugal • Spain •
Sweden • Switzerland • Turkey • United
Kingdom

Key Competitors

Goldman Sachs • J.P. Morgan • Morgan
Stanley

Employment Contact

www.ml.com/careers/europe
Campus Recruitment Hotline
Tel: +44 (0)20 7 996 3528

Pluses

• "Friendly and less hierarchical
environment"
• "Cooler than other banks"

Minuses

• Could have "better training and
healthcare"
• "Not that many women in top
management roles"

THE BUZZ
WHAT EMPLOYEES AT OTHER FIRMS ARE SAYING

• "Tough, very respected"
• "Renowned"
• "Ultra-aggressive"
• "Hampered by losses"

THE SCOOP

A merican financial services firm Merrill Lynch is a giant. Those not familiar with the firm's impressive Manhattan headquarters would be impressed to learn that Merrill Lynch, rather famously, occupies the entire 34 floors of the Four World Financial Center building. Just try and imagine how massive its Christmas party must be — and that's just one office in a global network that employs more than 60,000 employees.

It is one of the world's biggest financial services firms and is divided into two core businesses: global markets and investment banking (GMI) and global wealth management (GWM). GMI provides institutional sales and trading, advisory and capital raising services to corporations, governments and institutions, GWM offers wealth management services and products to individuals and businesses. Businesses within GMI include global markets, investment banking, global private equity and global leveraged finance.

The bigger they are ...

A hefty 23.2 billion US dollar writedown for 2007 was probably the biggest blow to Merrill during this year in banking, as declines in liquidity threatened at some points to sink the bank entirely. Investor confidence was struck in particular by the bank's fluctuations. When in October 2007, Merrill projected a colossal 4.5 billion dollar third-quarter writedown on collateralised debt obligations and subprime mortgages, before increasing the official number to 7.9 billion dollars, investors wondered how a bank could have misjudged its exposure to losses in such a big way.

Chief executive Stanley O'Neal eventually took personal responsibility for the overexposure to subprime rates, and the resultant impaired liquidity of Merrill Lynch. He was forced to retire in 2007, but do note that O'Neal got neither a bonus nor severance.

O'Neal was not the only major bank chief embroiled in post-subprime controversy in 2007. Citigroup's chief executive Charles O. Prince resigned after his company took an 11 billion dollar writedown and eventually joined O'Neal and Countrywide Financial founder Angelo Mozilo in the US Congress, defending the immense sums of money they had carried away with them from the burning wreckage of their respective firms in severance and stock options. O'Neal himself was given close to 160 million US dollars on his departure. The firm said, however, that the 160 million dollars was previously awarded stock-based compensation and not severance. The move may, however, have confused onlookers as Democratic Congressman Henry Waxman, chairman of the committee on oversight and government reform, said at the time: "The obvious question is how can a few executives do so well when their companies are doing so poorly?"

The subjectivity of the more complex and illiquid financial instruments was brought to light, and left a gaping hole in the perceived ability of Merrill to manage risk — its, and every investment bank's, nucleus. John Thain stepped into the breach following O'Neal's fall. Referring to the company's losses at fiscal year end 2007 in the company's annual report, he simply stated: "That must never happen again."

Rather humble origins

Charles E. Merrill arrived in New York City in 1907 and took a job at a textile company. He met Edmund C. Lynch in Manhattan, at the 23rd Street YMCA as Lynch needed a roommate. The pair became friends and Merrill went on to work in investment companies, opening his own firm in 1914. Lynch soon joined his comrade at the office and the firm was re-christened Merrill, Lynch & Co. in 1915. According to their contemporaries, they were perfectly suited to go into business together as Merrill liked to dream of what could be while Lynch enjoyed dwelling on what might go wrong. Decades after its founders' deaths and despite several mergers, Merrill Lynch continues to carry the two men's names into the frontlines of finance.

> " They were perfectly suited ... Merrill liked to dream of what could be ... Lynch dwelt on what might go wrong "

Showing them who's boss ...

Despite being at the epicentre of the global credit crisis, Merrill's GMI business won top awards in 2008, including first place in the *Forbes/Zacks* Investment Research Survey and second place globally in the inaugural 2008 *Financial Times/StarMine* analyst and brokerage awards. The 2008 *Global Custodian* also noted the firm's "astonishing performance", as clients ranked Merrill Lynch the No. 2 prime broker overall, from sixth position in 2007. Flexing its muscles in Asia, the firm was rated "Best M&A Adviser" in Japan, by *Asiamoney*, while at home, it leads *Barron's* "Top 100 Financial Advisors" for the fifth consecutive year, with 23 named advisors. Meanwhile *Euromoney* magazine named Merrill Lynch Best Global M&A House 2008.

According to data released by Reuters, Merrill Lynch was the world's joint-first top underwriter of stocks and bonds in 2007, along with Citi. Citi was first by volume, Merrill by reported fees. According to the 2007 Thomson Reuters Financial League Tables, Merrill Lynch was ranked No. 3 in global debt and equity capital markets underwriters for 2007, with 431.47 billion dollars worth of business. The firm also remained in the top ten M&A players around the world according to Thomson Reuters Financial: it took eighth place in global announced M&A, with 355 deals valued at 787.8 billion dollars, and ninth place in announced European M&A in 2007, with 179 deals, valued at 484.21 billion dollars.

The future's Turquoise

In response to increasing frustration with rising profit margins at European exchanges like the Deutsche Borse and the LSE, in November 2006, a consortium of banks launched plans for an alternative. Citigroup, Credit Suisse, Deutsche Bank, Goldman Sachs, Merrill Lynch, Morgan Stanley and UBS, who together account for around half of all equities trading carried out in Europe, announced plans for a user-owned exchange in November 2006. Named Turquoise, the new platform plan was seen by the exchanges as nothing more than sabre-rattling to drive down tariffs. By April 2007 however, when Turquoise found a post-trade partner in a new subsidiary of the Depository Trust and Clearing Corporation, it looked as though it might be more than an empty threat.

On June 3, 2008, a firm launch date was set for the platform. Its newly-appointed chief executive, Eli Lederman, stated that on September 5, 2008 the platform would offer 300 stocks across 14 European markets. Peter Gibbs, chairman of Merrill Lynch's Pension Fund, will be Turquoise's chairman.

Some pretty big deals

Merrill Lynch took centre stage in what was, at the time, the largest leveraged buyout ever: Blackstone Group's 39 billion dollar acquisition of Equity Office Properties Trust — the US's largest office landlord. While Blackstone had a number of financial advisors on its side, including Goldman Sachs, Bear Stearns and Bank of America, Equity Office had just one: Merrill. The deal, announced in November 2006, was followed by the notice that Merrill and J.P. Morgan would co-advise Freeport-McMoRan Copper & Gold in its 25.9 billion dollar purchase of rival Phelps Dodge.

Big deals didn't stop in 2007, as the 100 billion dollar acquisition of banking giant ABN AMRO by a consortium of three financial institutions was named best M&A deal of the year at *The Financial News* awards in December. Merrill Lynch led the trio of banks, including Royal Bank of Scotland, Banco Santander and Fortis, and raised the key financing for the transaction. Merrill was also named "European M&A House of the Year" and "European Investment Bank of the Year".

GETTING HIRED

The inside track

Merrill Lynch takes the majority of its full-time hires from its summer internship programmes, so if you're soon to graduate you might want to look into taking part. To do this you should apply around early September-December for programmes taking place the following summer.

The other starting points for graduates are the bank's full-time programmes. Hiring for these also takes place in autumn, so get your application in some time between early September and November, prior to your graduation. You can pursue a full-time position or summer internship in any of the following departments: global markets, global investment banking, global wealth management, global research, technology and human resources — although departmental availability varies with region.

As with many banks, you also have a choice of entry level: analyst, if you're due to complete an undergraduate degree, or as an associate if you've three years of work experience and an MBA or a PhD. The bank also has openings for you if you're pursuing a quantitative PhD and have an interest in working in financial services. The entry levels available in each department vary, so take a look at the list on the company careers page, under "Campus Candidates".

To apply for any position simply click "apply now" in the top right corner of each posting in the careers section of the site. You will be asked to complete an online application, within which you can specify your departmental and entry-level preferences.

Brushing up on your banking

The benefits of internships are manifold, but can be boiled down to two primary advantages: they're a very important introduction to the firm, and a high percentage of interns are offered a full-time job, according to insiders. "Many interns here enter their final year at university with a secure job ready for them when they leave university," a London-based worker comments.

As a student, "you're exceptionally well-paid" for your time spent interning and tasks range from "simple housekeeping," to "developing emerging market indices," together with a general involvement in the ongoing deals for the teams you work with.

Been there done that

If you have the experience to go straight into a position at Merrill Lynch, take a look at the experienced hires section of the careers page. You'll see that you can search for jobs in a variety of European and global locations, and that you can apply to the operations and chief financial office divisions as well as the preliminary six. Simply click on the region you're interested in working in, and take a look at the job postings.

You should also take a look at the firm's "Insight Programme," a two-year course taking place in London or Dublin that lets you explore the ins and outs of the chief financial office (CFO) and global markets and investment banking services department. You will be taken through two 12-month rotations in certain areas of each department, before receiving a permanent placement in one of them.

The Insight scheme is aimed primarily at full- or part-qualified accountants, to assist in developing their potential. If you are of, ideally, CIMA managerial level or ACCA level two, with finance experience in a blue chip organisation and an excellent academic record, contact Will Silverstone at Morgan McKinley who are the bank's recruitment partners for this programme, on +44 (0)207 759 9416, or alternatively, email your CV to wsilverstone@morganmckinley.com. The application deadline is early January 2009, and the programme begins in mid-March. Check the website for specific dates.

Ding! Round two

A first-year analyst tells us that the first round of the interview process at Merrill Lynch includes an online numerical reasoning test and two one-on-one interviews. The second round is an assessment centre and occasionally there is a third round where you meet people from the specific business group you've applied to.

Most employees reported five or more interviews with staff members of increasing seniority. If you're wondering quite what to expect in the interviews themselves, according to another analyst the first two rounds are "motivational and look at your background," with some "general market knowledge and maths questions thrown in." The final round is "purely technical," and you'll be given "a trading game and presentation exercise to complete at the assessment day if you're applying to the global markets division."

OUR SURVEY SAYS

Time flies when you're having fun

Working hours vary with department, with 60-70 hours per week being the average. The likelihood of weekend work also varies. "I never work on weekends as markets are closed" one source tells us, while "M&A people, just like in all major investment banks spend 24/7 in the office" according to another London-based source.

In busy periods "you can reach a similar level to the M&A people when there are lots of transactions going on that you need to handle," our source adds. "Generally, we start in the morning at 8am, and leave between 8 and 9pm."

"It's about 11 hours a day on average" a third-year analyst in investment banking tells us, "with a lot of scope to take breaks and step out for lunch. It all depends on your division — flow traders for example can't get out for lunch, but leave earlier."

All for Merrill and Merrill for all

Enthusiastic respondents in their first year see the bank as a meritocracy where you're given as much responsibility as you can handle. It's a "friendly, passionate" environment that is "very focused, demands hard work, but fosters a true sense of being part of a team."

The overwhelming majority of respondents emphasised the firm's dedication to a friendly and relaxed workplace fuelled by mutual respect, while managing to maintain a strong concentration on hard work and success. "There is a very friendly and less hierarchical environment at Merrill Lynch," says a second year analyst. "This I find crucial, as it gives you more opportunities to step-up and show yourself and to make decisions, even if you are in a junior position. This is the most important aspect of the culture at Merrill Lynch."

Diverse interests

The firm's London office in particular was praised by staff for its diversity, with one Asian staffer noting the high number of people from a range of ethnic minorities at the firm — he adds, "I myself have never encountered any issues relating to my race." In terms of diversity with respect to women, one female worker observes, "there are not that many women in top management roles."

There was one thing ...

Those staff who outlined potential for improvement focused on Merrill's need for "more efficient and concrete work without the need of long superficial hours at work." A first-year analyst pointed out that "top and middle management should be involved more in the business matters of each individual and also get to know them better." Other areas for improvement suggested by insiders surveyed, included: "Higher one-off signing and relocation bonuses at the analyst level in order to bring in the top talent from universities," and "better training and healthcare" were also brought up.

Travel in style

If you're working late, you can have a free dinner after 9pm and after 10pm a car service home. If you're travelling long-haul, you get to travel business class and stay in luxury hotels. For all employees, discounts on restaurants and theatres are available. "We also get a sizeable relocation package, regardless of whether we have to re-locate," one contented London worker says. "It's definitely cooler than other banks," a corporate financier concludes.

By order of the management

A third-year analyst tells us that at Merrill Lynch, compared to other banks, there is less hierarchy. This is "absolutely fantastic!" he exclaims. As an analyst, you can end up speaking to managing directors who will listen to you and give you things to work on directly, which, if you "work hard and deliver the goods, is great for your career. You can easily access very senior people."

Across the board, employees spoke highly of managers' accessibility, respect for junior staff and dedication to helping juniors develop. "You have to earn respect like anywhere else," says an analyst in London, "but when you prove yourself, you're treated very well." "My manager is always teaching me new things, even in the course of a normal conversation," notes another junior. □

SPRING WEEK
DEADLINE 17th
Jan.

DEUTSCHE BANK GROUP

Taunusanlage 12
Frankfurt am Main, 60325
Germany
Tel: +49 69 910 38080
www.db.com

The Stats

Employer Type: Public Company
Ticker Symbol: DBK (Frankfurt); DB (NYSE)
Chief Executive and Chairman: Dr. Josef Ackermann
2007 Revenue: €30.7bn
2007 Profit: €6.5bn
2006 Revenue: €28.4bn
2006 Profit: €6.1bn
No. of Employees: 78,291
No. of Offices: 1,889 in 76 countries

Departments

Corporate and Investment Banking • Private Clients and Asset Management

European Locations

Frankfurt am Main (HQ)
Austria • Belgium • Bulgaria • Czech Republic • Finland • France • Germany • Greece • Hungary • Italy • Luxembourg • The Netherlands • Poland • Portugal • Russia • Spain • Sweden • Switzerland • Turkey • United Kingdom

Key Competitors

Citi • Credit Suisse • Goldman Sachs

Employment Contact

www.db.com/careers

Pluses

• "Fast, dynamic atmosphere"
• "Mountain of responsibility from the word go"

Minuses

• "Can be political"
• Getting a position is "not very easy"

THE BUZZ
WHAT EMPLOYEES AT OTHER FIRMS ARE SAYING

• "Aggressive, young and impressive"
• "Well respected and famous for paying well"
• "Can get nasty on some desks"
• "German is mandatory"

THE SCOOP

A s the largest bank in Germany and one of the largest in the world, Deutsche Bank's two core business areas are corporate and investment banking (CIB), and private clients and asset management. CIB is further divided into corporate banking and securities, and global transaction banking. CIB is in charge of Deutsche Bank's capital markets operations, which comprise the origination, sales and trading of products including debt, equity and a range of other securities as well as corporate advisory, corporate lending and transaction banking businesses.

The corporate banking and securities subdivision of CIB deals with capital market products, corporate advisory and corporate financing businesses, asset finance and leasing and commercial real estate. The global transaction banking subdivision deals with the bank's trade finance, cash management and trust and securities businesses, and also counts financial institutions and corporations among its primary clients.

Divide and rule

Deutsche Bank's private clients and asset management division, known as PCAM, covers the bank's investment management business for both private and institutional clients, advisory for high-net-worth clients as well as more traditional banking services for private individuals and small and medium-sized businesses. It has two subdivisions: asset and wealth management, and private and business clients.

Asset management provides institutional clients — such as pension funds and insurance companies — with traditional asset management, alternative assets, sophisticated absolute return strategies and real estate asset management. The division also provides retail clients with mutual fund products through the bank's DWS and DWS Scudder franchises. Private wealth management provides particularly wealthy individuals with wealth management services such as portfolio management, tax advisory, inheritance planning and philanthropic advisory services. The private and business clients' subdivision targets small and medium-sized businesses in Germany, and seven other countries across Europe and Asia. Services include loans, current accounts, and deposit and payment services, in addition to securities, mutual funds and portfolio investment advisory. The bank has close to 1,500 branches, primarily located in Germany, Italy, Spain and Poland.

Great history

Founded in Berlin in 1870, Deutsche Bank branches spread rapidly across Germany and arrived in London in 1873. By 1876, Deutsche Bank had become the largest bank in Germany, as it remains today. The bank survived World War II and emerged as

Deutsche Bank AG, an amalgamation of German banks, and ventured into retail banking. From the 1960s through the 1990s, Deutsche Bank (DB) snapped up several European banks and financial services firms, opened offices in Asia and North America and went public on the New York Stock Exchange in 2001. In 2002, chief executive Dr. Josef Ackermann took up his post and embarked on a three-part management agenda designed to cut costs, streamline the bank and focus on its core businesses.

Great strength

As of 2008, the firm headlines the Association of German Banks' top-100 table as the first German bank ever to attain more than one quadrillion (1,000 billion) euros of assets. Headquartered in Frankfurt, the global banking giant boasts approximately 1,900 offices and more than 78,000 employees in 76 countries all over the world. Close to 40 percent of its workforce is based in Germany and another 29 percent work throughout the rest of Europe, with the remaining 31 percent divided between Asia and the Americas.

In 2007, Deutsche Bank reported a profit before tax of 8.7 billion euros, which was a five percent increase from 2006. Net income for the year was 6.5 billion euros, up seven percent from 2006. These figures are impressive, considering they were achieved in the wake of the subprime crisis that ran rampant across the banking sector. Fortunately for DB, it was not affected by the crisis as much as its competitors were. Also in 2007, Deutsche Bank was ranked No. 5 (tied with Citi) in European M&A by number of announced deals (187), which amounted to an impressive total of 536.5 billion US dollars. In addition, DB was in the top ten of firm rankings — ninth — for announced dollar volume of global deals, at 661.1 billion dollars.

Dodger bank

At a press conference in February 2008, Josef Ackermann calmed the nerves of employees and shareholders, stating, "The subprime crisis has up till now, in relative terms, had a very modest effect." Examined alongside the financial injuries suffered by Citi, UBS and Merrill Lynch, Deutsche Bank has successfully dodged the worst of the year's woes. This success was put down to the bank's risk management policies, which helped it to see out the drastic vacillation in financial markets. The rest of 2007 was an active time for the bank. Whilst strengthening its domestic market position, it also pushed its international brand through a series of foreign takeovers. At home, it acquired Berliner Bank and Norisbank, stepping its clients and asset management business up a gear, while lending support to its structured and retirement product offerings.

In Poland, the bank expanded its retail network, using the bolstered branch numbers to assist the launch of a new consumer finance platform. Also in 2007, DB picked up the Tilney Group and JPMorgan Chase's depository and clearing centre, both in the UK, enabling the development of DB's wealth management offering, as well as the broadening of services for money market instruments. In addition, new branches were opened in India, Dubai, Riyadh and Qatar. Separately, new partnerships were brought about with Hua Xia and Harvest Fund Management in China as well as Habubank in Vietnam.

Despite chief executive Josef Ackermann's assurances in May 2008 that DB had no plans for increasing capital, in June 2008, Bloomberg financial news service reported that a City analyst has said DB may need to raise three billion euros in new capital in order "to satisfy the regulators' desire for capital strength 'in a post crisis world,' Deutsche Bank's core equity tier 1 ratio of 9.2 percent, though 'robust' compared with European peers, fares 'less well' against US investment banks." The City analyst added that it's likely DB prefers to "get a new long-term investor on board, such as a sovereign wealth fund," rather than sell new shares.

Green credentials

While most banks are content with recycling paper in order to get their green credentials, Deutsche Bank is clearly miles ahead of the pack when it comes to environmental initiatives. In May 2007, Deutsche Bank announced it has partnered with the Clinton Climate Initiative, championed by the former US President Bill Clinton, and a coalition of municipal governments and private firms to launch a programme committed to reducing overall energy consumption in 15 major cities around the world. These are Bangkok, Berlin, Chicago, Houston, Johannesburg, Karachi, London, Melbourne, Mexico City, New York, Rome, São Paulo, Seoul, Tokyo and Toronto. As part of the programme, which seeks to reduce energy consumption and greenhouse gas emissions in these large cities, DB committed to arrange one billion dollars in financing for "energy efficiency retro-fitting projects for buildings" in the identified cities.

Highly decorated

In February 2008, *Asiamoney* awarded Deutsche Bank four of its 2007 "Country Deals" awards to conclude the year end results season, including "Deal of the Year" titles for transactions in Hong Kong, India, Pakistan and Singapore. Only a few months later, the German banking giant pulled *Global Finance's* Best Treasury and Cash Management Provider awards in January 2008, which bestowed the bank with "Best Overall Bank for Cash Management" and "Best Bank for Payments and Collections". Towards the end of 2007, *The Banker* Awards called it "Bank of the Year for Germany".

Red China News

As making headway in China becomes increasingly advantageous for major corporations, Deutsche Bank celebrated being the first foreign financial institution to appear on official Chinese postage stamps way back in 2003. The honour marked the bank's sponsorship of The China Youth School Football Project, a major national government youth initiative. One design shows the Deutsche Bank Cup, a symbolic award soon to be exhibited at Beijing's China National Museum while the other depicts Tiananmen Square.

GETTING HIRED

The world's your Deutsche

To apply for a job at Deutsche Bank, click the "careers" link on the company homepage at www.db.com, followed by the "application centre" link on the right. From here you can select your level of entry: school leaver, undergraduate/graduate, MBA or professional. Each link will take you through a slightly different process, based on which region you would like to work in, which level of qualification you are at and which division you would like to work in. Deutsche Bank recruits across all business lines.

Slipping into something a little more profitable

The firm has extensive opportunities for students at a range of levels. If you're an undergraduate, clicking "graduates/undergraduates" from the menu on the "careers" page, followed by "analyst internship programmes" will take you to a list of the programmes that are being offered in, at the time of writing, the Americas, Australia/New Zealand, China/Hong Kong, Germany, Japan, Singapore, the US and the UK. Requirements differ depending on what you're looking to do, but as a general rule you'll be offered a place on the analyst training programme — the next step up — if you do well. Simply click the link at the bottom of each programme's page to apply for an internship.

Doing your homework

As a top player in the employment market, getting a position with Deutsche Bank is "not very easy," a London-based worker tells us. You should try to attend a careers event as they seem to value this highly, he suggests. "I made some good connections at mine and it was very helpful as it gave me a lot of insight." However you still need to work very hard and "do a lot of homework to get the job!"

Internships "seem to be extremely important" an analyst says. If you want a good job, "My advice is start early — and look for an internship." It is worth noting that the firm "interviews its full timers and interns together," says a junior employee, "So they are judged on the same scale."

Teamwork and initiative

That said, insiders say that the interview process is very straightforward. One recently employed junior analyst in London says his interview "started off in the waiting room where a HR person explained what was going to happen and gave me some food, drinks and more documents." He recalls, "I waited for ten minutes and talked to other candidates during this time. Everyone was friendly." One insider says interviews can last between one and two hours recalling, "both the interviewers were from the division I applied to." He fondly remembers the interview started with "a handshake and a discussion about myself."

This conversation was followed by "yet another explanation of what I was going to go through." The skills part of the interview was entirely "competency-based", explains a junior employee in London. "It included a teamwork question and an initiative question. Before I finished I had a brief opportunity to ask some questions. They got back to me within 24 hours."

OUR SURVEY SAYS

Feet in the door

"Investment banks work you hard and long!" one weary employee in London tells us. "You'll have to make sacrifices, and if its quality of life and a nine to five work schedule you're after, then this place is definitely not for you." On the other hand, if you're a "glutton for punishment" and want to work in a "fast, dynamic atmosphere" — as well as have a "mountain of responsibility from the word go," — then a first year analyst advises you to "climb aboard!"

Another London employee notes that, "Deutsche Bank can be political." It's a huge company, he adds, "too big in my opinion." It can also be "very cliquey". One insider adds: "It's not always what but who you know that matters". He says, "Networking is key", and if you want to progress, "You need to be assertive and take ownership of your career progression." □

THE BLACKSTONE GROUP

40 Berkeley Square
London, W1J 5AL
United Kingdom
Tel: +44 (0) 20 7451 4000
www.blackstone.com

European Locations

London (HQ)
France • United Kingdom

The Stats

Employer Type: Public Company
Ticker Symbol: BX (NYSE)
Chief Executive: Stephen A. Schwarzman
2007 Revenue: $3.05bn
2007 Profit: $1.6bn
2006 Revenue: $2.6bn
2006 Profit: $2.3bn
No. of Employees: 1,020
No. of Offices: 12

Key Competitors

Goldman Sachs • J.P. Morgan • Morgan Stanley

Employment Contact

www.blackstone.com/careers

Departments

Advisory Services • Corporate Advisory Services • Corporate Debt • Distressed Securities Advisors • India/Asia Closed-End Funds • Long/Short Equity Investments • Alternative Asset Investments • Private Equity • Private Placement Advisory • Real Estate • Restructuring and Reorganisation

THE BUZZ
WHAT EMPLOYEES AT OTHER FIRMS ARE SAYING

• "Landmark private equity firm"
• "Sexy place to work"
• "Lost its boutique 'must work there' shine"
• "Well known private equity with terrible culture"

THE SCOOP

D espite the fact the firm was first founded as an alternative to traditional investment banking back in 1985, global investment firm The Blackstone Group has grown rapidly over the past two decades to become a force to be reckoned with in the industry. As an investment group, Blackstone says it maintains a small firm in order to give senior-level attention to clients, invests only in friendly takeovers rather than in hostile bids and grows through attracting professionals who create affiliated businesses.

The firm currently operates in alternative asset investing such as private equity, real estate, corporate debt and hedge funds, and in advisory including corporate advisory and restructuring advisory. It also invests significant amounts of its own money and puts an emphasis on the fact it avoids conflicts of interest in order to provide entirely objective advice.

Modest beginnings

The Blackstone Group was founded in 1985 by Stephen A. Schwarzman and Peter G. Peterson, two seasoned investment bankers who had worked their way up to high-level positions at Lehman Brothers investment bank. Schwarzman served as chairman of mergers and acquisitions and Peterson serving as chief executive of the firm. When Blackstone initially opened in New York City, it had a rather small staff of four and a modest balance sheet of 400,000 US dollars. The group of four persevered and through strategic investing, started to make heads turn. Fast-forward 20 years and Blackstone has offices in Atlanta, Boston, Chicago, Dallas, Los Angeles, San Francisco, London, Paris, Mumbai, Hong Kong and Tokyo, with headquarters in Manhattan on Park Avenue.

Private equity is where it's at

Blackstone's primary investment vehicle is its private equity business that handles more than 35 billion dollars managed in six funds: Blackstone Capital Partners I, II, III, IV, V and Blackstone Communications Partners. As private equity specialists, Blackstone has proven to be especially successful at raising capital, with the most recent fund, BCP V, boasting commitments of more than 19 billion dollars.

Blackstone invests in transactions around the world with investment levels between 250 million dollars and 1.25 billion dollars. Current holdings include such diverse companies as Celanese, CineWorld, Equity Office Properties, FGIC, Freedom Communications, Freescale, Graham Packaging, HealthMarkets, Orangina, SunGard, Travelport, TRW Automotive, TDC, United Biscuits, Universal Orlando, Vanguard Health Systems and VNU.

Corporate partnerships account for approximately one-third of the equity capital invested by Blackstone and corporate partners have included companies such as Time Warner, AT&T, Sony, Union Carbide, Union Pacific, USX and Vivendi. As of March 31, 2008, the total enterprise value of all transactions effected by the group's corporate private equity operations was a staggering 284 billion US dollars.

An impressive spread

Blackstone's business is comprised of eight other departments in addition to private equity. These are: real estate, corporate debt, marketable alternative investments, distressed security advisors, long/short equity, India/Asia closed-end mutual funds, corporate advisory services, and restructuring and reorganisation advisory services. The firm's real estate group has grown assets under management from three billion dollars to more than 17 billion dollars since 2002, while the corporate debt group (BCD) handles more than nine billion dollars of committed capital, investing in senior debt, subordinated debt, preferred stock and common equity. These investments are typically long-term-oriented, focused on assets with strong fundamentals and sustainable competitive advantages.

> " As of March 2008, the total enterprise value of Blackstone's transactions was $284 billion "

BAAM!

Blackstone Alternative Asset Management — or BAAM, as it is known is Blackstone's funds of hedge funds division and marketable alternative investments group. While the group was first used to manage Blackstone's internal investments, it is now open to clients. BAAM has become a leading fund of hedge funds, with more than 19 billion dollars under management and more than 90 percent of BAAM's assets originating in institutional investors. The long/short equity investment group formed in 2006 invests mainly in long and short equity investments, using a research-driven approach to capitalise on mis-priced or misunderstood securities. Meanwhile, the distressed debt group invests in the debt of financially distressed companies.

Black's pudding

The corporate advisory services division of Blackstone advises clients on often complicated transactions that range from distressed M&A to executive financings and fairness opinions. This can range from takeover defences to asset swaps to joint ventures and minority investments. Blackstone's advisors are behind a growing number of high-stakes M&A activity globally, and, to date, have handled transactions worth more than 500 billion dollars. The firm's impressive client roster over the years has included companies such as AIG, Merck, Reuters, Sony, Suez, Verizon and the State of New York.

Separately, under its restructuring and reorganisation advisory services, Blackstone has participated in some of the largest restructurings in history, to boot. These include Delta Airlines, Enron, Macy's, Transworld Airlines, Williams Communications and Xerox.

Pushing the envelope

On June 22, 2007, Blackstone Group had its moment in the sun, through an IPO listed on the NYSE which raised 4.1 billion dollars. This risky move paved the way for other private equity firms to test market waters. Blackstone's IPO, priced at 31 dollars — the top price in its expected range — raised interest through the fact that uniquely, its shareholders weren't given traditional voting rights and there would be no annual shareholder meeting.

With reasons behind the IPO to raise capital for expansion and to make further acquisitions, build the Blackstone brand name and give better incentives to employees, as of June 2008, the Blackstone share had dropped from its initial price of approximately 37 dollars 12 months previously, to approximately 20 dollars. That said, the group is famously astute and bets are on that Blackstone will be able to ride out the low.

European presence

Headquartered in London at a prestigious Berkeley Square address, Blackstone's European operations encompass five business divisions: private equity investing, real estate investing, corporate debt, marketable alternative asset investing (BAAM) and corporate advisory services. The office has more than 120 employees, including more than 60 professional staff. The French arm of Blackstone, located in Paris, only handles real estate investments at present.

GETTING HIRED

Romancing the stone

A list of vacancies can be found on the firm's careers page under "Open positions". When positions become available, Blackstone invites experienced candidates to complete this application to be included in this process. When it comes to recruitment

The Blackstone Group

in Europe, the firm's offices are considerably smaller than its US offices and recruitment is conducted on a case-by-case basis as a result. Its London office is home to four of its business units: corporate private equity investing, real estate investing, funds of hedge funds investing and corporate advisory.

If you're keen to work in the European offices then submit your CV and cover letter through Blackstone's online recruitment link, found under "How to Apply" on the Careers page. You should ideally have experience in one of the business areas listed and appropriate local language skills — or significant experience working in the region being applied to.

Laying the foundation stone

Blackstone offers two levels of internship programme, both of which typically take place in the summer. The summer analyst position is for graduates or those in their final year of study, while the summer associate programme is designed for second year MBA students, or students with one year of an advanced degree remaining.

Undertaking a number of the responsibilities of full-time analysts and associates, as an intern you'll get the chance to assist on a range of projects, and be part of the staff on several assignments at once. The comparatively small number of professional staff means that teams are small, and your role as an intern will be far from insignificant; on the contrary: you'll most likely be expected to take on an integral team position.

Internships last for ten weeks, and you should apply through the "How to Apply" link on Blackstone's careers page. First-round interviews tend to begin between late January and early February and are held on campus if your university is among those visited by the firm. Otherwise they are held in the firm's offices. Those selected in the first round are invited for a second interview. If you're made an offer, your programme will begin in early June.

Joining up

If you're looking to go into a full-time analyst or associate position, click the appropriate "How to Apply" section on the firm's careers page. Analysts are usually fresh university graduates who, as mentioned above, tend to get more of a look in on the action than one might expect at one of the larger banks.

Responsibilities typically include financial analysis, computer modeling, research, competitive analysis and the development of client presentations. Successful candidates kick off their tenure in July with a three-week training course that will take you through the fundamentals of accounting, corporate finance, corporate history and operations, financial modeling and a look at Blackstone's technology systems and database capabilities.

If you've just made it through an MBA programme, you might want to join Blackstone's Associate body. You'll get a panoramic exposure to the full range of financial and strategic issues, whilst working closely with senior members of the firm and seeing extensive client interaction. If offered a position, you'll typically start in early August. □

The Blackstone Group

57

LEHMAN BROTHERS

25 Bank Street
London, E14 5LE
United Kingdom
Tel: +44 (0)20 7102 1000
www.lehman.com

The Stats

Employer Type: Public Company
Ticker Symbol: LEH (NYSE)
Chairman and Chief Executive:
Richard S. Fuld Jr.
2007 Revenue: $19.3bn
2007 Profit: $4.2bn
2006 Revenue: $17.6bn
2006 Profit: $4bn
No. of Employees: 25,000+
No. of Offices: 55

Departments

Capital Markets • Corporate Division •
Investment Banking • Investment
Management

European Locations

London (European HQ)
France • Germany • Italy • Luxembourg •
The Netherlands • Russia • Spain •
Sweden • Switzerland • United Kingdom

Key Competitors

Goldman Sachs • Merrill Lynch • Morgan
Stanley

Employment Contact

www.lehman.com/careers

Pluses

• Working environment is "great"
• "Big egos and arrogance are
  discouraged"

Minuses

• Working weekends is a "frequent
  occurence"
• Could have "better hours" and "better
  compensation"

THE BUZZ
WHAT EMPLOYEES AT OTHER FIRMS ARE SAYING

• "Very good at securities and bonds"
• "Smart and focused"
• "Long working hours"
• "Good, but too formal"

THE SCOOP

Lehman put its success down to the faithful pursuit of its four-pillar business strategy: driving diversified growth, delivering the whole firm to its clients, managing risk, capital and expenses, whilst preserving and strengthening its culture. In the five years since 2003, Lehman's investment banking revenues have grown by 23 percent, equities capital markets by 40 percent and investment management by 36 percent. Alongside this, the firm has seen 38 percent growth in Asia and 36 percent growth in Europe. Lehman Brothers has now reported record results for the past five years, an impressive accomplishment in the 2008 economic climate.

The firm continues to develop and grow its franchise in Europe and the Middle East. The region achieved record net revenues for the third consecutive year, with 6.3 billion dollars of net revenues for the fiscal year 2007, an increase of 39 percent over the previous year. The firm strategically invested in new business areas and expanded into new markets in order to drive diversified growth and deliver superior returns. New offices were opened in Dubai, Turkey and Doha, in Qatar, and Lehman is also developing a presence in Russia. Lehman moved to larger offices in Paris and Madrid and in Switzerland it opened its second office, in Geneva, further highlighting the continuing growth and ongoing momentum across the region.

Lehman continues to focus on a "one firm" approach, coordinating and integrating its global businesses. The bank reported record earnings for 2007, despite the market difficulties that arose in the latter half of the year, which saw a US housing recession, a credit freeze and the drastic re-pricing of credit-related securities. The sharp decline in liquidity saw many of the world's leading banks report record losses and in some cases, go under completely.

Talk about history

Brothers Henry, Emmanuel and Mayer Lehman opened a commodities brokerage and trading firm in Montgomery, Alabama, in 1850. Eight years later, they opened an office in New York and in 1887, the Lehman Brothers listed their firm on the New York Stock Exchange. Almost a century later, in 1984, Lehman was bought by American Express and was subsequently spun off in 1994, becoming an independent operation again.

Today, Lehman Brothers is a full-service global investment bank, providing fixed income and equity underwriting, sales, trading, research, M&A advisory, public finance, private investment management, asset management and private equity. Lehman's first international office was inaugurated in Paris in 1960. Today, the firm's European headquarters are in London while its global headquarters are in New York City. The firm also has major offices in Madrid, Rome, Amsterdam, Milan, Frankfurt, Paris, Dubai, Tel Aviv and Zurich. Meanwhile, from its Asian headquarters in Tokyo, Lehman Brothers has also been building out its Asian business over the last five years, with a new Shanghai office having opened in 2007.

In league with the LSE

Lehman and the London Stock Exchange have a close relationship. In 2005, Lehman supported the LSE's successful defence against a 1.5 billion pound hostile takeover attempt by a consortium led by the Australian Macquarie Bank. Through summer 2006, Lehman set records for monthly equity volumes traded electronically on the LSE — in both June and July 2006, the firm executed more than two million transactions each month. As of 2007, Lehman had been ranked as the number one dealer on the LSE by trading volume for the third consecutive year.

Lehman and the LSE announced plans in early 2008 to create a pan-European Multilateral Trading Facility (MTF) for the execution of non-display orders. The MTF, to be named Baikal, will provide market participants with an unrivalled trading service for European equities, being the first to combine an innovative dark liquidity pool with sophisticated algorithmic trading functionality. Dark liquidity in European equities is estimated to account for around 12 billion euros in value traded per day and is expected to grow rapidly in coming years.

Big-time buying

Lehman has led more than its fair share of big-name M&A advisory roles. Two of Europe's biggest utility M&A deals saw Lehman take a large slice of the action: Endesa's defence following Gas Natural's 38.8 billion euro hostile takeover offer and E.ON's 56.2 billion euro hostile takeover offer. In February 2007, the firm was named advisor on the 90 billion euro Gaz de France merger with Suez, the world's number two water company, in a merger that would create the world's second-largest utility company. Perhaps best known of all, in 2007, Lehman advised ABN AMRO on its 71.3 billion euro acquisition by RBS, Santander and Fortis, as well as its 21 billion dollar sale of LaSalle Bank to Bank of America. The ABN AMRO acquisition was the largest ever global financial institutions purchase.

Who's the boss?

Lehman Brothers made headlines in mid-June 2008, when the firm ousted (and replaced) two of its top executives — its chief financial officer and chief operating officer — after reporting a net loss of 2.8 billion US dollars for the second quarter of 2008, its first as a public company. The staff changes at Lehman made international headlines, as the bank has been known for the length of service of its executive committee members and especially for having the longest-serving chief executive on Wall Street.

Some investors and analysts say that a management shake-up at Lehman was necessary considering the economic climate of the day. Advocates of the management changes say the move should reassure investors Lehman is coping strategically with the subprime crisis and is more than happy to assure Wall Street it was going to emerge from the unstable economic climate relatively unscathed. Writedowns at Lehman have been amongst the lowest in the industry and fears for its fate are looking increasingly unfounded, given its capital raising activities of mid 2008 and its strong balance sheet, with a record 45 billion dollars of available liquidity.

Looking up for Lehman?

Lehman's June 2008 problems were said to have stemmed from continued weakness in the mortgage and credit markets. Some analysts are convinced that Lehman may suffer into the future through the losses sustained by its assets, which makes securing decent leverage on them increasingly problematic. Some have speculated that a merger may be on the cards in the not-too-distant future. According to a *Forbes* magazine report in early June 2008, it has been rumoured that Barclays is interested in buying a slice or indeed all of Lehman, although this has been discounted elsewhere in the media. The bank ranked No. 6 in the Thomson Reuters 2007 league tables for debt and equity capital markets, having underwritten 395.04 billion dollars worth of transactions. In worldwide M&A, Lehman came ninth for announced M&A with a 17.1 percent market share at 767.19 billion dollars. In the European M&A rankings it scooped 12th place, with 350.97 dollars worth of transactions.

GETTING HIRED

Investing your time

Lehman offers a range of opportunities for undergraduates and graduates looking to get into the business. In the summer prior to graduation, you can get involved in the ten-week summer analyst programme. In case your academic calendar limits your summer availability, the London office also runs winter and spring internships available in its investment banking and capital markets divisions, with start dates in January and April respectively and a duration of 12 weeks. Additionally, a number of internships are also available in the European offices for up to six months.

If your application is successful, you'll join a business team and hold similar responsibilities to a first year analyst. You'll also receive training and hands-on experience — bear in mind that the internships are where the company looks first for individuals to fill its full-time analyst vacancies. If you have significant work experience and hold an MBA (or equivalent), or a PhD, Lehman's associate programmes in investment banking, capital markets, investment management and private investment management may appeal to you. These are available as a ten-week summer placement, or a full-time professional development scheme.

Application deadlines for London programmes vary by the season and business division you're applying for, so check the programme you're interested in on the company careers page. Applications in the firm's other European locations are accepted all year round; follow the link on the company careers page to complete the online application form.

Analysts away

If you're a graduate, or soon to be a graduate, you can apply for the full-time analyst programme. This is a two to three-year professional development scheme and it is available in the following business divisions: capital markets, investment banking, investment management, corporate advisory (legal, compliance and audit), finance, credit risk management, information technology and operations. Also available — in the UK only — is the Corporate Generalist Program, a two-year rotational scheme designed to build a pool of "talented future leaders who understand the factors required to manage complex and interrelated products."

A treasured job

As far as accessibility is concerned, many insiders consider Lehman Brothers akin to "a moated castle with armed guards." As one insider puts it, "The firm has enjoyed tremendous success in the past few years, leading it to be considered among candidates, and rightly so, as one of the world's most pre-eminent investment banks." He adds, "Accordingly, interest in working here [at Lehman] has increased substantially."

Another associate says his strategy for landing a coveted position involved attending "months of networking events at business school to get the interview for the summer position." Then, he says, he "excelled over the summer, and got the job". As one analyst points out, it is a highly competitive process, saying: "The number of applications Lehman receives has soared to record highs." The firm's interview process is described as having "a particular focus on diversity, academic achievement, leadership potential and high personal values." An associate notes that, "Aside from quantitative factors, such as grades and even past professional experience, the firm culture is truly very important and one must pass many levels of screening to ensure a good fit."

In a nutshell, the hiring process consists of two to three rounds of interviews. In each round, candidates are interviewed by three or four people, says a second-year associate. The first round tends to be in the candidate's local region with "analysts and associates conducting the interview followed by a final round in our regional headquarters in London with senior bankers."

Final rounds are normally "less technical and focus on personality and motivation." Lehman does not have standard question lists, such as those J.P. Morgan or Morgan Stanley use, but one insider tells us that in his experience "the first round is more skills-based" while "the final rounds are more personality and motivation focused."

Internships are an important part of landing a job with Lehman, and valuable experience for any banking career you might go into. "Yes, summer interns are heavily involved in projects within the team," says one first year analyst who had been involved in the internship programme. They are assigned analyst's tasks which enables them to get "a great insight and overview of investment banking activities." They also, depending on the deal flow, get involved in live transactions. "My summer internship was a great experience," he adds. "I was deeply involved on projects" and was working "like a full-time analyst alongside associates and directors on pitches." He adds, "The weekly compensation was also very competitive."

An associate in London tells us the internship was "extremely important" for getting hired, and that the selection process for full-time recruiting is "more difficult." Another insider notes that the importance of summer internships as a route to a full-time offer is increasing, "As Lehman aims to fill all of its associate positions through the summer internship programme."

Feet in the door

Lehman offers several opportunties for internships in London (winter, spring and summer programmes lasting up to 12 weeks) and other European offices (up to six months). The bank dedicates significant time and resources in recruiting to internships and developing top quality programmes that feed into its full-time hiring. A good number of sources have worked previously as Lehman interns. Internship work is described as "challenging" and "Lehman invests a lot of effort in training and creating opportunities for you to get to know various teams." The importance of landing a full-time position is high for interns as internships are the primary source for hiring full-time analyst and associates.

As an associate reports, "One has to excel at the internship, be motivated, show initiative and be self-driven" to receive a full-time offer. Another insider adds that the hiring of interns as full-time employees is "based on the individual performance [not] quotas [and there is] no cut-throat competition across the class." Overall, an internship at the firm is said to provide applicants as well as Lehman Brothers with a premium opportunity "to get to know each other and assess whether it's the right fit." One former lends some succinct advice: "You should view it as a prolonged interview process."

OUR SURVEY SAYS

On Lehman's terms

Hours vary with the division you work in. In the markets businesses – fixed income and equities, for instance, hours generally map to trading hours. For some other divisions, like investment banking, the hours are long. Analysts disclosed 50-hour working weeks at the low end of the spectrum, while several listed 80, 90, and in one extreme case 100-hour weeks as their generic maximum. Working weekends is a "frequent occurrence." That said, staff have indicated that they aren't always dismayed by the long and intense hours as they are generally offset by the "interesting characteristics of the tasks we are assigned to, such as live deals." You have to work long hours in investment banking another analyst notes, but the working environment is "great." An associate explained away the considerable time commitment, simply by stating, "it's a meritocracy."

You really feel like a part of the team "from the moment you start work," says an analyst in the London office. A director corroborates that the environment is highly competitive, "but there is a strong emphasis on the team. Big egos and arrogance are discouraged." Compared to other banks, one London-based analyst says, Lehman has a much flatter culture. Senior employees are very committed to the firm, while the typical Lehman employee is very smart, "successful at what he does" but "very down to earth at the same time." A satisfied (and somewhat thrilled) third-year analyst says the firm's culture is "the best thing about Lehman!"

Brothers and sisters

Employees at Lehman say the company has a "strong focus" on minorities and diversity, and makes consistent efforts to recruit talented people from ethnic minorities, says an insider. Others cited the firm's diversity aware internship programme, which specifically focuses on college students from African and Asian ethnic backgrounds. A female employee calls the firm's attitudes towards women "exceptional." Lehman is very strong in encouraging women to join and to stay in the firm she continues. "It also sponsors the Women in Business Research Centre at the London Business School". A male employee draws attention to the firm's special Diversity team, which is focused on hiring women in banking and describes it as being "very well organised and respected."

Improving the brotherhood

Despite the stoical acceptance of long hours being part and parcel of a career in investment banking, several employees, when asked what they would improve, state "better hours," as well as "better compensation." Other respondents gave more detail and one suggests "aligning compensation with where it's most deserved, to reduce attrition."

Maternity benefits should also be reviewed so as to be in line with competitor offerings, another source adds. "I am fully satisfied both professionally and personally," says a second year associate, adding: "I have been at the firm for five years and I strongly believe that it is a great place to work." Among the reasons to be satisfied, staffers list "great people", "a great culture" and "top pay", together with "an excellent learning curve".

Mutual respect

"I respect my seniors and the respect goes both ways" says a satisfied London worker. "They appreciate that I work long hours to get everything done on time. They also show that they really appreciate the work I do by giving me a lot of responsibility." Elaborating, he adds that all the seniors have started out as analysts. "My direct boss has been in the industry for over 20 years and I work with him on a day-to-day basis."

The satisfied employee adds, "The management know what an analyst can do, and what to expect from a second-year analyst." However, the analyst admits his management has been very good about training and encouraging in order to help junior employees advance. He says, "My manager advises me how to step up and get to the next level of the very steep learning curve I am on." Contributions are generally welcome by all levels in the organisation, a vice-president at the firm tells us.

One proud and patriotic insider proclaims, "Lehman may work you hard, but it takes care of you too." His gleeful anecdote might be because he's well-fed. Among the perks staffers in London were particularly thankful for include "free dinners and cars home when you work late." The quality and size of the cafeteria was also marked as a plus.

8 CREDIT SUISSE

Uetlibergstrasse 231
P.O. Box 700
CH 8070 Zurich
Switzerland
Tel: +41 1 332 6400

1 Cabot Square
London, E14 4QJ
United Kingdom
Tel: +44 (0)20 7888 8888

The Stats

Employer Type: Public Company
Ticker Symbol: CSGN (SWX); CS (NYSE)
Group Chief Executive: Brady W. Dougan
IB Chief Executive: Paul Calello
2007 Revenue: €39bn
2007 Profit: €7.7bn
2006 Revenue: CHF 38.6bn
2006 Profit: CHF 11.3bn
No. of Employees: 45,000
No. of Offices: 57

Departments

Asset Management • Investment Banking • Private Banking

European Locations*

*Not limited to IB locations

Zurich (Global HQ)
Austria • Czech Republic • Denmark • France • Germany • Gibraltar • Greece •

Guernsey • Hungary • Italy • Jersey • Lichtenstein • Luxembourg • Monaco • The Netherlands • Poland • Portugal • Russia • Slovakia • Spain • Sweden • Switzerland • Ukraine • United Kingdom

Key Competitors

Lehman Brothers • Merrill Lynch • Morgan Stanley • UBS

Employment Contact

www.credit-suisse.com/careers

For Graduate programmes
graduate.recruitment@credit-suisse.com

Pluses

• "Dynamic, stimulating culture"
• "Very collegial and friendly"

Minuses

• Weekend work
• Long hours

THE BUZZ
WHAT EMPLOYEES AT OTHER FIRMS ARE SAYING

• "Smart and innovative"
• "Good work ethic and friendly staff"
• "Graduate programme is not great, quite disorganised"
• "Not a very friendly environment"

THE SCOOP

Operating 57 offices in 26 countries, Credit Suisse has the impressive ranking of Switzerland's second-largest bank, after UBS. This Swiss giant has three central pillars to its business: investment banking, private banking and asset management. In each of these areas it provides securities and financial advisory services to corporations, governments and institutional investors. The range of Credit Suisse's expertise is huge. The bank provides services in equities, fixed income, prime services and research, and specialises in corporate client services including mergers and acquisitions, equity capital markets, debt capital markets, private placement, leveraged finance, industry-specific expertise and regional market issues.

The new craze

Over the past year, some of the world's top investment banks — Merrill Lynch, Goldman Sachs and Deutsche Bank to name a few — have been busy experimenting with the potentially big-money-spinning world of hedge fund replication. The practice is built around the view that hedge funds' performance is down to the movement of underlying assets, rather than human skill. If this is the case, it should be possible to clone hedge fund returns by mechanically recreating industry exposure to the underlying assets. To this end, in mid-March 2008, Credit Suisse teamed up with Professors William Fung and Naravan Naik of the London Business School and Duke University's David Hsieh. Drawing on the professors' academic expertise in the sector, Credit Suisse is putting together a product range designed to clone the major hedge fund strategies. The bank will launch three clones to mimic relative value arbitrage, tactical trading strategies and directional equity strategies.

Erasing errors

The Swiss bank came under fire in early 2008 when media reported on "pricing errors" by several of CS's traders, which led the firm to reveal losses of 1.93 billion euros on structured credit positions. The losses were blamed on the mispricing of asset-backed securities brought to light in the nick of time through the bank's internal control processes. In recent years, some industry analysts have said Credit Suisse has strived to clear its reputation for volatile results brought about by an excessive risk taking culture, a process assisted through awareness of Swiss rival UBS' huge losses. At the same time, Credit Suisse has been regarded as one of the best managed banks in Europe. The losses CS revealed in early 2008 only temporarily bruised this perceived stability, as well as stirring concerns about the investment banks' control processes, already shaky after Société Générale's 4.9 billion euro oversight of unauthorised trading in January 2008.

Hanging tough

A half-decade run of profits ended in the first quarter of 2008, as Credit Suisse announced its first quarterly loss in five years. The bank reported a net loss of 2.1 billion Swiss francs, compared to a 2.7 billion profit in the first quarter of 2007. It also wrote down 5.3 billion in losses linked to leveraged finance and structured products. Despite this setback, Credit Suisse fared better than many of its competitors in the troubled economy. Although its investment banking division recorded a first quarter loss of 489 million — the result of sharp drops in the fixed income business — other I-bank segments turned in solid performances. Leveraged finance and structured products did not fare well, but prime services and the global cash business saw strong revenues. Underwriting and advisory services declined slightly, though this change was in line with the drop in global market activity. Chief executive Brady Dougan called the 1Q08 results "clearly unsatisfactory", but insisted that Credit Suisse's balance sheet remained healthy and therefore, there was no need to rush into any capital-raising schemes.

Getting deals done

Even with a market-related decline in its advisory business, Credit Suisse managed to earn some impressive rankings on the 1Q08 banking league tables. In announced European M&A by value, Credit Suisse held on to the No. 6 position it had nabbed in the first quarter of 2007. In completed European M&A the bank was No. 3, just behind J.P. Morgan and Citi, and up one spot from its former ranking at No. 4. Credit Suisse also proved to be Europe's No. 3 advisor to the consumer staples sector – although, as the Thomson Financial tables noted, European M&A volume hit its lowest level since 2004 during the first quarter of 2008, so there simply weren't as many deals to go around. On the global stage, Credit Suisse ranked No. 2 in worldwide completed M&A by imputed fees, earning 342 million dollars on 69 deals to become Goldman Sachs' runner-up. By deal value, the banking giant was also No. 2 in worldwide completed transactions, but No. 6 in worldwide announced deals.

Settled at last

A long legal battle ended for Credit Suisse and fellow Swiss mega-bank UBS in June 2008, when the two institutions paid to settle a five-year lawsuit with Parmalat SpA, an Italian dairy and food conglomerate that collapsed under allegations of financial wrongdoing in 2003. It was the biggest bankruptcy in Italian history, and executives at the company promptly brought lawsuits against several multinational banks that had served as its financial advisors. Credit Suisse and UBS consistently denied any wrongdoing, but they agreed to pay 172.5 million euros and 184 million euros, respectively, to end the matter.

Facing East

In June 2008, Credit Suisse entered the nascent Chinese market. In a joint venture with Founder Securities, in which Credit Suisse holds 33.3 percent, the Swiss banking group will provide investment banking services to clients in the domestic Chinese market. The venture had to be approved by the China Securities Regulatory Commission and is expected to begin operations in early 2009. The deal is the first that has been approved since the China Securities Regulatory Commission set new regulations governing foreign investment in the sector, so it is a great coup for Credit Suisse.

Clear out your desk

In late June 2008, Credit Suisse announced it would slash 75 British investment banking jobs, prompting many analysts to speculate that more job cuts were on the way. Across the pond, the bank revealed it would make additional cuts in its US high-yield sales trading and leveraged loans departments, reducing its global investment banking staff to 19,000 employees. This wasn't the first round of pink slips Credit Suisse had handed out in 2008: earlier in the year, the bank laid off 1,000 investment bankers. In addition, at least 170 jobs were cut from the investment banking division in 2007 and 150 people were dismissed from the struggling Credit Suisse mortgage-backed securities unit.

Spare some change?

Giles Keating, the global head of research for private banking and asset management at Credit Suisse, showed Christmas spirit at the end of 2007 by implementing his idea for a free telephone service for homeless people in London. Managed by major homeless charity, St. Mungo's, it allows homeless people to pick up messages from phone points set up in around 100 drop-in centres across the capital. The scheme receives funding equivalent to 20,000 pounds per year and saw Keating named "Volunteer of the Year" by the City of London Corporation's Dragon Awards.

GETTING HIRED

It's a Suisse of cake

If you have some banking experience under your belt and want to apply for an entry-level position at Credit Suisse, follow the "experienced professionals" link on the company careers page. At the bottom of this page you'll find a link to search for job vacancies, each of which will contain a link to an online application form. While there is no separate investment banking careers page, you can specify the division you want in the search — investment banking itself is broken down into M&A, Global Markets Solutions and Financial Institutions. If you don't want to apply for a specific position but would prefer to just apply and see what happens, click "submit my profile" at the bottom of the job search page.

Foot in the door

Credit Suisse run a range of programmes and internships for European graduates at a range of levels. If you have a Bachelors or Masters degree in any discipline then you'll be all set for the analyst programmes. If you have completed an MBA and also have relevant work experience, then you're certainly potential associate material. Finally, if you're pursuing a PhD or Masters degree in a subject such as maths, physics, engineering, computer science or quantitative finance then you might have the skills for the quantitative programme. At all three levels (analyst, associate, and quantitative) you can undertake either a full-time programme or a ten-week internship to give you an idea of what's what. Each programme emphasises hands-on experience alongside structured training, with differing levels of responsibility.

To apply, select "training programmes" on the company website and click "apply now." From here, select the programme you're interested in — you'll need to register your details on the site and fill in an online application. Several of the divisions you may apply to will also require you to take an online verbal/numerical reasoning test, which will affect whether the bank decides to take you to the next stage of application.

Credit where credit's due

Once you've submitted your application, with any luck, you'll be called for an interview. This will involve one or more competency-based interviews, lasting around 30 minutes, either over the phone or face-to-face. You'll get some exposure to a range of people from the division you're interested in, varying in seniority and background. If you perform well here, you will be asked back for the final round of interviews which is designed to see which group you are best suited to, and to determine where your strengths lie. The firm will make sure you know exactly what your job will involve at this stage, and what your typical day-to-day duties will be. Soon after this, Credit Suisse will get in touch to let you know the results of your hard work.

"Credit Suisse has developed a more professional and structured hiring process since I joined," a member of the corporate finance team tells us. "The candidates see ten or more people and are tested on specific areas. They'll test your technical, numerical, communication and other soft skills as well as market awareness. You'll also have to present a case study to a panel (as a team) and do a numerical and English written test."

A lateral hire who joined the firm's sales team said the process was "fairly short". He explains, "I was hired from another firm to fill a gap in a team, so for me there were just four interviews with the heads of product and regional sales. The questions were very much focused on the job at hand, and my knowledge of the market and clients."

OUR SURVEY SAYS

A credit to the company

Insiders describe the company culture at Credit Suisse as "very professional", "dynamic", "challenging", "stimulating" and "rewarding". One London-based worker says the firm's office is "very collegial and friendly." The dress code on the whole is smart casual.

An experienced worker who disclosed that on average he works 70-to-80-hour weeks tells us, "It is truly a great environment to work in. I have had quite a bit of experience with other corporate cultures and for me Credit Suisse is the best in every aspect."

While the level of demand for weekend working will vary with departments, a sales department member tells us, "I only visit the office at weekends a few times each year."

"The culture is based on entrepreneurship and innovation," an experienced employee in the corporate finance department tells us, adding that the atmosphere in the office is "friendly". He says: "I have made good friends at the firm with whom I socialise outside work."

As far as remuneration goes, survey respondents were very happy with their yearly takings — and impressive bonuses. In addition to this, an insider tells us that "CS have recently enhanced an accelerated stock option scheme," adding "There are also various investment schemes that allow you to invest along with CS's private equity funds, together with the perks you'd expect. The most important in my view is the pension contribution."

9 UBS INVESTMENT BANK

UBS Global Headquarters
Bahnhofstrasse. 45
P.O. Box CH-8098
Zurich
Switzerland
Tel: +41 (0) 11 234 11 11
www.ubs.com

The Stats

Employer Type: Public Company
Ticker Symbol: UBS (NYSE, VTX)
Chief Executive: Marcel Rohner
IB Chairman and Chief Executive:
Jerker Johansson
2007 Revenue: CHF 31.9bn
2007 Profit (Loss): (CHF 3.8bn)
2006 Revenue: CHF 47.7bn
2006 Profit: CHF 12.7bn
No. of Employees: 80,000+
No. of Offices: 50+

Departments

Business Banking • Currencies and
Commodities • Global Asset
Management • Global Wealth
Management • Investment Bank (Equities,
Finance, Fixed Income and Money
Markets, Global Asset
Management, Legal and Compliance)

European Locations

Zurich (Global HQ)
London (Investment Bank HQ)
Austria • Belgium • Channel Islands •
Cyprus • Czech Republic • France •
Germany • Greece • Ireland •
Italy • Luxembourg • Monaco • The
Netherlands • Poland • Portugal • Russia •
Spain • Sweden • Switzerland • Turkey •
United Kingdom

Key Competitors

Morgan Stanley • Merrill Lynch • Credit
Suisse • Lehman Brothers

Employment Contact

www.ubs.com/careers

THE BUZZ
WHAT EMPLOYEES AT OTHER FIRMS ARE SAYING

• "Friendly teams in many departments"
• "Good and broad-based business"
• "Risky"
• "Hours are too long"

THE SCOOP

n 2007, *The Economist* famously described Swiss banking giant UBS as, "The world's biggest manager of other people's money." And while the firm remains a key player in the industry, quite a bit has changed since then.

Hit hard by the subprime crisis that ravaged the global banking industry, UBS has had a tough year in terms of losing money, share value, and having to face the reality of heavy job cuts — in March 2008 the firm announced that it would cut thousands of jobs at a time when revenue was dipping. The news was worrying for the group's 80,000-plus employees as UBS announced up to ten percent of jobs could go. London's *Telegraph* newspaper reported, "Some 1,500 jobs are being axed worldwide, with the brunt expected to be borne in London and New York. A third of [the firm's] 22,300 investment banking staff is based in London."A few months later, reports emerged that the firm was considering cutting a further 8,000 jobs.

Subprime shake-up

In July 2007 UBS's former chief executive, Peter Wuffli, stepped down just before the credit bubble burst amid complaints over his disappointing performance — and after being turned down for the chairman role. Marcel Rohner stepped into the breach as the new chief executive. By the end of the year UBS Investment Banking head Huw Jenkins had also stepped down, to be replaced by Jerker Johansson.

At the end of 2007 UBS admitted a colossal 18.4 billion dollar writedown related to the collapse of the American subprime mortgage market and a full-year loss of 4.3 billion Swiss francs. Hard on the heels of this shock came the announcement of a further 19 billion dollar writedown in April 2008, bringing the total loss close to the 40 billion dollar mark — the highest any bank has suffered since the crisis began.

Soon after this loss was announced and the Swiss major declared it would resort to a 7.57 billion pound rights issue in an attempt to salvage its balance sheet, UBS chairman Marcel Ospel stood down. Just a month earlier his pay had been cut by 90 percent following the bank's biggest ever loss, from 26.6 million to 2.57 million Swiss francs.

Mr Rohner, elevated to chief executive last July after the ousting of Peter Wuffli, said UBS was weathering one of the most difficult periods in the history of banking. Speaking in British newspaper *The Independent*, Rohner said, "I believe this capital increase and the creation of a separate vehicle to separate problem assets from the remainder of the business will allow us to return to sustainable value creation over time." Quite how much time he actually means remains to be seen.

Break it up, boys!

"UBS's reputation has been comprehensively destroyed," said former banking chief Luqman Arnold in early 2008. Making reference to UBS's spate of colossal writedowns, he called for an overhaul of corporate governance and risk controls at the Swiss giant as part of an activist campaign he is leading. He also called for the bank to sell its asset management arm to raise capital and to break up its private bank from its afflicted investment bank, as well as altering its board in order to reduce the power held by the chairman.

Arnold's investment vehicle, Olivant, owns a 0.7 percent stake in UBS. When in April 2008 it became clear that Arnold's comments were attracting qualified support from UBS shareholders, UBS agreed to meet with Olivant before the bank's general meeting that month.

Movers and shakers

With headquarters in Zurich and Basel, Switzerland, UBS operates in more than 50 countries and from all major international centres. Globally, UBS employs more than 80,000 people. UBS Investment Bank has three front-office business areas — investment banking, equities and fixed income, the last of which includes money markets, currencies and commodities.

It serves corporate, institutional, government and private clients worldwide, offering securities and commodities sales and trading, underwriting, mergers and acquisitions advice, debt and equity capital advice, research, risk management and a variety of foreign exchange transactions. It also provides access to a number of private equity and hedge funds.

As an integrated global financial firm, UBS creates added value for clients by drawing on the combined resources and expertise of all its businesses. UBS is a leading global wealth manager, a global investment bank and securities firm with a strong institutional and corporate client franchise and a key asset manager. The Swiss giant holds roughly a quarter of Switzerland's lending market and is the country's market leader in corporate and individual client banking.

Back in the day

UBS traces its roots to the early days of Swiss financing when a series of mergers, acquisitions and name changes brought a number of Switzerland's banks together as the Union Bank of Switzerland and the Swiss Bank Corporation. These entities merged in 1998 to form UBS AG and then, in 2000, the reborn bank acquired a securities arm by purchasing New York-based PaineWebber. A re-branding effort in 2003 brought all of UBS's activities under one streamlined umbrella.

Looking on the bright side

In spite of the subprime crisis and the losses it spread, UBS topped the league of financial advisers to mergers and acquisitions (M&As) in Asia-Pacific in 2007, according to figures released by data provider Mergermarket, with a total of 58 deals worth 85.5 billion dollars. The firm is also a reputable No. 2 by announced European M&As, with 233 deals worth 651.7 billion dollars in 2007. In the UK, UBS has the top placing in M&A with 111 announced deals worth 543.8 billion dollars. Last but not least, UBS remains included in the Top 20 Global Financial Institutions (at number 20), with a 38,167 million euros market value as of March 31, 2008.

Honours, awards and accolades

Despite the infamous credit crunch, the fact is that the majority of UBS has continued to perform very well and remains a leader in many areas. The firm is recognised as the number one European Equities House and last year was ranked No. 1 in Europe for M&A. So, despite the writedowns, UBS is one of the best capitalised banks in the world with a Tier One ratio of around 12 percent — higher than most of its competitors.

Some of the firm's latest credentials include the "2008 M&A Bank of the Year" by *Acquisition Monthly* Awards, "M&A Financial Advisor for Europe in 2007" by *The Financial Times* and *Merger Markets*, "Best Global Emerging Market Investment Bank" by Euromoney in 2007 and "Best Bank Overall" for the last 20 years by *Euroweek* 2007 Year Awards. In 2006, UBS was also voted the "Best European Equity House of the Decade" by *Financial News*.

The bank's good performance was also reflected in the Thomson Extel 2008 Survey results, which ranked UBS as the Leading Pan-European Brokerage firm for Equity and Equity Linked Research for the eighth consecutive year. The bank was also voted the first Pan-European Brokerage firm for Equity Trading and Execution, for Equity Sales and for Operations.

Mover and a shaker

Identifying an emerging demand in the market, in 2007, UBS partnered with global financial news service Bloomberg to launch a global commodity index published in both dollars and euros. The new index has become a basis for a range of investment products offered by UBS, further strengthening the Swiss giant's product offering and international growth. Through the UBS Bloomberg Constant Maturity Commodity Index, investors are able to scan and diversify their investments in global commodities by viewing the up-to-date economic commodity environment which has been designed to be a global benchmark for investment in the sector.

Everything's gone green

Speaking of indices, UBS seems to love them, and in April 2007, *The Financial Times* reported that UBS launched the world's first "Global Warming index", initially based on 15 major US cities. The index would allow businesses "most affected by the uncertainty of climate change — from ice-cream salesmen to makers of winter coats — to hedge their profits against it in a simple and transparent fashion. Retail and institutional investors will also be able to buy exposure to — or short sell — the index in much the same way that they would with the FTSE or Dow Jones stock indices. If temperatures rise, so will the value of the index."

> " You'll also benefit from senior managers giving you their perspective on firm strategy and goals "

That said, only months earlier, in November 2006, UBS unveiled the UBS World Emissions Index (UBS-WEMI), the first index for global emissions allowances markets. At its launch, UBS-WEMI covered several European emissions trading platforms, all of which are part of the European Emissions Trading Scheme — an early implementation of the Kyoto Protocols.

The index takes advantage of the rules implemented by the Kyoto Protocol, which 165 countries ratified in August 2006. Under these rules, industries that can easily reduce their emissions to regulatory levels can sell their unused emissions permits to other industries that need them.

GETTING HIRED

Working for Jerker

UBS offers a range of internships and graduate programmes to get the talent it wants into its offices. If you're looking for a summer internship or a full-time graduate programme, go to the company careers page and select "Graduates and Interns."

From here you can search for available training programmes in investment banking. In Europe, programmes are run in Zurich, Frankfurt, London, Madrid, Milan, Stockholm, Moscow and Amsterdam.

The bank also operates an academic sponsorship programme open to those in their first year or study, or the second year of a four-year course. You'll receive mentoring and regular correspondence with senior professionals, together with financial support throughout your university career, and a ten-week summer internship placement on graduation. If you're at MBA level you might be interested in the full-time and summer associate programmes that the bank runs.

Pick a programme

Lasting between 18 and 24 months, UBS's graduate programmes are available in global wealth management and business banking, investment banking, global asset management, and "corporate centre". With each programme you can expect an intensive education broken down into modules on the financial markets and UBS products, together with other topics central to the business.

Teaching methods include classroom instruction, case studies, presentations and practical exercises. You'll also receive on-the-job training, with assignment to a range of business areas enabling you to get a taste of day-to-day work and build up contacts. To assist in your development, you'll receive personal support from your managers. Some programmes will assign you a formal mentor.

Alongside work, the programmes incorporate a networking side with organised events and social occasions to bring you closer to your peers. You'll also benefit from senior managers giving you their perspective on firm strategy and goals.

Crème de la crème

UBS seeks out the best candidates from the top European schools and conducts a comprehensive screening process that initially consists of an online application and test, followed by interviews and an assessment centre. Information about careers and graduate opportunities at the firm can be found on the company's website at www.ubs.com/careers.

While the hiring process is clearly competitive, one insider involved in recruiting assures us that, "for all levels it's about potential and attitude as much as it is about existing achievements." Besides doing well on the logical and numerical reasoning tests and interviews, being multilingual also helps candidates get on the inside track — most new hires are fluent in more than one language.

That crucial internship

An internship is definitely an advantage. Many are hired by the departments in which they intern, and all of them seem to enjoy the programme. One recent hire explains, "I was given a variety of very engaging work, including modelling, sector analysis and deal coordination. It made it easier to be hired for a full-time position as it provides a greater opportunity to demonstrate your strengths than a short interview and case study."

Internships can also allow applicants who might not have scored the highest on the tests to shine. "The internship is what really got me hired as it allowed the team to assess me on the job rather than on tests where I probably didn't have the best scores of all," says one former participant. In fact, former interns seem to agree they were given a fair amount of freedom and that staff were open to their suggestions.

An intern can expect to shadow various team members to learn and eventually take on some of their routines. Duties include helping with day-to-day work as well as special projects. The programme also includes networking events, such as sports days and events with senior directors, along with internal training courses and breakfast meetings presented by senior managers that explain their department's function within the firm. These meetings also cover global asset management and wealth management in order to educate investment bank interns about all areas of business at UBS and thus show them career path options at the firm.

NM ROTHSCHILD & SONS

NM Rothschild & Sons Limited
New Court, St. Swithin's Lane
London EC4P 4DU
United Kingdom
Tel: +44 (0) 20 7280 5000
www.rothschild.com

The Stats

Employer Type: Private Company
Ticker Symbol: n/a
Chairman: Baron David de Rothschild
Finance Director: Isobel Baxter
2007 Revenue: £402m
2007 Profit: £63m
2006 Revenue: £356m
2006 Profit: £64m
No. of Employees: 979
No. of Offices: 65

Departments

Asset Management • Banking and
Treasury • Corporate Banking •
Investment Banking • Private Banking and
Trust

European Locations

London (HQ)
Belgium • Czech Republic • Channel
Islands • France • Germany • Greece •
Hungary • Italy • Luxembourg • Portugal •
Russia • Spain • Switzerland • Sweden •
United Kingdom

Key Competitors

Goldman Sachs • Merrill Lynch • Morgan
Stanley • UBS

Employment Contact

www.rothschild.com/careers

THE BUZZ
WHAT EMPLOYEES AT OTHER FIRMS ARE SAYING

• "Solid history"
• "British through and through"
• "Exclusive"
• "Has an 'upper class' feel"

THE SCOOP

L ondon-based, family-owned Rothschild Group is the world's largest independent merchant and investment bank and Rothschild & Sons is its investment banking arm. Rothschild's Continuation Holdings of Switzerland controls the Rothschild's empire. The firm's principal activities focus on M&A (including privatisations), debt advisory including restructuring, equity advisory, merchant banking, private banking and trust, as well as corporate banking. Over the last five years, Rothschild has been Europe's adviser of choice, working on more transactions than any other investment bank.

To serve and protect

With a history that stretches back more than two centuries, Rothschild's contribution to European banking is longstanding. As of 2008, the firm has a solid standing in the banking world, providing financial services to governments, corporations and individuals worldwide through 40 offices in more than 30 countries.

The firm's investment banking services include financial advice and execution expertise, as well as M&A (including privatisations), debt advisory as well as restructuring and equity advisory. One of Rothschild Investment Banking's notable recent transactions was the 71 billion euros acquisition of ABN AMRO by the RFS consortium comprised of RBS, Santander and Fortis.

Rothschild's corporate banking business department includes services like lending, treasury, asset finance, offshore banking and investor relations, while the private banking and trust provides independent advice on strategic planning, investment management, trust and fiduciary services as well as personalised banking services and credit solutions.

Financing history

In his book on the history of the Rothschild empire, *The House of Rothschild: Volume 1: Money's Prophets: 1798-1848*, historian Niall Ferguson has great words to describe the power and magnitude of the firm in its early years. He explains that for most of the nineteenth century, NM Rothschild was part of the "biggest bank in the world" as the English and French houses of the group NM Rothschild & Sons dominated the global bond market. Ferguson illustrated the significance of the bank's size at the time, writing: "For a contemporary equivalent, one has to imagine a merger between Merrill Lynch, Morgan Stanley, J.P. Morgan and probably Goldman Sachs too — as well, perhaps, as the International Monetary Fund, given the 19th century-Rothschild's role in stabilising the finances of numerous governments."

The Rothschild name is synonymous with art, culture, some of the most famous (and expensive) wines in the world and, of course, finance. In 1769, Mayer Amschel Rothschild founded the eponymous firm in Frankfurt and soon after enlisted his five sons to expand it throughout Europe. In 1814, the brothers would bankroll the Duke of Wellington's battle against Napoleon, purchasing gold coins throughout Europe, secretly sending them to Holland and then shipping them into Britain. The deal established Rothschild as one of the premier banks in Europe, and led to other monumental deals including bailing out Germany's banking system in 1825.

In 1875, Rothschild offered expertise to the British government during its acquisition of a large stake in the Suez Canal. In 1926, the firm helped finance London's underground transportation system. Like the British Empire it helped build, the firm's influence reached its apex in the 19th century. NMR never established a strong presence in the US market, but after the Cold War it assisted several companies in Eastern Europe to go private. As of 2008, Rothschild has offices in more than 22 countries all over the world, from Toronto to Tokyo, and headquarters in both London and New York.

A real M&A player

Since the days of smuggling and subway construction, Rothschild has become a significant force in the world of M&A advising. Enjoying a consistent presence among the top-ten global investment banks for M&A advisory, the firm's strength is centred in Europe (it has made little headway in the M&A market in the US, despite being a leader in restructuring). In 2007, it announced 360 deals worth a total of 566 billion US dollars — these included advising the Danish Ministry of Finance on the 6.6 billion euro merger of DONG and Elsam and the Government of Turkey on the 2.4 billion dollar cash offer for Telsim by Vodafone.

For the first quarter of 2008, according to Thomson Financial's league tables, Rothschild ranked No. 13 in worldwide announced M&A by deal volume, a slight drop from its position at No. 12 in the first quarter of the previous year. In completed M&A its rank was higher – No. 11, up from its previous spot at No. 13. The numbers were similar in European dealmaking, where Rothschild ranked No. 12 and No. 11 in announced and completed transactions, respectively. At home in the UK it cracked the top ten, placing No. 9 in announced M&A and No. 7 in completed deals.

Rothschild also played an important role in the 2008 mega-merger between Gaz de France and Suez, serving as co-adviser to Gaz de France alongside Merrill Lynch, Goldman Sachs, Lazard and Société Générale. The deal, two-and-a-half years in the making, is expected to wrap up in July 2008, with advisers to the two companies expecting a split of 290 million euros in fees.

All in the family

The Rothschilds have always strived to keep the business in the family, even arranging marriages in the early days. In April 2004, Sir Evelyn de Rothschild stepped aside as chairman of the firm to make room for his cousin, Baron David de Rothschild. Baron David had been running Rothschild's Paris-based bank and had chaired the firm's global investment bank, run jointly out of London, Paris and New York. Along with the handover came the unification of the NM Rothschild and the French side of the bank under one roof — a holding company called Concordia, which Baron David also chairs.

A balance of powers

Despite its excellent global reputation, the firm has struggled to keep up with larger banks. The Socialist government of François Mitterrand nationalised and renamed the Paris branch in 1982, but Baron David stayed in France and rebuilt the business. After taking control of the London business he pulled the plug on its weak-performing commodities trading unit after 200 years. In London, Rothschild had hosted the twice-daily ritual of waving small Union Jack flags to signal the price of gold.

> " The Rothschild name is synonymous with art, culture ... wines ... and of course, finance. "

Since the turn of the millennium, the Rothschild empire has gone through both reorganisation and consolidation. In September 2002, NM Rothschild Group combined 13 separate private banking units into a single worldwide private banking business. Later that year, in December 2002, the group sold the retail and institutional asset management businesses of Rothschild Asset Management to Insight Investment Management, the fund arm of British bank HBOS. The redistribution of power meant that the English and French sides of the family would have an equal stake in the company, likely mitigating family friction in the complex network of clan-run private companies that control Rothschild.

So long AMRO

At the end of 2007 Rothschild and ABN AMRO brought their 11-year equity capital markets partnership to an end, after Royal Bank of Scotland led a European consortium and bought the Dutch bank's investment banking assets. The banks will work together to complete all existing mandates, but new business origination was officially concluded on December 31, 2007.

Moving on, moving up

Two notable Rothschild executives made moves in late 2007 and early 2008. Franco Bernabè, a Rothschild vice-president, left the bank at the end of 2007 to take back his old job: head of Telecom Italia, which was struggling under a debt load of 35 billion euros. Bernabè had been forced from the position in a tense leveraged buyout, and found a home at Rothschild's investment bank in 2004. But when Telecom Italia found itself in trouble, Bernabè was persuaded to return.

Then in February James Fenwick, a 21-year veteran of the Rothschild investment bank who specialised in corporate advisory and corporate finance transactions (he got his start as a humble graduate trainee) was appointed as a client director. In his new role, Fenwick was tasked with developing Rothschild's private banking business in the North of England. Gary Powell, UK head of private banking, told reporters that the move was part of an effort to "forge closer links between our private banking and investment banking divisions in the UK."

Stacking up the awards

Each year, Rothschild boasts a host of awards and 2007 and 2008 were no exception. The firm was awarded "German M&A Adviser of the Year" and "Health and Pharma Adviser of the Year" by *Acquisitions Monthly* magazine in 2008, and in 2007 they scooped a handful of awards including *Financial News'* "French M&A House of the Year", *FT* Mergermarket Awards's "UK Financial Adviser of the Year" and *FinanceAsia.com*'s "Best M&A Deal of the Year" for its role in Tata Steel's acquisition of Corus.

Hard times mean more work

The global credit crisis has created some plum opportunities for Rothschild. In February 2008 Britain's fifth-largest mortgage lender, Northern Rock, hired Rothschild (along with consultancy McKinsey) to provide some much-needed advisory services. Northern Rock, which had been forced to borrow 25 billion pounds from the Bank of England in order to stay afloat after bad loans drained its capital reserves, was nationalised by legislation after the government failed to find a private buyer for the troubled institution.

Then in June 2008, news broke that Spanish real estate company Habitat planned to hire Rothschild for advice on debt refinancing, cost cutting — or a sale. Habitat had completed a 1.6 billion euro refinancing earlier in the year, but kept struggling in the depressed Spanish real estate market.

GETTING HIRED

A steep learning curve

Rothschild promises extensive opportunities for graduates, while warning of the steep learning curve involved in becoming a fully-fledged Rothschild banker. The company recruits graduates in investment banking in most of its offices, with the graduate training programme being run out of London (for Europe and all overseas offices excluding North America) and New York (North America).

The first six weeks in the London office consist of intensive classroom training to teach you the ins and outs of financial analysis, investment banking and related financial markets and legal issues. After this, UK graduates will carry out short placements in the investment and corporate banking divisions, where they'll be seconded to a range of teams and see live work. If you have applied for a position in, for example, Madrid or Paris, this stage will see you join an office in your chosen city.

Considering that Rothschild is not a conventionally hierarchical firm, you'll find yourself being given a lot of responsibility from the start. The majority of your tasks will include research and analysis, as well as financial modelling, such as investigating the likely effect on a company of an acquisition or disposal. The "steep learning", often mentioned on Rothschild's careers website, will of course require long hours, flexibility, and team-working skills.

In order to apply for a graduate role at Rothschild, you should have a very good degree in any academic discipline, from a recognised good university. Additional language skills are a bonus. Those who haven't achieved these results but have other key strengths that would be of interest to the firm are encouraged to submit applications as well. All applicants should also have a personal interest in the business of investment banking, and be well well-read on processes such as takeovers, mergers and capital flows.

Plant your seeds

Rothschild also offers a ten-week internship programme, based in London, Birmingham, Manchester or Leeds. Designed for those in full-time university education, doing well here will see you offered a position on the firm's full-time graduate training programme for the following year.

Applications for the UK and Spain programmes are made online, and open in the September the year before you want to start. Just click the link to the online application form under "Graduate Programmes" on the career page. It takes between 60 and 90 minutes to complete. Once submitted, you'll receive an email acknowledgement within 24 hours and a notification of interview soon after — if your application is successful, that is.

Le programme en France

Programmes in France last a minimum of six months, and applications have to be received about three to six months before the start of a position, though they are accepted year-round. Applications can be made in French only, and educational requirements are based on the French system, though a working knowledge of English is also encouraged. If your application is successful, you will face a two-stage interview process, at the end of which a decision about your recruitment will be made.

NM Rothschild also offers international programmes in the US and Asia. Check the careers website for details on details and deadlines for these.

Financial Advisory and Asset
Management
50 Stratton Street
London W1J 8LL, United Kingdom
Phone: +44 (0) 20 7187 2000

Financial Advisory
121, Boulevard Haussmann
75382 Paris, France
Tel: +33 (0) 1 44 13 01 11

Asset Management
Lazard Freres Gestion
11, rue d'Argenson
75008 Paris
Tel: +33 (0) 1 44 13 01 11

Financial Advisory and Asset
Management
Via Dell'Orso 2
20121 Milan, Italy
Tel: +39 (0) 2 723121

The Stats

Employer Type: Public Company
Ticker Symbol: LAZ (NYSE)
Chief Executive: Bruce Wasserstein
Chief Executive (Europe): Georges Ralli
2007 Revenue: $2.01bn
2007 Profit: $322m
2006 Revenue: $1.57bn
2006 Profit: $236m
No. of Employees: 2,490
No. of Offices: 329

Divisions

Asset Management • Financial Advisory

European Locations

London (HQ)
France • Germany • Italy • The
Netherlands • Spain • Switzerland •
Sweden • United Kingdom

Key Competitors

Lehman • RBS • Rothschild

Employment Contact

www.lazard.com/careers/careers.html

Paris: recruitment.france@lazard.fr
London: recruitment.london@lazard.com
Amsterdam: Benelux.office@lazard.com
Milan: italy.recruitment@lazard.com
Frankfurt, Madrid, Stockholm:
recruitment.roe@lazard.com

THE BUZZ
WHAT EMPLOYEES AT OTHER FIRMS ARE SAYING

• "Smaller, but has very good bankers"
• "Niche but effective"
• "Arrogant culture"
• "Poor perception in M&A space"

THE SCOOP

azard has been in existence for 160 years, starting in 1848 when the Lazard brothers opened Lazard Frères & Company, a dry goods business in New Orleans. However, this didn't last long, and the Lazards soon moved west with American gold prospectors, settling in San Francisco where they sold imported goods to the growing city and exported gold bullion. As demand for retail and commercial financial services grew, the Lazards expanded into financial transactions, including banking and foreign exchange.

After the gold rush

Quickly expanding from its base, Lazard opened an office in Paris in 1852 and one in London in 1870. By 1880, the Lazards' business consisted entirely of financial services, with the three "Houses" in New York, Paris and London operating independently under the overall control of Alexander Weill, a cousin of the Lazard brothers. Unification of these three entities came at the turn of the millennium at the hands of former chairman Michel David-Weill, creating Lazard LLC. Current chairman and chief executive Bruce Wasserstein became the head of Lazard in 2002. Wasserstein listed the firm on the New York Stock Exchange in May 2005 after it had enjoyed 157 years of private ownership.

The public face of Lazard

The firm's strong feature is considered to be its excellent financial advisory services, particularly when it comes to M&A and asset management. The firm has considerably expanded in Europe since it first entered the continent and its principal offices in the region are in the former "Houses" of Paris and London, as well as in Milan, Germany, France, The Netherlands, Sweden and Spain. Lazard serves corporate, partnership, institutional, government and individual clients around the world, advising on strategic and financial issues.

From the top

The firm's structure is easy to comprehend — Lazard's business is divided into two branches: financial advisory and asset management services. Within financial advisory, Lazard's renowned and busy M&A practice is organised into industry groups, including consumer goods, financial institutions, financial sponsors, healthcare and life sciences, industrial, power and energy, real estate and technology, media and telecommunications. Asset management provides equity, fixed income and cash management, alternative investment strategies, as well as merchant banking to institutional clients, financial intermediaries, private clients and investment vehicles.

In the financial advisory business, the majority of revenue typically comes from M&A; a smaller percent is generally derived from financial restructuring assignments, with the rest tending to come from other financial advisory work in capital raising. Geographically, 54 percent of revenue comes from Europe, 45 percent from the US and only one percent from the rest of the world. Lazard prides itself on a shrewd geographical spread, and while other competitors are weighted towards one side of the Atlantic or the other, Lazard is well placed to take advantage of booms in Europe or in North America.

Bruce knows best

In January 2008, Bruce Wasserstein was awarded a new five-year term as Lazard's chief executive and chairman. The announcement would certainly have been helped along by the bank's performance throughout 2007. When many banks took hard financial knocks from credit crunch fallout, Lazard posted record results. Net income for the fourth quarter showed a 43 percent increase from the previous year and Lazard's shares jumped by 9.1 percent in response to the good news. Revenues in M&A advice showed 27 percent growth in the fourth quarter to a record 313.6 million dollars, while asset management revenues rose 32 percent to a record 231.2 million dollars.

It was all going so well!

Despite an excellent end to 2007, Lazard did not quite make it out of the credit crunch wreckage unharmed. Losses on the value of bonds and equities took an unexpected swipe at the firm's profits in May 2008. Its corporate division reported outflow of 39.7 million dollars in the first quarter of 2008, compared to income of 18.7 million dollars in the same period of 2007. The losses were far smaller than those suffered by Lazard's major investment banking rivals. The firm's chief financial officer, Michael Castellano, noted in *The Financial Times* that the "first-quarter results are not, we believe, representative of the outlook for the year."

From many "Houses" to one firm

Lazard has been re-organising itself ever since its 2005 IPO. In September 2006, the head of the Paris office, Georges Ralli, was promoted to the newly created position of chief executive for European investment banking. London head William Rucker was named his deputy chief executive (both men retained their top posts in Paris and London). In addition, four bankers, Erik Maris, Matthieu Pigasse, Nicholas Shott and Antonio Weiss, were promoted to vice chairmen of the European unit. Firm chief executive Wasserstein said the moves were meant to fully integrate European investment banking and create "the next generation of management" for a new "one firm" model of Lazard banking. Moves at the top continued.

Ken Costa, previously head of European investment banking for UBS, joined as Chairman of Lazard International and Rodrigo de Rato, former head of the IMF, joined as a senior managing director of investment banking in Europe. Meanwhile Michael Grayer, from GE Finance, joined as head of debt advisory in London and Wouter Gabriels, previously chief of staff at Belgium Prime Minister Guy Verhofstadt's office, joined the firm's ranks in June 2008 as a managing director in Investment Banking.

Behind the big deals

Lazard has continually been in the spotlight since the turn of the millennium, becoming widely known for participating in a significant amount of high-volume transactions in Europe. These include advising Gaz de France on its 55 billion dollar offer for its rival on the utilities scene Suez in 2007, BAA on its 27 billion dollar-sale to Grupo Ferrovial in 2006 and the 10.8 billion dollar reorganisation and share sale between Caisse des Dépôts et Consignations and Caisse d'Epargne. Lazard advised Caisse d'Epargne on that deal, and again on its 30 billion dollar merger negotiations with Groupe Banque Populaire to create Natixis.

The high-profile deals for Lazard came thick and fast. The firm famously advised Eurotunnel as it contemplated a 12.6 billion dollar restructuring agreement with a consortium including Goldman Sachs, Barclays and Macquarie, and represented Eutelsat Communications in a major ownership restructuring that included the sale of more than half its share capital. Still, competition in the banking world was stiff, and Lazard cracked the top ten in the 2007 banking league tables for worldwide completed M&A, coming in at No. 10. For European announced M&A in the same year, Lazard came in at No. 12 and in terms of French M&A, it scooped seventh place, accruing 24.4 billion dollars worth of deals. Lazard also had a strong presence on the German M&A scene in 2007, ranking third in the announced deals with German participation transaction, with 44 deals announced, and tenth in completed deals with German participation transaction, with 25.5 billion dollars worth of transactions completed.

GETTING HIRED

Stiff competition

Lazard is well known for its presence on the university scene through a series of campus events with a view to picking up top graduates. Check the website for a list of dates and locations. With around 15 analyst vacancies each year, the competition is fierce — you'll need at least a 2:1 or equivalent to apply. The deadline to apply is generally mid-November, but you should check the company website at www.lazard.com for more specific details.

To give you a taste of the place, and the pace, Lazard offers 25 summer internship positions in its London office for undergraduates or post-graduates in their penultimate year of study. There are two seven-week internships run during the summer, one beginning in late June, and the other beginning in early August.

The firm also offers a one-year placement, during which participants complete the nine-week graduate induction programme, before joining a specialist team for the remaining time. The application process for both programmes is in February, but you should check the company careers page for precise dates.

Tricks of the trade

Once you're on the analyst programme, you'll find yourself working alongside bankers of varying seniority, including managing directors, directors, vice-presidents, associates and analysts. In London particularly, your job will see you assigned to a range of both generalist and specialist teams on a semi-annual basis.

The analyst programme in Paris and the rest of Europe likes its candidates to have an economics or business school background, in addition to a good academic background. The analysts' role here is to support transaction teams by carrying out financial and statistical analysis, research, due diligence work and the preparation of client presentations.

Lazard's graduate training programme consists of residential courses, master classes taught by practicing bankers, coaching on the job and visits to the firm's European offices. Twice a year the firm discusses individual employees' training needs, and arranges a selection of technical, personal, management, and business skills courses.

Campus to career

Applications for the one-year placement can be made online through the "Campus Recruitment" section of the company careers page. For internships in Paris, or the firm's other European offices, you should send your CV and covering letter expressing interest in any internship opportunities to the appropriate email address — Paris: recruitment.france@lazard.fr; London: recruitment.london@lazard.com; Amsterdam: Benelux.office@lazard.com; Milan: italy.recruitment@lazard.com; Frankfurt, Madrid and Stockholm internships can all be applied to by sending your CV and cover letter to: recruitment.roe@lazard.com.

The financial advisory group looks for professionals with M&A experience "from time to time," the firm says. The asset management team seeks applications from experienced buy or sell-side research analysts, and sales and trading professionals. To view vacancies for professional positions, go to www.lazard.com/careers/careers.html.

Lazard

Citigroup Centre
33 Canada Square
Canary Wharf
London, E14 5LB
United Kingdom
Tel: +44 (0) 20 7986 4000
www.citigroup.com

The Stats

Employer Type: Public Company
Ticker Symbol: C (NYSE)
Chief Executive: Vikram Pandit
2007 Revenue: $81.6bn
2007 Profit: $3.61bn
2006 Revenue: $89.6bn
2006 Profit: $21.5bn
No. of Employees: 320,000
No. of Offices: 7,500 offices in 104
countries on six continents

Departments

Consumer Banking • Global Cards •
Global Wealth Management •
Institutional Clients Group

European Locations

London (European HQ)
Belgium • Bulgaria • Czech Republic •
France • Germany • Hungary • Ireland •
Italy • Luxembourg • Poland • Romania •
Slovakia • Spain • Sweden • Switzerland •
Ukraine • United Kingdom

Key Competitors

Goldman Sachs • J.P. Morgan • Merrill
Lynch • Morgan Stanley

Employment Contact

www.careers.citigroup.com

Pluses

• "Easy going and relaxed" environment
• Very cosmopolitan

Minuses

• "Its internal processes are too
  bureaucratic"
• "Could have better perks"

THE BUZZ
WHAT EMPLOYEES AT OTHER FIRMS ARE SAYING

• "Extremely skilled"
• "Behemoth"
• "Unstable senior management"
• "Big, but unfriendly"

THE SCOOP

B efore it became an international banking powerhouse, Citi was a humble business. Established in London in 1818 as J. Henry Schröder & Co., Mr. Schröder is long gone and the firm that he founded was subsumed — along with dozens of others, including Citibank and Salomon Brothers — by the conglomerate now known as Citi.

The bank operates in 104 countries and offers its customers corporate and investment banking, transaction services, consumer and private banking, credit cards and personal finance. Citi was one of the first Western banks to establish a presence in post-Communist Eastern Europe, as Citi Handlowy, and now controls eight percent of Poland's corporate banking market and four percent of Polish consumer banking.

Citi's four main business areas are the Institutional Clients Group (ICG), global wealth management, consumer banking and global cards. Consumer banking includes retail banking, US consumer banking, loans and insurance. ICG includes global banking services (such as M&A advisory, debt,

> 66 Citi was one of the first Western banks to establish a presence in post-Communist Eastern Europe 99

equity, restructuring and underwriting), global capital markets, transaction services as well as alternative investments. Global wealth management encompasses the Citi private bank, Smith Barney American Private Wealth Management, and investment research.

Emerging markets

Citi has continued expansion into Central and Eastern Europe by opening its first Serbian representative office in Belgrade in 2006. The bank already operates Poland, Slovakia, Bulgaria, Romania, Hungary, Czech Republic, and Serbia where its Belgrade office provides corporate and investment banking products to Serbian corporations, institutions and public sector entities, as well as global transaction services, corporate finance and advisory services.

William J. Mills, chairman and chief executive of Citi's EMEA division, noted that Serbia had become attractive "due to its growth potential, geopolitical position ... and pace of development." Other Citi executives indicated the bank was committed to establishing itself in the Balkan region – which may be poised to become a global growth hot spot.

The chief formerly known as ...

November 5, 2007 will probably be forever etched in the memory of Charles "Chuck" Prince III, being the day he stepped down as chief executive of the largest bank in the world. His departure came amid colossal declines in the value of subprime mortgage related investments, and on the back of a simmering dissatisfaction with his capabilities among shareholders. In the third quarter of 2007, the bank had seen a 6.4 billion US dollar writedown — 500 million dollars more than predicted a few days earlier. Citi soon conceded that it would need to lose a further 11 billion dollars in the fourth quarter. In fact, it went on to writedown 18 billion dollars in that quarter.

Promoted into Prince's place is Vikram Pandit, who joined Citi in early 2007 after the world leader bought Old Lane, the hedge fund that Pandit set up after leaving Morgan Stanley. Commentators noted that in the wake of such underestimated losses, Pandit needed to address issues with Citi's risk management practices to win back the confidence of its investors and staff. In addition to this he needed to cut costs and upgrade the bank's technology systems. In Citi's 2007 annual report, investors read that Pandit had lowered the bank's dividend to 0.32 dollars, cutting, costs and allowing reinvestment in growth. Technological innovation was identified as another key area of focus going into 2008.

Taking a turn at the top

Two major executive shuffles came in March 2008. Michael Klein, former chief executive of markets and banking in the Europe, Middle East and Africa (EMEA) region, was appointed chairman of Citi's institutional clients group (which includes markets and banking and Citi Alternative Investments). John Havens, formerly chief executive of Citi's alternative investments unit, was tapped as the group's chief executive; he was simultaneously named chairman of Citi Alternative Investments. Citi head Vikram Pandit also asked Klein to lead a company-wide client relations committee aimed at "delivering one Citi to all clients."

Could've been worse

Few global banks had good news to report at the end of the first quarter of 2008, but Citi managed to find a bright spot of sorts: its writedown of 15 billion US dollars fell below analyst expectations that ranged as high as 22 billion dollars. However, the bank also posted a 5.1 billion quarterly loss, the result of shaky performance in the fixed-income business and the ongoing consumer credit crunch. The markets and banking division was the biggest drag on Citi's bottom line, posting a 4.48 billion loss due to writedowns on subprime exposures, commercial real estate, leveraged loans and other securities.

The news prompted immediate reaction from Citi brass, who announced in April 2008 that they would sell the bank's commercial lending and leasing business to General Electric for an undisclosed sum, part of an effort to secure much-needed capital. Other holdings put on the block included Diners Club International and Citi's stake in Redecard SA, a Brazilian credit card company. To no one's surprise, Citi also announced that it would reduce its global head count by 9,000 — this came after it cut 4,200 jobs in the final quarter of 2007. The markets and banking division lost 1,800 employees in March 2008 alone, but in London job losses were measured in the hundreds, not the thousands. Citi currently employs approximately 320,000 people worldwide, with around 11,500 of these working in London.

Keeping up on deals

Financial woes notwithstanding, Citi made its presence known on the banking league tables for the first quarter of 2008. According to Thomson Financial, Citi was the world's No. 8 mergers and acquisitions advisor for the quarter, by imputed fees. In specific industry deals, Citi was the world's No. 1 materials sector advisor, and the No. 3 advisor on deals in the financial and energy sectors. By deal value, Citi ranked No. 2 in worldwide announced deals, just behind Goldman Sachs. In worldwide completed deals it was No. 3, narrowly edged out by Credit Suisse and J.P. Morgan.

In European deal-making, Citi ranked No. 2 in both announced and completed M&A by deal volume, ceding the top spot to Deutsche Bank and J.P. Morgan, respectively. Looking at UK deals, Citi was again runner-up in announced transactions (Lehman Brothers took first place); in UK completed mergers and acquisitions it slipped below the top five, coming sixth.

Citi's global head of mergers and acquisitions, Frank Yeary, was widely credited with the bank's strong performance on the league tables — but in June 2008 he announced his resignation, decamping from Citi to accept a position as vice-chancellor of the University of California, Berkeley. Yeary's resignation becomes effective in mid-July, at which point Raymond McGuire, global co-head of investment banking, will fill the role on a temporary basis until a replacement is found.

Cut some to save others

In May 2008, Citi pledged to trim 400 billion US dollars of assets worldwide in order to shore up its core businesses, and one of the first big cuts came in the UK consumer sector. The bank announced it would eliminate nearly 25 percent of its UK consumer employees, shuttering its CitiFinancial personal loan business and mortgage intermediary Future Mortgages. The Citi and Egg consumer brands — as well as the

97

UK investment banking operation — escaped unscathed, and will likely reap benefits from the cost-cutting elsewhere.

At the same time, the bank made plans to sell off three billion dollars' worth of new shares: since the end of 2007, Citi has had to raise more than 36 billion dollars in capital to replace its losses from subprime mortgages and other debts.

Trimming the hedges in the shape of a … loss

In June 2008, the bank announced plans to close Old Lane Partners following two years of flat returns that caused 200 million dollars of writedowns in the first quarter. The closure will mark close to four failures for Citi's hedge fund management unit.

The difficulties hedge funds currently face are a sign of how tricky global markets have become, and how hedge funds have lost their previous rosy tint. The hedge funds within several major banks, such as Goldman Sachs, have begun to pile up losses.

Don't relax yet

Despite its aggressive streamlining efforts, Citi chief financial officer Gary Crittenden warned that the second quarter of 2008 would likely bring more losses. At a June 2008 conference hosted by Deutsche Bank, Crittenden said Citi's writedowns on collateralised debt obligations would be lower than they were in the first quarter of the year, but writedowns related to leveraged loans and bond insurers would continue to be steep. Overall credit costs are also expected to stay high, the result of continued turmoil in the global mortgage markets.

GETTING HIRED

Bright lights, big Citi

Clearly, working for a firm as international and as huge as Citi means that opportunities for young professionals and graduates are plentiful. Information about careers and graduate opportunities at Citi can be found on the company's website at www.careers.citigroup.com.

Akin to a marathon

The company recruits at top business schools and universities around Europe. Applying for a position begins with an online registration form followed by uploading a CV and

Citi

cover letter. While the exact hiring process will vary with the position you're applying for, the basic system is the same. There's one day of interviews with either directors or managing directors, a case study presented to senior business executives and a group case study, plus a numerical test, we are told by survey participants. The questions asked address "core competencies like teamwork, leadership skills, creative thinking and motivation," says a recent hire in London. The process will also vary with location.

A recent hire recalls: "They asked technical questions such as accounting and valuation, as well as questions about my CV." An experienced hire in Madrid tells us, "I interviewed with all senior members in the office, for a total of ten interviews." "In small offices it is particularly important that the new hire fits in with everyone," he adds. "The questions I was asked covered different

> 66 The difficulties hedge funds currently face are a sign of how tricky global markets have become 99

methods of valuation, such as comps, precedents, DCF and LBO and how multiples evolve." There were also a lot of "personal questions, about my motivation, my reasons for moving jobs and my expectations." "I had seven interviews with senior members of my M&A team," says an analyst in the London office. "Two interviews were technical and the rest were more casual, to get an impression of my personality and fit within the team." The respondent muses that, "in this job it is not just your aptitude but your attitude that matters."

"I know a lot of people who failed at the interview stage," says an insider in the sales department. Those who are lucky or brilliant enough to make it through the first round of interviews go to an assessment centre for additional interviews and a battery of competency tests, which includes a group discussion, an essay and a case study. "I was asked the expected questions about my motives in joining an investment bank, what attracted me to Citi and M&A in particular, etc," another insider said. "There were also 'competency questions' along the lines of 'When have you received negative feedback and how did you deal with it?'"

Interviewing for a position at an investment bank isn't simply being tested for some quantitative and analytical skills. Citi, like other banks, is interested in how you deal with real-life situations and what makes you stand out from the crowd. Be prepared to answer questions about your degree and your extracurricular activities.

Summer in the Citi

If you do a summer internship it "really does set you in good stead for a graduate job," says a London-based analyst. He adds that performing well over the summer and having a good appraisal at the end of it translates into a very good chance of being offered a graduate position. "My summer was so much fun!" he exclaims, noting that he had to learn the day-to-day tasks, but also assess the efficiency of the team and present, at the end of the internship, a plan to improve efficiency. "Citi hired based upon our appraisal and our performance in this interview," he surmises. "I think I might not have my graduate job if I hadn't done the internship." A banker in Frankfurt emphasises that all of the full-time positions in London are filled with summer interns.

The assessment day agenda usually entails interviews with management, a maths test, a group exercise and a presentation, according to one former intern who now works for the firm's M&A division. He elaborates: "For the internship, I had two 20- to 30-minute first-round interviews, then an assessment centre for the final round. The most junior interviewer was an associate and the most senior was the head of German/Austrian investment banking."

A former intern who is now a trading analyst says interning was crucial in his landing a position at the firm. He says, "Overall, I found it relatively easy to get hired after completing the internship, not only because of the experience that you can use to your advantage, but also because you understand the business much better." He adds, "During my ten-week summer internship in 2005, I spent the majority of my time shadowing traders and working on quantitative projects such as financial instrument pricing and analysis."

Another former intern, now in the sales department, describes the internship as really being a "ten-week interview." He says that during the internship he worked on the sales desk, "did lots of administrative work," and spent time moving around the floor to find out what everyone did and how things worked. And then, his ten weeks of anticipation was greeted with an answer: "On the last day they told us if we'd been hired or not."

But remember, there's no guarantee that an internship will lead to an offer. "Internship gets your foot into the door, but whether you make it in depends on performance in [the] summer," explains one analyst. "As far as I am aware, only 50 percent got an offer."

The cream of the crop

Some sources say it can be tough to land a job with Citi. Most investment bankers in the firm's London office are graduates of top universities such as Oxford, Cambridge or the London School of Economics. It's also interesting to note that in the era of the MBA, most Citi staffers surveyed don't have one — although a large percentage do hold other advanced degrees.

To work in corporate finance for Citi's corporate and investment banking division, applicants need strong grades from a "good" university. And like most other firms, Citi also looks at skills, experience and commitment. A successful applicant doesn't need to have a background in economics and finance, but the firm definitely wants employees who possess strong quantitative skills, a superior academic background and good communication skills.

Unless you are exceptionally brainy and have some way to prove this in the application process, an internship and work experience become rather necessary. That said, although getting hired at Citi isn't easy, it isn't impossible either. "It is a huge firm so there is always demand for staff," says one recent hire. "The selection criteria and application process are no harder or easier than at any other bank."

OUR SURVEY SAYS

Putting in the hours

The working hours disclosed by survey respondents ranged from a 40-50 per week average, all the way up to 80-90 hours. While workers admit, "we work very hard," a respondent in Moscow notes that the work schedule can be flexible, depending on the employee's ability to get work done in an efficient manner. "I would suggest that it's more self-imposed pressure rather than corporate,"

> ❝ Citi is interested in how you deal with real-life situations and what makes you stand out from the crowd ❞

another worker ventures. "Some of our team choose to come in earlier and leave later. The average for most is an 11-hour day, although some of us do more." When it came to weekend work, the number of people giving up their own time for work varied with department: "People rarely work weekends in the Syndicate team. This is not true, however, in Origination," a London banker notes.

Overall there was a mix of attitudes in respondents, ranging from one Poland-based worker's comment, "If I want to leave early it is not a problem. It is more important to do the job, not to stay at work," to a Frankfurt banker's more single-minded observation: "In investment banking in general, you have to sacrifice everything to work."

Diversity hats on, everyone

The firm is very cosmopolitan, a London staffer says. "The trading floor resembles the United Nations — it's very good." Across the board respondents note an impressive commitment to diversity. In the Belfast office "one in every five people is a foreign national."

On the whole, the firm's diversity with respect to women was praised. "As a female on the desk, I haven't seen anything but a positive attitude towards diversity," one worker tells us. "Over half the MDs in my department are female and there are woman-focused programmes that you can get involved in too, should you choose."

A female employee lauded the firm's maternity arrangements as "really good!" She says: "I was given six months maternity leave on full pay and there is a 97 percent return rate of employees after maternity leave."

Please Citi, can we have some more?

It's not all hard work and if you're in the office late you can expect a free meal and car ride home. A Madrid-based employee was happy about "go-kart races to celebrate deals — and for any success the whole office gets together for drinks." A worker in Moscow was glad the firm provided relocation expenses, while a London insider noted you often get, "free places in boxes at concerts or other high profile events, as well as free Nobu lunches and free team dinners."

A Madrid-based employee tells us: "I've participated in good deals — for Spain, once in a lifetime deals — and the people I work with are exceptional professionals." However, "many things could improve," he goes on. There are "small details and lifestyle issues that, if improved, would make this the perfect place to work."

On the whole staff are pleased with the firm, but have a range of suggestions for improvements. Higher bonuses, more frequent raises, fewer hours, more client contact and more responsibility for juniors were among the major changes sought after. "It [Citi] should provide a better career support and mentoring scheme," a first-year analyst informs us, while a worker in Madrid tells us, "its internal processes are too bureaucratic," and there needs to be "better work organisation by the managing director to improve workers' lifestyle. Promotion and ranking for this location is like a black box."

Many employees gave the impression that compared to other banks, Citi were pretty stingy with their perks. There were additional calls for things as simple as "free fresh coffee and tea, and even fruit," and complaints about the gym in the London office. "It's pathetic that a building with ten thousand people in it has a ten by ten feet gym with six treadmills permanently in use!" exclaimed an exasperated, but undoubtedly healthy banker. "Move it to a bigger area and make it better!" he suggests, with some urgency.

Do it yourself

An employee in the firm's Istanbul office reports that on a weekly basis, "I meet with my boss and discuss work and how to improve in my job," noting, "It really helps my personal development and the work I am doing." A source in Madrid admits that managers are well qualified, but the only problem can be that they "don't manage themselves appropriately" and "often fail to set feasible deadlines."

A London-based worker was happy with the general lack of autocracy among managers. "I am given a lot of authority with what to do daily and how to do the job." Sometimes the managers are "not as involved or motivational as I'd hoped," but says that overall, "I'm given plenty of room to do it my way." This does of course mean a significant level of responsibility." As another London worker notes, "You need to be able to cope with "large amounts of uncertainty." He says this means your manager "may often expect you to take things away, find out the root cause of a problem or issue, devise a solution and then report back."

I'm Spartacus!

From respondents' comments, hard work would appear to be the mainstay of the culture at Citi. Ranging from one Madrid-based banker's view that you should "work as hard as you can — it's a pure meritocracy," to the almost worrying catechism "work is more important than anything else in life," volunteered by an employee in Belfast, you should be prepared to knuckle down. However, voices in the London office assert that the firm is very "easygoing and relaxed" and "seems less political and hierarchical than in other firms," so culture clearly varies with location.

BARCLAYS CAPITAL

5 The North Colonnade
Canary Wharf
London, E14 4BB
United Kingdom
Tel: +44 (0) 20 7623 2323
www.barcap.com

The Stats

Employer Type: Public Company
Ticker Symbol: BARC (LSE); BCS (NYSE); 8642 (Tokyo)
Group Chief Executive: Robert "Bob" Diamond Jr
2007 Revenue: £23bn
2007 Profit: £5bn
2006 Revenue: £22bn
2006 Profit: £5.1bn
No. of Employees: 5,500 in Europe
No. of Offices: Locations in 29 countries

Departments

Distribution • E-commerce • Financing • Indices • Investment Banking • Private Equity • Research • Risk Management

European Locations

London (HQ)
France • Germany • Ireland • Italy • The Netherlands • Portugal • Spain• Switzerland • United Kingdom

Key Competitors

Goldman Sachs • J.P. Morgan • Lehman Brothers • Merrill Lynch

Employment Contact

www.barcap.com/campusrecruitment

Pluses

• "Very pleasant teamwork atmosphere"
• "Sensible work/life balance"

Minuses

• Poor retention policy
• Long hours

THE BUZZ
WHAT EMPLOYEES AT OTHER FIRMS ARE SAYING

• "Good to work for"
• "Innovative and aggressive"
• "Not M&A focused"
• "Old school"

THE SCOOP

B arclays Capital is the investment banking arm of Barclays Bank PLC, a parent company with more than 1.2 trillion pounds on its balance sheet at the end of fiscal year 2007, and clearly capable of offering considerable support. Globally, Barclays Capital has offices in 29 countries and over 16,200 employees —resources it devotes to debt market financing and risk management for sovereign, corporate and institutional clients. Offering global corporates, government organisations and financial institutions advice in undertaking financing opportunities, Barclays Capital offers services to both issuer and investor clients, with a focus in the cash and derivatives markets.

Trading is at the core of the firm's business model and primarily involves the generation of profit through the purchase and sale of financial instruments. It also stands among Europe's leading mid-market private equity investors.

Child of the 1980s

While Barclays Bank PLC traces its roots to 18th century London, Barclays Capital grew out of its parent company's continuing global expansion in the 1980s, and the founding of an investment capital division in 1986 called BZW Investment Management. Today, Barclays Capital is one of the world's leading investment banking divisions and in recent years it has increased the range of its investment banking activities to taking income from mortgage-backed securities, equity products, commodities and derivative products across all asset classes. In January 2008, Barclays Capital won five "Deal of the Year" awards at the *Islamic Finance News* awards, recognising its contribution to increasing accessibility in the Islamic market for global investors.

BARXing up the right tree

Among the most lauded of Barclays Capital's specialities is its leading e-commerce execution platform service, known as BARX. More than 3,000 clients, particularly corporations, institutional investors and financial institutions use the service; annual transactions are firmly hitting the three trillion pound mark, and in November 2005, BARX was voted overall winner in the European Banking Technology Awards in *Banking Technology* magazine. Continually adding features to the system since its inception, in 2006 BARX became the first to offer electronic CME Eurodollar options, with CME citing BARX's "tremendous distribution network and sophisticated functionality" as reasons for the partnership. CME Eurodollar options averaged nearly 750,000 contracts a day in 2005, and are known to be the world's largest interest rate options market, as well as the most actively traded, exchange-listed interest rate options globally.

In 2006, the service was cited by *Euromoney* as one of the "series of innovative measures" that led to Barclays Capital winning the "Foreign Exchange House of the Year Award". It was shortlisted alongside the gargantuan Deutsche Bank and only slightly less major contender Citi. In 2006, Ivan Ritossa, Barclays Capital's head of foreign exchange said in *Euromoney* magazine, "Back in 2001, we weren't in the Euromoney top-ten ... People didn't look at us as a major FX bank. We just weren't seen as relevant in the market. Now we're number four in the *Euromoney* poll and we're the only bank in the top 20 that's gone up every year in the last five years. We've done that in a consolidating environment where the big are getting bigger."

Yes, subprime minister?

More recently, in January 2008 in the wake of the subprime crisis and subsequent credit crunch, Barclays Capital said goodbye to co-president, and head of the division which pioneered the SIV-lite investment vehicle, Grant Kvalheim. He quit following the bank's losses in subprime mortgages amid net writedowns of 1.3 billion pounds in November 2007, leaving Jerry del Missier as sole president, and sole clear heir to chief executive Bob Diamond.

In another league

Barclays Capital ranked eighth in Global Debt and Equity Capital Markets in Thomson Financial, bringing home 352.8 billion US dollars in proceeds at the end of 2007. This figure was the result of 960 deals, and marked a 0.2 percent change in market share.

Barclays Capital has for the past 11 years kept its distance from mergers and acquisitions — it is currently ranked 156th according to Dealogic. Its hiring raid on ABN AMRO of 40 bankers in May 2008 however, means that for the first time in 11 years it will have an M&A advisory capacity. The bank has played down the move as a fresh M&A start, and is referring to the new team as "corporate advisory", but several commentators have seen the move as the bank's return to M&A activity.

GETTING HIRED

Maths and English

Barclays Capital offers three types of positions to graduates of varying levels. The fundamental position, "analyst," requires an undergraduate degree and occasionally a masters. The firm's website lists intelligence, numeracy and communication skills among its sought-after qualities for this role, and notes fluency in more than one language as a definite asset. Barclays Capital lists 18 specific avenues that are available for those aiming for the analyst role, including compliance, corporate communications, facilities management finance, and trading and technology.

The "associate" is a more specialised role, calling for applicants who are working towards a business school MBA. Alongside this, you must have undergone a period of professional work and be able to demonstrate your progression, project work responsibility, leadership, teamwork and international awareness. Jobs at this level are available in the areas of strategy and planning, investment banking and debt capital markets, research, sales, structuring and trading.

If you're more interested in a cutting edge technical role developing mathematical models for trading and risk management activities, then you might want to go for the "quantitative associate" level position. Candidates for these positions should have gained or be studying towards a PhD (or equivalent) in a highly technical discipline like maths, physics or engineering. If you're not at this level, you're still in

> " Barclays Capital lists 18 specific avenues available for those aiming for the analyst role "

with a chance if you're studying at a post-graduate level and have a good understanding of numerical methods, coding, probability and stochastic calculus as well as fantastic analytical skills. Your study would have to be primarily research-driven and include original work. You must also have defended a thesis before an advisory panel. If you're at this level, you'll find jobs in quantitative analytics, research, global financial risk management, structuring and trading open to you.

Capital interns

Summer placements are available for each of the three levels, while analysts have the option of the spring session, which is designed more to give participants as much exposure to what goes on in investment banking as possible. The spring placement is available only to those in the first year of an undergraduate degree at a European university, (or to those in the second year of a four-year course) and takes place towards the end of March.

Those interested in a technology-related role will find a range of industrial placements available to them; these typically last between six and 12 months and begin in March. Other internship opportunities may be investigated by clicking the "Positions Wizard" on the online application form. To apply for internships you need to click the "Register and apply" link in the top right and complete the online application form. The deadline for all summer internships and the spring session is January 31, 2009, but they do begin screening applications as early as September.

Pro(fessional suc)cess?

The application procedure for full-time positions is the same as that for internships. Once you've completed the online application form, there is also an online aptitude test. Firstly you'll be given a numerical reasoning test. Within 24 hours, you'll receive an email letting you know if you passed. If you did, you'll be invited to complete the verbal reasoning test.

Successfully completing both tests within five days will enable you to proceed to the next part of the recruitment process. Once your application has been screened, you may be asked to participate in a telephone interview. At this stage the company mainly want to hear about your motivation for applying. If you impress, you'll be asked along to a final assessment event, where you'll meet senior management and have a chance to show off your strengths and skills though some team and individual exercises.

The interview process for graduate and internship positions is more structured than that for experienced hires which, "can be said to be tough and robust", explains a London-based manager.

The first round "is completely about your CV", points out a London-based analyst developer. He adds that it was for more than an hour and that the interviewers ask "a lot about your experience in previous companies and general questions like why you were leaving your previous job." There are also questions, one junior insider tells us, such as, "What was the most and least enjoyable part of your previous job." The same source declares: "The person who interviewed me was young and very friendly."

For the second interview you can expect to meet the prospective superior staff of the area you're applying to.

OUR SURVEY SAYS

Stepping in

"Not all that glitters is gold," goes the saying, and this is also the case with Barclays Capital. Even if overall satisfaction levels are high at the bank, some respondents pointed towards several aspects in need of improvement.

A London-based respondent discloses that the firm's "retention policy is non-existent. IT has a high attrition rate and one gets the impression that management think interns can come in and fill any role." The same insider adds that, at the same time, "people never get fired unless they're really bad." This has downsides to it as people who don't really make an effort and have "hung around long enough to know everybody" can still "stick around and be a burden to their colleagues."

Even with this in mind, he goes on to say, "Overall it's a good place to start a career in, or a mid-career stop over to get some business exposure. Long-term prospects depend on you and whom you work with!"

Happy bankers …

Staff are overall very happy with their experience at Barclays Capital. A "growing multicultural environment", "possibilities of growth", "a relaxed dress code", "a sensible life-work balance", and a "very pleasant teamwork atmosphere" were among their reasons.

A London-based analyst reflects that working at "Barcap" is a "very pleasant experience". "I've met many people from different areas and 80 percent of them are keen to spend time with you." Diversity at the firm "is huge", he explains, adding "there are people from virtually everywhere, with no single predominance." The dress code for trading is smart casual, "nothing really special." He adds that, "hours are not too bad, so one can still have a life. Well, maybe 50 percent of a life."

Another insider, a junior analyst developer states that career growth "looks good" and there is flexibility to switch to various departments inside Barclays. The company growth also looks very good, he adds. Barclays Capital has offices in 29 different countries and 16,200 employees and is constantly maintaining its expansion. But its size doesn't mean you'll get lost in the bureaucratic shuffle — it means there are "more areas for you to explore."

8 Canada Square
London, E14 5HQ
United Kingdom
Tel: +44 020 7991 8888
www.hsbc.com

The Stats

Employer Type: Public Company
Ticker Symbol: HSBA (LSE); HBC
(NYSE); 0005 (Hong Kong)
Group Chairman: Stephen K. Green
Group Chief Executive: Michael F.
Geoghegan
2007 Revenue: $87.6bn
2007 Profit: $20.5bn
2006 Revenue: $70.1bn
2006 Profit: $16.9bn
No. of Employees: 330,000
No. of Offices: 9,800+

Departments

Asset Management • Commercial
Banking • Consumer Banking • Credit
Cards • Insurance • Leasing • Securities
Trading

European locations

London (HQ)
Armenia • Belgium • Cyprus • Czech
Republic • France • Germany • Greece •
Guernsey • Hungary • Ireland • Isle of
Man • Italy • Jersey • Luxembourg •
Malta • Monaco • The Netherlands •
Poland • Russia • Slovakia • Spain •
Sweden • Switzerland • Turkey • United
Kingdom

Key Competitors

Barclays • Citi • Lloyds TSB

Employment Contact

www.hsbc.com/hsbc/careers/hsbc-
in-europe

For graduate information:
www.hsbc.co.uk/1/2/graduatecareers/home

Pluses

• "Committed to a good work/life
  balance"
• "Collegiate" culture

Minuses

• Too bureaucratic
• Difficult to make a difference

THE BUZZ
WHAT EMPLOYEES AT OTHER FIRMS ARE SAYING

• "Very strong presence in the UK "
• "Good reputation; worldwide
  presence"
• "Weak investment banking "
• "Weak in Europe"

THE SCOOP

Y ou'd be hard-pressed to find someone that doesn't know HSBC, the global banking giant. HSBC Holdings is the world's fourth-largest bank by assets — boasting 1.86 trillion US dollars as of December 31, 2007. It is also Europe's biggest bank by market value. The international firm owns the Hong Kong and Shanghai Banking Corporation, France's CCF (formerly known as Credit Commercial de France) and 62 percent of Hong Kong's Hang Seng Bank.

In total, HSBC has almost 10,000 offices and a presence in 76 countries, providing a full range of financial services, including consumer and business banking, asset management, investment banking, securities trading, insurance and leasing. HSBC also has almost a 20 percent stake in the country's fifth-largest lender, Bank of Communications Co. — and an eight percent piece of the Bank of Shanghai. National branch numbers in Europe ranging from two branches in Slovakia to nearly 2,000 in Great Britain. In mainland China, Hong Kong and Shanghai Banking Corporation has 24 outlets.

Not so fine thanks to subprime

Like all other global banking firms, HSBC has suffered due to the subprime mortgage crisis in the US. In March 2008, the bank admitted to 8.7 billion pounds worth of bad debts from 2007, but pre-tax profits were high enough — jumping ten percent from the previous year — to absorb these debts. Why were HSBC's profits so high? According to analysts, it was because HSBC is both an expert at diversification and increasingly pouring its energies into its Asian operations. According to the *International Herald Tribune*, these emerging markets operations were a "more-than-ample buffer" against subprime writedowns. Close to half of HSBC's 24.2 billion dollar profits in 2007 came from the Asia-Pacific region, particularly China, India and Hong Kong.

Financial oasis

In March 2008, it became known that HSBC was looking at bulking up its presence in sub-Saharan Africa, as the importance of the region to the bank's extensive network of Asian and Indian clients increases dramatically. Speaking in *The Financial Times*, HSBC's chief executive of the bank's Asian region said: "We would like to be a bigger player in Africa going forward. As an emerging markets bank, it is a logical place for us to be."

Rising on up the charts

In April 2008 HSBC broke the ice in global rankings, and was named the top underwriting bank in global initial public offerings (IPO) by deal volume. The new high was in large part due to its close connections with Asia and the Middle East, and strong deal flow from the regions. The value of the bank's role on the six listings this year amounted to 4.4 billion dollars. It acted as sole bookrunner on Saudi energy firm Petrorabigh's 1.2 billion dollars listing in January, and the 500 million dollar IPO of Qatari holding company GIS.

In terms of global M&A deals, HSBC was ranked No. 13 on the 2007 Thomson Reuters Financial League Tables, with 314.87 billion dollars worth of announced deals. When it came to European M&A, HSBC was also ranked No. 13 in 2007, with 276.38 billion dollars worth of announced deals to its name. In the UK HSBC ranked tenth for announced M&A activity in 2007, conducting 29 deals with a combined value of 235.4 billion dollars.

Back in time

The origins of HSBC date back to the 19th century, when the Hong Kong and Shanghai Banking Corporation Limited were founded in 1865, and opened offices in Shanghai and London. Thomas Sutherland, Hong Kong Superintendent of the Peninsular and Oriental Stream Navigation Company, saw a need for local banking branches in Hong Kong and along the China Coast. Through the next several decades and into the 20th century, the company opened branches in China and Southeast Asia, eventually expanding into the Indian sub-continent, Europe and North America.

In 1959, the Hong Kong and Shanghai Banking Corp. took on the British Bank of the Middle East (originally the Imperial Bank of Persia, which had a number of operations in the Gulf States) and the Mercantile Bank, which had operations in India and South East Asia. Six years after that dual purchase, the company bought a controlling interest in the Hang Seng Bank which has been based in Hong Kong since 1933. Through the 1980s, the banking behemoth focused on moving into new markets, establishing the Hong Kong Bank of Canada in 1981 and the Hong Kong Bank of Australia five years later.

Then, in 1987, New York-based Marine Midland Bank became part of Hong Kong and Shanghai Banking's holdings and part of the company's US operations. A few years later, in 1991, this fragmented global constellation of operations was brought together under the ownership and control of a new company, HSBC Holdings.

Taking on the household chores

In 1992, HSBC kept the ball rolling by buying UK-based Midland Bank and forming the HSBC Investment Bank. This acquisition brought together the company's London merchant and securities banking businesses. Throughout the 1990s, HSBC expanded into Brazil and Argentina.

Just after the millennium came another high-profile deal for the bank, when, in March 2003, HSBC finalised its monster-sized 14.2 billion dollar acquisition of Household International. The latter company is a major provider of consumer finance and a top-ten issuer of credit cards in the US. In December 2004, Household International merged with Household Finance Corporation, the holding company for Household's US-based consumer finance operations, and then changed its name to HSBC Finance.

Spreading all over the world

In July 2006, approval came through from the China Banking Regulatory Commission for HSBC to proceed with plans to open a branch in Xi'an. Just weeks later, the huge banking group announced it had entered into an agreement with Grupo Banistmo S.A., the leading banking group in Central America, to acquire all outstanding shares. As Banistmo was the owner of Primer Banco del Istmo, the largest bank in Panama, this complemented HSBC Bank Panama S.A.'s presence in the country.

More movement in the summer of 2006 saw HSBC ink a deal to buy Panama's largest bank, Grupo Banistmo, for 1.77 billion dollars in cash. This gave the bank a foothold in five Latin American countries. HSBC rounded off 2006 by acquiring the mortgage loan portfolio of Champion Mortgage, Parsippany, a New Jersey-based division of Key Bank with a loan portfolio valued at about 2.5 billion dollars and 30,000 customers. Then, in December 2006, HSBC Bank Australia inked a deal to sell its broker-originated mortgage book to FirstMac, but still retaining the majority of its Aussie residential mortgage portfolio.

HSBC the eco-warrior

In 2006, the bank was named "Sustainable Bank of the Year" in the first *Financial Times* Sustainable Banking Awards. Since then, its green practices have blossomed. In May 2008, HSBC opened its new "green" US headquarters in a 560,000 square-foot building in the Chicago suburbs. The building was constructed to minimise resource consumption and environmental impact and houses 3,100 employees.

Among many other sustainability policies, the bank has also signed up to the United Nations Principles for Responsible Investment, a set of voluntary principles for asset owners and investment professionals. The principles provide a framework for incorporating environmental, social and governance issues into investment decision-making and ownership practices. Responsible investment, HSBC claims, is key to sustainability for the bank, its clients and society at large.

HSBC has numerous awards to its name, unsurprisingly for such a big bank. In 2007, just a handful of the accolades the bank's various divisions scored included *Euromoney*'s "Best Cash Management House" and "Best Risk Management House", *The Banker*'s "Interest Rate Derivatives House of the Year", along with being ranked first in treasury outsourcing in *Euromoney*'s Foreign Exchange Poll. HSBC's prowess in the Middle East also clearly shone through, with its HSBC Amanah division scooping several of *Euromoney*'s Islamic Finance awards in 2007, including "Best International Islamic Bank", "Best Sukuk House" and "Best Project Financing Deal". In April 2008, the bank hit the big-time, unsurprisingly, being ranked top of the *"Forbes* Global 2000" list of the world's biggest companies. This was the first time a non-American firm had led these rankings since 2004.

GETTING HIRED

Easy as HSBC

On HSBC's careers page you'll find an extensive range of opportunities for students and graduates. You can search for a programme by the region you'd like to work in, or by the business sector your experience relates to. There is also an international programme, which is focused around giving you experience in several of HSBC's global locations. At the internship level HSBC offers paid work placements to undergraduate students in their first or penultimate years. You can undertake a seven-week placement on the first or penultimate year programmes, which are centred around retail and/or commercial banking, or sign up for a year-long undergraduate placement in the bank's operations or IT departments. There is also a ten-week IT summer programme.

Out of the library into the bank

HSBC's graduate programmes are popular among graduates as they span a range of departments and divisions, including commercial management, operations management, executive management, insurance broking, information technology, corporate banking, marketing, human resources and trainee financial planning manager programmes. These last between 18 months and two years and while requirements vary, the majority require a 2:1 degree (2:2 for retail or commercial management).

To apply, simply select the region or business area you are interested in from the "student careers" section of the HSBC careers page, select your preferred programme, and click "find out more." This will take you to the page associated with your chosen region, and a link to complete the online application form. The application process opens in June each year, but for specific dates check the website at www.hsbc.co.uk/1/2/graduatecareers/home.

Country-hopping

HSBC sub-divides its graduate offerings further with a placement aimed at those who want to globetrot. In the international management programme, after an initial seven-week residential training programme in the UK, you'll be given your first two assignments. Together these last 18 months and span a number of roles and locations. Following your third assignment you'll be asked to settle on a business area, whilst remaining internationally mobile. For this role you'll need a 2:1 and have at least two languages to an operational level — one of which must be English. Simply click the "Apply Now" link on the company careers page to put yourself in with a chance.

OUR SURVEY SAYS

Is HSBC for me?

One insider says it's important when joining HSBC to work out beforehand if you are an HSBC "type of person," adding that "If you aren't, then you probably will not last very long." Another experienced hire says the firm is a good "solid" company to work for, "But not for those who really want to make a difference or with too much energy." That said, another staff member says, "It can be quite difficult to keep projects progressing as senior managers tend to want to sign off on everything."

An outspoken London banker tells us he believes that HSBC could improve how the firm communicates its "aims and goals" — and "where it perceives itself in the global marketplace." He adds, "This is also a positive, in the way that the bank is diversified throughout the global environment and economy, with profits tending to break down quite evenly between Asia, the Americas and Europe."

All in all, the bank is "committed to a good work/life balance, and has an ongoing campaign to be on the 'Best Place to Work list'," one London staffer tells us. A junior insider adds that HSBC's culture is "collegiate" and the dress code "smart". Perhaps a great indicator of the multicultural and international staff in HSBC offices, one insider describes the office vibe as having, "Quite an expat flavour, with people rotating round the business into new areas even at senior levels ."

THE ROYAL BANK OF SCOTLAND GROUP

RBS
36 St. Andrews Square
Edinburgh, EH2 2YB
United Kingdom
Tel: + 44 (0) 131 556 8555
www.rbs.com

The Stats

Employer Type: Public Company
Ticker Symbol: RBS (LSE)
Chairman: Sir Thomas F.W. McKillop
Group Chief Executive: Sir Frederick A. Goodwin
2007 Revenue: £31.1bn
2007 Profit: £7.7bn
2006 Revenue: £28bn
2006 Profit: £6.5bn
No. of Employees: 170,000
No. of Offices: 2,720 offices and branches

Departments

ABN AMRO • Global Markets • Group Manufacturing • Regional Markets • Group Functions • RBS Insurance

European Locations

Edinburgh (Global HQ)
Austria • Belgium • Czech Republic • Denmark • Finland • France • Germany • Gibraltar • Greece • Italy • Ireland • Luxembourg • Monaco • The Netherlands • Norway • Poland • Portugal • Romania • Russian Federation • Slovakia • Spain • Sweden • Switzerland • Turkey • United Kingdom

Key Competitors

Barclays • Citi • HSBC Holdings

Employment Contact

Graduate recruitment RBS Group:
www.makeitrbs.com
Graduate recruitment Global Markets:
www.rbs.com/gmgraduates
Careers: www.rbs.com/careers

Pluses

• "Modern, accepting atmosphere"
• "People work together and respect each other"

Minuses

• Work pressure equivalent to American investment banks
• Pay could be better

THE BUZZ
WHAT EMPLOYEES AT OTHER FIRMS ARE SAYING

• "Important UK corporate bank"
• "Strong in capital markets "
• "Big but unexciting"
• "No customer care"

THE SCOOP

T o say the least, 2007 was a fruitful year for RBS. Sure, the Scottish banking giant's 19 percent increase in net profits was good, but leading a consortium of European banking heroes to victory in the largest — and perhaps most highly publicised — takeover in financial services history was clearly the icing on the cake.

While talks concerning a possible takeover of Amsterdam-based ABN AMRO by British bank Barclays had begun in March 2007, the offer made by the RBS-Santander-Fortis consortium proved more appealing to the Dutch bank. The consortium's winning bid was nearly ten percent higher than Barclays' bid, at 70 billion euros, more than three times RBS' annual revenue in 2007.

The offer was formally accepted by ABN AMRO's shareholders in early October 2007. At that point, the three musketeers, RBS, Santander and Fortis, divided ABN AMRO's operations between them. Fortis took ABN's retail banking operations in The Netherlands and its global private clients and asset management businesses, while Santander gained ownership of the Latin American operations and Antonveneta in Italy. RBS took ABN's wholesale and corporate banking business, its Asian operations and the rest of the Dutch bank's European banking operations.

Stop the press!

This was big banking news. In addition to the sheer size of the deal, it was the first hostile cross-border takeover of a big European bank and the first bidder break-up of a big lender — most bankers and investors believed a break up on this scale was impossible. But spearheaded by the incredibly suave RBS, the takeover actually happened rather smoothly.

Shortly after the deal was confirmed, RBS senior executive Mark Fisher was named chief executive of ABN Amro. Fisher had led RBS' integration of NatWest. John Varley of Barclays, speaking in *The Financial Times*, said of the deal: "Victory at any price was not something we were prepared to contemplate", while Sir Fred Goodwin of RBS said: "It's true that the people who win pay more than the people who don't win."

Making it happen

The Royal Bank of Scotland group (RBS) is the third-largest financial institution in Europe and the ninth-largest in the world. RBS, a FTSE 100 company, is also the sixth-largest bank in the world by assets. Founded in Edinburgh by royal charter in 1727, the company opened its first branch in 1783. Today, its branch network blankets the British Isles. The history of RBS has really become synonymous with the history of British banking itself.

With the acquisition of National Westminster Bank (NatWest) in 2000 — the biggest takeover in the history of British banking — and the August 2004 purchase of Charter One Financial, the 40th-largest lender in the US, RBS continues to grow its businesses around the world. In January 2006, RBS joined a consortium and took a ten percent stake of one of China's largest banks, the Bank of China.

A failed expedition launches a financial superpower

RBS can trace its roots back to the Darien Company, which launched a disastrous expedition to establish a Scottish trading company in Panama in 1699. England compensated the Scottish creditors eight years later —

> ❝ The history of RBS has really become synonomous with the history of British banking itself ❞

because it had promised support and then pulled out, which ultimately led to the expedition's failure. The entrepreneurial creditors began lending the money they were given and eventually, in 1727, received a charter and became The Royal Bank of Scotland.

RBS opened a London branch in 1874 and almost a century later merged with the National Commercial Bank in 1968. Then, in 2000, after a long takeover battle with arch-rival Bank of Scotland, RBS finally (and famously) bought NatWest. RBS proceeded to sell off the Gartmore Investment Management fund management division to Nationwide Mutual Insurance Co. and NatWest's Equity Partners unit, launching NatWest Private Banking to provide services to the wealthy.

For the love of Europe

RBS operates offices throughout the world. RBS' French and German offices have been open since 1998, providing products and services to corporations and institutions. The firm's Greek branch opened in 1973 and is now the world's leading lending bank to Greece's shipping market. In Spain, RBS opened an office in 2001 and an Italian branch opened in 2002 quickly followed by a branch in the Nordic region in 2004.

RBS is comprised of five divisions that in turn are made up of 41 brands. Between its two retail banking arms, The Royal Bank of Scotland's retail banking and NatWest's retail banking, RBS operates 2,720 branches. Private banking customers have six options to choose from, including Coutts & Co, Adam & Company, The Royal Bank of Scotland International and NatWest Private Banking.

Where it's at

Ranked 22nd on the Thomson Reuters Financial League Tables in terms of global M&A announced deals, RBS M&A operations in 2007 had a value of 146.21 billion dollars and ranked 25th on the European league table of announced deals. RBS Global Markets is a major player on the global banking and markets scene. Global markets comprise two entities: global banking and markets (GBM) and global transaction services (GTS). GBM provides a range of services to large corporate and institutional customers in the UK and overseas. RBS claims its position as the leader in the UK corporate market, with a significant presence in the US, Europe and Asia Pacific. GTS is a market-leading international payments business providing transaction banking and merchant acquiring services.

Since the turn of the millennium, RBS has transformed its capital markets capabilities, taking bold steps and expanding rapidly into new markets. As a result, it has shifted from being a UK firm with ambition and an eye to expansion into a genuinely worldwide organisation that is a leading banking partner to major corporate and financial institutions worldwide.

Land of the rising market

RBS joined a consortium in 2006 and bought a ten percent share in the Bank of China. The group shelled out about 3.1 billion dollars for a stake in China's second-biggest lender, with RBS investing 1.6 billion dollars. RBS's goal is to build on Bank of China's distribution strength and expand its credit card, wealth management, corporate banking and personal insurance business lines in China.

The two banks will co-operate in the key areas of corporate governance, risk management, financial management, human resources and information technology. Bank of China went public on the Hong Kong and Shanghai exchanges in June, diluting RBS' stake from ten percent to 4.26 percent. The Chinese government holds a 67 percent stake. In June 2006, RBS also launched a US dollar swap, trading via Bloomberg during Asian business hours. The launch is a step closer towards providing a fully global electronic offering for interest rate derivatives. RBS is a leader in US dollar IRD electronic liquidity, providing trading functionality during European, US and Asia-Pacific trading hours.

Scan here, sir

In May 2008, RBS announced a four million pound investment supporting the acquisition of a cutting edge scanner for The University of Edinburgh's Queens' Medical Research Institute and NHS Lothian. As well as funding the acquisition, RBS contributed to the machine's operating costs. In return, RBS' staff will gain access to 25 percent of the scanner's capacity.

One of the world's most-advanced CT scanners; it will add 4,000 extra scans per year to the NHS' current capacity, as well as increasing the university's access to cutting edge research. It can scan an entire organ in a fraction of a second, and reduce radiation exposure by around 80 percent, compared to standard CT scans.

Royal bank of the environment

Taking steps to reduce its harmful effects on the environment, RBS bought 74 percent of its UK and Ireland electricity from renewable sources, and reduced its carbon footprint by 210,000 tonnes in 2006. Among the bank's plans going forward is a further reduction of its carbon footprint — primarily by purchasing 100 percent of the electricity it uses in Great Britain from renewable sources. RBS is also investing 55 million pounds in making its premises more environmentally friendly. This includes piloting emerging technologies such as biomass boilers, solar roofs and wind turbines.

GETTING HIRED

Make it RBS

Dedicating a whole domain name solely to graduate recruitment, RBS offer www.makeitrbs.com to save you the hassle of hunting around on a labyrinth-like website to track down that oft-dimmed window of graduate opportunity. They even offer you an anagram quiz. Investment banking opportunities in global markets can be accessed directly at www.rbs.com/gmgraduates.

More importantly, RBS run a total of 30 different graduate programmes, ranging from global markets including all areas of investment banking activities, finance, risk and retail to group technology and technology integration, and offering international placements, professional qualifications and rotation opportunities.

Test the waters

If you're a penultimate year student with a heart set on banking, you should look into RBS' ten-week summer internships, available in global markets covering all investment banking opportunities, finance, human resources, internal audit and risk. Or, if you're studying an IT-related degree, you can opt for the "group technology and technology integration industrial placement programme," a one-year industrial placement programme offered in Dublin, London and Edinburgh.

Good performance here could see you fast-tracked onto the next programme up: the GT graduate programme. The placement will see you involved in a team working on IT services or IT development, and receive technical training. To apply for this, your degree needs a year-out placement requirement. In global markets RBS offers a two-week Easter Insight work experience to first year students allowing candidates to get exposure to two areas of the global markets business.

Skills to pay the bills

There is a myriad of opportunities for graduates looking for a way into a banking career, primarily in the form of one- to three-year programmes. All the programmes RBS offer can be found on www.makeitrbs.com. Global markets opportunities can be found at www.rbs.com/gmgraduates. The entry requirements vary from programme to programme, but as a general rule, most require a minimum 2:1 honours degree in any discipline — or a 2:2 plus a Master's degree for the Ulster Bank programmes. Some, such as risk management, need more specific skills, and require a more technical qualification, such as mathematics, statistics, economics or engineering. They all require some work experience, so you should make sure you pave your way with a pre-graduation internship.

Sign here ...

Applications are submitted online — simply click the "apply now" link, which can be found on every page of the graduate portal. You'll need to register first. Selection processes may vary from division to division, but if you meet the minimum requirements, you'll be asked to complete an online competency questionnaire, a numerical reasoning test and a telephone or face to face interview where you should discuss how your past work experiences relate to what you're applying for.

The final assessment step is a graduate assessment centre in all divisions. These are located in London, Edinburgh and Dublin. RBS notes that for some business areas they will hold a pre-assessment dinner — and will stress that it is not assessed. So don't worry too much about how you were holding your fork when you spilled your wine on the chief executive — but do use the opportunity to ask those in the know about what it's like to work for RBS. Overall, the assessment will involve a numerical reasoning test, a group challenge, a presentation, a face-to-face interview and a planning and organising exercise.

The number of interviews you'll participate in can vary with your location and your role, say global markets insiders. A respondent in Paris reports having gone through "seven interviews, all with operational people", while a London-based worker tells us he had to "meet eight people and go through many interviews." In Milan, a staffer says that in addition to HR recruitment staff, he met "Senior business representatives, the chief operating officer and my future line manager."

A more experienced worker relates that he was hired as an experienced professional with five to six years of work experience, including two years in the job he interviewed for. Consequently, the interview process was limited to the top-four managing directors of the unit, as well as the head of the local branch. "I also got to meet two future colleagues at the same level of seniority, to get a better idea of processes and the work environment," he notes.

Get a little insight

Good performance during an internship is definitely an advantage but is not a pre-requisite for gaining a position, an associate director tells us. "They're a good way to prove yourself," notes a staffer in Stockholm, adding: "They are a good way for people at university to get on the graduate scheme without having to apply the same way as everyone else."

On top of this, internships are becoming increasingly important as the competition for graduate jobs continues to increase, a London-based associate tells us. They serve a dual purpose: they're viewed as an important tool — both for the participant, for identifying opportunities and interests and for the bank to "gauge the candidate's attitude and ability."

In terms of what you'll get up to on an internship, one associate tells us "I was placed on one team for the duration of the internship." He says his work consisted of "Putting presentations together, manipulating data in excel, attending various client meetings and reading legal documents to understand the structure of our deals." A source in Paris tells us that interns get a package similar to banking peers in the market. "They assist us in all documentation-related work (know-your-customer checks) and market research, but also get exposure to client pitching and sometimes financial modelling if they perform exceptionally well."

Thinking globally

RBS Global Markets is made up of global banking and markets (GBM) and global transaction services (GTS). GBM provides a diverse range of debt financing, risk management and investment services to leading corporations and financial institutions, and has a presence in all leading global financial centres. GTS is a market leading, international payments business providing transaction banking and merchant acquiring services. Detailed information about career opportunities within RBS global markets can be found on the company website at: www.rbs.com. Follow the "Careers" link.

OUR SURVEY SAYS

Your weekends are yours

Working 40 to 60-hours a week is the norm at RBS, with most respondents reporting weekend work as a rare occurrence. Hours are worked "as required" say insiders, but "normally these are reasonable by City standards," an associate director tells us. There is less of a focus on work hours and more on achieving results, he adds, and while this may mean working all night, experienced hires assure us that, "There is limited face time." The majority of respondents made reference to the high importance the bank puts on its employees' work/life balance. "It's not necessary to stay as long — or longer — than your boss," one employee says. "However, it is expected that you can assess whether something can wait until the next day or not."

Getting it done and keeping you happy

A senior manager tells us that RBS corporate culture is very much team-oriented. The co-operation between employees at work is facilitated by the numerous off-sites that the bank organises. A respondent in London called the culture "very professional," saying that, "deals get done".

In Paris, one staffer tells us, "The office is probably a bit more 'French' — more hierarchy and seniority-driven — than in London, but certainly less so than its French competitors." In London, employees say RBS offices have a "modern, accepting atmosphere". One junior insider boasts, "I soon found a role I enjoyed and was given respect and responsibility quickly afterwards." Another more experienced hire explains, "The culture has a steely determination about it and strives to succeed without being too harsh on the employees."

A second-year analyst describes the firm as "very relaxed", adding, "It's not as intense as the American bank I interned with. I'm incredibly lucky and thankful that people in the bank are not too set in their ways and offered a fresh graduate the opportunity to work in trading." Another junior employee reveals, "The bank is a lot more conservative in terms of risk taking than other big banks, but I see it as a good environment in which to learn."

In terms of things to improve, employees mention that the "working hours" and "work pressure" are "equivalent to American investment banks", adding that as a result of this, "the pay should be equivalent too."

Welcome, one and all

Workers in London as well as continental RBS offices consider the firm as being a diverse place to work. "RBS has in excess of ten different nationalities within its staff in the region," said one Stockholm-based banker.

When it comes to male/female diversity, a female insider tells us, "There is a true meritocratic promotion process, irrespective of gender." She adds, "As proof of this, there are many women in senior positions within RBS in the Nordic Region." That said, another female banker says the London office is "male dominated" adding, "I would like to see a woman as one of our sector directors."

With managers like this, who needs friends?

A London employee happily tells us, "I have received great respect from all my managers and superiors," adding "they are brilliant — very motivational and always there to help." The same respondent did however note that, "In other areas people are sometimes not as supportive as they should be."

Junior staff are expected to do "the menial tasks" but are also given "lots of responsibility", a Paris-based senior discloses. "There's a great atmosphere and I have friendly colleagues." Another experienced insider says, "This is definitely not your average investment bank. People work hard but work together and respect each other. There is significant focus during interviews on candidates' potential fit within the team to this end."

A respondent who'd taken some time off notes: "They are very understanding and were supportive to me during a period of ill health and in general. They are demanding, but not excessively so." Another employee says, "It is variable: relations are sometimes good, sometimes strained," adding, "The difficult period in the banking industry has perhaps put more pressure on relationships."

They've got it, oh baby they've got it

Profit-sharing, free breakdown cover, moving expenses and company cars (once you're a director) were high on the employee's lists of preferred perks. "You also get an annual personal budget for gyms or training," says an employee in Frankfurt. Among employees' reasons to be satisfied with the firm were the "enormous prospects" it offered, and a work/life balance that "appears better than at many of its peers". A Frankfurt-based worker says, "RBS gives you every chance to perform and develop according to your knowledge and your ambitions." □

16, Boulevard des Italiens
Paris, 75009
France
Tel: +33 1 40 14 45 46
www.bnpparibas.com

The Stats

Employer Type: Public Company
Ticker Symbol: BNP (Euronext Paris);
8664 (Tokyo)
Chairman: Baudouin Prot
2007 Revenue: €12.2bn
2007 Profit: €7.8bn
2006 Revenue: €10.8bn
2006 Profit: €7.3bn
2007 No. of Employees: 162,700
2006 No. of Employees: 140,000
No. of Offices: 2,200 branches

Departments

Asset Management and Services •
BNP Paribas Capital (Private Equity) •
Corporate and Investment Banking •
Retail Banking

European Locations

Paris (HQ)
Austria • Belgium • Bulgaria • Cyprus •
Czech Republic • France • Germany •
Greece • Hungary • Ireland • Italy •
Jersey • Luxembourg • Monaco •
Norway • The Netherlands • Poland •
Portugal • Romania • Russia • Serbia and
Montenegro • Slovakia • Spain • Sweden •
Switzerland • Turkey • Ukraine • United
Kingdom

Key Competitors

Crédit Agricole • Lazard • Société
Générale

Employment Contact

careers.bnpparibas.com
www.recrutement.bnpparibas.com

THE BUZZ
WHAT EMPLOYEES AT OTHER FIRMS ARE SAYING

• "Great strategy, great management"
• "Strong brand"
• "Very French"
• "Not truly global"

THE SCOOP

One of France's biggest banks, BNP Paribas, actually got its name from the phrase "Paris et Pays-Bas", literally meaning Paris and The Netherlands. The bank traces its roots to the Banque de Paris et Pays-Bas, which was founded in 1872. BNP Paribas was founded via a series of mergers beginning in 1966, when Comptoir National d'Escompte de Paris (CNEP) and Banque Nationale pour le Commerce et l'Industrie (BNCI) joined to form Banque National de Paris (BNP). The Paribas Group formed in May 1998 following a long stretch of French banking nationalisation and reorganisation. The group included the Banque Paribas, Compagnie Financière de Paribas and Compagnie Bancaire. In 1999, with the approval of the French financial markets authorities, BNP took control of the Paribas Group. The final product was one of the largest financial institutions in Europe.

As of 2008, BNP Paribas is the largest European bank by total assets, the second-largest by market capitalisation and the 16th-largest company in the world. With a foothold in 88 countries, the bank has a strong global reach. In its home market, BNP Paribas has 2,200 branches and manages 54 billion euros of the estimated total 500 billion euros of assets in the French market.

In 2007, according to the Thomson Reuters Financial League Tables for global M&A, BNP Paribas ranked 12th worldwide, with 384.6 billion dollars worth of announced deals. As for European rankings, BNP came tenth, with 376.44 billion dollars worth of announced deals. The French banking giant's business is divided into three sectors: corporate and investment banking, asset management and services and retail banking.

BNP Paribas takes on the world

Known for its domination of the French retail banking business, BNP Paribas has been aggressively expanding its services into the rest of Europe since the turn of the millennium. Part of this growth has derived from its increased focus on internet technology and online banking products, and part derives from BNP Paribas's prominent position in the banking world which allows it to buy up other banks.

In all the right places

In fact, BNP Paribas' muscle has been particularly visible since early 2006. After a failed bid by Spain's BBVA in July 2005 and the Bank of Italy's rejection of Italian insurer Unipol's bid in February 2006, BNP Paribas successfully claimed a stake of Banca Nazionale del Lavoro (BNL), its biggest competitor in Italy. It made an initial acquisition of 48 percent of the company. By May 2006, the bank had increased this share to 97 percent. BNL is Italy's sixth-largest bank by deposits and loans. In a move to further boost its visibility in the region, in June 2006, BNP offered one billion euros to the Italian car company Fiat to take over half of Fidis, its finance division, but was beaten by Crédit Agricole, France's largest banking group.

BNL was responsible for 2.23 billion euros to BNP's group revenue for the first nine months of 2006. Retail banking, a key part of the business, makes up about 60 percent of total revenue. Approximately 25 percent comes from corporate and investment banking and 15 percent from asset management services. French retail banking accounts for almost half of all of BNP's retail banking income, with six million customers able to access 2,200 branches and 3,400 ATMs.

In Paris, where the firm is headquartered, BNP has 15 percent of the retail market. "We are increasing our retail activity in three key places — Italy, Ukraine and Turkey," said BNP Paribas' chief executive Baudouin Prot in January 2007. "The acquisition in 2006 of BNL has made Italy our second domestic market. Over the next three years in Italy, our plan is to exploit synergies and leverage the strong pre-existing product platform of BNP Paribas." In December 2006, BNP acquired the Paris-based private banking arm of Franco-Belgian bank Dexia in a deal worth approximately 200 million euros. With close to 200 staff, Dexia had revenue of almost 19 million euros and net profits of 3.6 million euros in the first half of 2006.

The near east ...

In April 2006, BNP bought up 51 percent of UkrSibbank, the fourth-largest bank in the Ukraine. In the same year, BNP also became one of the leading bidders in the battle to acquire 80 percent of the Bank of Alexandria in the Egyptian government's sell-off of this state-owned institution. However, Italy's then Banca Sanpaolo was the eventual winner. Three months later, BNP arranged a 400 million dollar, three-and-a-half year loan for Rinat Akhmetov's System Capital Management (SCM), the largest financial-industrial conglomerate in the Ukraine.

Other news-making moves by BNP Paribas in the former Soviet region included a 300 million euro cooperation agreement with Russia's Vnesheconombank (VEB) in November 2007. This amounted to a credit loan for Vnesheconombank to finance purchases of Western European goods and services by Russian importers.

... and the far east

In April 2006, BNP acquired a 5.6 percent stake of the Shinhan Financial Group in South Korea for 800 million euros. It later boosted its stake to 9.4 percent, making it the largest single shareholder of the Group, which is Korea's second-largest financial company, focusing on asset management, insurance, leasing and consumer credit.

In January 2007, BNP pulled out of its securities joint venture with the Chinese firm Changjiang Securities after a squabble over strategy, selling its 33 percent stake to Changjiang for an undisclosed sum. BNP's involvement with Changjiang was among the first between a Chinese securities firm and a foreign partner — only Goldman Sachs, Morgan Stanley and UBS had been there before. But curtains haven't gone down on BNP's adventures in China. At the time of press, the French bank still had a 19.2 percent stake in Nanjing City Commercial Bank, the eighth largest commercial bank in China.

Awards and applause

BNP Paribas' corporate finance division was named No.1 M&A house in France by *Euromoney* in 2007, and in the same year, its global finance division was named "Best Credit Derivatives Provider" in Asia by *Global Finance Magasine*. The bank has also won a slew of other awards, including *Euromoney's*

> ❝ BNP Paribas' corporate finance division was named No. 1 M&A house in France by *Euromoney* in 2007 ❞

"Best Project Finance Division in Gulf Countries in 2007", the 2006 *Financial News* "European M&A Deal of the Year" for its role of advisor in France Télécom's acquisition of Spanish phone operator Amena, and *Acquisition Monthly's* "Emerging Market Deal of the Year" in 2005 for its advisory role in the privatisation of Turk Telecom. In 2007, the bank rated first in announced French M&A deals by volume at 39.3 billion US dollars, and eighth in Europe with 375.1 billion US dollars.

SOS for BNP

The US subprime mortgage crisis reached global proportions in July 2007, bringing chaos the business world. As market liquidity evaporated as a result of the global effects of the crashing US subprime lending markets, on August 9, 2007, BNP Paribas announced it was impossible to value the underlying assets of three of its major investment funds, worth approximately two billion euros.

With many other European banks experiencing similar problems, the European Central Bank was forced to step in to ease market worries, pumping 96.8 billion euros in low-interest credit into the Eurozone. Luckily crisis was averted, and BNP Paribas ducked banking disaster, announcing in November that the credit crisis had a total impact of just 301 million euros on the group, according to *The Telegraph*. Though banks remain cautious about the current market environment, BNP is optimistic about its rejuvenation, projecting positive results over 2008-09.

GETTING HIRED

Be the best for BNP

If you want to find yourself working for the French finance giant, visit www.graduates.bnpparibas.com to explore its corporate and investment banking graduate opportunities as well as entry-level professional positions around Europe and internationally. The spectrum of available openings is so wide that the bank's HR itself says that it is "impossible to list all of the careers available within BNP Paribas." For most positions, a degree is the minimum qualification required, though many of their employees have pursued their studies at least until master's level. In the corporate and investment banking sphere, the firm adds, "A previous internship in finance is a real advantage." This you can also find at BNP.

The banking group offers graduate programmes, internships and summer positions across a wide range of activities, from retail banking to corporate finance, including market finance and non-finance related areas like marketing, information systems, auditing and management control. Recruitment is de-centralised, however, with HR offices in different countries offering their own programmes and options.

Vive la France

On its French recruitment website www.recrutement.bnpparibas.com, for example, BNP offers extensive internships, work experience and VIE (Volontariat International Enterprise) — 16-month work abroad experience schemes — to students with native and near-native fluency in French as well as the appropriate qualifications. In the UK, BNP offers long-term and summer internships for students in their penultimate year.

On its corporate and investment banking website, www.graduates.bnpparibas.com, BNP offers graduate programmes, long-term and summer internships for students in their penultimate year, as well as paths to join the company as analysts (if you have a 2:1 in any discipline) and associates (if you have an MBA or PhD). Opportunities are available globally.

To discover the kinds of options available at BNP in your area, follow the careers link to the country of your choice, where you'll be able to browse positions by location and business area. You can subsequently register your CV and cover letter online and submit it to the local HR office. If your application is successful, expect interviews with HR managers, group case study exercises and further interviews with line managers. For graduate programmes in corporate and investment banking, go directly to the www.graduates.bnpparibas.com website and apply online.

BANK OF AMERICA

5 Canada Square
London
E14 5AQ
United Kingdom
Tel: +44 (0) 20 7174 4000
www.bankofamerica.com

The Stats

Employer Type: Public Company
Ticker Symbol: BAC (NYSE)
Chief Executive: Kenneth D. Lewis
2007 Revenue: $68.07bn
2007 Profit: $14.9bn
2006 Revenue: $73.80bn
2006 Profit: $21.1m
No. of Employees: 210,000
No. of Offices: 6,000

Departments

Europe Card Services • Global
Investment Banking • Global Markets •
Global Middle Office • Global Product
Solutions • Risk Management •
Technology

European Locations

London (HQ)
France • Germany • Greece • Ireland • Italy •
The Netherlands • Spain • United
Kingdom

Employment Contact

www.bankofamerica.com/careers

THE BUZZ
WHAT EMPLOYEES AT OTHER FIRMS ARE SAYING

• "Top international firm"
• "Impressive size"
• "Weak investment banking franchise"
• "Uncommitted to Europe"

VAULT career
library

THE SCOOP

F
ew people know that US banking giant Bank of America has had a growing presence in Europe since 1922. As of 2007, the company employed more than 8,350 people in Europe. Of this number, approximately 2,850 worked in legacy Bank of America businesses based in the UK, Belgium, France, Germany, Greece, Italy, The Netherlands, the Republic of Ireland and Spain. Close to 5,500 employees work for Bank of America's Europe Card Services division (i.e. Legacy MBNA).

Many of the services that company offers to corporate and institutional clients, are provided through its US and UK subsidiaries — Banc of America Securities LLC and Banc of America Securities Limited. The company's global corporate and investment banking group (GCIB) division covers a range of industries,

> ❝ Bank of America boasts business relationships with 80 percent of the Global Fortune 500 ❞

including consumer and retail, financial institutions, financial sponsors, global industrial, healthcare, media and telecommunications, natural resources, real estate and gaming.

GCIB focuses on companies with an annual revenue of more than two-and-a-half million US dollars, as well as middle-market and large corporations, institutional investors, financial institutions and government entities. GCIB provides innovative services in M&A, equity and debt capital raising, lending, trading, risk management, treasury management and research.

How America took shape

The banks that eventually became Bank of America were the first banks in the new nation back in the late 18th century. In 1784, the Massachusetts Bank was chartered followed in 1791 by the Providence Bank in Rhode Island. These banks grew with the country, expanding and merging with smaller companies over decades. Two centuries later the modern roots of Bank of America can be found in the 1960s, when North Carolina National Bank (NCNB) began an aggressive plan of expansion based on a "hometown bank" model that would allow each branch to be fully shaped by the needs of its community.

In 1991, NCNB merged with C&S/Sovran Corporation to form NationsBank. Then in 1998, NationsBank acquired BankAmerica to become Bank of America, creating a bank whose business reached across the country. The banking giant took another big step in 2004, when Bank of America acquired FleetBoston Financial for 47 billion dollars. The following year, Bank of America acquired MBNA, a commercial bank with operations in the US, England, Scotland, Ireland and Canada, for 35 billion dollars. As of 2008, Bank of America is ranked among the world's largest financial institutions, serving individual clients, small and middle-market businesses and large corporations in more than 175 countries. It can also boast business relationships with 80 percent of the Global Fortune 500.

Expand and conquer

Bank of America serves clients in 175 countries and has relationships with 99 percent of the US Fortune 500 companies and 83 percent of the Global Fortune 500. Internationally, the bank targets European clients with strong US interests and issuer and investor clients with whom the bank already has a strong relationship in the US. Leveraging its balance sheet, Bank of America is able to help clients meet their financial goals and, by expanding its product groups, it provides clients with a full, global product suite.

Welcome aboard

The Dow Jones industrial average is one of the world's best-known financial bellwethers, but it rarely alters the mix of stocks it indexes. In February 2008, the Dow made its first alteration since 2004 adding Bank of America and Chevron Corporation to its list of 30 public companies. The two newbies replaced the Altria Group and Honeywell International, which were dropped from the index.

Bearing up well

In June 2008, Bank of America made the most of the credit crisis to pick up five senior executives who were clawing their way out of Bear Stearns' wreckage. Among them were David Glaser, Bear's co-head of investment banking, who will chair Bank of America's global mergers and acquisitions department. Along with the new managing directors from Bear Stearns, Bank of America has taken on Phil Barnett from Morgan Stanley as head of its financial institutions unit.

The new appointments come amid a shake-up at the bank, after a 92 percent fall in profit at the start of 2008. An estimated 650 jobs were cut from its global markets and global investment banking businesses, chief executive Kenneth Lewis declared in January 2008. This followed a round of 3,000 pink slips in November 2007 after dismal 3Q07 results.

Although the downsizing attracted plenty of media attention, Bank of America's operations in Europe were largely unaffected — the job cuts were focused in the US. Continuing the theme of realignment, Bank of America put its hedge fund trading and financing unit up for sale in early 2008. A few months later, in June, French banking giant BNP Paribas stepped forward with an offer of 300 million US dollars. The deal is set to close in the second half of 2008.

Down, down, down

The first quarter of 2008 brought more bad news for Bank of America, which reported a 77 percent drop in profit and a steep writedown: 1.3 billion dollars in trading losses and provisions against bad debts. Still, chief executive Kenneth Lewis sounded an optimistic note soon after the earnings announcement, telling a *Wall Street Journal* conference in June that 2Q08 could be "one of the three or four best investment banking quarters that we've had."

Picking up the pieces

In January 2008, Bank of America announced plans to acquire Countrywide Financial, the biggest mortgage lender in the US and a leading player in the ill-fated subprime market. At the time of the announcement, Country-wide was said to be on the verge of bankruptcy, felled by record losses and foreclosures — and under

> " Early 2008 brought bad news for the bank — a 77 percent drop in profit and a steep writedown "

investigation by US prosecutors who questioned its lending practices. Regulators approved the acquisition in June 2008 and Bank of America said the bailout deal would be finalised on July 1, 2008.

At first Countrywide was valued at four billion dollars, but just two weeks before the deal was set to close, Countrywide's dwindling stock value prompted Bank of America to cut its offer by a quarter. The new valuation priced Countrywide at 5.13 dollars per share, reducing the final stock swap value to approximately three billion dollars.

Analysts touted the importance of rescuing the troubled lender to stem further bleeding in the global credit sector, but Bank of America's chief executive Kenneth Lewis admitted he was taking on a big challenge. "We are aware of the issues within the housing and mortgage industries," he said in a statement after the acquisition was made public. "The transaction reflects those challenges."

Under the terms of the deal, Countrywide's shareholders will receive 0.1822 of a Bank of America share for each unit of Countrywide stock. Bank of America claims it will see after-tax savings of 670 million US dollars from the deal by 2011.

GETTING HIRED

America calling

Bank of America has a global careers page, so you'll have to go to www.bankofamerica.com/careers. From here you can search for vacancies and complete an online application by clicking the link at the end of your chosen position. Vacancies arise across the bank in a number of departments and divisions, including: administration, group/finance, communications, consumer banking, customer care, human resources, operations, risk management, sales and technology.

Bank of Opportunity

The bank offers a wide variety of undergraduate and graduate programs across its locations in Europe. Internship opportunities are available, but occur mainly across the US and the UK. All of the opportunities for graduates and undergraduates can be viewed on the company's "Campus Recruitment" page, which you'll find on the company's careers page.

Graduate opportunities include full-time or summer analyst positions — for which you'll need a 2:1 degree — and for those with an MBA, full-time or summer associate programmes are available. The analyst programmes can take place in any of the bank's European locations, depending on the banking sector you choose, but common locations are London, Frankfurt, Milan and Paris. For either level you can select from the following banking sectors: investment banking, capital markets, sales and trading, product services, technology, risk management and global middle office. The associate program is essentially a more advanced version of the analyst program.

The summer analyst and associate programmes last for ten weeks. To apply for these, or any other programs on the Campus Recruitment page, simply select the position you're interested in from the drop down tab and click the link to complete the application form. ☐

29 Blvd. Haussman
Paris 75009
France
Tel: +33 (0) 42 14 20 00
www.socgen.com

The Stats

Employer type: Public Company
Ticker Symbol: GLE (Euronext)
Chief Executive: Frédéric Oudéa
2007 Revenue: €21.9bn
2007 Profit: €1.6bn
2006 Revenue: €22.4bn
2006 Profit: €5.78bn
No. of Employees: 151,000
No. of Offices: locations in 82 countries

Departments

Corporate and Investment Banking •
Global Investment Management and
Services • Retail Banking and Financial
Services

European Locations

Paris (HQ)
Austria • Belgium • France • Germany •
Ireland • Italy • The Netherlands •
Norway • Poland • Portugal • Spain •
Sweden • Switzerland • Ukraine • United
Kingdom

Key Competitors

BNP Paribas • Crédit Agricole • Natixis

Employment Contact

www.recrutement-
societegenerale.com/jpapps/sg

Pluses

• Good opportunities both to switch
  teams and focus
• Weekend work is rare

Minuses

• Seniority counts more than it should
• Career progression not as rapid as
  desired

THE BUZZ
WHAT EMPLOYEES AT OTHER FIRMS ARE SAYING

• "Excellent in derivatives"
• "Kerviel aside, a strong organisation"
• "Lot of noise around its scandal"
• "Typical 'French and only French' bank"

THE SCOOP

I t makes for great trivia, that French banking giant Société Générale (SocGen) was formed by a decree signed by France's then-emperor Napoleon III on May 4, 1864, founding the firm in order to "foster the development of trade and industry in France." Over the past two centuries, that's what SocGen has done.

SocGen fast evolved into a leading European financial services company and a major player in the global market. The firm began its international expansion in 1871 with the opening of a London branch. By 1913, the booming banking powerhouse had established 1,400 branches and established itself as a network bank. The company remained private until 1945, when the bank's capital stock passed into the hands of the French government. Then in 1970, Société Générale stepped up its international development, concentrating on Asia and Eastern Europe. Ten years later, in 1980, the bank had branches in 54 countries.

The new wave of global expansion

SocGen's capital markets subdivision was created in 1987 and Société Générale was privatised soon after. The next year, and following the lead of many commercial banks, the firm acquired an investment banking arm by purchasing New York-based Cowen & Company (now called SG Cowen). The following

> 66 SocGen fast evolved into a leading European financial services company and a major global player 99

year, SocGen set up retail banking outside France, expanding into Romania, Bulgaria and Madagascar. The firm's Central European operations, combined with SocGen's acquisitions in Africa, have headed up the bank's external growth.

Central and Eastern European expansion continues briskly, with the bank acquiring 70 percent of a leading bank in Moldova for 18.4 million euros, as well as banks in the Republic of Macedonia and Albania in early 2007. In December 2007, Société Générale paid 860 million pounds to increase its stake in Russian rival Rosbank, in a move that will give it a controlling stake in the company, which has more than 600 branches and is one of the biggest private banks in Russia.

After the millennium

Long-established as a powerhouse in financial services for the Eurozone, as of April 2007, SocGen was the fifth-largest French company by capitalisation in the region, with worldwide employee numbers in excess of 150,000. As a bank, SocGen operates more than 2,900 branches in France as well as an additional 2,300 branches throughout the rest of the world. By 2008, the bank has carved out a niche in 82 countries worldwide, with its retail banking and specialised financial services business serving approximately 27 million customers. In 2007, the bank had a net banking income of 21.9 billion euros.

A Générale feeling

SocGen Group is divided into three main businesses: retail banking and specialised financial services, global investment management and services, and corporate and investment banking. In France, the bank's retail banking division runs two distribution networks in tandem, Société Générale and Crédit du Nord. In Europe, the specialised financial services activities of the bank have seen it become a major player over the past five years.

Globally private

SocGen's global investment management and services division is huge, encompassing five complementary business lines: Société Générale Asset Management, SG Private Banking, Société Générale Securities Services, Newedge, a multi-asset brokerage business and Boursorama, an online banking platform. This division employs approximately 12,500 people worldwide. Private banking is particularly on the up for SocGen, with the group having averaged a growth in managed assets of 35 percent per year since this department's creation in 1998.

SG Private Banking has, as of 2008, offices in 24 countries offering wealth management services to clients with a net worth of more than one million euros. SG Private Banking was ranked as among the world's top 15 players in private banking by *Euromoney* in 2008 with assets under management, as of December 2007, of 76.9 billion euros, all of which are in the capable hands of 2,600 employees in Europe, Asia-Pacific, North America and the Middle East.

A strong bond

SocGen's corporate and investment banking business is based around three central pillars: euro capital markets, derivates and structured finance. The bank is one of the leading players in the euro debt capital markets and in the equity capital markets in France. This side of SocGen's operations claimed the title of "Euro Bond House of the Year" from IFR Magazine in December 2007. The firm also claims it is the world leader in export, project and structured commodity finance with global expertise in numerous sectors.

Problems au générale

No matter how capable and stable a bank may seem, there can be cracks in the system. In January 2008, the European business world was rocked by scandal. One man had lost Société Générale 4.82 billion euros in one of the biggest frauds in European banking history. Jérôme Kerviel, a junior trader at the bank, had stolen computer codes and falsified documents to place more than 50 billion euros in futures trades. Alongside the bank's two billion euro writedown from the US subprime slump, the 4.82 billion euro loss caused major concern and remained a global talking point for a good while after.

In the wake of the scandal, the bank's shareholders criticised how it had been handled. While chairman Daniel Bouton claimed that the incident was "isolated", both internal and external investigations, the latter by PricewaterhouseCoopers, found that there had been a lack of key controls at the bank which might have allowed Kerviel to get away with his fraudulent behaviour. Bouton, chief executive since 1997, has a long history in finance, including a spell as the head of the Budget Department in the French Ministry of Finance — and he was under pressure to resign. He also had to fend off speculation about SocGen being taken over by other European banks. Bouton resigned as chief executive in May, remaining as the bank's chairman, with Frédéric Oudea, former chief financial officer, taking over as chief executive.

The scandal was so high-profile that even French politicians were involved in discussing the bank's future. French Prime Minister François Fillon vowed that Société Générale would remain a "great French bank" and would be protected against any "hostile raids" from foreign companies. The fraud exposed banks' vulnerability to market misjudgements and revealed SocGen's lack of internal and external monitoring. Risk management software is likely to get far more sophisticated in the wake of this humungous bungle, with the bank likely to make reforms that will cost in the region of 100 million euros.

Time to go

There were also reforms when it came to personnel. Aside from Kerviel's immediate supervisors being fired, the head of investment banking, Jean-Pierre Mustier, was replaced at the end of May 2008. His replacement was Michel Péretié, the former chief executive of Bear Stearns in Europe. Mustier's resignation was demanded along with that of Bouton, but it looks as though he will take up a position elsewhere in SocGen.

As for SocGen itself, the bank has suffered its shares dropping by 28 percent since the start of 2008, but in general, the embattled French giant seems to be holding up, especially given the 2008 economic climate, in which all banks across the board were at lower ebb than usual.

Société Générale

In the leagues

That said, at the end of 2007, Société Générale ranked 17th in worldwide announced mergers and acquisition activity, according to Thomson Financial. Moving up one place from the previous year, this ranking represented 73 deals and a rank value of 231.7 billion US dollars. For European involvement the firm ranked 15th, and 11th for involvement in France.

GETTING HIRED

Voulez-vouz travailler avec SG?

Société Générale is generous with its work experience offers, and recruits actively in France as well as internationally. In its home country, the group's approach is based on pre-recruitment via work-study programmes and internships within various business lines and sales training. These programmes are offered to over 1,000 graduates yearly. The placement may be part of a sandwich course or an initial posting immediately after your degree, lasting three to six months or more. A significant proportion of trainees are offered a permanent position at the end of their placement, staying on to pursue their careers in one of the bank's many different fields.

SocGen also holds various recruitment forums in France throughout the year, a schedule of which can be found at the following link: groupe.socgen.com/recrut/reseau/etudiants_forums.php.

If you are a European citizen interested in international work experience, Société Générale also offers the V.I.E. for people between the ages of 18 and 28, who have a minimum of a Bachelor's degree. The programme involves assignments of six to 24 months throughout the international SG network and applications can be submitted via the Civi Volontariat International website, at www.civiweb.com.

Pack your suitcase

The SG CIB Graduate International Programme is a two-year structured development scheme that focuses on one of three areas that a successful candidate can choose to explore: capital markets, corporate finance, or structured finance. The Capital Markets path covers equity sales and trading, fixed income and currencies, the commodities market and market risk. The Corporate Finance career path covers equity capital markets, debt capital markets, M&A and strategic and acquisition finance; finally, the Structure Finance path covers cash-flow lending, asset-based lending and access to market. The programme also includes a two week induction course at the INSEAD business school for all trainees.

Discover Europe

Graduates typically spend three periods in Paris, London and possibly another European city such as Madrid, Milan or Frankfurt. In order to be considered for the program, you must be a recent university, business school or engineering school graduate with an excellent academic record, entitled to work in France or in the UK, be fluent in English and have excellent working knowledge of French. A solid educational background in business, economics and finance, engineering or quantitative mathematics is a plus.

At the end of the programme, participants can be offered a permanent position in one of SG CIB's European offices under a local contract. The company has a specific interest in recruiting graduates who are fluent in both Japanese and English. Successful applicants will join the programme to spend two years in Europe and upon completion will be offered a position in Japan under a Japanese contract. The initial applications are usually due in December, and can be submitted through the SG CIB Graduate International Programme at www.sgcib-gip.com.

The leg work

A worker on the graduate international programme says application consists of: "An online application, a telephone interview, behavioural tests and an assessment centre." In the telephone interview they ask about your CV and how you would act in different kinds of situation under pressure. The assessment centre involves, "one team exercise, a numerical test, a presentation skills test and two interviews."

An analyst confides, "The interview process in Paris is very weird." He adds, "You have to pass a psychometric examination but frequently you will have already started work by the time they get around to doing this." In theory, no one in the whole organisation can override the psychometric exam. "If you fail it, they push you out (using the probationary period loophole). I do know one person who had been working a few months before he could take the test, and out he went, having already resigned his previous job."

OUR SURVEY SAYS

Where diversity is key

The office culture is quite diverse, and depends on which team you fall into and who your manager happens to be, a worker in Paris says, adding "I've had three different managers, and feel like the culture, hours and career growth differed amongst the three." On the whole "hours vary a lot," he adds. "Don't expect a 35-hour week, it's more like 50-60 with peaks being higher. Weekend work is rare however, and in fact you need your boss's permission to do it." An employee on the graduate international programme is pleased that the corporate culture is not as stressful as is often the case in American Banks, saying "There is time to have a chat or coffee with your colleagues."

With respect to diversity, an analyst in Paris observes there is good ethnic diversity within the French employees at the firm, as well as "a surprising number of foreign staff". In the London office particularly, a graduate international programme worker says, "The teams I worked in were up to 50 percent women, from analyst to MD, and also included people from different cultures and backgrounds."

When it comes to advancement, "seniority counts here more than one might think it should" a banker in the Paris office confides, "meaning you may not rise as rapidly as you like. On the other hand, he goes on, there's a lot of lateral mobility within the organisation. There's a "conception of mobility where you're expected to move departments every three to four years (less often once you are more senior). This does give you a lot of different things to try out." A worker in London corroborated, noting, "you are able to switch teams and focus, especially in the Paris office."

Bringing home the bacon

Salaries are raised yearly, and you can expect to receive an annual performance-based bonus, as well as a signing-on bonus. On top of pay, on a French contract you can look forward to 25 days holiday per year, plus 16-18 days off for overtime, thanks to the French 35-hour week. In the UK, you'll receive 25 days off per year. "Once a year, employees can buy stock-options for a preferential price" an employee adds, other perks also available include "gym memberships and additional health insurance".

MACQUARIE GROUP

CityPoint, Level 35
1 Ropemaker Street
London
EC2Y 9HD
United Kingdom
Tel: +44 (0) 20 7065 2000
www.macquarie.com/eu

European Locations

London (HQ)
Austria • France • Germany • Ireland •
Italy • The Netherlands • Switzerland •
United Kingdom

The Stats

Employer Type: Public Company
Ticker Symbol: MQG (Sydney)
Chief Executive: Nicholas Moore
Executive Director Europe: Andrew
Hunter
2008 Revenue: AUS $8.2bn
2008 Profit: AUS $1.8bn
2007 Revenue: AUS $7.2bn
2007 Profit: AUS $1.5bn
No. of Employees: 13,000+
No. of Offices: 60+ in 25 countries

Employment Contact

www.macquarie.com
(Click on "Careers")

Email:
londongraduates@macquarie.com

Pluses

• Everyone is part of the team
• "Good opportunities to travel"

Minuses

• Nearly all senior positions are held by
  Australian employees
• "Long hours expected at all times"

Departments

Banking and property • Equity markets •
Financial services • Funds Management •
Investment banking • Treasury and
commodities

THE BUZZ
WHAT EMPLOYEES AT OTHER FIRMS ARE SAYING

• "Strong in infrastructure"
• "Nice people, good pay"
• "Aggressive and feisty Australian bank"
• "Getting there in the UK"

THE SCOOP

N ot many people know that the iconic Australian bank Macquarie's roots are actually in England. In 1969, London merchant bank Hill Samuel & Co. established a subsidiary branch, Hill Samuel Australia (HSA), in Sydney. The banks name changed in 1985, following the deregulation of the financial markets in the 1980s when HSA gained a banking license in 1985. The new name was chosen in honour of Governor Lachlan Macquarie, the man credited with transforming Australia from a penal colony into the bustling nation it is today.

Listed on the Australian stock exchange, Macquarie has grown from an Australian investment bank to a firm with an international financial services presence. While the bank's global headquarters are in Sydney, its European headquarters are in London. Continental European offices are in Austria, Germany, Ireland, Italy, Switzerland, Russia and The Netherlands. Further offices can be found in New Zealand, Asia, Africa and the Americas.

The Aussies come north

Although Macquarie is a diversified investment bank and financial services provider in Asia, Australia and New Zealand, its focus in Europe and the Americas is more selective. The bank is, by all accounts, growing at a fast pace. In the year to March 2008, approximately 55 percent of the group's revenue was generated from business outside the Asia-Pacific. To support its international business, Macquarie expanded its workforce by more than 30 percent in 2007/8.

Making the rankings

The 2007 banking league tables showed Macquarie was well positioned on the worldwide banking ladder. At the end of the year, it ranked No.15 in worldwide-announced mergers and acquisitions, with an announced total deal value of 264.24 billion dollars. This was a market share of 5.9 percent and two spots up from its 2006 ranking of No.17. In European announced M&A, Macquarie climbed to No.16 from its 2006 spot of No.20, and in the UK it came in at No. 12 for announced deals. The bank also cracked the Spanish M&A rankings, landing No.25 for announced deals and No.24 for completed deals in the Spanish market in 2007.

Don't fence me in

The massive Macquarie system is divided into six operating groups. The management system of the bank has been labelled unique — it is non-hierarchical, allowing each business group to operate freely, albeit within defined risk limits. The bank calls this strategy "freedom within boundaries". Operating groups include Macquarie Capital (advisory and specialised funds management), securities, treasury and commodities, banking and property, funds management and financial services.

Macquarie Capital (formerly the investment banking group) includes Macquarie's wholesale structuring, stock broking, underwriting and advisory capabilities. Its services include project financing, M&A and restructuring advisory, equity capital management, specialised infrastructure and fund management, specialised leasing and asset financing.

I'll take that

In early 2006, Macquarie stepped up to the bidding table with a surprise 1.5 billion US dollar takeover bid for the London Stock Exchange. Although the bid was rejected, as LSE stockholders demanded a higher price, Macquarie strode ahead with other deals in Europe. In 2006, the bank was the co-adviser to the high profile takeover of BAA by Ferrovial, and in August 2006 it bought Corona Energy, one of the UK's largest suppliers of energy to industrial and commercial customers. Macquarie said the move would expand its presence in the European energy markets business.

> 66 Macquarie stepped up to the bidding table with a surprise $1.5 billion takeover bid for the LSE 99

Still intent on creating a force to be reckoned within the UK, only two months passed before Macquarie's utilities corporate advisory team advised Kemble Water — a consortium led Macquarie's European Infrastructure Funds — in a bid to acquire Thames Water. In March 2007, Macquarie announced it would acquire Giuliani Capital Advisers — the boutique investment bank headed by New York's famous former mayor. More UK deals came in April 2007, when Macquarie and its managed funds were involved in a series of deals including the acquisition of the off-street car parking business of National Car Parks, the digital transmission networks of National Grid Wireless and the emergency communication provider Airwave.

Acquisition mania looks set to run and run. In May 2007, the bank announced it had raised 7.5 billion euros in two new infrastructure funds to focus on investments in Europe and North America.

Wizards of Oz

Things kept on moving at a brisk pace, with Macquarie teaming up with the international business school INSEAD in Autumn 2006, to launch a global Master of Finance program for Macquarie's investment banking managers. The opportunity to study for a Master of Finance degree via this route is open to analysts joining Macquarie Capital, which can be undertaken while working. Jointly designed by Macquarie and INSEAD, the degree is tailored specifically to a career in investment advisory. It includes residential on-campus study at INSEAD's Europe, Asia, Australia and US campuses.

Conquering Europe

Clearly a bank on the move, Macquarie's real estate trusts and joint ventures are also gaining headway in Europe. Macquarie Real Estate Europe established a management agreement with self-storage operator Storage King. Its joint venture, Macquarie Global Property Advisors, has recently opened offices in France and Germany and made significant investments in Poland, France and Germany.

From Moss to Moore

After 15 years as head of "the millionaire factory" — as Macquarie was enviously dubbed, Allan Moss must have been relieved to be among the very small number of chief executives stepping down un-hounded by a frowning boardroom and a balance sheet in tatters. His decision came in May 2008, as Macquarie reported record profits from its global operations, including a 60 percent increase in consolidated post-tax profit attributable to ordinary equity holders. Nicholas Moore, head of the group's investment banking division, stepped in to replace him.

Macquarie chairman, David Clarke, said in *The Financial Times* "Nicholas has led the development of our Macquarie Capital business, which provides more than 50 percent of the group's profits." Mr. Moss himself said: "We have an ideal successor in Nicholas and I feel that this is the right time for me to hand over...Our holdings of cash and liquid securities are more than three times normal liquidity levels."

GETTING HIRED

Chasing the sun

Macquarie has full-time opportunities available for graduates in a range of areas, including: Macquarie capital, treasury and commodities, securities, fund management, finance, risk management, information technology and real estate. The firm also runs several summer internship programmes, which will take you through a comprehensive training course and hands-on experience. All programmes offer intensive, hands-on work on specific projects alongside senior figures and are an excellent way to orientate yourself in the Macquarie world.

Those who do well are offered places on the company's graduate programme. To view the available graduate programmes in Europe, you'll need to click "search jobs", and tick the "graduates and undergraduates" box on the search form — just click the programme you're interested in and follow the links to apply online. The opportunities vary widely, from analyst vacancies in the IT department in Frankfurt, to summer interns wanted for Macquarie Capital in London. You'll need to search and investigate what's on offer.

To browse opportunities at Macquarie go to the company website, click "careers" and select the country you're interested in. Here you'll find specific links for graduates and experienced professionals.

OUR SURVEY SAYS

Getting ahead in banking

Employees at Macquarie called the firm "risk-averse". Hours clearly vary according to what projects are being worked on. One employee remarks, "Obviously when we are working on large deals, hours can be longer." A number of staff surveyed tell us that "long hours are expected at all times". Some workers express dissatisfaction that "virtually all senior positions at the firm are filled by Australian employees — and the firm generally is very Australian-centric." According to a worker in London it has "a very young workforce", while another London-based employee calls the company culture "very cliquey."

A nice way to say "Thanks"

In terms of perks and benefits, employees seem happy overall. An associate boasts: "We get a season ticket loan and contributory pension scheme, as well as 25 days holiday." An insider at the firm's London office notes, "Everyone is part of the team, not just part of IT or finance." Staff also admit the firm offers them "good opportunities to travel". One satisfied employee tells us: "There are some nice touches, like beer on Fridays." □

"I Feel the need, the need for speed"

Top Gun, 1986

Shift your career into higher gear:

Visit Vault for a copy of our 2009 European guides:

● **Employer Guides:**

The Vault Guide to the Top 50 UK Law Firms
The Vault Guide to the Top 25 Banking Employers
The Vault Guide to the Top 25 Consulting Firms
The Vault Guide to the Top Engineering Firms
The Vault Guide to the Top UK Accounting Firms

● **Industry Guides:**

The Vault Career Guide to Investment Banking
The Vault Career Guide to Consulting
The Vault Career Guide to Investment Management
The Vault Career Guide to Private Equity

● **Regional Guides:**

The Vault Guide to the Top UK Employers
The Vault Guide to the Top Spanish Employers
The Vault Guide to the Top German Employers
The Vault Guide to the Top French Employers

● **Interview Guides:**

The Vault Guide to Finance Interviews
The Vault Guide to Case Interviews

www.vault.com/europe

GREENHILL & CO

Lansdowne House
57 Berkeley Square
London
W1J 6ER
United Kingdom
Tel: +44 20 7198 7400
www.greenhill.com

The Stats

Employer Type: Public Company
Ticker Symbol: GHL (NYSE)
Chairman: Robert Greenhill
Co-Chief Executives: Scott Bok, Simon Borrows
2007 Revenue: $400.4m
2007 Profit: $115.3m
2006 Revenue: $290.6m
2006 Profit: $75.7m
No. of Employees: 225
No. of Offices: 6

Departments

Financial Advisory • Merchant Banking

European Locations

London (European HQ)
Frankfurt • United Kingdom

Key Competitors

Goldman Sachs • Lazard • Rothschild

Employment Contact

In London:
For Analysts:
londonanalystrecruit@greenhill.com
For Associates:
londonassociaterecruit@greenhill.com
For Lateral Hires:
uklateralhire@greenhill.com

In Frankfurt:
For Analysts:
frankfurtanalystrecruit@greenhill.com
For Associates:
frankfurtassociaterecruit@greenhill.com
For Lateral Hires:
frankfurtlateralhire@greenhill.com

THE BUZZ
WHAT EMPLOYEES AT OTHER FIRMS ARE SAYING

• "Great people, great relationship"
• "Good quality boutique"
• "Painful to work with"
• "Unknown"

THE SCOOP

Compared to the huge players that often seem to dominate the finance scene, Greenhill is small; a fact the bank makes a virtue of. In contrast to its multi-faceted, sprawling competitors, the compact and independent Greenhill is divided into just two divisions: financial advisory services and merchant banking. The firm prides itself on its total autonomy from large institutions and its focus, both of which have enabled it to excel in merger, acquisition and restructuring advice for a growing list of large international clients. As part of its merchant banking division, Greenhill's private equity funds are sparking interest by participating in an increasing number of high stakes deals around the globe.

Need some advice?

First and foremost, Greenhill is an advisory firm, with financial advisory services contributing approximately 72 percent of total revenue. The firm's mergers and acquisitions practice offers sell-side and buy-side advisory, merger advisory and cross-border advisory, leveraging the talent drawn together from the firm's international network of offices. With M&A activity heating up around the globe, Greenhill has reaped the rewards in increased revenue from advisory services.

A mountain out of a Greenhill

Greenhill is relatively new to banking, founded a little over ten years ago by current chairman Robert F. Greenhill. Before he started up his own firm, Greenhill was chairman and chief executive of investment bank Smith Barney. Prior to this, he had spent more than three decades at Morgan Stanley where, amongst other things, he founded the M&A group and ran the establishment of Morgan Stanley's private equity group.

An energetic banker now in his seventies, Greenhill's involvement in, well, Greenhill, is impressive. He serves on the firm's management committee and on Greenhill Capital Partners' investment committee. He himself was chief executive until October 2007, when he stepped down and handed control over to Scott Bok in New York and Simon Borrows, based in London, who now reign as co-chief executives.

Only two years after the opening of its first office in New York, Greenhill opened a second office in London to serve European clients and to boost the company's fast-growing transatlantic business. Greenhill Capital Partners, the firm's private equity arm, was launched in early 2000 and subsequently raised 423 million US dollars in investment capital. Later the same year, Greenhill opened a second European office, this time in Frankfurt, Germany's financial centre. A financial restructuring practice was added in January 2001, expanding the firm's advisory practice. Greenhill opened more North American offices in Dallas and Toronto in 2005 and 2006, and San Francisco in 2008, bringing its total number of offices to six, firmly securing the firm as a global player.

The mergers magician

Just a few of the transactions Greenhill has advised on, in early 2008, include the 1.5 billion US dollar acquisition of Ambac Financial Group in March by a consortium of global financial institutions and investors. This consortium included Bank of America Securities, Citigroup Global Markets and Dresdner Kleinwort. It also advised on the 3.4 billion dollar acquisition of US medical test maker Ventana Medical Systems by Roche Holding, a Swiss pharmaceuticals company, which was finalised in the same month.

> ❝ First and foremost, Greenhill is an advisory firm. Financial advisory contributes 72 percent of revenue. ❞

Greenhill's restructuring advisory division guides debtors, creditors and acquirers, both inside and outside of formal bankruptcy, through a range of restructuring activities. The range of advice includes reorganisation proceedings, the identification of targets or buyers, sales or court proceedings and recapitalisations.

Meanwhile, Greenhill's restructuring clients, like its M&A clients, come from a range of industries. Advised restructurings include the colossal Chapter 11 proceedings of General Motors suppliers Delphi and the restructuring of US-based Delta Air Lines, specifically in connection with strategic and labour issues relating to its Chapter 11 proceedings.

Getting the management on board

The firm's private equity arm, Greenhill Capital Partners, manages two private equity funds as of mid-2008. These two funds have together raised 1.3 billion US dollars in capital, approximately 25 percent of which comes from Greenhill & Co and its employees themselves. GCP aims for long-term growth in middle-market companies, focusing primarily on the financial services, energy and telecommunications industries.

The strategy of this fund is to invest in companies where managerial staff holds equity stakes in their businesses. This puts management teams in the reins when it comes to financial success. The company also does its level best to avoid direct conflict with Greenhill's advisory clients in its investments. Recent GCP investments include the newly formed global insurance company Ironshore Insurance Ltd and the recapitalisation of credit card issuer First Equity Card.

In 2006, the company reported increased revenue from financial advisory services, which it attributed to high levels of M&A volume. Merchant banking revenue also increased, mostly due to investment gains and higher asset management fees. Earlier that year, the firm closed its first venture capital fund, Greenhill SAVP, after raising 101.5 million dollars in committed capital.

Leading lights of Europe

In 2006, Greenhill established a European primary merchant banking business, based in London. The new business acts as the European equivalent of Greenhill Capital Partners and focuses on small and mid-cap opportunities in Europe. Prior to this, Greenhill was only involved in advisory services for Europe, where major clients included leading UK retailer Tesco plc, German commercial vehicles and industrial equipment group MAN AG and the international pharmaceuticals and industrial group Bayer AG.

In 2007, Greenhill Capital Partners Europe (GCPE) was launched, with 191 million pounds in commitments. Out of this amount, 35 percent of total capital was contributed by Greenhill and its management. The fund, headed by Brian Phillips, now one of the firm's managing directors, focuses on investments in the leisure, consumer, services and healthcare sectors in Europe and the UK.

GETTING HIRED

A steep hill?

Greenhill offers full-time positions at both analyst and associate level. The analyst role is designed for university graduates looking to start a career in investment banking. Working in small teams, you'll be involved with M&A advisory assignments, restructuring assignments, and merchant banking opportunities. There's a high chance you'll get a look into a range of business practices during your time on the programme.

In addition, there is the opportunity to do a summer internship sometime between June and September, however for this you must be about to enter your final year at university or grad school.

A good thing to keep in mind is the advantage in Greenhill's size. The relatively small size of the firm means you'll be rubbing shoulders with senior professionals on a daily basis rather than toiling away in anonymity. This also means you'll get more of a chance to pick up skills from the people at the top.

The best options

For analyst positions in Frankfurt, you'll need to submit an English language cover letter and CV to frankfurtanalystrecruit@greenhill.com. Interviews are held at the firm's offices in Frankfurt, though there are some opportunities for initial interviews in London to maximise candidates' convenience. You will need written and spoken fluency in German to be eligible for this position, and should provide appropriate assurance of this in your cover letter.

In London, the analyst programme lasts for three years before moving up to associate level. If you're keen, send your CV and cover letter along to londonanalystrecruit@greenhill.com.

For associates, Greenhill looks at candidates from graduate business schools worldwide. If you're interested, send your CV and cover letter to either londonassociaterecruit@ greenhill.com or frankfurtassociaterecruit@greenhill.com. Once again, for Frankfurt you should be able to convince the firm you are fluent in both English and German. For those above analyst and associate levels, send your CV and cover letter to uklateralhire@ greenhill.com or frankfurtlateralhire@greenhill.com.

DRESDNER KLEINWORT IB

Theodor-Heuss-Alle 44-46
60486 Frankfurt
Germany
Tel: +49 (0) 69 713 0

30 Gresham Street
London
EC2P 2XY
United Kingdom
Tel: +44 (0)20 7623 8000
www.dresdnerkleinwort.com

The Stats

Employer Type: IB division of Dresdner
Bank AG
Ticker Symbol: DRB7 (Frankfurt)
Chairman: Herbert Walter
Chief Executive: Stefan Jentzsch
2007 Revenue: €1.63bn
2007 Profit (Loss): (€659m)
2006 Revenue: €3.11bn
2006 Profit: €548m
No. of Employees: 5,500 (Corporate and
I-Banking)
No. of Offices: 50

Departments

Business Support • Capital Markets
(Emerging Markets, FICC, Global
Distribution, Global Equities, Hedge Fund
Solutions, Research) • Global Banking
(Client Coverage, Global Finance) •
Global Loans and Transaction • Services •
Strategic Advisory

European Locations

Frankfurt, London (Joint Global HQs)
Austria • Belgium • France • Germany •
Greece • Hungary • Italy • Latvia •
Luxembourg • The Netherlands • Poland •
Russia • Spain • Switzerland • Turkey •
Ukraine • United Kingdom

Key Competitors

Deutsche Bank • Commerzbank •
Morgan Stanley

Employment Contact

www.dresdnerkleinwort.com
(Click on "careers")

THE BUZZ
WHAT EMPLOYEES AT OTHER FIRMS ARE SAYING

• "Great second-tier bank"
• "Dominates small/mid-caps"
• "Not exciting"
• "No clear strategy of main shareholder
  Allianz"

THE SCOOP

I n June 2008, Dresdner Kleinwort was granted the retail-coordinator role for what is likely to be the biggest European IPO of the year. German rail operator, Deutsche Bahn will proceed with its 7.7 billion dollar flotation with Dresdner Kleinwort assisting on the retail aspects, including coordinating the sale of shares to Deutsche Bahn employees. The bank had hoped for the more lucrative global coordinator role, but this fell to Morgan Stanley, Deutsche Bank, UBS and Goldman Sachs. In its other key home market of the UK, Dresdner Kleinwort also worked on the four billion pound rights issue of HBOS in July of 2008.

Size and shape

Dresdner Kleinwort (DKIB) is Dresdner Bank AG's commercial and investment banking arm, a subsidiary of German financial services giant, Allianz Group. It offers services to corporate, institutional and governmental clients worldwide, and is headquartered in both Frankfurt and London, whilst operating branches in major financial centres such as New York, Tokyo and Hong Kong.

While focusing primarily on deals in Germany and the UK, Dresdner Kleinwort has a presence in France, Italy, Luxembourg, Poland, Russia, Spain and Switzerland, as well as Brazil, China, Japan and the US. The Allianz Group connection means that Dresdner Kleinwort's corporate family includes thousands of offices around the world.

A series of successive mergers and acquisitions brought the bank into being, beginning in 1961 with the merger of two small family-owned banks: Robert Benson & Lonsdale and Kleinwort and Sons. The result, named Kleinwort Benson, became central to the privatisation of British industries (including British Telecom and British Gas) in the 1980s.

Dresdner Bank AG stepped in and acquired Kleinwort Benson in 1995, subsequently merging with the US boutique Wasserstein Perella in 2001. The combined investment bank Dresdner Kleinwort Wasserstein was created, but later dropped the "Wasserstein" to become simply, "Dresdner Kleinwort" on June 29, 2006.

In that year, and in 2007, the investment bank integrated some of Dresdner's corporate banking services, mainly in Germany. The firm now has three divisions: global banking, capital markets and business support.

Rolling in the green

DKIB struck an environmentally minded deal with Gazprombank, the arm of one of Russia's leading energy conglomerates, in 2007. The two firms embarked on an innovative carbon trading joint venture fund to invest in mainly Russian and Eastern European projects that create carbon credits, in line with the Kyoto Protocol. Under the UN agreement, companies that invest in Eastern Europe-based projects that cut emissions receive credits for each ton of carbon dioxide that is effectively cancelled out. The credits can then be sold to EU states and other countries that emit more than they were allotted from 2008 to 2012. The venture could generate up to one billion tons of credit that could be worth 15 billion euros.

In the Bleak Midwinter

Hard on the heels of 60 credit-related job cuts in December 2007, plus a general end-of-year review process which led to other exits across the bank, the German investment bank said it was looking to take on an additional 60 staff in Moscow, London and New York, to expand its Russian franchise. Dresdner Kleinwort regards Russia as its third most important market after Germany and the UK. It has worked on big deals there in the past for Gazprom, Rosneft and others, but also has a growing business in local trading and structured produts.

> ❝ Dresdner Kleinwort is Dresdner Bank AG's commercial and investment banking arm, subsidiary of financial services giant Allianz ❞

Former Dresdner board member in Russia Matthias Warnig departed during 2007 in order to lead Nordstream, the project to construct a natural gas pipeline from Russia to Germay. During October 2007, Dresdner also lost three of its bankers to Gazprombank, lured to open its investment banking arm, Gazprom Financial Services, in London.

Breaking the Allianz

The big news in Germany in 2008 was Allianz's decision to split Dresdner Bank into two distinct units for private clients, retail banking and corporate/investment banking with a deadline of August 31, 2008. It was further rumoured that Allianz was also in talks with various parties as potential merger partners for the bank, either as a whole or on the retail side. Deutsche Bank and Commerzbank were two parties approached directly by Allianz. Commerzbank, Lloyds TSB and Santander are all names which appeared in presss reports, with Commerzbank talks said to be at an advanced stage at the time of writing. A three-way merger involving Commerzbank, Dresdner Bank Postbank was also possible.

Recognised for achievement

DKIB picked up significant awards in 2007. It was named "Best Investment Bank in Central & Eastern Europe", "Best Equity House in Russia" by *Euromoney*; "German M&A Bank of the Year" in *Financial News*. In 2008, it collected *Acquisitions Monthly's* "Domestic Deal of the Year" for advising and financing Macquarie on its joint 1.6 billion euro bid for Techem in Germany. The bank's deals have also garnered recognition, and in 2006 it won "IPO of the Year" from *Financial News* for Rosneft's 10.7 billion dollar flotation. According to Dealogic, Dresdner Kleinwort has ranked No. 2 in German IPO's since 1995 and 2007 is no exception. It is also No. 2 for German equity transactions.

As well as deal accolades, the bank is well-regarded in the sphere of research. In May for example, *Boersenzeitung* gave it top award for "Best Recommendations - German Mid/Small Caps". More broadly, in the latest Thompson Reuters Extel survey published in 2008, Dresdner Kleinwort ranked number ten in the category of leading pan-European brokerage firms for equity and equity-linked research, and had fifteen research teams score top five positions. Additionally, in the latest *Euromoney* Credit and Fixed Income research poll, it ranked number five overall.

GETTING HIRED

Step up to stiff competition

Dresdner Bank as a whole puts high value on vocational traineeships, with a view to permanent employment at their conclusion in its recruitment policy. In 2006, 491 vocational trainees were taken on, with 131 being offered full-time positions with the company once their training was complete. The quality of employees' qualifications is viewed by the bank as directly related to its success, so it takes pains to train its potential staff well.

To apply for an internship, follow the "careers" link on the company's homepage, click "graduate", and then select the country in which you would like to undertake an internship using the links at the top of the page. Selecting "apply" will take your through the details of the various internships available, and give details on how to apply. In London, as a general rule, the Summer Internship online application form opens on November 12, 2008, and should be submitted before February 8, 2009 but it's worth checking the website for any changes to these dates. Successful interns will begin in June 2009.

In Frankfurt, interns are recruited all year round, so there is no official deadline for applications. However, applicants are advised to submit their applications three or four months before they plan to start, due to the popularity of the schemes. To find out more about the careers or graduate programmes at Dresdner Kleinwort, visit the company's careers link at www.dresdnerkleinwort.com/eng/careers/index.html.

All's fair in love and banking ,

Dresdner Kleinwort visit a selection of the top universities throughout Europe each academic year and set up careers fairs for undergraduates thinking of working in banking. Details of the specific campuses visited and the dates they will be run are listed by city — either London or Frankfurt — on the "Events" link found in the Graduates section of the company's "careers" website.

Swapping gowns for suits

For graduates seeking work with Dresdner Kleinwort, you must have achieved or be expected to achieve a 2:1 honours degree (of equivalent) in any discipline; have 300 UCAS points at A-level (or equivalent); have Maths GCSE at Grade A or B and be fluent in English. If you meet these criteria, you are invited to apply online: from the "careers" link, select "graduates," either "London" or "Frankfurt," then "apply" from the menu on the left, followed by "apply online". The applications are divided into specific banking sectors: capital markets, global banking, finance, IT and risk management — extensive details on each of these sectors and the various employment opportunities within them, are to be found on the website under the "graduate" link on the careers homepage

Pay close attention to the opening and closing dates for applications. For London, currently the online application form for graduates opens in September and must be submitted by November 8, 2008. If you meet the firm's selection criteria, you'll be asked to complete its online numerical reasoning test; success here will see you invited to attend a first round assessment centre (these take place in September). Here again you will be given further numerical tests, and interviews if successful. You will be invited to a second round assessment centre if you put in a good performance in the first round; these are currently scheduled for November.

Dresdner describes its assessment centres as processes "to identify candidates with the right academic skills and personal attributes for our business." It also makes clear that the specifics of assessment tasks and exercises will depend on which business division you have applied to. In Frankfurt, the process is the same but graduate applications can be submitted throughout the year, with the exception of Risk

Management applicants, who should apply by February. In general, the bank advises applicants to submit applications three to four months before you plan to start.

If you require more information on the company's recruitment process, they offer a 12-page PDF document on their "Apply" page to answer applicant queries. Experienced professionals can browse and apply for current vacancies listed in the "Experienced Hires" section of DK's careers site. □

Dresdner Kleinwort IB

25 Gresham Street
London, EC2V 7HN
United Kingdom
Tel: +44 (0) 20 7626 1500
www.lloydstsb.com

The Stats

Employer Type: Public Company
Ticker Symbol: LLOY (LSE); LYG (NYSE)
Chairman: Sir Victor Blank
2007 Revenue: £29.6bn
2007 Income: £3.28bn
2006 Revenue: £29.09bn
2006 Income: £2.8bn
No. of Employees: 70,000
No. of Offices: 2,000 branches

Departments

Central Support Functions •
Group Finance • Insurance and
Investments • IT and Operations
UK Retail Banking • Wholesale and
International Banking

European Locations

London (HQ)
Belgium • Cyprus • Gibraltar •
Luxembourg • Monaco • The
Netherlands • Spain • Switzerland •
United Kingdom

Employment Contact

www.lloydstsb.com
(Click on "careers with us")

Key Competitors

Barclays • HSBC • HBOS • RBS/NatWest

Pluses

• Hours are fairly flexible

Minuses

• Conservative

THE BUZZ
WHAT EMPLOYEES AT OTHER FIRMS ARE SAYING

• "Competent high street bank"
• "Growing in the UK"
• "Major but boring work culture"
• "Old and serious"

THE SCOOP

L loyds Bank was founded in 1765 by John Taylor and Sampson Lloyd in Birmingham, England. Two sons of the original partners formed Barnetts Hoares Hanbury and Lloyd in London, which became a part of the Lloyds Banking Company.

The bank had numerous takeovers by 1923 and by the early 1990s it was a banking empire to be reckoned with. By the turn of the millennium, Lloyds had offices worldwide. The strength the bank held in its position as National Bank of New Zealand was reinforced by the 1994 takeover of the Rural Bank, making Lloyds the leading provider of agricultural finance. A 1985 Act of Parliament created the Trustee Savings Bank (TSB), and merged all UK savings banks under TSB Bank plc. TSB had deeper roots, in a savings bank founded in 1810 by Henry Duncan in Scotland.

Shuffling banks

In 1995, the Lloyds bank group welcomed Cheltenham & Gloucester (C&G) as a member, before merging with TSB Group to form what is now known as the Lloyds TSB Group plc. A thorough re-branding followed, in which all TSB and Lloyds Bank branches in England and Wales were re-branded Lloyds TSB by June 1999, while bank branches in Scotland received the new brand name, Lloyds TSB Scotland. Scottish Widows, the insurance provider, entered the new group in March 2000, to form one of the UK's largest providers of life, pensions and unit trust products and services.

In October 2003, Lloyds TSB Group sold subsidiary NBNZ Holdings Limited, comprising the Group's New Zealand banking and insurance operations, to Australia and New Zealand Banking Group Limited. In another move towards slimming down and focussing on its core businesses, the group also sold its Argentinean business to Banco Patagonia Sudameris S.A and its Colombian business to Primer Banco del Istmo S.A. in July 2004. As if this weren't enough activity, in December 2005, the firm announced a deal to sell part of its credit card business Goldfish to Morgan Stanley Bank for 175 million pounds in cash.

Cushioning the crunch

Lloyds TSB rode the storm of the credit crunch with considerable style, avoiding the excesses of damage which hit its rivals. The bank reported 2007 pre-tax profits of four billion pounds, a drop of six percent from 2006, but still better than analysts' predictions. According to some, the lack of focus on corporate and investment banking, meaning less exposure in high-risk areas, is what kept Lloyds TSB head and shoulders above its competition. Having a strong retail banking core enabled the firm to stay buoyant, as this segment was responsible for 42 percent of its 2007 pre-tax profits. This division was helped along by strong sales growth and tight cost control.

Inroads into Germany

When Allianz announced that Dresdner Bank was up for sale in 2008, market speculation suggested that Lloyds TSB was certainly interested, if not quite throwing caution to the wind, in making a purchase. It was reported that the British bank made a non-binding offer for the German powerhouse in June 2008, determined to make the most of opportunities left in the post credit-crunch retail banking market. As one among the few banks left relatively unhurt by the credit crisis, Lloyds TSB was rumoured to be investigating a fully-fledged bid for the six billion pound German bank to do what it can to consolidate its advantage.

Around the same time, media reports indicated that Lloyds TSB has also been eyeing Postbank as a potential acquisition — the German firm is likely to be on the market before the end of 2008 — as well as taking an interest in Citigroup's German operations. However, there is stiff competition from Germany's Commerzbank, which is reported to be in serious talks over the purchase of a merged Postbank and Dresdner Bank package.

Some onlookers say that among Lloyds TSB's arguments in favour of the Dresdner buy are its lengthy experience in retail banking and its capacity to manage a major retail customer franchise. Commentators have speculated that Lloyds TSB might swap its Scottish Widows life assurance operation for Dresdner's retail operations, although this is thought to be less likely as bancassurance is held by Lloyds TSB to be central to its identity and strategy for growth. While Allianz has looked abroad for buyers, a German-only deal is thought to be more than possible — German politicians have certainly expressed their enthusiasm for a domestic buyer.

Is this your 69 million pounds, madam?

In June 2008, Lloyds TSB announced a nationwide drive to reunite customers with approximately 69 million pounds held in over 120,000 unused savings accounts, commercial accounts and personal accounts. The bank appointed a specialist search agency to help track down customers with accounts that have been active for 15 years or more. "These accounts have been long forgotten and our aim is to reunite as many customers as possible with their cash," said the bank's group executive director of UK retail banking, Helen Weir, speaking in *The Independent*. The search will cover unclaimed assets in Lloyds TSB and Cheltenham & Gloucester accounts. The average amount that Lloyds TSB hopes to return to its owners is 575 pounds, with one in ten accounts having a balance in excess of 1,000 pounds.

GETTING HIRED

Taking the Lloyds road

There are a number of routes into landing one of the 150 vacancies Lloyds TSB has open for graduates. Applications are taken online from September for graduates, industrial placements and interns. To browse vacancies for more general roles and positions, adverts are placed on the Lloyds TSB website at www.lloydstsbjobs.com/ career_opportunities.asp. Insiders agree it is easier to land a job at Lloyds after having a summer internship, but it is far from required, as many current graduates and employees did not undertake an internship at Lloyds TSB. However those that did join as an intern spoke highly of the experience. One contact says his internship involved working on the management of private banking client's portfolios, commenting that the work was diverse. The experience, he adds, "Certainly helped me in getting back into the organisation, as I knew how the bank operated."

While some insiders maintain that Lloyds TSB is not an overly selective firm, one associate says the company is "in an aggressive growth phase. It is arguably the UK's fastest growing institution, so its recruitment is very selective at present." Sources say the interview and selection process is relatively standard and potential hires are subject to competency tests. A contact describes his hiring experience as a "very straightforward process."

So many options

There are a number of different training programmes at Lloyds TSB: business specialist programmes for those without a degree, the new Graduate Leadership Programme for those with a 2:1 undergraduate degree or above, as well as other opportunities for industrial placements and the summer vacation internship scheme.

On the competitive (and fully revised in 2008) graduate leadership programme, you will spend two years developing your technical expertise, leadership and management skills in selected assignments. The revised programme has a greater emphasis on senior support, giving participants access to a senior manager and a dedicated graduate development specialist. Your career journey will include formal training, one-on-one reviews and placements where you can employ your management capabilities. Some of the placements also include study towards a professional qualification. The specific streams of the programme are: general management, finance, corporate markets, human resources, retail leadership and IT. To join this programme, you'll need a minimum 2:1 in any discipline, together with all the qualities that make for strong leaders: judgement, drive, the ability to influence and successfully put plans and ideas into action.

The summer internship is for those expecting to receive a minimum 2:1 in any discipline, and consists of a paid 10-week placement. Doing well here could see you fast-tracked to the leadership programme when you graduate. These programmes tend to begin in June, but check the website for specific dates. The year-long industrial placement programme is for those in the penultimate year of their degree with an expected 2:1. It will give you excellent exposure to real work and responsibility in all Lloyds' major business functions.

Applications should be made online, simply click any of the "apply now" links on the Lloyds TSB career page and complete the online application. Deadlines for programmes vary, so make sure you carefully research the application dates for the programme you are applying to.

We'd love to have you

Insiders in the investment banking and trading teams told us about their experiences with the hiring process and culture at the firm. A member of the trading team tells us his interview consisted of three rounds of interviews with senior management and assessment centre exercises. Final interviews, he says, are usually with the managing directors of the business area you're interested in working in and its partner business areas.

A trainee describes the process of securing a summer internship as having four stages: an online application form, a numeracy test, a telephone interview and attendance at a one day assessment centre.

OUR SURVEY SAYS

Talking your way in

In what employees described as a "progressive, intellectually challenging and entrepreneurial culture that embraces change," hours are fairly flexible. One trader "works the hours required to develop [himself] and [his] business," in a 60-70 hour week. Elsewhere in the bank, others work less than 40 hours a week and happily reveal, "There is no pressure to work long hours." Another insider notes the organisation is: "very flexible and offers compressed hours and flexitime to some employees." Benefits of working at the firm listed by staff include private healthcare and a gym membership discount. A London-based trainee calls the firm "very conservative, yet innovative at the same time, with a constant quest for improvement." He goes on to praise the firm's "good work/life balance and frequently 9-5 culture."

Piazza Cordusio
20123 Milano
Italy
Tel: +39 02 88 621
www.unicreditgroup.eu

The Stats

Employer Type: Public Company
Ticker Symbol: UCG (Milan)
Chief Executive: Alessandro Profumo
2007 Revenue: €29.6bn
2007 Profit: €6.6bn
2006 Revenue: €23.3bn
2006 Profit: €6.13bn
No. of Employees: 170,000
No. of Branches: 9,000+

Departments

Asset Management • Central and Eastern
Europe • Corporate Banking
Markets and Investment Banking • Poland
Markets • Private Banking •
Retail Banking

European Locations

Milan (HQ)
Austria • Bosnia and Herzegovina •
Bulgaria • Croatia • Czech Republic •
Estonia • France • Germany • Greece •
Hungary • Ireland • Italy • Latvia •
Lithuania • Luxembourg • Macedonia •
The Netherlands • Norway • Poland •
Romania • Russia • Serbia • Slovakia •
Slovenia • Spain • Switzerland • Turkey •
Ukraine • United Kingdom

Employment Contacts

www.unicreditgroup.eu/DOC/jsp/navigati
on/include_content.jsp

Head of HR:
Rino Piazzolla
Head of Human Resources
Via San Protaso, 3
20121 Milano, Italy
Fax +39 02/8862 2324
info@unicreditgroup.eu

Key Competitors

BNP Paribas • ING • Grupo Santander

THE BUZZ
WHAT EMPLOYEES AT OTHER FIRMS ARE SAYING

• "Becoming increasingly European"
• "Increasingly powerful"
• "Spivvy"
• "Large but regional"

THE SCOOP

Formed from the gradual coalescence of more than a hundred banks throughout more than 500 years of Italian history — a process discussed in extremely small detail on the group's website — UniCredit has become one of Europe's largest players in banking and financial services, reporting annual revenue of almost 30 million euros for 2007.

Operating a mammoth network of branches, representative offices and small banking subsidiaries in 50 countries worldwide, UniCredit is a market leader in diverse geographical areas, including Bavaria, Austria and Italy, one of Europe's richest regions as well as the hotbed of economic growth that is Central ar Eastern Europe. It operates via a series of business divisions, two of which dedicated solely to banking in Poland and the remainder of Central East Europe respectively. Altogether this has led to the business' characterisatior the strong diversification of its revenues, both in its business types and geographical spread.

Leagues ahead

According to Thomson Financial, in announced mergers and acquisitions in Eu at the end of 2007, UniCredit ranked 11th for Italian involvement, stepping up 17th place the year before. As well as bringing in proceeds to the tune of 52.2 bi US dollars in its home territory, the group was also busy in Eastern Eu UniCredit moved into 12th place in 2007 from 13th place in 2006. Celebrating a year in the region, the bank carried out 22 deals and saw profits of 10.4 billio dollars. The bank's merger with Capitalia was also ranked seventh in the worldwide announced deals in 2007.

From Holy Roman Empire to wholly banking empire

The hundred or so banks that came together to form the entity that is UniCre had prior to this final union existed as Credito Italiano, Caritro, CariVero Cassamarca, Cassa di Risparmio di Carpi, Rolo Banca 1473, Cassa di Risparm di Torino, Banca dell'Umbria, Cassa di Risparmio di Trieste. Several of the traced their origin back to the 15th century — and all of them belonged to t four original Italian bank categories of state pawn agencies and Banch Monte, savings banks, credit societies and cooperatives, and commercial t The Amato Law of 1990 brought about a drastic conversion of the na banking model, shifting it to match the corporate model of publicly entities. This enabled the coming together of the nine banks into a arrangement in 1998.

The 2005 merger of UniCredit with the German HVB group was soon followed by the 2007 acquisition of Capitalia, the third-largest banking group in Italy, allowing UniCredit to cement its position in Western Europe. Thanks in part to HVB's prior merger with Bank Austria (which was well represented throughout "new" post-communist European markets); UniCredit began to market itself as "the new truly European bank".

CEE you at the top

UniCredit's rise to market dominance in Central and Eastern Europe began in 1999 with the acquisition of Poland's Bank Pekao, soon followed in 2000 with the acquisition of Bulbank (Bulgaria) and Unibanka (Slovenia). In 2002, it picked up Zagrebacka Banka (Croatia), Demirbank Romania (Romania), and Živnostenska Banka (Czech Republic), Turkey's Yapi Kredi in 2005, while 2007 saw it establish a presence in Ukraine, Kazakhstan, Tajikistan, and Kyrgyzstan. With the CEE region reporting the highest economic growth rates in Europe, UniCredit saw fit to allocate its management to the sub-holding Bank Austria, while Poland would be managed directly by UniCredit.

Doffing their Capitalia

In spring 2007, UniCredit grew into the euro zone's biggest bank by market capitalisation, with the 21.8 billion euro acquisition of Capitalia SpA, its largest deal to date. Expected to be accretive by 2009, the deal also marked UniCredit's ascension to the second largest lender in Germany, holding a five percent market share, the No.1 bank in Austria, and the second biggest retail banking provider in Italy, after Intesa Sanpalo SpA.

Here's looking at .eu

In 2006, UniCredit re-launched its website with an .eu suffix, in an attempt to emphasise its desired identity as a pan-European entity, as opposed to an Italian bank with operations in a range of European nations. This step towards inclusion in the global elect may be seen partly in response to domestic consolidation and resulting competition, most notably the formation of Intesa Sanpaulo, UniCredit's direct rival Italian bank. It may also be seen as being a part of Profumo's vision for an Italian banking "champion" to compete with the French, British and American leaders. Its plan for 2008 focuses strongly on retail banking markets in Italy, Germany and Austria, together with cost reduction at HVB.

Good Unidea

Pro-active about financing goodwill projects, UniCredit set up the private foundation Unidea to further intervention in social and humanitarian matters, "particularly medical, educational and environmental aid in developing countries, and transition economies." Unidea lists among its objectives the promotion and sustenance of co-operation and humanitarian aid projects which promote community development and a self-sufficient society, while also consulting for not-for-profit organisations. Viewed alongside the bank's expansion into the high growth economies of CEE, cynics may perceive a link to the company's business strategy of investment in developing nations. One of Unidea's focus regions is Central and South Eastern Europe, with its remit entailing aid through these nations' economic transitions into becoming EU countries.

GETTING HIRED

Whetting the banking appetite

UniCredit offer internships to degree-holders to help them pick up some banking experience and discover if banking is the career choice they are looking for. A trainee's progress is followed by a company tutor who provides assistance throughout the scheme. The programmes are promoted through universities and schools, local school authorities and provincial employment authorities and range from six to 12 months in duration. Those interested should check the website of their university or the careers division of their educational institution for more information. This information can be found on the company's careers page, by following the "Students" link.

Location Location Location

Clicking on "Work With Us" on UniCredit's careers page will take you to the online application where you can apply directly for work at either it or one of its subsidiaries in primarily CEE locations, but also in Ireland, Italy, Germany and Austria. Most of the pages are in the vernacular of each nation as well as English, with the exception of Bosnia, which specifies that speaking English is "mandatory." For work in Italy, you can select "Vacant Positions", "Submit Your CV" or "Update Your CV". For all other nations, you will be taken to the regional or subsidiary website and given instructions from there. □

AIB Bank (CI) Ltd • Anglo Irish

KGaA • Banesto • Bank of Ir

Caisse d'Epargne, Groupe • Ca

Group • Close Brothers • Coll

Credit Agricole S.A. • Danske

Fortis • Fox-Pitt, Kelton • HB

CAP • ING Groep N.V • Intesa

KBC Group • Landesbank Berlin

Corporate Bank • Natixis • Nor

• Petercam • Grupo Banco Popu

kets • Sabadell, Banco • Sal.

ander, Grupo • Sberbank • Sta

AIB Bank (CI) Ltd • Anglo Irish

KGaA • Banesto • Bank of Ir

Caisse d'Epargne, Groupe • Cal

THE
BEST OF THE
REST

ALLIED IRISH BANKS

Bankcentre
Ballsbridge
Dublin, 4
Ireland
Tel: +353 (0) 1 660311
www.aibgroup.com

The Stats

Employer Type: Public Company
Ticker Symbol: AIB (NYSE)
Chief Executive: Eugene Sheehy
2007 Revenue: €4.86bn (FYE 12/07)
2007 Profit: €2.508bn
2006 Revenue: €4.33bn
2006 Profit: €2.62bn
No. of Employees: 23,700+
No. of Offices: Offices in 14 countries

Departments

Asset Finance • Commercial Banking
Compliance and Money Laundering •
Finance • Legal and Central Securities •
New Accounts • Operations and
Technology • Property and Facilities
Risk

European Locations

Dublin (HQ)
Ireland • Poland • United Kingdom

Employment Contact

careers@aib.ie

Key Competitors

Bank of Ireland • HSBC Holdings • RBS

Pluses

• Regionally strong, Lots of opportunity

Minuses

• Limited European opportunities

THE SCOOP

Allied Irish Banks (AIB) is the leading banking and financial services organisation in the Republic of Ireland. In addition to its Irish operations, the bank operates in Britain, Poland and the US. Ranked No. 61 in the Top 1000 World Banks by Tier One Capital in *The Banker* July 2008, the bank offers a full range of banking services, including commercial and retail accounts and loans, financing, leasing, pension, financing and trust services.

Additionally, the bank also offers a range of general insurance products, including home, travel and health insurance. AIB has approximately 270 retail outlets in Ireland and an additional 52 in Northern Ireland, where it operates First Trust Bank.

Four-leafed clover

Comprised of four main divisions, AIB has positioned itself to cater to all types of customers. AIB Bank Republic of Ireland, encompasses all retail and commercial activities in Ireland, the Channel Islands and the Isle of Man; AIB Bank Great Britain and Northern Ireland provides retail and commercial banking services in the two countries, and AIB Capital Markets oversees the global treasury and international, investment banking and corporate banking activities, as well as the Allied Irish America Network. AIB's fourth segment is the Poland division, which is comprised of AIB's majority shareholding in Bank Zachodni WBK.

Allied Irish Banks was formed in 1966 from the union of three Irish Banks: Provincial Bank, Royal Bank of Ireland and Munster & Leinster Bank. The banks merged to overcome the traditionally fragmented nature of the Irish banking industry, as well as to strengthen their position in the global business era.

A stronger platform for competition with North American banks — which were just beginning to enter Ireland — was increasingly necessary. In November 2006, Allied Irish Bank was voted "Britain's Best Business Bank" in a biannual survey of the business sector, commissioned by the Forum of Private Business.

Spreading roots

In order to remain competitive, AIB looked to expand internationally. In July 1991, the merger of AIB Group's interests in Northern Ireland with those of TSB Northern Ireland created First Trust Bank. In 2003, the company sold troubled Maryland-based bank Allfirst Financial (which was formed by AIB's merger of First Maryland Bancorp and Dauphin Deposit Corp.) to New York-based M&T Bank Corp.

As part of the deal, AIB acquired a 22.5 percent stake of M&T. Today, AIB has a significant presence in the US, Poland and the UK, with more than half of AIB's operating profit generated from outside the bank's Republic of Ireland division.

Bulgarian banking

In February 2008, AIB took a firmer foothold aboard the CEE (Central and Eastern Europe) investment banking bandwagon and bought a 49.99 percent stake in the Bulgarian-American Credit Bank (BACB) from the Bulgarian-American Enterprise Fund (BAEF) for 216.2 million euros in cash. The acquisition came as many banks look to the CEE region for growth, thanks primarily to its abundant supply of high-growth economies.

AIB became the second bank from Western Europe to pick up a stake in Bulgaria's burgeoning lending market in the last 12 years. In 2007, Belgium's KBC took on 72 percent of Bulgaria's Economic and Investment Bank (EIBank).

GETTING HIRED

AIB usually operates a graduate recruitment programme to bring university leavers into its banking fold. It consists of an induction programme, training on the job, and a variety of training courses. If you're in the final year of a degree in business, accountancy, technology or a related discipline, a recently qualified graduate (minimum 2:2), or if you're studying towards a postgraduate or Masters qualification, AIB would like to hear from you.

The Learning and Development Programme is at the centre of the programme. Candidates are taken through structured on-the-job experiences to help graduates bolster their practical knowledge, whilst receiving support and coaching on personal goals from their Line Manager. A series of evening classes, or "master classes", are run in order to give candidates the knowledge they will need, whilst allowing them to rub shoulders with senior management and their fellow graduates.

As well as building knowledge and experience, the graduate training programme works to develop your competencies, the firm says, through a series of workshops in things such as: career management, teamwork, customer relationship management, strategic thinking and time and task management. Once you're through the programme, the company will assist you in selecting the most appropriate banking sector for you based on your strengths. If you're keen to get on board, make sure you check the bank's careers website at www.aibgroup.com (click on the "Careers" link).

The bank recruits into the technology, business and personal credit, business and private banking, finance and financial management, general business and corporate governance sectors.

Pots of gold

Among the perks you'll receive working for AIB are a performance-related promotion structure, market-related salary and 21 days leave per year. You'll also be able to participate in the bank's profit sharing scheme and be eligible for preferential rates on personal loans. Employees at the bank are encouraged and financially assisted to pursue further studies and also benefit from an exciting range of sports and social activities and special rates for car and house insurance.

Get in touch with the bank's HR department for further information on opportunities at the bank. If you're looking for entry level positions, you can check vacancies on the bank's careers page. Careers information is sorted in four categories: Ireland, capital markets, Northern Ireland and Great Britain. □

ANGLO IRISH BANK

Stephen Ct., 18/21
St. Stephen's Green
Dublin, 2
Ireland
Tel: + 353 (0) 1 6162000
www.angloirishbank.ie

The Stats

Employer Type: Public Company
Ticker Symbol: ANGL (Dublin, LSE)
Chairman: Sean FitzPatrick
Chief Executive: David Drumm
2007 Revenue: €1.8bn
2007 Profit: €1.2bn
2006 Revenue: €1.2bn
2006 Profit: €658m
No. of Employees: 1,900+
No. of Offices: 20 in Europe

Departments

Business Banking • Retail Banking •
Treasury • Wealth Management

European Locations

Dublin (HQ)
Austria • Ireland • Switzerland •
United Kingdom

Employment Contact

www.angloirishbank.ie/careers

Key Competitors

Allied Irish Banks • Bank of Ireland •
Close Brothers

Pluses

• Good team atmosphere
• "Open door policy from
  management"

Minuses

• Hours can be long
• Formal dress code

THE BUZZ
WHAT EMPLOYEES AT OTHER FIRMS ARE SAYING

• "Commercial bank"
• "Small, regional"

THE SCOOP

Anglo Irish Bank Corporation, headquartered in Dublin, offers business and private banking services with operations divided into three main business units: business banking, wealth management and treasury. These business units are supported by a group services function. The business banking unit is primarily a commercial lending business, while the treasury unit focuses on funding, liquidity and FX and interest rate risk management for corporate customers, capital markets and international finance. The bank's wealth management division provides private banking services to high net worth individuals.

Founded in 1964 and a publicly listed company by 1971, in addition to Ireland, the UK and Isle of Man, the bank has offices in the US, Austria, Germany and Jersey. In the UK, Anglo Irish has locations in London, Manchester, Birmingham, Leeds, Banbury, Glasgow and Edinburgh. Additionally, Anglo Irish has a treasury relationship with a network of 350 banks located worldwide. Anglo Irish Bank's organic growth was complemented by a series of strategic acquisitions. The bank purchased the Austrian Royal Trust Bank in 1995 from the Royal Bank of Canada and in 1996, the bank bought Ansbacher Brothers, which was established in Dublin in 1950. Two years later it snapped up Credit Lyonnais, an Austrian bank that could be neatly combined with its other Austrian operations, resulting in an entity that provided funding and wealth management services. In Ireland in 1999, the purchase of Dublin-based Smurfit Paribas Bank completed this acquisition phase.

Thank their lucky charms

The bank has been an active user of the capital markets as its growth continues. As an example of such transactions, it raised 416 million euros in January 2006 to support its growth, placing 33.6 million shares priced at 12.40 euros per share, the largest placing ever by an Irish-listed company. At the time, chief executive David Drumm said, "It further strengthens the bank's capital base and positions us well to take advantage of future organic growth opportunities in each of our core markets." Much of the bank's lending is supported by commercial real estate collateral. One example of Anglo Irish Bank's activity in the US was a deal in October 2006, where 149 million US dollars was raised to buy two Midtown Manhattan-based hotels in New York — the Beekman Tower Hotel and Eastgate Tower Hotel, as part of the Peninsula Real Estate Fund I. This fund was created to allow Irish investors make commercial real estate buys in the US.

The bank's property dealings were just as swanky in the UK. An example of a deal made in the UK is Thistle Hotels, for whom the Anglo Irish Bank arranged and structured a debt facility for the purchase and refurbishment of 28 hotels, in major UK cities. The same year also showed how strong the bank's wealth management division is. In 2004, on behalf of clients, the wealth management division acquired a 50 percent share of the retail development around the Royal Opera House in London's Covent Garden. This high-profile investment, when sold three years later, generated a return in excess of 200 percent for the bank's clients.

In 2007, Anglo Irish Bank had a good year. Pre-tax earnings grew 46 percent to 1.24 billion euros, breaking the billion euro mark for the first time. Investors trembling over the effect of the subprime crisis and property slowdown on profits were reassured, as share prices rose. David Drumm, the bank's chief executive, noted in *The Irish Times*, "Our stellar results are not going to fix the market, but it might silence a few people."

The results were largely due to a healthy growth in business lending, which saw a 37 percent increase to 67.1 billion euros. The bank also enjoyed an increase of 46 percent in customer deposit growth in 2007, taking it up to an impressive 16.7 billion euros. Also surely a pleasure to report in the Bank's annual fiscal round-up was that it was the 22nd consecutive year of uninterrupted earnings growth, with core capital equity growing by 1.4 billion euros to reach in excess of four billion euros.

For 2008, however, Drumm predicted a growth of 15 percent in earnings per share (EPS), a forecast reiterated in May 2008. This lower growth rate can be attributed to borrower and investor caution associated with the credit crunch and the bank's stated approach of prudent management of its core activities. On a brighter note, Drumm added that Anglo Irish actually stood to gain from the credit crunch in some ways, due to other lenders dropping out of the market.

Setting the record straight

Anglo Irish Bank and its share prices, fell victim to the circulation of false rumours concerning its funding and liquidity throughout the opening months of 2008. The latest in a serious of tall stories reported that Merrill Lynch had withdrawn a two billion dollar credit line from the Irish bank.

A previous rumour gone awry saw the Irish Financial Services Regulatory Authority (IFSRA) investigating unusual trading and false rumours when the bank's share price collapsed on St. Patrick's Day. The latest gossip proved the last straw for the bank, which filed a complaint in the High Court in London, alleging an employee of stock broking firm Mirabaud Securities sent an email in February 2008 stating Merrill Lynch had pulled the credit plug. Share prices were left reeling in the 12 day period following the receipt of the email, and since the start of the year the bank's share price has plummeted by 38 percent.

GETTING HIRED

Something for everyone

Anglo Irish Bank runs two graduate recruitment programmes. The 24-month Graduate Development Programme is based in the Dublin head office and in London, the bank operates the Graduate Programme UK, which also takes 12 months to complete. Graduates from all degree disciplines are welcome to apply — enthusiasm and a genuine interest in banking are the key qualities the bank is looking for. The closing date for applications is towards the end of November each year, but check the company website for updates and exact deadlines. One experienced insider says, "Anglo Irish Bank is well aware of how important it is for graduates to gain a thorough grounding in how the bank and its systems work."

Benefits offered by bank include life assurance and a contributory pension scheme and private healthcare. Also, employees are entitled to buy shares at a discount price through through A SAYE scheme, a perk that works, since 90 percent of employees are bank shareholders. The bank also runs active sports and social clubs. Jobseekers can view the bank's vacancies at www.angloirishbank.com/careers. Applications are divided according to the bank's main divisions: business banking, wealth management, group services and treasury. More information on divisions and vacancies for entry level positions can be found by clicking these respective links.

Stepping into Anglo-Irish Bank follows the same process as other banks in the sector. Insiders say at interviews applicants must expect: "lots of questions on performance and relative experience," as well as questions about why they want to join the bank's workforce. Hours are slightly higher "than competitors," but are "still not far from the norm," says a Dublin-based manager. According to surveys assessed, these might range from 40 to 60-hours per week. Anglo Irish Bank prides itself in having a strong corporate culture. As stated by a junior insider, a "can do" attitude is essential at this firm, adding that employees must strive "to be the best and put the customer first."

OUR SURVEY SAYS

Shiny, happy people

One Dublin-based insider claims to keeping an "open door policy from management" that "helps keep a flat structure," which helps maintain a good "team atmosphere". Some insiders grumbled that "dress is formal at all times". ☐

B. METZLER SEEL. SOHN & CO. KGaA

Grosse Gallusstrasse 18
60311 Frankfurt am Main
Germany
Tel: +49 (0) 69 21 04 0
www.metzler.com

The Stats

Employer Type: Private Company
Ticker Symbol: n/a
Chief Executive: Friedrich von Metzler
2007 Revenue: n/a
2007 Profit: n/a
2006 Revenue: n/a
2006 Profit: n/a
No. of Offices: 11
No. of Employees: 750

Departments

Asset Management • Corporate
Finance • Equities • Financial Markets
Private Banking

Key Competitors

Berenberg • MM Warburg • Sal
Oppenheim

European Locations

Frankfurt/Main (HQ)
Germany • Ireland

Employment Contact

Email your inquiries or CV to
jobs@metzler.com

For internship information contact
Margit Weber at:
Tel: +49 (69) 21 04 - 3 08

Or write to:
B. Metzler seel. Sohn & Co. KGaA
Personalabteilung
Herrn Michael Diedrich
Grosse Gallusstrasse 18
60311 Frankfurt am Main
Germany

THE BUZZ
WHAT EMPLOYEES AT OTHER FIRMS ARE SAYING

• "Private bank, good reputation"
• "Good local firm in Germany"

THE SCOOP

Headquartered in Frankfurt/Main, Metzler seel. Sohn & Co. has been in business for more than 330 years and today has offices all over the world. It was founded by Benjamin Metzler in Frankfurt/Main in 1674 and is the oldest German bank still managed by the family that created it. It is run by 11th-generation descendant Friedrich von Metzler. In 1760, Metzler made the transition from trading house to merchant banking house and in 1779 it began issuing its first loan stocks.

By the end of the 19th century, Metzler had successfully transformed into a private bank, switching its focus from balance-effectual business tactics to individual finances. While it started as a trading company, it now functions as a bank offering financial services, as a partner in securities transactions, as an asset manager for private clients and as a corporate finance consultant. Germany entered the 20th century with roughly 2,000 independent banks and through strategic restructuring B. Metzler managed to survive two World Wars, the Great Depression and the Third Reich. Today, it is one of 55 German private banks to survive the turbulence of the 20th century. The firm has 39 billion euros under management, with 80 percent coming from institutions, as its specialty is fund administration and pension management. In 2001, the bank opened a Tokyo office to target Japanese institutional investors and is going to open an office in Beijing soon.

A variety of services

Metzler Bank offers an extensive menu of services. The firm's Asset Management division manages substantial assets for institutional clients, segregated funds and mutual funds. Metzler Private Banking comprises portfolio management and investment advisory services for private clients as well as wealth management services such as asset allocation and portfolio controlling for wealthy individuals and foundations. Brokerage services are covered by the equities division, which includes such features as equity research, advice and trading. The corporate finance arm covers mergers and acquisitions, IPO consulting, advice on the privatisation of companies and structured financing. Metzler's bond and currency management, special customer advisory services and bank relations operations are combined in its core financial markets business area.

Metzler North America Corporation, Seattle, which was founded in 1976, and Metzler North America GmbH, Frankfurt/Main, act as asset managers for US and Canadian institutional real estate portfolios. In addition to managing direct investments and closed-end funds, Metzler acts as a consultant for segregated real estate funds.

Based in Los Angeles, Metzler/Payden, LLC is a 50-50 joint venture between Metzler Bank and Payden & Rygel with two billion US dollars in assets under management. The combination offers customers access to the expertise of the two partners. Metzler's proven knowledge of the European capital market is complemented by Payden & Rygel's expertise in North American bonds. Payden & Rygel has 54 billion dollars in assets under management and is one of the largest independent investment managers in the US. In addition to Los Angeles, the firm has offices in London, Dublin and Frankfurt/Main.

In April 2007, Metzler/Payden reported that it's European Emerging Markets Fund (MPYMX), which invests in Eastern European and Russian publicly traded companies, produced a year-to-date return of 22.05 per cent through March 31, 2006. The firm's flagship mutual fund, the Metzler/Payden European Emerging Markets Fund (MPYMX), has a five-star Morningstar rating.

Heir apparent

There has been speculation the bank is grooming von Metzler's nephew as the heir apparent. Metzler family members are expected to learn the tools of the trade: Friedrich von Metzler gained banking experience at Schroder Wagg in London, Smith Barney in New York and at Deutsche Bank in Germany. Experience aside, the next head of the family empire will also need cash, as they'll have to buy out shares of another family member to gain a controlling stake, as the bank is privately owned.

Taxing times

Employees at Metzler and several other German banks were caught up in the mammoth German tax evasion scandal that hit the news in February 2008 concerned with undeclared savings in Liechtenstein. Three employees at the German bank were under investigation after it was alleged they abetted tax fraud of close to six million euros, although prosecutors took pains to assert that the banks themselves were not under investigation. By March, the scandal had reached the eyes of Ecofin, the EU's high command of economics and finance ministers, who met in Brussels to agree on a strategy to tackle the EU's tax havens.

GETTING HIRED

All about the right people

Metzler offers opportunities to graduates in its Investment Trainee Programme, a 12-month paid scheme where you'll receive on-the-job training in the banks core business areas: asset management, private banking, equities, corporate finance and financial markets. The first six months will consist of orientation to these areas, so you can get your head around what working in each of them equates to. At the end of this period you'll discuss with your line manager which of the business areas suits you best, and spend the following six months developing your knowledge of this area, and receiving further training.

To be eligible you'll need a good economics or computer science degree, as well as a good knowledge of finance, business analysis and portfolio theory. You'll also need excellent spoken and written English and German.

Further information is available in the information brochure, which can be downloaded from the "Investment-Trainee-Programme" link. To apply, post your application to B. Metzler seel. Sohn & Co. KGaA, Personalabteilung, Herrn Michael Diedrich, Grosse Gallusstrasse 18, 60311 Frankfurt am Main, Germany.

Getting the hang of it

Metzler provides a range of internships, and welcomes students working towards finance related degrees, but will consider students involved in any discipline. The positions currently on offer can be found by clicking "Praktikanten und Studenten" on the company careers page. To apply, send a CV and references to praktikum@metzler.com, or for further information contact Margit Weber on (+49 69) 21 04 - 3 08.

Test your Metzler

Metzler has opportunities available for managers and specialists in an array of core business disciplines and offers positions at entry level as well as at senior levels. Job vacancies are available on the company's German site, under the "Offene Positionen" link. At the bottom of each vacancy you'll find a contact email address where you can send your CV. The company also accepts applications by post at the following address: B. Metzler seel. Sohn & Co. KGaA, Personalabteilung, Herrn Michael Diedrich, Grosse Gallusstrasse 18, 60311 Frankfurt am Main, Germany.

It should be noted that career opportunities at Metzler are only available on the German version of its site; you'll need some skill in the language to be eligible for employment.

GRUPO BANESTO

Avenida Gran Vía de
Hortaleza, 3
28042 Madrid
Spain
Tel: +34 91 338 15 00
www.banesto.es

The Stats

Employer Type: Public Company
Ticker Symbol: BTO (Madrid)
Chairman: Ana Patricia Botín-Sanz de
Sautuola
2007 Revenue: €2.2bn
2007 Profit: €764.5m
2006 Revenue: €1.9bn
2006 Profit: €1,4bn
No. of Employees: 9,923
No. of Offices: 1,844

Departments

Business and Trade • Communication •
Corporate Banking • Finance • Human
Resources • Marketing, Particulars •
Personal Banking • Private Banking •
Small and Medium Companies

Locations in Europe

Madrid (HQ)
Germany • Spain • Switzerland

Employment Contact

www.banesto.es

Key Competitors

Bankinter • Banco Sabadell

THE BUZZ
WHAT EMPLOYEES AT OTHER FIRMS ARE SAYING

• "Significant Spanish player"
• "Local retail bank"
• "Great at SME

THE SCOOP

F ew people know that Banesto, one of the biggest banks in Spain, was founded by a French financier. The origins of this sizeable financial group date back to the middle of the 19th Century and the efforts of Parisian Isaac Pereire. Despite the fact the bank was created with French capital, the company's aim was to cover Spain's budget deficit through the acquisition of public debt and the financing of public sector companies. For this reason it was given a Spanish name: Sociedad General de Crédito Mobiliario Español.

With new income going to Spain from overseas and some reforms made by the Spanish government at the beginning of the 20th century, some shareholders decided to sell off the company and create a new financial entity. It was May 1902 when the new company was founded, located in the centre of Madrid. The name was Banco Español de Crédito, or Banesto. Commercial banking is Banesto's main field of business in Spain — principally retail banking and banking with small and medium-sized enterprises. The Spanish finance giant also conducts wholesale banking and activities in the capital markets.

A Whirlwind Past

In the 1920s, Banesto started to expand, opening 30 new branches by the end of 1921. The group also started to absorb existing banks, such as Banco Comercial Español de Valencia, Burgos and Oviedo, Gijonés de Crédito and Mercantil de Las Américas.

The period of inflation in the wake of World War I, together with the credit crisis across Europe, led the French group to lose its shares to Banco Español de Crédito in 1927.

In just a few years, the bank already had 103 branches throughout Spain and by 1935 there were a total of 400. This was the beginning of what would be one of the largest bank branch networks in Spain. In spite of the outbreak of the Spanish Civil War in 1936, the bank was able to deal with the complicated state of affairs and managed to continue to function relatively well, continuing its strategy of absorbing smaller entities and creating new ones.

By 1955, Banesto had taken over Banco de Vitoria and at the end of 1970 the company acquired Banco Coca. At the beginning of the 1980s, the firm also had shareholdings in Banco Abel Matures Torres, Banco Catalán de Desarrollo, Bandescom Banca Garriga Nogués, Banco Guipuzcoano, Banco de Madrid, Banco Trelles and Banco de Vitoria.

By this time Banesto was an attractive entity and in 1986 Banco de Bilbao made an offer to merge with its competitor. However, this was rejected by its board of directors so the bank made a public acquisition offer for Banesto just a few days later, only to be rebuffed again.

A small trip

On the Día de los Santos Inocentes (the equivalent of April Fool's day in Spanish-speaking countries) in 1993, Banco de España suspended Banesto's banking activities because of inconsistencies in its accounts — unfortunately for the bank it wasn't a joke. Banesto's administrators were removed from their posts by representatives of each of the major Spanish banks and the then president, Mario Conde, was sent to prison. His replacement was Alfredo Sáenz.

In spite of this setback, Banesto moved forward. In 1994, the Deposit Guarantee Fund awarded 73.45 percent of Banesto to Banco Santander. In 1998, Santander launched a takeover bid for the remaining shares of Banesto, increasing its stake to 97 percent and making Banesto part of one of Spain's largest banks. That year, Banesto ended the Plan de Saneamiento (cleaning-up plan), writing an end to an era and starting a new one in which the company will hobnob with the biggest bank firms in Spain.

Woman in charge

In February 2002, Banesto's board appointed Ana Patricia Botín-Sanz de Sautuola director and chairman of the company, making her the most powerful woman among all of Spain's largest companies. The economist was named the "Most Outstanding Businesswomen in Europe" by the UK daily newspaper *The Financial Times* for two years in a row. The newspaper called Ana Patricia's management of Banesto "exemplary", especially due to her efforts to expand the company.

GETTING HIRED

Show them your stuff

At Banesto, for every 200 applicants, only 30 are invited for an interview, to attend the company's evaluation centre and demonstrate their skills in a variety of banking scenarios. Banesto operates a 12-month programme in which new employees receive training in technical areas, personal skills and the company's values.

Each recruit is specially trained according to the department they will work in, such as business, trade or personal or private banking. To check out Banesto's job board you should log into the company's website, www.banesto.es, and follow the "Empleo" link. It should be noted that this link is only available from the Spanish site, where several options to check the vacancies, upload your CV and find more information are shown. ☐

Grupo Banesto

BANK OF IRELAND

Lower Baggot Street
Dublin, 2
Ireland
Tel: +353 1 661 5933
www.bankofireland.com

The Stats

Employer Type: Public Company
Ticker Symbol: BKIR (LSE), IRE
(NYSE)
Chief Executive: Brian J. Goggin
2007 Revenue: €6.4bn
2007 Profit: €1.7bn
2006 Revenue: €5.3bn
2006 Profit: €1.2bn
No. of Employees: 16,190
No. of Offices: 250

Departments

Asset Management • Corporate
Banking • Corporate Finance • First
Rate Enterprises • Global Markets •
Securities Services

European Locations

Dublin (HQ)
France • Germany • Northern Ireland •
United Kingdom

Employment Contact

www.bankofireland.com/about_us_ne
w/career_opportunities/index.html

For graduate recruitment queries:
gradrecruitment@boimail.com

Key Competitors

HBOS • Allied Irish Banks • Anglo
Irish Bank

THE BUZZ
WHAT EMPLOYEES AT OTHER FIRMS ARE SAYING

• "Small player, but aggressive"
• "Regional"

THE SCOOP

T he Bank of Ireland (BoI) opened its doors by Royal Charter in 1783, in an office at Mary's Abbey in Dublin. The regally approved bank, which was named official banker to the Irish government in 1922, diversified in 1966, adding asset management and investment banking businesses to its offerings. As of 2008, the bank is the largest in Ireland by total assets and boasts the status of being the highest-rated listed Irish financial institution. While its headquarters are in the charming old city of Dublin, the bank's 16,000-plus employees are spread out over 250 offices in eight countries worldwide.

BoI is a fully diversified financial services group, offering corporate banking, global markets services, asset management, corporate finance, securities services and first rate/foreign currency services. The Irish charmer also has personal and business retail banking lines. For the fiscal year 2006, 64 percent of BoI profits came from the Republic of Ireland, 22 percent from the UK and 14 percent from the rest of the world. In February 2008, Bank of Ireland's Asset Management Division (BIAM) announced a new milestone in the bank's history. For the first time, the booming firm's indexation business managed in excess of ten billion euros of Irish institutional investors' funds. Established in 2001, this key division operates in conjunction with State Street Global Advisors, the investment management division of the largest institutional fund manager in the world, State Street Corporation.

New people, new divisions

In 2006, BoI created a new capital markets division, which incorporated operations from both the bank's experienced wholesale financial services and asset management services. The division is led by Denis Donovan, who, until then had been the head of wholesale financial services. BoI chief executive Brian Goggin, a banker throughout his long career and a graduate of Trinity College Dublin, noted that the realignment was "a logical strategic development of our ambitious international growth strategy," as it combined two of the bank's main growth businesses.

Trading spaces

According to a BoI-commissioned study of Irish mortgages, the "mover purchaser" — a customer who is moving from a starter home to a bigger, better house — represents a huge segment of the market. The same research also showed that over half the people surveyed described securing a mortgage and moving house as "stressful" — unsurprising, really. Stress was put down to the unexpected costs of trading up, including decorating a bigger space, moving costs and agency fees, together with the overwhelming number of financial and legal organisations involved with the process. Responding to this trend, customer-oriented Bank of Ireland launched a Trade Up mortgage programme in 2006, specifically aimed at these stressed-out customers. The programme offers personalised assistance, booklets explaining the organisations and regulations involved with mortgages and real estate, as well as step-by-step advice for the transition to a better home.

Heart of gold

BoI has a long history of supporting educational and charitable organisations in Ireland. Established in 2000, its Millennium Scholars Trust is a relatively recent project, providing annual scholarships to qualified students who cannot otherwise continue their education because of poverty or disability. The bank is also the proprietary sponsor of the Special Olympics Network, committing funds and five full-time staff members to manage the promotion and organisation of the Special Olympics and the World Summer Games. The altruistic side of this big bank hardly stops there, as BoI is a major supporter of the Irish Cancer Society, the Irish Rugby Football Union and many local and national charities selected by its staff through a staff and charities matching fund. The bank also preserves rare 18th century tapestries in its art collection and sponsors an annual football tournament.

Troubled times

Along with the rest of the banking sector, the Bank of Ireland was bitten by the 2007 subprime crisis. By early 2008, despite its usual robust performance, the bank's shares had dropped to half the value of the previous year, plummeting to a five-year low of less than nine euros each. However, there have been plenty of bright spots for the bank during this difficult period. Among them, Bank of Ireland Asset Management launched three new enhanced cash funds, aimed at investors with longer term investment horizons. These are sure to boost both the bank's reach and standing. Another division of the bank, Bank of Ireland Business Banking, launched a 75 million euro fund dedicated to the Irish nursing home sector.

GETTING HIRED

A menu of opportunities

Bank of Ireland group offers a great selection of graduate programmes, outlined on its careers site, open to those in their penultimate year of a degree, or graduates with a 2:2 honours degree or better in any discipline. Be warned though, some of the individual programmes demand a 2:1 or higher. The programmes available include the Group Graduate Development Programme, the Finance Professional Development Programme, the Bank of Ireland Life Actuarial Programme, the Business Banking Professional Development Programme, the Capital Markets Graduate Programme and the GB / NI Graduate Development Programme.

Application deadlines are mid-November but make sure you check online for precise dates. Each of the programmes offers hands-on, intensive experience, although some, like the 18-month Group Graduate Development Programme, also expose you to a broader range of banking activities. If you're looking for in-depth training in a specific field or skill, look for programmes like the two-year Bank of Ireland Life Actuarial Programme. More details can be found on the company careers page.

The job application process begins with "an online application system" and applicants who meet the minimum requirements are invited to complete an online ability testing and an online personality profile, explains one insider. The next stage is to attend an assessment centre and competency based interview. Offers are typically made to successful candidates between late December and early January.

Rich rewards

Employees at BoI have plenty of perks. Depending on their contract, staff perks include: a staff mortgage scheme, preferential loans, club subscriptions, free banking, a staff study scheme, an employee stock scheme and VHI cover. You can browse Bank of Ireland's vacancies on its main careers page by clicking "Current Opportunities." Positions are available across the following sectors: sales, finance, administration, mortgage, pensions and insurance, IT and customer service.

OUR SURVEY SAYS

Good times

Once you're in, you can look forward to a "strong culture; the scale of the organisation and the options available are good," one employee in Dublin tells us. The bank's laidback atmosphere is reflected in its casual Fridays policy, however in some areas wearing jeans is not permitted. Perks of working with this firm include a range of financial incentives such as stock options, free banking and reduced lending rates. You also get to enjoy lifestyle benefits like reduced gym membership, health insurance, a subsidised canteen, reduced rates and holiday pay.

GRUPO BANKINTER

Paseo de la Castellana, 29
28042 Madrid
Spain
Tel: +34 91 339 75 00
www.bankinter.com

The Stats

Employer Type: Public Company
Ticker Symbol: BKT (Madrid)
Chairman: Pedro Guerrero
2007 Revenue: €949m
2007 Profit: €361m
2006 Revenue: €819m
2006 Profit: €208m
No. of Employees: 4,530
No. of Offices: 885

Departments

Clients and Networks • Development •
Direction and Investor Relations •
External Communications and
Corporate Reputation • Financial
General Secretary • Innovation •
Markets and Products • Media •
People and Business • Quality • Risk

Locations in Europe

Madrid (HQ)
Spain • United Kingdom

Employment Contact

www.grupoacs.com
(Click on Human Resources)

Key Competitors

Banco Sabadell • Banesto

THE BUZZ
WHAT EMPLOYEES AT OTHER FIRMS ARE SAYING

• "Domestic retail bank"
• "Top at commercial"
• "Not a global player"
• "Regional"

THE SCOOP

I t may be a little-known fact, but Bankinter was one of the first banks in Spain to offer telephone and internet banking services. In fact, this Spanish banking group is one of the most technologically-advanced banks in Spain according to its French competitor Credit Agricole. Apart from that, the main businesses of this 43 year-old banking company are the mutual and pension funds, mortgages, leasing and securities brokerage, in addition to personal banking products and services.

Founded in June 1965 as a Spanish industrial bank with equal investments by institutions today known as Banco Santander and Banco de América, Bankinter didn't become an independent commercial bank until it was listed on the Madrid Stock Exchange in 1972. When it was created, the bank was ranked 107th in Spain but has since made huge headway, becoming one of the top six Spanish players in the new millennium according to Forbes magazine, joining an elite club with such important players as Banco Santander, BBVA, Banco Popular, Banco Sabadell and Banco Pastor.

Strategising pioneers

Bankinter's history is characterised by progressive growth and the ability to capitalise on regulatory changes, emerging economic situations and new market niches. As an example of this adaptive strategy, in 1987 Bankinter became the first bank to launch a high interest Special Deposit account, which enabled it to double its balance sheet in the following two years. As part of the company's

> " Bankinter became one of the first banks in Spain to offer alternatives to traditional forms of banking "

expansion plan, a special emphasis on technology and a multi-channel strategy in regards to the distribution of financial products and services was made by the company throughout the last decades of the 20th century.

Mission: possible

In the 1990s, Bankinter became one of the first banks in Spain to offer alternatives to traditional forms of banking. Today this forms an essential part of Bankinter's multi-channel network as well as serving as an example for the rest of the banks in the country. The technological revolution involved incorporating telephone and mobile banking, virtual banking, agent network and internet in addition to the usual face-to-face customer service offered at branches.

Grupo Bankinter

197

The Spanish firm's internet banking website offers a range of financial products and services in addition to customer counselling, aggregators, product simulators and a variety of value-added services. Over the years these new avenues of banking proved worthwhile for both the company and the consumer, revolutionising the modern electronic banking system. In 2007, more than 60 percent of transactions in Spain happened through internet, telephone or electronic and mobile technology. Around 46 percent of Bankinter's transactions are carried out online.

Banking on insurance

Bankinter and Mapfre, Spain's largest insurance firm, came to an agreement in March 2007 through which both parties would develop an entire line of life insurance packages together, including everything from accident cover to pension plans. The bank agreed to share 50 percent of its life insurance-focused society, Bankinter Seguros de Vida, with Mapfre. Bankinter retained exclusive rights to distribute the products throughout its commercial networks.

This landmark purchase was worth more than 197 million euros, excluding two additional payments of 20 million euros each that Mapfre paid once the deal closed. The main purpose of this agreement was to achieve better market penetration. Mapfre manages the process, lending its experience in the design and creation of the insurance products. Thanks to this purchase, Bankinter secured earnings of 251 million euros in the first months of 2007 alone — that's 113 percent more than in the same period in 2006.

Goodbye to an old ring-master

Bankinter's chairman, Juan Arena, once drew a parallel between the bank and a world-famous circus, Cirque du Soleil, saying that it was the bank's objective to be, much like the famous circus, the defining bank in Spain. This light-hearted aspiration has not been easy to put into reality, as Bankinter is not currently the leader in Spain. That is a title currently held by Banco Santander. Nevertheless, Bankinter has performed its share of amazing feats in the industry, growing in size ten-fold in only 16 years and increasing its profitability for shareholders by close to a thousand times, thanks in large part to Arena's management.

Having spent 37 years with the bank, five of these as chairman, Arena declared he would be retiring from his post in 2007. Spanish newspapers reported that he wept as he made his decision public to Bankinter's board of directors.

Despite its growth and its successful banking model, the market speculates that a buyout of Bankinter is looming. Since Arena became chairman in 2002, rumours about the buyout have not subsided. The latest company to show interest in the bank was Banco Sabadell, whose chairman, Josep Oliu, declared in November 2006 that his company was interested in Bankinter on the condition that his bank leads the merger operation. Bankinter chief executive Jaime Echegoyen responded by stating the bank was not considering a merger. His statement came in the wake of Bankinter's unveiling a new logo, as an affirmation of its independence.

GETTING HIRED

You gotta recognise

The Great Place to Work Institute's Spanish branch rated Bankinter as the sixth best company to work for in Spain, from a top-30 ranking. In fact, Bankinter was the only Spanish company in the top six and the best in the financial field. The American institution bases the list on the quality of companies' work environment, the relationship between managers and employees, between workers with their company and between employees.

Bank on a career

According to the 2007 Morgan Stanley European Banks Conference, there are 28 different nationalities among Bankinter's workforce and 72 percent of this workforce are university graduates. The report also noted that a total of 1,014 new graduates were hired at the bank in 2007. This multi-channel and interactive bank seeks new graduates and young professionals who are fluent in Spanish but also have a good level of English and can be innovative, dynamic and eager to learn.

To be considered for any vacancies at Bankinter, you should submit your CV to the human resources department through the company website. Simply click on the "Join us" section at www.bankinter.com.

BBVA S.A.

Plaza de San Nicolás, 4
48005 Bilbao (Vizcaya),
Spain
Tel: +34 91 374 60 00
www.bbva.com

The Stats

Employer Type: Public Company
Ticker Symbol: BBVA (Madrid); BBV
(NYSE)
Chairman: Francisco González
2007 Revenue: €18.1bn
2007 Profit: €6.0bn
2006 Revenue: €15.7bn
2006 Profit: €4.7bn
No. of Employees: 111,913
No. of Offices: 8,028 in 31 countries

Divisions

Asset Management. • Corporate
Banking • Finance • Global Markets •
Human Resources • Investment
Banking • Marketing and
Communication • Private Banking •
Retail Banking • Technology and
Computing Systems • Wholesale
Banking

Locations in Europe

Bilbao (HQ)
Belgium • France • Germany • Italy •
Portugal • Russia • Spain • Switzerland •
United Kingdom

Employment Contact

www.bbva.com
(Click on "Employment")

Key Competitors

Banco Sabadell • Banco Santander

Pluses

• Enormous amount of opportunity
  internationally
• Very respected

Minuses

• Limited opportunities in UK
• Spanish language skills are needed

THE BUZZ
WHAT EMPLOYEES AT OTHER FIRMS ARE SAYING

• "Significant regional player"
• "Impressive in Latin America"
• "Not a big hirer in London"
• "Needs to break with bureaucracy"

THE SCOOP

O nly a year after a group of banking players merged to create the global banking giant known as BBVA, the firm was chosen in 2000 as the "World's Best Bank" by American business magazine *Forbes* — quite an accomplishment in such a short period of time. The group of banks that would merge in 1999 to become the global financial services group known as Spain's BBVA (Banco Bilbao Vizcaya Argentaria) date back to 1857, when the Spanish Board of Trade established a currency-issuing and discount bank called Banco de Bilbao.

Commercial bank Banco de Vizcaya, was created several decades later. After more than a century of mergers, growth and expansion, Banco de Bilbao and Banco de Vizcaya merged in 1988 and formed BBV. Then, a year later BBV announced its intention to merge with Argentaria, another consortium of private Spanish banks. The deal was completed in 2001, and the new group became BBVA. Current BBVA chairman Francisco González was previously chairman of Argentaria.

Best in a long line of banks

Today's BBVA is one of Spain's largest banks, and is the product of the merging and acquisition of 150 banks over 150 years of history. While most of its European operations are concentrated in Spain, Portugal, the UK, France and Italy, the bank also has offices in Belgium, Germany, Switzerland and Russia. This equates to approximately 8,000 offices in more than 30 countries. BBVA has also come to dominate Latin America, where it has busy subsidiary operations in ten countries. BBVA's services include retail, corporate and institutional banking, investment banking, asset management and insurance.

Size isn't everything

BBVA has carved out a niche market by creating branches specialising in small and medium-sized enterprises (SMEs). BBVA's SME branches provide customised services and financial products created especially for SME owners. These products and services include foreign trade, cash-flow management solutions, payment collection, tax and social security products and transfer mechanisms.

The bank also offers special discount lines, loans, advances, liability services and flotation to SMEs — and each SME client has a BBVA advisor assigned to his or her company to personally handle all service requests and questions. Much of BBVA's SME business relies on the bank's extensive online banking systems.

Eyes on the east

Like other major European banks, BBVA has been scoping opportunities in eastern markets. In 2005 the Spanish banking giant unveiled a so-called "Asia plan" aimed at becoming the biggest Spanish and Latin American bank in the region.

In November 2006 BBVA announced a crucial move forward in its Asia plan, purchasing a five percent stake of China CITIC Bank with an option to increase to 9.9 percent and acquiring a 15 percent stake in CITIC International Financial Holdings. By spending a combined 989 million euros on these deals, BBVA made the biggest investment in mainland China and Hong Kong by a Spanish company to date. The alliance between BBVA and CITIC will include retail and corporate banking in mainland China and Hong Kong as well as investment banking and treasury business throughout Asia.

By the end of 2007, BBVA was busy executing its Asia plan and opened new representative offices in Taipei, Seoul, Sydney and a liaison office in Mumbai. It also converted its Shanghai representative office into a branch and expanded existing branches in Hong Kong, Tokyo and Singapore, as well as plans to hire new staff throughout Asia. In 2008 the Asia plan continued, with BBVA identifying India as a key Asian market, and making plans to forge a real presence there through a joint venture with a public sector bank. The bank's road map for the country over the next three to four years consists of a mutual funds venture, followed by projects in consumer finance, credit cards, and eventually, life insurance

BBVA has begun talks with Bank of India and Corporation Bank, and noted that it is particularly looking for banks with a wide distribution and a sufficient scale to be of use to its mutual funds business, and also to be of assistance in its planned consumer finance and credit card ventures. The bank remarked that it would need strong risk management processes to be in place in India before embarking on the later stages of its plan, but added that its current exposure to Indian corporate is already noteworthy, totalling one billion US dollars.

Growth and expansion

While BBVA already has a strong presence in South America, expansion in the US is a big part of BBVA's strategy. In October 2007, as part of BBVA's 150th anniversary, bank chairman and chief executive González and other BBVA executives visited Washington for a series of meetings.

According to him, the US will be one of the bank's main focuses moving forward, and by October 2008, BBVA's USS franchise will account for almost ten percent of the total group earnings. González added that BBVA will have merged the four banks it bought in the US into a single company by October 2008.

In February 2007 the Spanish bank acquired Compass Bancshares, established in 1970 and with presence in the retail, wholesale and private banking segments with 417 branches in the US. This transaction was the largest announced in BBVA's history and presented an excellent strategic fit with the bank's acquisition in the US from 2004 to 2006 — Valley Bank, Laredo National Bancshares, Texas Regional Bancshares and State National Bancshares. The bank financed the acquisition approximately 9.6 billion dollars — through a capital increase of 196 million shares of BBVA, internal resources coming from the sale of selected stakes and internal capital generation.

BBVA entered the demanding Dow Jones Sustainability Index (DJSI) in 2001. The Spanish bank achieved the highest score in the index in September 2007, reinforcing the group's commitment to development. The DJSI rewards companies' best practices in the field of corporate responsibility.

GETTING HIRED

The right opportunities

BBVA Group offers fantastic training for graduates through its internships. The bank has signed many agreements with different universities and business schools both in Spain and abroad. To those who are in the last years of their undergraduate or postgraduate degree such as a Masters or MBA, the banking entity offers the chance to work within the company in different areas such as legal, economy and business administration, communication, marketing and publicity and statistics among others.

If you are offered an internship at BBVA, you will be required to sign a contract for an initial period of six months as well as creating a schedule that will be compatible with completing your studies, whether it is through full-time or part-time employment. Fortunately, there are always opportunities for full-time permanent employment after completing the internship programme.

Under the "employment at BBVA" link at www.bbva.com, candidates can check out job opportunities for all skill levels, from university graduates to experienced professionals and fill an electronic CV/resume form. The bank notes on the site that they no longer accept paper applications. If your application is successful you'll be invited in for an interview.

BBVA (Banco Bilbao Vizcaya Argentaria S.A.

GROUPE CAISSE D'EPARGNE (GCE)

50 avenue Pierre Mendes
Cedex 13
Paris, 75201
France
Tel: +33 (0) 58-40-41-42
www.groupe.caisse-epargne.com

The Stats

Employer Type: Semi co-operative
Ticker Symbol: n/a
Chairman: Charles Milhaud
2007 Revenue: €9.8bn
2007 Profit: €1.4bn
2006 Revenue: €10bn
2006 Profit: €1.4bn
No. of Employees: 260,000
worldwide
No. of Offices: n/a

Divisions

Commercial Banking • Investment
Banking via Natixis • Retail Banking

European Locations

Paris (HQ)
Locations throughout France and
Europe

Employment Contact

www.groupe.caisse-epargne.fr/recrute

Key Competitors

BNP Paribas (CIB) • CIC • Société
Générale (CIB)

THE BUZZ
WHAT EMPLOYEES AT OTHER FIRMS ARE SAYING

• "Small, French, nice"
• "Quite regional"

THE SCOOP

G roupe Caisse d'Epargne (GCE) is one of the largest retail banking networks in France, comprising the Caisse d'Epargne banks, Crédit Foncier, Banque Palatine and OCÉOR banks as well as several more specialised subsidiaries. As a huge full-service bank, GCE is popular among individuals and professionals in mainland France and overseas, offering a full range of financial services. The enormous GCE boasts close to 56,000 employees spanning 4,700 branches and 26 million customers globally.

Backed by 20 billion euros in consolidated equity, a net income of 3.8 billion euros and credit ratings that rank among the best in the French banking sector, Groupe Caisse d'Epargne has a solid financial profile. In 2007, it was ranked 169th on the Global Fortune 500 list. Following a general trend in the banking world, the group is actively pursuing consolidation in order to make itself a stronger player. It has also pledged to step up its commitments to corporate social responsibility. The regional Caisses d'Epargne own 80 percent of CNCE, which is a limited or incorporated company (known in French as a "société anonyme")

> 66 As of spring 2007 Natixis has already attracted more than 2.86 million individual shareholders 99

governed by a management board and a supervisory board. The Federation Nationale des Caisses d'Epargne is a non-profit association representing the individual Caisses d'Epargne and their cooperative shareholders. Natixis, which is owned jointly by GCE and the Banque Populaire group, now spearheads the group's investment and corporate, asset management and financial services divisions.

Natixis in action

It took less than three months to bring this project — of major importance for the future growth of Groupe Caisse d'Epargne — to a satisfactory conclusion. Created legally on November 17, 2006, Natixis, the new investment and project bank jointly owned by Groupe Caisse d'Epargne and Groupe Banque Populaire, made its successful debut on the Paris Bourse on December 5, 2006.

As of spring 2007 Natixis has already attracted more than 2.86 million individual shareholders, according to the firm. As the largest operation in the French financial market in 2006 in terms of value, it was also the banking industry's most attractive investment since 1999. Close to 670,000 Groupe Caisse d'Epargne customers, including almost 390,000 Caisses d'Epargne cooperative shareholders, have bought shares in Natixis.

Growth frenzy

GCE has experienced enormous growth in a slew of sectors by making several key deals. In addition to the creation of Natixis, 2006 saw some other big developments for Groupe Caisse D'Epargne, with particular emphasis on Portugal. The group acquired an 80 percent interest stake in the French and Luxembourg subsidiaries of Millenium bcp, a Portuguese bank. Groupe Caisse D'Epargne also created two new banks, Banco Primus in Portugal, adding to its portfolio a specialist in loan restructuring, as well as its own joint subsidiary in Italy, which specialises in consumer credit. Also, Groupe Caisse D'Epargne acquired interest in Crédit Immobilier et Hôtelier (CIH) in Morocco, in a joint transaction with the Moroccan bank Caisse de Dépôt et de Gestion. The acquired bank specialises in family banking services, adding still more diversity toGroupe Caisse D'Epargne's practical services repertoire.

In April 2007, Groupe Caisse D'Epargne signed a memorandum of understanding with Nexity for the purpose of generating power in the real estate market. The transaction between Nexity and the CNCE, completed in July 2007, saw CNCE transferring 25 percent of Crédit Foncier, 100 percent of Groupe Caisse D'Epargne Immobilier's services division and 32 percent of Eurosic, a real estate company, to Nexity. In return, CNCE gained 38.2 percent of Nexity, making it the key shareholder. The agreement took place in order to make Nexity, a real estate developer, with a genuine global reach and for it to act as a real estate stronghold for Groupe Caisse D'Epargne.

100,000 is the magic number

In terms of corporate social responsibility, Groupe Caisse D'Epargne has got quite a lot to shout about. It lays claim to the Caisses d'Epargne Foundation for Social Solidarity, which has become one of France's largest public-interest organisations. Created in 2001, the foundation heads up a network of 76 establishments for the elderly including 68 residential homes that operate alongside significant home support services, and in early 2008, the generous giant put 100,000 euros funding towards six separate projects that work on combating illiteracy.

GETTING HIRED

A fountain of French opportunities

All of Groupe Caisse D'Epargne's graduate internship and traineeships are offered in French and are searchable individually, along with jobs, on their recruitment website with a position description and application procedures. The company also offers sandwich year opportunities to French students. You can sign up to the company's alerts mailing list to ensure you don't miss out on any new career postings by visiting Groupe Caisse D'Epargne's recruitment website at www.groupe.caisse-epargne.fr/recrute. □

CALYON

9 Doumer:
9, quai du Président Paul Doumer
Paris La Défense Cedex, 92920
France
Tel: +33 1 41 89 00 00
www.calyon.com

The Stats

Employer Type: Subsidiary of Crédit
Agricole
Ticker Symbol: CAGR (Euronext, LSE,
Berlin, XETRA, Frankfurt, Munich,
Stuttgart, Virt-Z, Düsseldorf,
Hamburg)
Chairman: Georges Pauget
Chief Executive: Patrick Valroff
2007 Revenue: €3.4bn
2007 Profit (Loss): (€714m)
2006 Revenue: €5.9bn
2006 Profit: €1.8bn
No. of Employees: 14,000
No. of Offices: 55+

Departments

Acquisition Finance • Brokerage and
Investment Banking • Capital Markets •
Cash Management • CDO •
Commodities • Corporate Banking •
Credit Markets • Debt Capital Markets •
Equity • Financing Structured Finance •
Foreign Exchange • Fund Derivatives •
Global Corporate Finance • Global
Equity Capital Markets (ECM) •
Interest Rate Derivatives • Loan
Syndication • Treasury

European Locations

Paris (HQ)
Austria • Belgium • Bulgaria • Czech
Republic • Denmark • Finland • France •
Germany • Greece • Ireland • Italy •
Hungary • Luxembourg • Monaco •
Norway • The Netherlands • Poland •
Portugal • Russia • Slovakia • Spain •
Sweden • Switzerland • Ukraine •
United Kingdom

Employment Contact

www.calyon.com/hr/job-opportunities-
on-line.html

Key Competitors

BNP Paribas (CIB) • Citigroup Global
Markets Europe • Lazard • Société
Générale (CIB) • UBS (IB)

THE BUZZ
WHAT EMPLOYEES AT OTHER FIRMS ARE SAYING

- "French, growing slowly"
- "Top at credit"
- "Second-tier French bank"
- "Local focus with European Cap
  Market capabilities"

THE SCOOP

C alyon grabbed headlines back in 2005 as a relative newcomer, ranking first in European Initial Public Offerings (IPOs), notably advising the French government on the privatisation of Electricité de France — a nuclear energy giant and one of the most important European IPOs since the late 1990s. The wholly owned subsidiary of France's largest financial institution, Crédit Agricole Group, Calyon combines the corporate and investment banking businesses of Crédit Agricole Indosuez and Crédit Lyonnais.

The offshoot's operations are organised into two major divisions: capital markets, brokerage and investment banking — which grew 29 percent in 2007 — and financing, which rose 14 percent. The strong 2007 growth was reflected in a pre-tax net profit of 2.3 billion euros (a 35 percent rise on the previous year), and a net banking income increase of 22.4 percent to 5.4 billion euros overall.

Complex division

Calyon's two divisions are divided further into several subdivisions: capital markets is in charge of a network of 30 trading rooms around the world with product lines including foreign exchange, commodities, interest rate derivatives, debt capital markets, credit markets and collateralized debt obligation (CDO), treasury, equity and fund derivatives. Investment banking, on the other hand, is organised into global corporate finance, which is responsible for executing all merger and acquisitions transactions; global equity capital markets (ECM), which conducts primary issues, IPOs, secondary market offerings bond issues and also global sector groups, which are linked together by industry. Financing is Calyon's second division, and is divided into structured finance, loan syndication, corporate banking and cash management, and acquisition finance.

Calyon announced plans in early 2007 to merge its brokerage activities with those of Société Générale. The newly formed entity, Newedge, controlled equally by Société Générale and Calyon, is expected to be a world leader in the execution and clearing of listed financial futures and options. Calyon previously carried out these activities through its subsidiaries Cheuvreux, CLSA and Calyon Financial.

Simply assets

Calyon emerged from French bank Crédit Agricole S.A. in 2004, as the new brand and corporate name for its financing and investment banking business. Assets were partially transferred from the newly acquired Crédit Lyonnais to Crédit Agricole Indosuez, the bank's internationally focused banking arm. Prior to its acquisition, Crédit Lyonnais was in business for over a century. Well-established, upon its launch Calyon had assets of approximately 380 billion US dollars — as well as offices in 60 countries around the world.

Impressive IPO portfolio

In recent years, Calyon has established a leading role in French IPOs. In addition to the EDF deal of 2005, Calyon was a bookrunner and lead manager for Gaz de France's IPO, which was the world's largest share sale at 4.5 billion euros. Then in 2006, Calyon acted as co-arranger for several IPOs, including Legrand and Ansalso, and in rights issues including Vinci and Swiss Re. The Legrand IPO was a high-profile offering, due to an unexpected surge in demand for Legrand shares. Legrand SA, the world's largest manufacturer of power plugs and switches, sold off about 20 percent of its stock in order to raise funds for takeovers. About 57.8 million shares were launched on the Paris bourse, which were sold to yield a total of 972 million euros. Calyon played a major role as bookrunner for the initial public offering of Rexel, the first worldwide distributor of electrical supplies. The IPO amounted to a total value of 1.02 billion euros.

There goes another one

As Calyon announced a 5.9 million euro rights issue following subprime writedowns, chief executive Marc Litzler became the latest senior European banking figure to step down. He had only been the bank's premier since July 2007. Litzler had previously been directly responsible for Calyon's fixed-income and equities-derivatives divisions, and it was therefore logical that he should take the fall for the bank's losses, a senior banker noted in *The Financial Times*. He also faced opposition from the bank's more conservative shareholders and board members, who were more concerned about the bank's involvement in risky markets. The bank's new chief executive, Patrick Valroff, is considered by most in the industry to be a more traditional establishment figure.

Calyon's accolades

In 2005 and 2006, Calyon's increase in both the volume and scale of M&A deals garnered increased prominence in global rankings. In 2005, Calyon was ranked seventh in France for M&A advisory services and first for initial public offerings in Europe — primarily due to the firm's role in advising the French government on the long-awaited privatisation of nuclear giant Electricité de France — widely regarded as the most important European IPO since the late 1990s, according to *Thomson Financial* and *Capital Finance*.

210

The next year also fared well for the firm as Calyon advised 26 deals for a total value of 91 billion dollars, an increase of rank value of 152 percent. The trend continued into 2007, with Calyon receiving the *Euromoney* "Project Finance Deal of the Year" award for a refinery and petrochemical plant financing, on behalf of Petro Rabigh. In May 2008, it was also distinguished by the Club of Thirty (representatives of large French companies) for its initiation and advice of French construction giant Lafarge's acquisition of its smaller competitor Orascom.

GETTING HIRED

Focus your goals

Calyon helpfully lists its available vacancies on the careers section of its website under "job opportunities" and interested applicants can apply online. To browse jobs in specific areas, under the "job type"menu, you can choose from accountancy and finance, audit, capital markets, compliance, credit risk management, coverage, distribution, investment banking, IT and project management, M&A and structured finance, to name but a few.

You can also specify which continent, country, and region you would like to work in, but be aware that job descriptions themselves are entirely in French, so your French skills need to be up to scratch if you want to be in the running. You'll be asked to register your name and email address, before being taken through an online application.

Be the enVIE of your friends

Calyon offers a selection of internships and student internships, as well as its Volontariat International en Entreprise, or VIE programme. The successor to the CSNE (Coopération du Service National à l'Etranger), the civilian version of national service, it is aimed at Europeans between 18 and 28 years of age who are either entry level job seekers, recent graduates or students. VIE positions are offered in a range of countries and can last between six and 24 months. Calyon include a number of testimonials from scheme participants on its website, so you can read about the various pros and cons from first hand sources.

To apply for an internship or a VIE placement, you need search on the "job opportunities" page, making sure you select "VIE" or "internship" in the "contract type" box. Positions in different regions and at different levels have different durations, requirements and specifications, so have a look and see what suits you.

CIBC WORLD MARKETS

European Headquarters
Cottons Centre
Cottons Lane
London SE1 2QL
United Kingdom
Tel: +44 20 7234 6000
www.cibcwm.com

The Stats

Employer Type: Public Company
Ticker Symbol: CM (Toronto, NYSE)
Chief Executive: Richard Nesbitt
Head of Bank, Europe: Scott Wilson
2007 Revenue: CAD $12.1bn
2007 Profit: CAD $3.3bn
2006 Revenue: CAD $11.4bn
2006 Profit: CAD $2.6bn
No. of Employees: 1,145
No. of Offices: 21

Divisions

Fixed Income and Currencies • Global
Equities • Investment and Corporate
Banking

European Locations

London (European HQ)
Dublin • United Kingdom

Employment Contact

recruitment@cibc.co.uk

Key Competitors

Citi • RBC • HSBC

THE BUZZ
WHAT EMPLOYEES AT OTHER FIRMS ARE SAYING

• "Very markets focused"
• "Not a big hirer in London"

THE SCOOP

C IBC World Markets is the investment banking division of the Canadian Imperial Bank of Commerce. As an investment bank, CIBC World Markets helps large companies, governments and other institutions to obtain capital and credit. CIBC World Markets provides capital solutions and advisory services across a wide range of industries, as well as merchant banking and top-ranked research. In the European market, CIBC World Markets operates as both CIBC World Markets and CIBC World Markets plc, with three core businesses: fixed income and currencies (FIC), investment banking, and global equities.

Home-grown institution

CIBC World Markets was formed in 1988 when the Canadian Imperial Bank of Commerce acquired a majority interest in Wood Gundy Inc, one of Canada's leading securities dealers and the foremost Canadian dealer on the international scene. The combination of CIBC capital and Wood Gundy's underwriting reputation created an investment banking arm that soon became one of

> 66 World Markets' research is well-knownfor its breadth and quality 99

the leading investing institutions in Canada. The result, CIBC Wood Gundy Inc., formed the core of CIBC World Markets, which was created in 1997. As of 2008, the company had approximately 1,145 employees around the world.

It's all about the details

At the CIBC World Markets London office, the fixed income and currencies division provides clients in Europe, the Middle East and Asia with services such as advisory, syndication, trading and sales. The business uses an integrated, multi-product approach, offering cash and derivative products in fixed income, securitisation, credit, foreign exchange, commodity and equity markets. Meanwhile, the European investment banking group operates on the direct investment side, working in financial advisory services and mergers and acquisitions.

Key industry sectors for CIBC include gaming, lodging and leisure, infrastructure finance, mining, oil and gas, and power and utilities. The third segment, equity sales and structured products, has a targeted focus in the trading of US and Canadian cash equities and is known as a leading distributor of North American equity products in the European market. The equity sales and structured products division also offers equity-linked notes and commodity-linked notes.

Top-notch research

CIBC World Markets has more than 50 analysts around the world conducting equity, fixed income and economics research. World Markets' research is well known for its breadth and quality, with the Canadian fixed income research team ranking number one in Canada. Economics is another strong point in the research department — CIBC World Markets' chief economist, Jeff Rubin, is one of Canada's foremost economists and is quickly becoming the international leading voice on oil. His long and well-earned reputation of being ahead of the curve has attracted the attention of industries, investors and governments across the globe.

Enron Shmenron

In 2005, disaster struck as CIBC's involvement in the Enron scandal resulted in the company having to shell out 2.5 billion CAD dollars in litigation expenses and settlements. That year, CIBC World Markets reported a loss in net income of 1.67 billion CAD dollars. A year later, the firm was back in the black.

Fortunately, in December 2006, the US Federal Reserve terminated the enforcement action against the bank over its transactions with Enron prior to its infamous collapse in 2001. The enforcement action, which CIBC signed four years earlier in December 2003, had prohibited it from engaging in certain types of structured finance deals.

Go Canada!

In 2007, CIBC's advisory team won the number one spot in the Canadian national daily newspaper, *The National Post*, for the greatest volume of Canadian M&A activity as well as the highest level of Private Equity deal activity in Canada. Since 2001, the advisory team has also led on eight of the country's top transactions. The firm has also consistently been recognized as Canada's top equity underwriter having led the greatest deal activity in Canada as measured by value for six of the past seven years.

CIBC's equities research team also picked up the first place in 2007 for *Financial Post/StarMine's* brokerage and analyst rankings, with 19 top-analysts named on the success of stock picks and earnings estimate accuracy. For its efforts as exclusive financier to Fortis on its 3.7 billion US dollar acquisition of Terasen Inc., the firm was named as Canadian Dealmaker of the Year. It also carried out the top deal in Canada, according to *The Banker*, for the 10.3 billion CAD dollar sale of Placer Dome to Barrick Gold.

Big deal

Among CIBC World Markets' major deals in 2007 were Rio Tinto's 44.9 billion US dollar acquisition of Alcan, cited as one of the top-five deals of 2007 by *Time Magazine* and Fortis' 3.7 billion US dollar purchase of Terasen's gas distribution business, in which the investment bank acted as lead advisor, credit provider and underwriter to the Belgian acquirer. This transaction went on record as the largest domestic utility distribution acquisition to date. One of the largest debt transactions in Canadian history — the issue of a nine billion dollar bond from the Canada Mortgage Bond Program for Canada Housing Trust No. 1 — was also brought about thanks to the bank's handiwork as lead manager.

GETTING HIRED

Taking the first step

While the company provides an online search form for its opportunities outside Europe, to apply for opportunities within Europe you'll need to send your CV to recruitment@cibc.co.uk. You might want to have a look at the non-European form to give yourself an idea of the jobs on offer though, and you'll find it on the company careers page under "Recruitment."

The world market's your oyster

CIBC World Markets offers a selection of summer programmes for both undergraduate and MBA students, but it should be noted that on the whole they take place at company offices in Canada. Undergraduates in their final year of a business related degree will find summer analyst programmes in credit capital markets, global equities and investment banking.

For first year MBA students, the company offers summer associate programmes in equity research, investment banking and merchant banking. All of these courses offer on-the-job exposure to real-life banking situations. Applications open at the start of August. Alternatively, talk to CIBC at one of its many university visits. The group is a keen and active recruiter, although in Europe, it only visits UK universities at time of press.

CRÉDIT INDUSTRIEL ET COMMERCIAL (CIC)

6, avenue de Provence
75452 Paris Cedex 9
France
Tel: +33 (0)1 45 96 96 96
www.cic.fr/en

The Stats

Employer Type: Public Company
Ticker Symbol: CC (Paris)
President: Michel Lucas
2007 Revenue: €4.2bn
2007 Profit: €1.1bn
2006 Revenue: €4.4bn
2006 Profit: €1.3bn
No. of Employees: 22,938
No. of Offices: 1,990 in France,
3 branches and 37 offices abroad

Departments

Capital Development • Market
Financing • Private Banking •
Retail Banking

European Locations

Paris (HQ)
Belgium • Czech Republic • France •
Greece • Germany • Italy • Portugal •
Poland • Romania • Russia • Spain •
Sweden • Switzerland • Turkey •
United Kingdom

Employment Contact

www.cic.fr/fr/banques/le-
cic/recrutement/index.html

Key Competitors

BNP Paribas (CIB) • Société Générale
(CIB)

THE SCOOP

A veritable dinosaur in the banking world, CIC emerged as a result of a Royal Decree signed by Napoleon III in 1859. Created as a Franco-English financial institution, the Société Générale de Crédit Industriel et Commercial has survived into modernity as the oldest investment bank in France. Founded in part to help ease the financial burden on businesses developing railroads during the Second Empire industrial boom from 1852-1871, CIC was behind the creation of many regional banks across France and later abroad.

Having developed beyond investment into a full range of insurance and financial services (including mortgages, asset management and securities) upon its buyout by bank Crédit Mutuel, CIC is now the fourth-largest banking group and the number one provider of bancassurance in France.

Consisting of six regional high-street bank chains which operate across France in a network of almost 2,000 branches, CIC continues to play a large role in economic and business spheres in France. Its customer base numbers 2.7 million individuals as well as nearly a third of all French companies.

Bankosaurus CIC

Its considerable age is not the only thing that makes this group a mammoth player in the French financial sector. If other banking groups are more like Godzilla, with an insatiable appetite for M&A, the CIC is a less vicious but no less ambitious player — perhaps strategically, more of a gatherer than a

>   " CIC's network has been based around six regional hubs that individually oversee their own franchises "

hunter. CIC began its expansion beyond French borders by opening its first branch abroad in London in 1895, and at the turn of the century, the group participated in the creation of several banks around the world, including the Banks of Romania, Madrid, New Caledonia, Réunion and Madagascar.

Choosing to sow its seeds in France and beyond, through ventures like the creation of the Union of Regional Banks for the Crédit Industriel (UBR), which brought together 18 regional and local banks around the CIC in 1929, the network saw significant expansion between the 1940s to 1970s. Growth has continued steadily into the 21st century, with branches as of 2007 numbering 1,990. CIC continued developing its international presence with its acquisition of a stake in Bank of Tunisia, as well as with partnerships with Banco Popolare di Milano (Italy) and Bank of East

Crédit Industriel et Commercial (CIC)

217

Asia in the early 21st century. Its foreign branches and representative offices are now present in 35 countries across the globe.

Le tug of war

The CIC system grew to be both far-reaching and well-integrated by the late 20th century, which is probably what appealed so much to investors like GAN (Groupe des Assurances Nationales), a French insurance group — which at a point in the 1990s owned almost the entire company — and its latest majority holder Crédit Mutuel Centre Est Europe. Crédit Mutuel managed to wrangle away the insurance company's stake after it was nationalised in 1982 and then privatised in 1998, merging its own operations with CIC, resulting in a more than 98 percent ownership. Crédit Mutuel's director general, Michel Lucas, still remains CIC's president today, even though the two companies are marketed separately.

Since 2004, CIC's network has been based around six regional hubs that individually oversee their own franchises. These are: the CIC Bank in eastern and central (Île-de-France) regions, the CIC Bank Scalbert Dupont and CIC Bank CIN network in the northwest, the south-east network managed by CIC Bank Lyonnaise, the southwest network run by CIC Company Bordelaise and the western network managed by Bank CIO and CIC Bank BRO.

The bank has been thriving since being bought out and it continues to work on consolidating and improving operations, with its 2006 net income growing 120.4 percent from 2005. The growth was due to a surge in retail banking, after CIC increased the number of individual, self employed professional and corporate clients by over one million in 2006. Alongside renovating or enlarging more than half of its existing branches, it has also opened 336 new ones.

C is for culture

Despite being a very different institution than it was in the 19th century, CIC embraces its, and French, history. The banking group pays homage to its far-reaching heritage by supporting various cultural and historical endeavours. They are partners, for example, in the Grand Tournoi de l'Histoire, a history quiz show broadcast on the television channel France 3, as well as supporting several documentaries about the life and work of great composers and classical musicians. CIC also directly sponsors young classical musicians, going as far as paying for instruments for especially prodigious students. In addition, the group is financing the renovation of a collection of 17th century frescoes and murals commissioned by Louis XIV, in the Hôtel National des Invalides (Army Museum) in Paris, as well as arranging summer concerts at the historic building.

GETTING HIRED

A history of appeal to graduates

CIC group has long offered graduate employment schemes to students seeking to start a career in France's financial sector. They welcome about 200 young people into their sandwich course programmes and more than 1,500 recruits into their trainee programmes each year. CIC specifically targets recruitment toward students who have a Bac+2 to Bac+5 (Baccalaureate plus two-to-five years of higher education) qualification, preparing for diplomas in the fields of commerce, economics, finance or banking.

You can begin the application process online by requesting a particular traineeship and mentioning your availability dates and the region in which you would like to train. Your trainee period will alternate between teaching periods and on-site training within CIC's commercial network.

Applicants must have a high level of French in order to apply for any of these positions, as the online application procedure is entirely in French. Those looking to submit their CV speculatively for internship applications and entry level positions, should click on the "déposer une candidature spontanée" link on the "recrutement" page of CIC's French site (www.cic.fr/fr/banques/le-cic/recrutement/index.html). Here you will be prompted to pick one of eight regional banks to work for, as well as to upload your CV and letter of motivation.

To view current vacancies for entry level positions, internships and trainee programmes, click the "nos offres d'emploi, de stages et d'alternance" link on the "recrutement" page. ☐

Crédit Industriel et Commercial (CIC)

CLOSE BROTHERS

10 Crown Place
London EC2A 4FT
United Kingdom
Tel: +44 20 7655 3100
www.closebrothers.co.uk

The Stats

Employer Type: Public Company
Ticker Symbol: CBG (LSE)
Chief Executive: Strone Macpherson
2007 Revenue: £606m
2007 Profit: £136m
2006 Revenue: £536m
2006 Profit: £112m
No. of Employees: 2,600

Departments

Corporate Finance Advice • Deposits
and Treasury Services • Investment
Funds • Securities Trading • Wealth
Management

European Locations

London (HQ)
France • Germany • United Kingdom

Employment Contact

www.closebrothers.co.uk

Pluses

• Performance-based career
  progression
• "Hands off" attitude towards
  management

Minuses

• Easy to get overloaded with work
• Very long hours

THE BUZZ
WHAT EMPLOYEES AT OTHER FIRMS ARE SAYING

• "Small, UK-focused IB"
• "Small but successful franchise"

THE SCOOP

C lose Brothers Group is one of the UK's leading independent investment banks and stands proud among the top 200 listed companies in the UK. While most of its competitors have been bought up by larger global banks over the years, Close Brothers has managed to hold onto its independence by providing services to the oft-neglected small and medium-sized business segment.

The group is comprised of some 30 businesses, each with its own management team and board of directors. Operating in four primary segments, the bank has literally a wealth of experience in each. These segments are asset management including wealth management and investment funds, corporate finance, securities and banking, including treasury services and lending.

Close Brothers has got even more to its range, offering a range of specialist services to niche areas of industry. One of these areas is the British Armed Forces, specifically, the Army, Royal Navy and Royal Airforce, to whose members the bank offers financing facilities.

Take advice from the Brothers

Close Brothers' corporate finance business offers advisory services to corporate and institutional clients in four areas: mergers and acquisitions, structuring and raising debt, special situations and IPO advisory. The firm has an especially strong reputation in middle market transactions (with values up to 500 million euros), where it is one of the most active advisers in Europe on the basis of announced deals.

Close Brothers' special situations team concentrates on one-of-a-kind deals and has notably been engaged in high-profile financial restructurings for huge companies such as British Energy and Parmalat. While it holds its strongest presence in the UK, Close Brothers has expanded its corporate finance business into France, Germany, Italy and Spain. The bank operates further abroad through a series of exclusive alliances with investment banks in other countries, including leading middle market mergers and acquisitions bank Harris Williams in the US.

Those brothers were so Close

The origins of the modern Close Brothers Group date back to 1878 when William Brooks Close and his brothers founded a banking and investment firm. The Close family had over 100 years of banking in its blood, including James Close, an advisor to Neapolitan King Ferdinand II. The brothers began their enterprise by investing in cheap land in the American Midwest, which was then sold at a remarkable profit to the growing number of settlers heading west. The partnership, based in London, thrived on exploration, buying land and financing the White Pass & Yukon railway between Alaska and Canada's northern Yukon territory. As the firm expanded, it added banking, investment and lending as sources of income, offering these services primarily to a select group of wealthy individuals.

Following World War II, Close Brothers began investing in traditional mining, utility, property and banking projects. A major chunk of the bank was acquired by London & Western Trust in 1972, following years of slumping profits. This stake was reacquired in a management buyout in 1978. In the 1980s, Close Brothers launched a series of acquisitions which greatly expanded its areas of operations. The company capitalised on the UK recession of the early 1990s, acquiring a specialist in Business Expansion Scheme (BES) transactions (now Close Brothers Investment) and automobile financing operations (now Close Consumer Finance).

> ❝ The partnership thrived on exploration, buying land and financing the White Pass & Yukon railway ❞

One of Close Brothers' most significant additions was Winterflood Securities, which it acquired for 19 million pounds in 1993. Winterflood specialises in small company stocks, and as a market-maker, positioned Close Brothers to capitalise on the emerging high-technology stock bubble of the late 1990s. In 2000, profits from the Winterflood operations comprised almost 60 percent of Close Brothers' entire operating profits.

Close of play?

In March 2008, it came to light that a group of Close Brothers' shareholders were planning to depose 54-year old group chief executive Colin Keogh in a management coup, due largely to ongoing dissatisfaction in the wake of a string of failed takeover bids. When takeover talks with Cenkos Securities collapsed, the confidence of a raft of major shareholders was lost in the rubble.

A senior insider at Close, speaking in *The Independent*, declared: "Staff are totally disaffected with what's been going on. The bid from Andy Stewart at Cenkos Securities had popular internal support. This process has gone on far too long — something has to give." When bidding opened, Andy Stewart upped his original offer of 9.50 pounds per share to 10.50 pounds per share. Close closed at 5.91 pounds per share in early March, partly as a result of the failed bid.

I'm bored ...

According to reports, Andy Stewart's takeover bid eventually bordered on the hostile. Stewart said that Close Brothers' underperformance was down to the demotivation of its staff, which, he speculated, was largely due to the fact that they were not given equity ownership of the business. Speaking in *The Times* in January 2008, Close Brothers' chief executive of corporate finance, Stephen Aulsebrook strenuously denied this, saying "Our staff are as engaged with the business now as they ever have been. Lack of equity is not why people have moved on to other companies over the years."

In March 2008, *The Telegraph* reported Close Brothers were working on a new incentive scheme for staff, after rejecting plans to sell the business or accept a takeover. As part of its efforts to rebuild business and rejuvenate its staff morale, it will devise an incentive plan akin to equity, payed out if the value of the business rises. The same month, Close Brothers acquired two niche lending businesses — the Commercial Acceptances Group and Amber Credit, a specialist insurance finance business — that boasted a combined loan book value of 145 million pounds.

Who's the boss?

In June 2008 Close Brothers Group announced that it's long-serving chairman and chief executive Rod Kent was stepping down from his role, and would be replaced by Kent's deputy chairman, Strone Macpherson. The move was reported to be so that Kent could become executive chairman of UK mortgage lender Bradford and Bingley.

GETTING HIRED

Keeping it real

The firm is not especially forthcoming about career opportunities on its website, but accepts written and speculative applications which you should send the old-fashioned way to 10 Crown Place, London, EC2A 4FT, or by email to enquiries@cbgplc.com. The firm discloses that it does operate internships and graduate programs in some of its departments, but again, you should write to the departments you're keen on working with and ask directly.

Joining the brotherhood

The hiring process at Close Brothers follows the norms of the sector. One respondent, a Paris-based analyst, explains that he had "seven interviews with directors and partners over a four month period."

According to the same source, Close Brothers does not provide formal training. He states: "Junior analysts are hired from other banks where they have received formal training. Interns receive negligible training; they mainly work on company profiles and multiples. Few are hired as analysts".

OUR SURVEY SAYS

Manage your workload

Unsurprisingly, working hours are rather long at Close Brothers. Commenting on this inevitable aspect of corporate life, a Paris-based respondent says: "I would get there before 9am, eat lunch in front of my computer and leave around 10pm. Some weeks, I would leave at 2am. I would usually come back during the weekend."

Regarding the company work ethic, the same source states: "You can easily get overbooked if you do a good job: the better your job, the more managers give you assignments. It is important to sometimes say no because you will not be forgiven if your work is not perfect or not ready for the deadline."

Independent-minded people might find working at Close Brothers gives them a great chance to flourish. The company boasts a "hands-off" attitude towards managing, reveals an insider in London.

Keeping up appearances

Regarding the growth opportunities inside the company, a Parisian respondent reflects: "You start as a junior analyst. It takes one to two years to get promoted to senior analyst, one to two more years to become manager but it all depends on your performance and the perception of your performance by managers and partners."

"I want the truth!"

"You can't handle the truth!"

A Few Good Men, 1992

The truth is in the Vault:

- Browse 5,000+ company profiles and 100's of industry overviews.

- Access "insider info" on interviews, culture, compensation and hours.

- Read employee surveys.

- Browse "Day in the life" of employee profiles and Q&As with recruiters.

- Find a job.

- Browse our video career library.

- And much more!

www.vault.com/europe   V∧ULT

COLLINS STEWART

Collins Stewart Europe Limited
8th Floor
88 Wood Street
London EC2V 7QR
United Kingdom
Tel: +44 (0)20 7523 8000
www.collinsstewart.com

The Stats

Employer Type: Public Company
Ticker Symbol: CLST (LSE)
Chief Executive: Joel Plasco
2007 Revenue: £233.9m
2006 Profit: £79m
2006 Revenue: £160m
2006 Profit: £61.2m
No. of Employees: 720
No. of Offices: 17

Departments

Capital Markets • Corporate advisory
Securities • Wealth Management

European Locations

London (HQ)
Channel Islands • Isle of Man • France •
Ireland • Switzerland • United
Kingdom

Employment Contact

www.collinsstewart.com/cs_careers.asp

For information on graduate
programmes email:

recruitment@collinsstewart.com

For experienced hires:

recruitment@collinsstewart.com
(for London, Paris, Geneva and
Dublin)

paulinewilliams@collinsstewart.com
(for the Channel Islands)

Key Competitors

Cenkos • Evolution • Investec •
Numis Securities

THE BUZZ
WHAT EMPLOYEES AT OTHER FIRMS ARE SAYING

• "Good quality boutique"
• "Not very well known`"

THE SCOOP

L SE-listed Collins Stewart (CS) organises its operations around four business divisions: capital markets, wealth management, securities and corporate advisory. The firm's corporate advisory capability incorporates London-based Hawkpoint, which it acquired in 2007.

They have a significant research capability both for large corporates and smaller companies, most of which they also raise capital for, the securities division includes "Quest" — a database and modelling system which serves the other divisions by offering a method for analysing corporate value creation and valuation. Quest covers 2,600 companies in 27 countries across the UK, the US, Europe and Asia Pacific.

Collins Stewart serves more than 400 institutional clients across North America, Asia Pacific and Europe, with sales teams in London, Paris, Dublin, Geneva and New York distributing its research product. Its London operation boasts a full service investment trust and funds team, as well as convertible and preference trading desks.

As one of the leading stockbrokers for small and mid-cap equity fundraising in London, in 2008, Collins Stewart's capital markets division added two new products in the London market: the Accelerated IPO (AIPO) and the Special Purpose Acquisition Corporation (SPAC). In 2005, this division worked on award-winning transactions for Foseco and Media Square, which collected *Shares Magazine's* "IPO of the Year" and at the AIM Awards, recognition for "Best Use of AIM" prizes respectively.

The firm's wealth management division manages more than four billion pounds and provides stockbroking and investment management services to private clients, trusts, charities, pension funds and private companies. Collins Stewart's advisory business, incorporating Hawkpoint, advises governmental bodies, private equity houses and financial institutions in the areas of M&A, capital markets and debt restructuring.

The rest is history

Collins Stewart was founded in 1991 as a partnership with Singer & Friedlander Securities. Starting out as a private client business by acquiring Greig Middleton's Channel Islands and Isle of Man business in 1996 along with the New York business, it became incorporated in 1999.

In October 2000, Collins Stewart listed on the London Stock Exchange, and a year later, in 2001, it bolstered its private client offering with the acquisition of NatWest Stockbrokers' private client business. As the inter-dealer broking sector expanded throughout the early 21st century, CS acquired Tullett Liberty in March 2003 and Prebon in October 2004 to form the then Collins Stewart Tullett. It is today named Tullett Prebon and is the world's second largest inter-dealer broker.

At the end of 2006, Collins Stewart demerged from Collins Stewart Tullett and was listed on the main list of the London Stock Exchange as Collins Stewart plc. Growing through acquisition, it picked up independent corporate advisory business Hawkpoint Partners in January 2007, followed by New York investment bank CE Unterberg Towbin in July.

Capitalising on Catalist

In the opening months of 2008, Collins Stewart opened an office in Singapore to get a foot in the door of Asia's new rival to London's alternative investment market: Catalist. Catalist's predecessor, the less-catchy Sesdaq, was revamped to provide more flexible trading and a faster registration process to bring more small and quickly-growing companies onto its books. As for many financial institutions, the scent of Asian high-growth economies is proving difficult to resist, and Collins Stewart was no exception, becoming the first UK sponsor for Catalist.

> " Its London operation boasts a full-service investment trust and funds team "

Added to the potential for growth is the opportunity for a bespoke service that a global trading presence would provide: "We want to be completely agnostic when we advise a client about where they should list — in North America, Asia, the UK or Europe, based on what will be the best for them" said chief executive Joel Plasco in *The Financial Times*. "No matter where a company is based, if it has a high exposure to the Asian markets and visibility to Asian investors it might well want to seek a listing in Singapore or a dual listing in London/Singapore," he added.

GETTING HIRED

The new deal

Collins Stewart is introducing a graduate recruitment programme, building on the success of the Hawkpoint scheme which has been running for five years. The joint graduate recruitment programme will commence in September 2008 with eight graduates in total, five who will be working for Hawkpoint and three for Collins Stewart. Applications for 2008 are now closed, however both Collins Stewart and Hawkpoint welcome applications for entry in September 2009 from October 2008 onwards.

For further information and to apply for a graduate role or any other role, email the following: for Collins Stewart, recruitment@collinsstewart.com; for Hawkpoint, recruitment@hawkpoint.com; and for the Collins Stewart Channel Islands office, email Pauline Williams at: paulinewilliams@collinsstewart.com. □

COMMERZBANK

Kaiserplatz
60261 Frankfurt
Germany
Tel: +49 69 136 20
www.commerzbank.com

The Stats

Employer Type: Public Company
Ticker Symbol: CBK (Frankfurt)
Chief Executive: Klaus-Peter Müller
2007 Revenue: €2.5bn
2007 Profit: €1.9bn
2006 Revenue: €2.6bn
2006 Profit: €1.6bn
No. of Employees: 36,767
No. of Offices: 820

Departments

Commercial Real Estate • Corporate
and Investment Banking • Public
Finance and Treasury • Retail Banking
and Asset Management

European Locations

Frankfurt (Global HQ)
Belarus • Belgium • Croatia • Czech
Republic • France • Germany • Hungary •
Ireland • Italy • Luxembourg • The
Netherlands • Poland • Russia •
Slovakia • Spain • Switzerland •
Ukraine • United Kingdom

Key Competitors

Deutsche Bank • Dresdner Bank •
HVB Group

Employment Contact

www.commerzbank.com
(See "A Career" section)

THE BUZZ
WHAT EMPLOYEES AT OTHER FIRMS ARE SAYING

• "Mid-sized German player"
• "Large commercial bank"
• "Regional focus"
• "Poor IB profile"

THE SCOOP

U ntil 2004, Commerzbank surveyed its domain from the top of the Commerzbank Tower in Frankfurt, Europe's tallest tower, dreamed up by British architectural mastermind Norman Foster, creator of London's "Gherkin." The tower was also Europe's first ecological skyscraper, including features such as natural ventilation and lighting, multi-storey "sky gardens" and innovative eco-friendly heat and power systems. By all accounts, an appropriate vantage point for the second-largest bank in Germany after Deutsche Bank.

This major German player caters primarily to private customers and small to medium-sized companies in three major areas: retail banking and asset management; corporate and investment banking; and commercial real estate, public finance and treasury. The high profile acquisition of Eurohypo, Europe's largest specialist real estate bank, increased Commerzbank's assets by more than 50 percent. One of the DAX 30, the blue chip index of the leading 30 companies listed on the Frankfurt Stock Exchange, the company has around 290,000 shareholders, with more than 70 percent of its capital in the hands of non-resident investors.

Worldwide commerz

Tending to Commerzbank's primarily German market are its 820 domestic branches, but the bank conducts business worldwide through operations in Western, Central and Eastern European markets, and in the Americas and Asia. The bank makes its presence known in more than 40 countries, operating through subsidiaries, branches and representative offices. At present, it benefits from a network of more than 5,000 correspondent banks worldwide.

Commerzbank's retail banking division provides investing services to roughly 5.5 million customers. The division offers asset management, home loans, account management, an officially certified selection of funds, Eurocards and Visa cards to private and business customers. Its direct subsidiary, Comdirect bank AG, is Germany's number one online broker. Commerzbank's asset management arm, Cominvest, spends its time managing securities-based funds for investors, while its Ebase subsidiary manages fund procurement and custody accounts.

Mittel ground

Mittelstand, or medium-sized companies, comprise a significant slice of Commerzbank's business. It is unique among banks in Germany in being the only one to devote an entire division to mittelstand business. Commerzbank provides services to over 60,000 small to medium-sized companies with an annual turnover of more than 2.5 million euros. In its corporate and investment banking division, Commerzbank's mittelstand business is concentrated in 166 branches, while its approximately 800 larger corporate clients are served in five specialised corporate centres.

In the wars

Founded in 1870 by individual and merchant bankers in Hamburg, Commerzbank merged with Berliner Bank in 1905 and moved its headquarters to Berlin. After a succession of mergers with German banks, the name Commerzbank Aktiengesellschaft was officially adopted in 1940. The bank suffered a loss of 45 percent of its premises with the division of Europe after World War II, and was divided into three regional banks. These entities were reunited in 1958 under a central headquarters in Düsseldorf. The bank gradually shifted its headquarters to Frankfurt in the 1970s and established its centre of operations in Germany's financial centre in 1990. In 1971, Commerzbank was the first German bank to establish a branch in New York City. Throughout the 1970s, Commerzbank successfully opened offices in London, Chicago, Paris, Brussels, Tokyo, Hong Kong and Madrid.

> " In 1971, Commerzbank was the first German bank to establish a branch in New York City "

The Eurohypo acquisition

In March 2006, Commerzbank acquired Eurohypo, a Germany-based European real estate bank, purchasing the remaining 66.2 percent of the company for a total price of 4.56 billion euros. The bank now owns a 98 percent share in Europe's largest institution for public sector financing and real estate lending. Commerzbank purchased the Eurohypo interests from Deutsche Bank and Allianz/Dresdner Bank at an average price of 19.60 euros per share.

In order to finance the acquisition, Commerzbank issued new shares to institutional investors at the price of 23.50 euros per share, which was met with an overwhelming demand. The bank was able to sell 57.7 million new shares in just two hours. The purchase was Commerzbank's largest acquisition in the last 50 years, increasing the bank's balance sheet total to almost 700 billion euros. The addition of Eurohypo boosted the bank's balance sheet and helped Commerzbank report a net profit of 1,597 million (1.59 billion) euros in the 2006 fiscal year.

GETTING HIRED

Different strokes for different folks

Commerzbank offers a range of opportunities for students, including training programmes in financial markets, in its in-house operations from its headquarters to its branches, and in its IT division.

If you've just graduated, or completed the Vordiplom exam in Germany, you'll find paid eight-week internships available to you. Helpfully, to apply for any kind of employment with the bank, from training programmes to full time positions, simply click the "a career" link on the company homepage, followed by "apply for a job online." You can direct your application to service departments, corporate banking, investment banking, group management, retail banking and asset management divisions, as well as to the trainee programmes.

If you fancy a virtual tour of the bank and receiving guidelines on what criteria you need to fulfil to work at Commerzbank as an intern or trainee, click the "hotstaff" link in the menu on the left.

Jump straight in

You can also browse the company's vacancies on the careers page by clicking "looking for a job", and specify your desired capacity, division and working location. Note that many job descriptions are in German. □

CRÉDIT AGRICOLE GROUP

91-93 Blvd. Pasteur
Paris, 75015
France
Tel: +33 43 23 52 02
www.credit-agricole.com

The Stats

Employer Type: Public Company
Ticker Symbol: CAC (Euronext)
Chief Executive: Georges Pauget
2007 Revenue: €16.8bn
2007 Profit: €4.5bn
2006 Revenue: €16.1bn
2006 Profit: €4.8bn
No. of Employees: 157,000
No. of Offices: locations in 40
countries

Departments

Asset Management, Insurance and
Private Banking • Corporate and
Investment Banking • French Retail
Banking - Regional Banks • French
Retail Banking - LCL • International
Retail Banking • Specialised Financial
Services

European Locations

Paris (HQ)
Albania • Austria • Belgium • Bulgaria •
Cyprus • Czech Republic • Denmark •
Finland • France • Germany • Greece •
Hungary • Ireland • Italy • Luxembourg •
Monaco • The Netherlands • Norway •
Poland • Portugal • Romania • Russia •
Serbia • Slovakia • Spain • Sweden •
Switzerland • Ukraine • United
Kingdom

Employment Contact

www.crédit-agricole.fr/recrutement

carrieres.emploi@crédit-agricole-sa.fr

Key Competitors

BNP Paribas (CIB) • CIC • Société
Générale (CIB)

THE BUZZ
WHAT EMPLOYEES AT OTHER FIRMS ARE SAYING

• "Very strong sales team"
• "Wholesale bank"
• "Regional"
• "Small French player"

THE SCOOP

D espite its rather provincial name, Crédit Agricole can be found on almost every French high street. With 28 percent of France's consumer market, Crédit Agricole is Europe's leading banking group in terms of retail banking revenues, and is ranked sixth as a banking group worldwide in terms of shareholder equity. A co-operative venture from the outset, the bank owns a 25 percent stake in each of 39 regional banks, which between them own more than half of Crédit Agricole. The bank offers retail and business banking, and lending and deposit services at more than 9,130 branches throughout the country, including those of subsidiary Le Crédit Lyonnais (LCL), which it acquired in 2003. With more than 150 further banking entities in 70 countries, this giant group is notable for having established a significant presence in the Middle East and Southeast Asia.

French fare

Crédit Agricole S.A. was created in 2001 to represent the Crédit Agricole Group as a central body and central bank. When it became a listed company in December 2001, it was organised to represent all of the group's business lines and entities — it owns 25 percent of each regional bank, along with all of the group's specialist subsidiaries and foreign entities. With 5.7 million customers, the firm's 2,583 local banks make up the backbone of its organisation. The local banks micromanage the

> ❝ Calyon is the investment banking division of Crédit Agricole ❞

capital of the regional banks, which are cooperative organisations acting under the Crédit Agricole umbrella. As the overarching entity, Crédit Agricole S.A. has three main purposes: to ensure uniformity in the operation of its diverse entities, to ensure their financial unity, and to ensure consistent commercial development throughout them.

Calyon is the investment banking division of Crédit Agricole, formed in 2004. It combined the corporate and investment bank Crédit Agricole Indosuez with the corresponding division of LCL, allowing LCL to focus solely on its retail operations. Calyon offers brokerage and investment banking services worldwide, with 13,000 staff in 58 countries.

Surviving the worst of times

Crédit Lyonnais dates back to 1839, when the French banker Henri Germain and several other prominent local businessmen founded a bank in Lyon. The firm grew over the next 25 years and in 1865 it added branches in Paris and Marseilles. The

235

company survived the Franco-Prussian War of 1870 – 1871, but after the siege of Paris by the Prussians in the winter of 1870, Germain felt Crédit Lyonnais could benefit from geographical diversity and so a London office was promptly established.

Winning Euro-vision

By the end of the 1880s, Crédit Lyonnais was the leading bank in France and had branches in London, Constantinople, Alexandria, Geneva, Madrid and St. Petersburg. A new Paris headquarters opened in 1883, shortly after the firm led the French banking industry through a liquidity crisis. At the beginning of World War I, Crédit Lyonnais was the largest bank in the world with nearly 400 branches — including 13 branches located in cities outside of France.

Like much of France, Crédit Lyonnais was devastated by the war; branches were closed and nearly 1,600 of the company's employees died in the conflict. As the war was drawing to a close the firm was touched by the tide of history once more, as revolutions in Russia and Turkey closed branches and put foreign debt in doubt. Crédit Lyonnais actually fared better in World War II than in the previous continent-wide conflict.

> ❝ After the siege of Paris by the Prussians in the winter of 1870 a London office was promptly established ❞

Fewer branches were destroyed in the fighting, and the company focused on safer investments during the uncertain time. Post-war Crédit Lyonnais provided financial help to the rebuilding efforts. In the 1980s, the company benefited from deregulation mania and expanded its capital markets presence.

Italian expansion

In May 2005, Crédit Lyonnais bought a 63 percent stake in Banca Intesa's asset management unit Nextra for 850 million euros. Crédit Lyonnais had been hoping to strengthen its links with Banca Intesa, while the Italian bank wished to sell its subsidiary, which suffered considerably as a result of its involvement with the Parmalat scandal in 2004, in which the Italian food corporation was accused of a multi-million euro fraud.

In February 2007, Crédit Agricole bought 654 bank branches from Banca Intesa for 5.96 billion euros. This purchase, which went ahead after EU regulatory approval, gave Crédit Agricole ownership of 654 banks previously owned by Banca Intesa — 310 from Cariparma, 140 from Friuladria and 193 from Banca Intesa itself. It also cleared the way for Banca Intesa to finally complete its merger with domestic rival Sanpaolo, which was subject to both banks' ability to comply with European antitrust regulations.

International shopping trips

In March 2006, the bank signed a 220 million euro deal to buy JSC Index Bank, one of the Ukraine's leading banks. Crédit Agricole has had a 13-year presence in the country, and was already one of the leading corporate and investment banks there, but the deal moves it into retail banking for the first time.

Crédit Agricole also bought a majority stake in Greece's state-run Emporiki Bank in. This deal increased Crédit's existing stake in Greece's fourth-largest bank, from 11 percent to 51 percent. The bank then boosted its stake to more than 70 percent in August 2006, beating out the Central Bank of Cyprus. The same month, Crédit Agricole made another astute regional move, acquiring more than 70 percent of Serbia's Meridian Bank for 34 million euros as part of a strategic partnership in the financial services market in Serbia.

Crédit Agricole kept the momentum going in November 2007, by purchasing 14.99 percent of Bankinter, the sixth-largest bank in Spain for 809 million euros, thereby reinforcing its European influence. The bank also asked Bankinter SA Chairman Pedro Guerrero for two seats on the bank's board, *El Economista* reported, as well as asking the Bank of Spain to allow Crédit Agricole to hike its stake to 30 percent.

However, not all of Crédit Agricole's buys were focused on banking. It bought champagne producer Taittinger from the eastern US-based investment management group Starwood Capital for 660 million euros in June 2006. The deal included ownership of California wine maker Domaine Carneros and French sparkling wine producer Bouvet-Ladubay.

Crédit Agricole broke into the Chinese banking market by forming a joint venture with the Agricultural Bank of China (ABC) in January 2007, taking a 33.7 percent stake, with ABC holding 51.3 percent and Chalco, the second-largest aluminium producer in the world, taking 15 percent. However, not all of the bank's deals panned out. In May 2006, rumours hit the press that Crédit Agricole was planning a bid for the UK's seventh-largest bank, the Alliance & Leicester building society. But after scrutinising A&L's books, Crédit Agricole decided not to bid on it.

Out of credit

As the subprime mortgage financial crisis, which began in the US in 2006, reached global proportions in July 2007, concerns about Crédit Agricole's investment banking subsidiary Calyon began to surface. They proved to be well-founded as the company reported a steep drop in profits after a 546 million euro writedown on its portfolio of asset-backed securities. Its business in France subsequently became undermined by its stronger rivals BNP Paribas and Société Générale In December 2007, the beleagured Crédit Agricole had to admit to a further loss of 1.6 billion euros over 2007 due to the impact of the US subprime meltdown.

Taking a new approach

There was significant reshuffling at Crédit Agricole in 2006 — in April, the firm announced that the bank's alternative investment products group would be re-branded as Crédit Agricole Asset Management. The division is a leader in the alternative funds industry, and manages 13.6 billion euros for both French and international investors.

The following June, CPR Private Equity was renamed Crédit Agricole Asset Management Capital Investors and the bank committed itself to a drive to develop its business scope and client base. Focused on the management of private equity funds for institutional and retail investors, the Capital Investors Asset Management fund has 1.2 billion euros under management. That same month, Crédit Agricole announced the launch of a venture fund dedicated to investing in renewable energies, and a 400 million euro fund to invest in infrastructure financed by public-private partnerships.

GETTING HIRED

Attracting the right crowd

Crédit Agricole offers several trainee programmes which are geared towards graduates who have a Bac (Baccalaureate) and four or five years of higher education. The company mostly recruits those with a background in commerce and engineering, as well as other areas from well-respected French schools, whose career fairs it often attends — a full listing of visited schools can be found on the company's website.

Its internship programmes, for example, last a minimum of six months and provide rotations through different departments within the company in areas such as commercial credit analysis, product marketing, sales, project finance and private client consultancy.

The company sponsors the VIE (Volontariat International en Entreprise) programme, as well as L'ELDE (Expérience Longue Durée à l'Etranger) — a long-term internship abroad. To find out more about graduate and career opportunities at Crédit Agricole, check out the company's site at www.Crédit-agricole.fr and click on "recrutement".

You can also go directly to the recruitment websites of Crédit Agricole's subsidiaries through the same link, but be warned that despite offering graduate opportunities at its offices throughout the world, Crédit Agricole's recruitment info is only available in French (any questions or enquiries can be forwarded to carrieres.emploi@Crédit-agricole-sa.fr). □

Crédit Agricole Group

DANSKE BANK GROUP

Danske Bank Group
Holmens Kanal 2-12
DK-1092 Copenhagen
Denmark
Tel. +45 33 44 00 00
www.danskebank.com

The Stats

Employer Type: Public Company
Ticker Symbol: DANSKE
(Copenhagen)
Chief Executive: Peter Straarup
2007 Revenue: DKr 45bn
2007 Profit: DKr 15bn
2006 Revenue: DKr 43bn
2006 Profit: DKr 15bn
No. of Employees: 23,632
(worldwide)
No. of Offices: Offices throughout
Denmark and the rest of Europe.

Departments

Asset management (Danske Capital) ·
Banking · Corporate Banking ·
Financial markets (Danske Markets) ·
Institutional Services · Retail Banking

European Locations

Copenhagen (HQ) · Denmark ·
Estonia · Finland · Germany · Latvia ·
Lithuania · Luxembourg · Norway ·
Northern Ireland · Poland · Republic
of Ireland · Russia · Sweden · United
Kingdom

Employment Contact

HR Contact:
arbejdspladsen@danskebank.dk
Careers website:
www.danskebank.com
(Click on "Jobs")

Key Competitors

Danmarks Nationalsbank · Jydske
Bank · Nordea

THE BUZZ
WHAT EMPLOYEES AT OTHER FIRMS ARE SAYING

· "The best Nordic bank"
· "Increasing international presence"
· "Not very prestigious"
· "Small, regional player"

THE SCOOP

Founded in 1871 by a saddle-maker who later became a talented broker, as Den Danske Landmandsbank, today's Danske Bank stands among the world's leading banks. The Dankse Bank Group is Denmark's biggest financial enterprise by total assets and one of the largest in the Nordic region. Operating in banking, mortgage finance, insurance, leasing, real estate brokerage and asset management, this Danish dazzler focuses on retail banking and boasts nationwide branch networks in Denmark, Sweden, Norway, Northern Ireland, the Republic of Ireland, Finland and the Baltic states of Estonia, Latvia and Lithuania. Within Denmark, it stands among the market leaders, holding a market share of close to a third in banking, mortgage finance and life insurance.

The Great Dane

The late 19th century saw the founding of three important banks in Denmark. Privatbanken, founded in 1857 by leading figures in Copenhagen's business circles, was Denmark's first private bank. In 1871, Gottlieb Hartvig Abrahamsson Gedalia, the saddle-maker and broker, established Den Danske Landmandsbank, which translated, means the Danish Farmer's Bank. A third large bank, Handelsbanken, was

> " Founded by a saddle-maker who later became a talented broker, Danske Bank is among the world's leading banks "

launched in 1873 by merchant D.B. Adler, one of the co-founders of Privatbanken. By 1910, Den Danske Landmandsbank had grown to become the largest bank in Scandinavia, under the management of the Glückstadt family.

Despite the post-war depression, Den Danske Landmandsbank grew healthily between 1920 and 1950, renaming itself Den Danske Bank in 1976. Competitors Handelsbank and Privatbanken grew at a similar rate. Between 1960 and 1990 all three benefited from a gradual rationalisation in the national banking laws. While restrictions on product development, marketing and technological innovation loosened, competition from abroad grew fiercer. In 1990, Den Danske Bank, Handelsbank and the then Provinsbanken (born through a merger of Fyens Disconto Kasse and Privatbanken in 1967) merged into Den Danske Bank, which became Danske Bank in 2000.

Border crossing

The Danske Bank Group began its Nordic expansion strategy in 1997. Aiming to consider the entire Nordic region as its home market, it acquired Östgöta Enskilda

Bank, now called Danske Bank Sweden. In 1999, it took on Norway's Fokus bank to achieve a seven percent market share in Scandinavia. Shifting its sights further south, the group purchased Ireland's Northern Bank and National Irish Bank in 2004.

The Big Finnish

Returning to its original policy of Nordic conquest, in November 2006 the group acquired Finland's third-largest bank, Sampo, for 30.1 billion Danish kroner (4.05 billion euros, 5.15 billion US dollars), together with its subsidiaries in the Baltic states and Russia. The Danish high-flyers also bought into investment companies Mandatum Asset Management, Sampo Fund Management, Mandatum and Co. and Mandatum Stockbrokers. Market commentators criticised Danske's over-eagerness to expand geographically as the source of paying in excess of the three billion euro price-tag affixed by most analysts to the Finnish company.

Speaking in *The Financial Times*, UBS analyst Anders Hakansson noted: "It's a very expensive deal ... Danske has realised that it has 30 percent of the local market and that profit growth there is going backwards, so it has do something outside, or just be a boring bank." Dankse's chief executive cited the Finnish bank's "scarcity value" as the only bank for sale in Finland, as a selling point. Another selling point was the access the purchase offered to the developing Eastern European markets.

Keeping IT in the family

The bank group is hailed for its innovative IT management strategy. Operating one single shared platform across Northern Europe, its customers benefit from products that function across borders and units. As a result, the IT platform actually plays a large role in driving the group's business strategy, as the acquisition and integration of new financial businesses and services is felt by customers system-wide.

GETTING HIRED

If you speak Danish ...

The jobs offered on Danske Bank Group's main website are based in Denmark and many of them require fluency in Danish. For jobs in other locations through the banking group's subsidiaries and regional operations, you need to check out the particular website that relates to the region you are interested in. Links to these sites can be found on the "jobs" page by following the "current vacancies" link, and selecting any of the firms operations in other countries from the drop-down menu at the bottom of the page, under the heading "other jobsites."

Danske Bank Group offers opportunities to students including employment for undergraduates and a thesis project for Masters students in collaboration with Danske Bank divisions. For these opportunities, follow the "jobs" link on the company homepage, select "student" from the list at the top of the page and either "student jobs" or "write your thesis."

For student jobs, the company offers benefits including an attractive salary and pension, holidays and time off, part-time schemes and maternity leave, health insurance, a share purchase programme and other financial advantages. Students will be thrilled to learn that the bank only requires them to work 20 hours per week — with reduced office time requirements during exam periods. For opportunities to integrate your thesis, keep an eye on the website from the start of autumn, as this is when the company advertises for applicants. Participants in the scheme benefit from an insider's perspective on the firm, interviews with senior staff and extended stays within company units. For further information on this opportunity you can send an email to danskespeciale@danskebank.dk.

Trainees for high fees

Danske Bank Group is especially fond of graduates from economics, financing, IT, business development, accountancy, marketing and human resources backgrounds. The group offers courses, conferences and on-campus recruitment information to job-hunters preparing to leave university. The bank's divisions which welcome applications include Danske Capital, Danske Markets, group finance, group credits, IT development, internal audit, group HR and communications and business development and marketing. Information on each of these can be found under the "group units" link on the Jobs page on Danske Bank's website.

Get with the programme

Dankse Bank Group operates a 12-month graduate trainee programme beginning each September, with applications due in by the preceding March. Applicants to the programme must have recently obtained a Masters degree and be fluent in Danish. Once on the course, participants are taken through their paces and will be involved in a range of tasks, courses and network activities alongside other graduate trainees and colleagues across Danske Bank Group.

Employed in a specific area as part of the programme, participants are put on an equal footing with more experienced colleagues and will see involvement in other departments within the company, including those outside Denmark. A range of courses and seminars together with a common education programme are run under the program. Every participant, together with their line manager, gets the chance to put together a plan establishing which courses will be most relevant for development in their desired career path. Under the "graduate" section on the Jobs page, select "graduate trainee" for more information.

The IT development department also has a graduate programme divided into three lines: IT development, test management and business development. The programme contains a 21-month development plan with a mixture of practical assignments and internal training. Non-Danish speaking graduates are also accepted at this programme.

Feeling special

Under the "specialist" link on the "jobs" page, Danske outlines the range of specific roles available at the bank. These include analyst, controller, IT developer, dealer, IT business developer, advisor and HR consultant. Clicking any of the links next to these positions will take you to further details on each function. Information on the culture and working environment at the firm, including its views on leadership and individual development, can be found by following the "work life" link.

Climb aboard

When applying to the firm, make sure you indicate why you are interested in a specific job and what opportunities you feel it will offer you. Danske Bank Group likes to hear about applicants' relevant experiences along with what opportunities they see for themselves in the job. It also focuses very much on what your motivations are for wanting to work with the group. Subtlety, honesty and differentiation from other candidates, through proof of your exceptional characteristics, are prized qualities in applications.

Applicants will be notified after the application deadline as to whether they have been invited to an interview. The preliminary interview is an opportunity for the bank to brief you in more depth about the position in which you would be working. After giving you an idea of job specifics and likely scenarios in that role, you will get the chance to explain your motivation and experiences that make you the best candidate.

Making your mark

Success at this stage will get you invited to a further in-depth interview, where the bank will glean the particulars about your skills and look to identify your personal preferences for your work situation. Before attending, the company will ask you to complete a personality test online. Do expect it to be used as a point of discussion in the interview. Successful or unsuccessful, Danske Bank Group asserts it will notify all applicants personally as to their application status once the recruitment process is complete.

Danske Bank Group

DEXIA SA

Place Rogier, 11
B - 1210
Brussels
Belgium
Tel: +32 2 213 57 00
www.dexia.com

The Stats

Employer Type: Public Company
Ticker Symbol: DEXB (EBR)
Chief Executive: Axel Miller
2007 Revenue: €6.8bn
2007 Profit: €2.6bn
2006 Revenue: €7.0bn
2006 Profit: €2.8bn
No. of Employees: 35,200
No. of Offices: n/a

Departments

Credit Enhancement • Financial
Markets • Investment Management
Insurance Services • Personal Financial
Services • Public/Project Finance •
Treasury

European Locations

Brussels (HQ)
Austria • Belgium • Bulgaria • Czech
Republic • Denmark • France •
Germany • Hungary • Ireland • Italy •
Jersey • Luxembourg • Monaco •
Netherlands • Poland • Portugal •
Romania • Russia • Slovakia • Spain •
Sweden • Switzerland • Turkey •
United Kingdom

Employment Contacts

www.dexia.com/e/
you-are/candidate.php

Dexia Crédit Local
www.workatdexia-cl.com

Dexia Bank
Contact: recrut@dexia.be

Dexia Banque Internationale à
Luxembourg
Contact: recruitment@dexia-bil.com

Dexia Asset Management
Contact: Andre.Gaublomme

Key Competitors

Fortis • ING • KBC

THE BUZZ
WHAT EMPLOYEES AT OTHER FIRMS ARE SAYING

• "Belgian/French focused"
• "Regional retail bank"

THE SCOOP

Created through the coming together of two major European public sector finance operators in 1996 — Crédit Communal de Belgique and Crédit Local de France — Dexia is the 15th-largest financial institution in the eurozone. Its operations have a dual focus: retail banking in Europe and public and project finance globally. Boasting a customer base of 5.5 million customers in Europe, the bank's clients include individuals, institutional clients and small and medium-sized businesses. Globally, Dexia provides asset management, investor services and insurance, and is active in capital markets.

With approximately 1,000 branches in Belgium and 40 in Luxembourg, the bank's personal financial services work covers private and retail banking. It reaches into Turkey through a 99.8 percent participation in DenizBank, as well as into France, Switzerland, Slovakia and Spain, through a mixture of participations, joint operations and representative offices in

> " Dexia climbed to an enviable third place in Thomson Financial's "Global Project Finance Review" "

these countries. The mainstay of Dexia's income, however, is its public/project finance division. Accounting for 54 percent of the group's net income, it has a presence in 30 countries and 24,000 employees.

On July 3, 2008, Dexia announced it was planning to change its status to that of a European company, so it will become known as Dexia SE. This change is intended to assert the European foundations of the company along with simplifying the way it is run, in order to boost commercial efficiency.

European alliance

Crédit Communal de Belgium was created in 1860 and governed the granting of credits to municipalities for use in investment. Over the span of a century, the firm developed into a professional network of savings banks, offering accounts to private individuals. In 1987, the French Crédit Local de France was created. It expanded throughout the 1990s, with the opening of a US branch, and further growth planned in the UK, Spain, Germany, Italy, Austria, Scandinavia and Portugal.

The two expanding firms, Crédit Communal de Belgium — now bolstered with its acquisition of a 25 percent stake in Banque Internationale à Luxembourg (BIL) — and Crédit Local de France, came together to form Dexia in 1996. At this point Dexia comprised two holdings: Dexia France and Dexia Belgium. This was simplified in 1999 when Dexia Belgium took over Dexia France.

Expansion continued into the 21st century and the group began to focus on two main markets, public finance and retail, in 2003. Growth proceeded with the opening of new public project finance outposts in Poland, Japan, Mexico and Canada in 2004, followed by an alliance with Royal Bank of Canada concerning their institutional investors businesses, to form RBC Dexia Investor Services in 2005. Moving into Turkey in 2006, the group took on a 75 percent controlling interest in ithe country's sixth largest privately owned bank, DenizBank, for 1.89 billion euros.

Climbing the ranks

In 2007, Dexia climbed to an enviable third place in Thomson Financial's Global Project Finance Review, from its previous position at 13th. For Dexia this was in some part due to its having generated 9.2 billion dollars in proceeds across 61 issues, and taking its 2.2 percent market share to nearly double its size at 4.2 percent. The ranking looks at the leading arrangers on loans, and the power industry remains one of the most active sectors.

Dexia sees a particularly active involvement in project financing in the power sector, with an emphasis on wind energies, funding projects in France, Australia, Belgium, Spain, the US, Italy, Morocco, Portugal and the UK.

GETTING HIRED

Continental opportunities

Dexia make frequent appearances at careers fairs, the majority of which take place on university campuses in the bank's domestic regions: France, Belgium and Luxembourg. In addition to this you'll come across Dexia JobDays, a Dexia specific recruitment event which will give you an insight into the full range of Dexia activities and where a career could take you. Candidates should be aware that many of the information pages on these events on the company website are in French or Dutch.

You can apply for a job directly on the main Dexia website by following the "employment opportunities" link, and submitting your CV. To apply to a specific company subsidiary, your best bet is to follow the application instructions on the subsidiary website. □

EUROHYPO AG

Helfmann-Park 5
65760 Eschborn
Germany
Tel: +49 (0)69 25 482 1452
www.eurohypo.com

The Stats

Employer Type: Public Company
Ticker Symbol: NHY (Frankfurt)
Chief Executive: Bernd Knobloch
2007 Revenue: €588m
2006 Revenue: €653m
2007 Employees: 2,404
2006 Employees: n/a
No. of Offices: 25

Departments

Public Finance • Real Estate • Treasury

European Locations

Eschborn (HQ)
Austria • Belgium • Czech Republic •
Denmark • Finland • France •
Germany • Greece • Hungary • Italy •
Luxembourg • Netherlands • Poland •
Portugal • Romania • Russia • Slovakia •
Spain • Sweden • Switzerland • Turkey •
United Kingdom

Employment Contacts

Jana Schäfer
CC Human Resources
Tel. +49 (069) 25 48-2 17 80

Klaus Langstroff
CC Human Resources
Tel. +49 (069) 25 48-2 14 22

Link to online email form:
www.eurohypo.com/en/site/header/ka
rriere/index.php

THE BUZZ
WHAT EMPLOYEES AT OTHER FIRMS ARE SAYING

• "Small European player"
• "Mortgage bank"

THE SCOOP

The largest issuer of mortgage bonds in Europe, global specialist bank Eurohypo has, since 2005, been 98 percent owned by Commerzbank after the banking major bought out Dresdner Bank and Deutsche Bank's stakes in the firm. This acquisition by Germany's second-largest bank was Commerzbank's largest ever mergers and acquisitions purchase and was touted as a celebrated entry into the commercial lending sector.

Eurohypo, which divides its business into real estate and public finance specialisations, stands as Germany's tenth-largest bank. Boasting over 240 billion euros in total assets and 5.9 billion euros in equity, it stands among the top bond issuers on the capital market. The bank operates a network of real estate finance focused offices extending across Western and Eastern Europe, the US and Asia, together with public finance centres in Frankfurt and Rome.

Finest at finance

In 2002, Deutsche Bank, Dresdner Bank and Commerzbank finalised their agreement to merge their holdings in Eurohypo, Rheinhyp and Deutsche Hyp to form Eurohypo AG. By 2006, the bank had been named Best Global Commercial Bank in Real Estate in the *Euromoney* Awards of Excellence; a title it defended successfully in 2007. With the bank consolidated into one body, brought together under one roof in the Vitrium in Eschborn in 2004, and finally acquired in its entirety by Commerzbank in 2005, it was ready to begin expansion in earnest.

> 66 The bank operates a network of real estate finance focused offices across Europe, the US and Asia 99

Eyes on the East

With considerable Western European operations in full swing, Eurohypo looked to Asia and Eastern Europe, primarily to establish strongholds in regions that promised growth and pose attractive prospects for real estate developers. In 2006, the bank opened its first office in Tokyo. In early 2007, the firm opened a representative office in Hong Kong, planning to cement its future involvement in China's rapid growth, and begin earnest advances into establishing its network of operations throughout Asia and South-East Asia.

Gold war

Eurohypo has joined the clamour of firms emphasising the growth potential of the Baltic region, thanks to the region's rapid economic development. Most commonly considered among these are the Baltic states of Estonia, Romania, Latvia and Lithuania and Poland. Romania, in particular, has shown especially high growth rates in real estate investments.

In 2007, the company's operations in Eastern Europe were given a boost by the opening of an office in Bucharest, followed by subsequent real estate financings of major projects in the region. Romania's entry into the European Union, effective from January 1, 2007, has been a further incentive for investment.

The activities Eurohypo is conducting in the region have included the 150 million euro funding of two shopping centres in Bucharest, the "Bucuresti Mall" and the "Plaza Romania", considered by Eurohypo to be the nation's two most important shopping complexes. This investment was soon followed up with a high profile Russian investment; a 747 million dollar investment and development financing facility to fund the North Domodedovo Logistics Park, Europe's largest class A logistics complex. The deal was struck with Russia's largest developer of industrial real estate, Eurasia Logistics, and sought to increase activity in the rapidly growing Russian economy as well as creating closer ties with Russian businesses.

> ❝ Eurohypo looked to Asia and Eastern Europe to establish strongholds in regions that promised growth ❞

Easy as HSBC

In mid 2007, Ahsan Ellahi left his position as HSBC's managing director and head of real estate Europe to head Eurohypo's newly created European Structured Finance group. Marrying the financing arms of the real estate investment banking and European debt capital markets teams, the new body focuses on putting together complex financial transactions, including syndications and mezzanine loans. Its primary objective was to offer greater clarity in financial transactions, particularly for international clients as Eurohypo increased its global reach, but also for those more disposed towards using commercial mortgage-backed securities as their financing strategy.

Eye for the arts

The 2007 Georg Baselitz retrospective at London's Royal Academy of Arts, the most comprehensive body of Baselitz's work brought together into one exhibition to date benefited from Eurohypo sponsorship. One of the leading representatives of German painting, the exhibition displayed works from a creative period of over half a century.

GETTING HIRED

Bright lights at the tunnel's end

Eurohypo offers both a graduate training scheme and the opportunity for recent graduates to start work directly, as well as internships for students and training for school-leavers. The graduate training scheme lasts 12 months and a job is guaranteed afterwards in the particular field in which training focuses.

Applicants must have either studied banking or have completed an internship in this area, as well as being fluent in both German and English. Experience in the field of property banking is particularly advantageous and may put you ahead of the pack. The scheme includes both on-the-job training and formal teaching in the form of workshops and seminars. Applications are made via the online system (in German) or by email or post and start dates for the scheme are published on the company website.

The right experience

Internships lasting between two and six months are available to those who have already completed two to three years of study in a banking-related discipline. Applications can be made online for specific openings advertised on the company's job database; if no suitable internship is shown, it is also possible to make a speculative application online or register with the personnel department, who will contact you if an opportunity that matches your candidate profile arises.

All staff at Eurohypo receive both fixed and performance-related pay and the group is known for its flexible working hours. Working together with the "Familien Service" agency (www.familienservice.de), it offers particular assistance with the provision of various forms of childcare, as well as advice on looking after elderly dependents. Around 15 percent of staff is located outside of Germany, with the largest numbers being in New York (6.2 percent) and London (3.2 percent), so there are some opportunities to get a taste of the Eurohypo experience abroad.

FORTIS SA/NV

Rue Royale 20
1000 Brussels,
Belgium
Tel: +32 (0)2 565 11 11

Fortis N.V.
Archimedeslaan 6
3584 BA Utrecht,
The Netherlands
Tel: +31 (0)30 226 26 26
www.fortis.com

The Stats

Employer Type: Public Company
Ticker Symbol: FORB (Euronext
Brussels), FORA (Euronext
Amsterdam)
Chief Executive: Jean-Paul Votron
2007 Revenue: €30.8bn
2007 Profit: €4.0bn
2006 Revenue: €29.5bn
2006 Profit: €4.4bn
No. of Employees: 65,000+
No. of Offices: Offices in more than
50 countries

Departments

Asset Management and Private ·
Banking · Insurance Belgium ·
Insurance International · Insurance
Netherlands · Merchant Banking ·
Retail Banking

European Locations

Brussels, Utrecht (HQ)
Austria · Belgium · Czech Republic ·
Denmark · Finland · France ·
Germany · Guernsey · Greece ·
Hungary · Ireland · Isle of Man · Italy ·
Luxembourg · Monaco · The
Netherlands · Norway · Poland ·
Portugal · Romania · Russia · Spain ·
Switzerland · Turkey · Ukraine · United
Kingdom

Employment Contact

www.fortis.com/career

THE BUZZ
WHAT EMPLOYEES AT OTHER FIRMS ARE SAYING

· "Large commercial bank"
· "Getting bigger and bigger"
· "Coming back, hire good people"
· "Regional"

THE SCOOP

A t its core, Fortis provides a two-pronged service: banking and insurance. But that's not the only reason the firm might give you double vision — Fortis has dual head offices in Belgium and The Netherlands, and its presence is strong in both countries as it continues to expand across Europe and internationally. The bank even has a "twinned share" structure for its stocks, trading on the Brussels and Amsterdam Euronext exchange. Building on its market leadership in financial services in the Benelux countries, Fortis has developed an extensive European footprint and successfully combines banking and insurance skills in growth markets in Europe and Asia.

The Benelux giant has been around in different incarnations for centuries, but it was in 1990 when Fortis really solidified as an entity. The Dutch insurer N.V. AMEV and Dutch bank VSB merged and were followed in financial matrimony by Belgian insurer AG Group. The uniting of the three units marked the first financial merger that crossed national borders.

Transformational acquisition

Fortis seized the unique opportunity in 2007 to be part of what was hailed as the largest and most ambitious takeover in the financial industry to date. The Royal Bank of Scotland, Banco Santander and Fortis together spent 70 billion euros to acquire ABN AMRO in a long and fraught deal that finally saw completion in October 2007. The final piece of the arrangement was Fortis' completion of its 13 billion euro rights issue. ABN AMRO was divided up among the three buyers and for Fortis, the acquisition of the Dutch retail and business operations of ABN AMRO and its global private clients and asset management activities can be described as truly transformational. The move will allow Fortis to accelerate the growth strategy it launched in 2005, underlying its position as one of Europe's most dynamic and sustainable financial services providers.

The tricky part of the process began in earnest once the transaction itself was complete. Fortis acquired ABN's global private clients, global asset management and Dutch retail operations, along with 20 retail branches in Indonesia, four in Malaysia and five in Singapore. In the Netherlands, RBS and Fortis are disentangling those portions taken by Fortis from the wholesale banking division taken by RBS. Fortis will rebrand its current Dutch retail bank with the ABN AMRO name.

With ABN AMRO's Dutch retail operations now in the Fortis family, Fortis has become the number one merchant bank in the Benelux, lending hope to its ambitions to become the best bank in Europe servicing international mid caps and corporates.

Clients of Fortis will have access to its integrated international network of 175 business centres across 20 countries. Additionally, with its unique expertise, Fortis has become a leader and in some cases, an internationally respected leader, in niche markets such as carbon bank trading, trust, renewable energy, commodities, shipping and hedge fund administration.

The historic acquisition clearly set the stage for an exciting future for Fortis. Next to the transition process of disentangling and integrating the ABN AMRO activities, Fortis can look forward to solid long-term growth prospects. The deal will bolster its Benelux core competencies and will give the company the opportunity to leverage its capabilities in bancassurance. The transaction will also create strong asset gathering platforms making Fortis a No. 4 European player in private banking and a top-tier European asset manager.

China, meet Belgium

In November 2007 Chinese insurance firm Ping An became Fortis' largest shareholder after it acquired a 4.18 percent stake in the Belgian bank for 1.8 billion euros. Ping An is based in the South Chinese city of Shenzhen and has a market value of close to 34 billion pounds, it is also 16.8 percent owned by HSBC. Peter Ma,

> " The historic acquisition clearly set the stage for an exciting future for Fortis "

chairman of Ping An, said in *The Times*, "The deal will realise valuable benefits because of Fortis's and Ping An's shared business model of an integrated banking and insurance platform."

Fending off the credit curse

In the global credit turmoil that began in earnest in 2007, Fortis did not emerge unscathed — although it did demonstrate resilience. A 1.5 billion euro writedown on the value of securities affected by the US subprime mortgage market crash took 2007 net profits down by 30 percent. In the wake of this, Fortis's chief executive, Jean-Paul Votron, reassured *The Financial Times* that Fortis had "Taken appropriate steps to curtail [its] CDO activities," while adding that markets would most likely, "Remain challenging for the foreseeable future."

In March 2008 Fortis revealed that Ping An, the Chinese insurer, had upped its stake in Fortis from 4.18 percent to 4.99 percent. It also bought half of Fortis's asset management business for 2.15 billion euros. The new joint asset management business will be re-launched as Fortis Ping An Investments, and will have more than 300 billion euros in assets under management. The deal was part of Fortis's strategy to rebuild its capital base, which took hits from the 2007 writedowns and from the costs of integrating ABN AMRO's operations. Fortis is projected to add approximately 1.4 billion euros to its cash reserves in the coming years — so more deals may be on the way. It's also thought that Ping An may raise its stake in Fortis as high as seven percent in the near future.

The Benelux haven

Earnings fell 31 percent in the first quarter of 2008, Fortis reported, with net profits of 808 million euros compared to 1.167 billion euros in the first quarter of 2007. Total income dropped four percent to 30.7 billion euros, and the bank admitted it lost at least 380 million euros to the world credit meltdown. Chief executive Jean-Paul Votron noted that the damage could have been far more severe: the company's core operations remain in Belgium, The Netherlands and Luxembourg, countries with historically-strong credit, and that insulated Fortis from some of the trouble in global markets. The leading cause of losses in Fortis's banking units were the credit writedowns, but according to Votron, underlying business remained strong.

That said, Fortis's strong balance sheet, robust recurrent earnings and sustained client activity have proved a diversified business mix, confirming the validity of its business model and strategic direction. Votron affirmed, "The environment remains challenging, but we remain firmly committed to delivering on our strategic business plans, including the successful integration of ABN AMRO and the development of our new partnership with Ping An."

More pieces of the ABN AMRO pie

In May 2008 Fortis announced it was planning to take over a 51 percent stake in ABN AMRO Verzekeringen (AAV) from Delta Lloyd, The Netherlands' sixth-largest insurance company. The deal, if completed, would involve a circuitous transaction — because of the ABN AMRO takeover by consortium, ABN AMRO can exercise call option rights to buy back Delta Lloyd's stake in AAV. Fortis's goal is to have ABN AMRO transfer that stake, along with the remaining 49 percent of AAV, to Fortis's business in The Netherlands. According to Fortis, the plans will be final by the end of 2008, with the transaction set to close in the first quarter of 2009.

Clearing across Europe

A Fortis subsidiary won a plum assignment in May 2008: the European Multilateral Clearing Facility (EMCF), a wholly-owned Fortis subsidiary, was selected by the NASDAQ OMX Group to provide clearing services for the NASDAQ OMX Pan-

European Market. A new platform, slated to be the first to connect European liquidity pools with pan-European routing, is scheduled to launch in September 2008 with 300 of the most popular blue chip stocks in Europe. According to Jan Booij, EMCF's managing director, Fortis has "a strong determination to substantially grow the clearing businesses."

For sale: Dutch banking units

After picking up its share of ABN AMRO's business in late 2007, Fortis agreed to unload some of its new purchases in order to comply with the European Commission's anti-trust regulations — as did the other banks involved in the deal. However, it was easier said than done. By mid-2008, reports surfaced that Fortis was struggling to find a buyer for ABN's Dutch commercial advisory and corporate client units. Germany's Deutsche Bank was the only institution to express an interest in the assets and the terms it offered were described as "ridiculous conditions" by Dutch newspapers.

Fortis had pledged to sell the ABN units by July 1, 2008, but that deadline wasn't just about satisfying European regulators. The bank also needed the capital from the sale to finance its ongoing integration with ABN AMRO, which is set to continue through the end of 2009, and to replenish its losses from the credit crisis.

Fortis was finally forced to sell to Deutsche Bank, who paid 300 million euros under the net asset value of the business, taking the Dutch banking operations for 709 million euros in cash. Fortis also agreed to insure ten billion euros worth of risk-weighted assets against unexpected losses for an undisclosed period of time, which some critics could say is a worrying agreement in a time when unexpected losses are rather frequent.

World, meet Fortis

Solidifying its position as a European powerhouse, in June 2008 Fortis launched its first fully-integrated global advertising campaign, adopting the mantra "Life is a curve". The ads, designed by London's Grey Group, were designed to reach viewers via billboards, print media and television programming. The hook? A frank acknowledgement of the risks banking clients face, accompanied by images of rising and falling curves and an exhortation to make thoughtful choices.

Adrian Martorana, head of Fortis's branding and communications department, told the *International Herald Tribune* that in the current economic climate, "Clients don't want picture-perfect promises of something that isn't real." By sounding a note of honesty in its ads, he said, **Fortis** hoped to build trust with consumers, investors and businesses around the world.

GETTING HIRED

Make it fit

Fortis offers a tailor-made programme for graduates, which gives you the chance to broaden your horizons and gain insight in your own abilities. You can get started focusing on one of our businesses being retail banking, asset management and private banking, merchant banking and insurance — or you can start a general management, finance or project and process management route for example.

You get the opportunity to acquire work experience, gain in-depth knowledge and create an extensive network of contacts. A common part provides you with general expertise but each route gives you the opportunity to receive specialised professional training according to your competencies and personal interests. To view what's on offer just click "Students" on the firm's careers page.

Quick Taste

Fortis offers internship opportunities in a range of areas which are available in Belgium and The Netherlands for students in their penultimate year. Bear in mind that preference is given to those pursuing certain disciplines such as economics and law. To apply simply complete the form, in Dutch or French, on the company's website. Job opportunities at Fortis can be found on the company website. Simply click the "apply/vacancies" link to be taken to a job search engine.

Fortis SA/NV

FOX-PITT KELTON
COCHRAN CARONIA WALLER

25 Copthall Avenue
London
EC2R
United Kingdom
Tel: +44 (0) 207 663 6000
www.fpk.com

The Stats

Employer Type: Private Company
Ticker Symbol: n/a
Chief Executive: Giles Fitzpatrick
2007 Revenue: n/a
2007 Profit: n/a
2006 Revenue: n/a
2006 Profit: n/a
No. of Employees: 232
Number of Offices: 7

Departments

Advisory • Corporate Broking • Equity
Capital Markets • Equity Research •
Equity Sales • Equity Sales Trading •
Equity Trading • Finance • Operations •
Legal • Compliance • Technology •
Human Resources

European Locations

London (European HQ)
United Kingdom

Employment Contact

www.fpk.com/x?careers.html

Graduate applications:
graduateinfo@fpk.com
Experienced hire applications:
experiencedhires@fpk.com

Key Competitors

Berstein • Billings • Friedman • KBW •
Ramsey Group • Sanford C

THE BUZZ
WHAT EMPLOYEES AT OTHER FIRMS ARE SAYING

- "Great FIG house with skilled workforce"
- "Narrow focus on financial institutions and research"

THE SCOOP

F ox-Pitt Kelton Cochrane Caronia Waller, or FPKCCW, is an investment bank well regarded for its equity research, which covers the stocks of more than 400 companies and institutions around the globe. The bank plays an important role in high-profile transactions worldwide as an investor, advisor and as a researcher, specialising in banking, insurance and related industries.

Vying for a more established presence in the US, together perhaps with the wordiest moniker on the banking scene, Fox-Pitt Kelton merged with Cochran Caronia Waller on September 4, 2007 to form Fox-Pitt Kelton Cochrane Caronia Waller (FPKCCW). Chicago-based boutique CCW was long known for its specialisms in the property-casualty, life and health industries, and for its research, equity sales, alternative capital raising and M&A advisory product offering.

Since the buyout, FPK has been diversifying from its mainstay as an equities specialist to offer a greater variety of services to its clients. CCW joined forces with FPK after considering sale to other banks. Its co-founders, George Cochran and Len Caronia are co-chairmen of the combined company, while its remaining founder, John Waller, is president. FPK's chief executive, Giles Fitzpatrick, runs the group.

Services provided by the firm include equity brokerage and trading, capital markets services, and mergers and acquisitions advice. FPK clients consist of pension funds, mutual fund managers, insurance companies, bank investment departments, hedge funds and private client asset managers. The bank prides itself on its position as the only vertically integrated investment bank in the world specialising in the financial services industry.

Made in England

FPK was founded in 1971, by Oliver Fox-Pitt and Robin Kelton. The bank was originally built upon the idea of placing American bank and insurance equities with institutions in Europe. Nine years later, the founders opened two more offices in New York and Hartford, Connecticut. In 1985 a corporate finance division was introduced in the New York office, to manage the company's growing list of corporate clients.

Three years later, FPK launched European Financials Product, to focus on European equities. The European corporate finance division was launched in London in 1996, to complement the company's US corporate finance offerings. FPK continued its global expansion in 1998 with the launch of an Asian Financials Product division and opened a corresponding office in Hong Kong in 2000. A Boston office was opened in 2004, FPK's third US office alongside New York and Hartford, Connecticut.

Look who's boss

In the top spot at the London office is chief executive Giles Fitzpatrick, who joined FPK in 2005 as the head of global equities, where he oversaw FPK's equity research, sales, sales trading and equity capital markets divisions.

Prior to joining FPK, Fitzpatrick secured more than 20 years of equity markets experience running trading, heading up sales and then secondary equities at the UK broker Hoare Govett. He later worked as global head of trading and head of European equities at Amsterdam-based ABN AMRO. Fitzpatrick was also a member of the London Stock Exchange Markets Committee and The LIBA Securities Trading Committee.

Trickle-down equity

Between 1999 and February 2006, FPK was owned by the famous reinsurer Swiss Re — the firm that commissioned the iconic London Swiss Rebuilding, also known (and identified) as "The Gherkin". At that time, in February 2006, Swiss Re announced its intention to sell FPK to a consortium led by private equity firm J.C. Flowers & Co. and

> “ It was originally built upon the idea of placing American bank and insurance equities with institutions in Europe ”

FPK management. However, Swiss Re retained a minority stake in the company. Based in Zurich, Swiss Re provides reinsurance and risk management products to clients in more than 30 countries.

The transfer of ownership, which was completed in June 2006, greatly reinforced the firm's independence by putting equity in the hands of FPK staff and managers, a crucial component of the firm's ability to deliver objective research and advice. Globally, FPK is considered a "Co-Lead of Choice" in the primary market for financial services equity issuance, where it has acted as the co-lead manager with companies such as Morgan Stanley, Goldman Sachs and Merrill Lynch.

GETTING HIRED

Ticking all the boxes

To apply to FPK you'll need to have achieved more than 300 UCAS points (that's three Bs or better at A level) or equivalent — as well as a 2:1 honours degree. The company also wants candidates with strong analytical and quantitative skills, proficiency in English and another European language, together with relevant work experience.

Keep in mind that FPK's only European office is in London, so you'll need the right to work in the UK to be eligible for a position. To be considered for a vacancy, send your CV and a covering letter along to graduateinfo@fpk.com. Experienced hires should send CVs and covering letters to experiencedhires@fpk.com.

HBOS

The Mound
Edinburgh
EH1 1YZ
Scotland
Tel: +44 (0) 131 470 2000
www.hbosplc.com

The Stats

Employer Type: Public Company
Ticker Symbol: HBOS (LSE)
Chairman: Lord Dennis Stevenson
Group Executive Director: Andrew
Hornby
2007 Revenue: £21.2bn
2007 Profit: £4.1bn
2006 Revenue: £22.7bn
2006 Profit: £3.9bn
No. of Employees: 74,000
No. of Offices: Offices throughout the
United Kingdom and worldwide

Departments

Asset Management • Corporate
Banking • Insurance • Investment
Retail Banking • Treasury Management

European Locations

Edinburgh (HQ)
Offices in 17 countries globally

Key Competitors

Abbey National • Lloyds TSB • Royal
Bank of Scotland Group

Pluses

• Good opportunities for
  advancement
• "Relaxed but professional culture"

Minuses

• Conservative dress code
• Limited meritocracy

Employment Contact

For graduates:
www.hbosbeamazed.co.uk
www.hbosplc.com (Click on
"Recruitment")

THE BUZZ
WHAT EMPLOYEES AT OTHER FIRMS ARE SAYING

• "Strong presence in the UK"
• "Mid-sized Uk retail bank"
• "Mortgage expertise"
• "Markets oriented"

THE SCOOP

Formed from Halifax's 2001 merger with Bank of Scotland, the UK's oldest commercial bank, HBOS plc is the holding company of the HBOS Group, a UK-based banking and insurance company. Prior to Halifax's acquisition, Bank of Scotland was riding high in its home country with both a strong retail banking business and a strong corporate banking business.

At the time of the acquisition, Halifax was a UK giant: the largest provider of mortgages and savings in the country, offering credit cards, life assurance and general insurance products among its services. The merger was greeted by the industry, media and analysts as the creation of a fifth superpower in UK banking, as HBOS had the wherewithal to rival the established "Big Four" UK retail banks.

Who's the boss?

As of 2008, the firm claims to be the UK's biggest mortgage lender. The new and improved incarnation of the Bank of Scotland also boasts the biggest private shareholder group in the region. Primarily active in UK and Australian markets, the company operates in five business divisions: retail, corporate, insurance and investment, international, and treasury and asset management.

Alongside Halifax and Bank of Scotland, some of HBOS' most recognisable brands include Intelligent Finance, which offers consumer banking via the internet and telephone. Birmingham Midshire, which offers lending, savings and general insurance, and Colleys, a surveying business. The British banking giant is ranked No. 14 in Commercial & Savings banks on the much-respected Fortune Global 500 list, which is ranked by worldwide annual revenue. Impressively, the bank is also ranked in eighth place on *Fortune Magazine*'s 2007 list of Ten-Most "Accountable Big Companies. Ranked ninth in 2006, HBOS was awarded such a high ranking due to the fact that it publishes a list of 48 social and environmental performance metrics and ties 25 percent of senior managers' bonuses to meeting goals according to these measures.

Hot gossip

HBOS share prices plunged by 17 percent in March 2008 after false rumours were spread that it had sought emergency funding from the Bank of England. The rumours were strongly denied by HBOS and the joint Bank of England and the industry watchdog Financial Services Authority's (FSA) investigation into possible stock manipulation was soon underway. HBOS itself approached experienced stockbroker and founder of Schroders Securities, Richard Wyatt, for assistance on detecting any possible unlawful trading. In *The Financial Times*, HBOS representatives were quoted as saying: "The FSA is in the driving seat, but we are trying to help them ... It is important that the culprits are caught. What happened last week was very serious indeed, not just for our stock but for the banking system in general."

That said, the HBOS share price recovered in no time at all and confidence was aided when 250 of the bank's loyal senior managers bought six million pounds worth of shares.

Investing in food

A year earlier, in February 2007, HBOS made headlines when it announced that it had bought an additional five percent of the shareholding in Sainsbury's Bank, an upcoming contender on the banking scene, for 21 million pounds. Sainsbury's Bank is now a 50-50 joint venture between HBOS and Sainsbury's, as opposed to the 55–45 structure which previously existed. The board of Sainsbury's Bank consists of eight directors — three from both HBOS and Sainsbury's and two from Sainsbury's Bank.

> ❝ HBOS plc has donated more than £19.5 million in philanthropic gestures ❞

A helping hand

Charity is hardly a token consideration at the firm. Since the early nineties, HBOS plc has donated more than 19.5 million pounds in philanthropic gestures through its charity credit cards. In this scheme, HBOS donates to a charity of the customer's choice every time the card is used. In fact, in 2000, Halifax entered the legendary *Guinness Book of Records* as the world's most successful charity card provider. The group has actively donated to Cancer Research UK, the National Society for the Prevention of Cruelty to Children and the Scottish Society for the Prevention of Cruelty to Animals, as well as to various homeless charities. In 2006, the company announced it would install 100 new fee-free ATMs in poor and rural areas in Scotland and England.

Great Scot!

HBOS' corporate headquarters is one of the most recognisable buildings in Scotland. Located on the hillside that rises in the middle of Edinburgh, The Mound, HBOS' headquarters are an important city landmark. More than 200 years old, aside from housing HBOS, the building displays specially commissioned works from contemporary Scottish artists.

In June 2006, HBOS acquired the draft of the last will and testament of Scottish novelist and poet Sir Walter Scott, whose own history is actually closely linked to that of the Bank of Scotland. In 1826, Scott came to the defence of the bank when Parliament attempted to prevent the issue of notes for under five pounds. Scott wrote a series of letters to the *Edinburgh Weekly Journal*, which were collected and reprinted as a pamphlet. The letters served to force the government to relent and allow banks to continue issuing those always useful one pound notes.

GETTING HIRED

A summer to write home about ...

HBOS offers a retail, insurance and investment internship and a summer placement scheme for university students in their penultimate year. You'll need a predicted 2:1 degree and some prior work experience under your belt, and the internship should form a requisite part of a degree course. The retail programmes division is HBOS' core project management function for retail operations. The course lasts for one year and will give you a grounding in project management and a range of retail business areas.

The summer placements begin in June and last for eight weeks. They give candidates the opportunity to work alongside human resources teams on real projects, covering areas including resourcing, learning and development, graduate recruitment and business area change programmes. Both programmes are paid and based in Halifax, West Yorkshire.

Anything you say, HBOS

HBOS provides a full range of graduate training schemes, which vary in length from the standard two years to a maximum of seven years for the actuarial scheme, depending on how long you take to qualify. Schemes are available in the following divisions: actuarial, commercial leaders, risk, IT (technical), IT project management, corporate finance, financial markets, treasury, front office sales and trading, financial markets treasury, business leaders, HR, legal, marketing, audit and sales management .

Application requirements range from a 2:2 in any discipline to a 2:1 in a technical discipline such as maths or engineering. Select "the graduate schemes" on the graduate careers page and take a look at the schemes on offer from the drop-down menu to see specific details. Closing dates for application are in late March but make sure you check the website for exact dates, as they can vary.

Online application includes a competency test. If you're successful here you'll be asked to complete a numerical reasoning test, followed by a telephone interview if you make it this far. The final stage will see you invited to a graduate training centre, where you'll be given a range of tests.

Stake out your personal page

Check out the "recruitment" link at www.hbosplc.com to learn about open positions for graduates and experienced professionals. From there, you can use the "search and apply" function or register and receive your own "personal pages," where you'll have the opportunity to upload everything from a standard CV to a PowerPoint presentation for the firm to peruse. An analyst in Edinburgh confides that getting into HBOS is "not too difficult" if you're prepared. With one interview session consisting of an MS Excel test, a GI Analysis test, a group exercise, a presentation, a formal interview and verbal and numerical reasoning tests, it is reasonably rigorous however.

Interview experiences run the gamut, sources report. One insider says he "did not get asked job-specific questions" and that "they have the same questions for every vacancy." Another contact says "the interview process can be a nightmare" with "meaningless aptitude tests and endless streams of questions that make it nearly impossible not to repeat answers. By the end of the interview, the interviewer and the interviewee are totally exhausted." The insider goes on to add that "I learned later that some managers bypass normal procedures to make the interview process more effective and streamlined."

OUR SURVEY SAYS

Life on the inside

Employees' perspective on HBOS' office culture vary. One employee in Edinburgh calls the bank "a fairly good place to work," while another calls it "nepotistic," and bemoans the absence of a meritocracy.

The dress code is "conservative" but it will come as a relief to prospective employees that "you're not expected to work late every day," a senior analyst tells us. Opportunities for advancement are good, according to another analyst and "after working as an analyst for a year to two years, you can assume a senior analyst role." However, he goes on to say "from there on it is up to you as to when and if you are promoted."

A Leeds-based employee calls the firm "a good employer, with a relaxed but professional culture." While diverse, the workforce is "a bit on the young side," he adds. "The firm's main strength is the time it invests in training and developing the workforce" he goes on to say, "Closely followed by its massive client base and the high potential to increase your earnings."

Money, money, money

At HBOS, you can look forward to free private health care with BUPA, 28 days annual holiday, unlimited sick days, discount dental, free HBOS shares and a range of discounts, according to Edinburgh sources. Other bonuses mentioned included a study leave package and a "pretty good year end bonus."

HYPOVEREINSBANK / UNICREDIT GROUP

Arabellastr.12
81925 Munich
Germany
Tel: + 49 89 378 0
www.hvbgroup.com

The Stats

Employer Type: Public Company
Ticker Symbol: HVM (Frankfurt)
Chairman, Supervisory Board:
Alessandro Profumo
Chief Executive: Wolfgang Sprissler
2007 Revenue: €3.03bn
2007 Profit: €2.05bn
2006 Revenue: €2.25bn
2006 Profit: €1.64bn
No. of Employees: 25,363
No. of Offices: 850

Departments

Corporates • Markets & Investment
Banking • Retail • Wealth Management

European Locations

Munich (HQ)
Germany • Luxembourg • Russia •
United Kingdom

9,714 subsidiaries worldwide of which
729 are in Germany and 429 in
Bavaria

Employment Contact

See "Jobs & Karriere" section on
www.hvbgroup.com

Key Competitors

Commerzbank • Deutsche Bank •
Dresdner Bank

THE BUZZ
WHAT EMPLOYEES AT OTHER FIRMS ARE SAYING

• "Mid-sized German player"
• "Get a lot of business from small cap
  clients"

THE SCOOP

HypoVereinsbank/UniCredit Group is ranked No. 7 on the Association of German Banks' top 100 banks and has some solid statistics to its name: more than 25,000 employees, 850 branch offices and 4.3 million customers. HVB focuses on European retail and mid-cap customers and also works in capital market and trading activities. It is a leading real estate lender in Europe with a loan portfolio of 325 billion euros. HypoVereinsbank is divided, as is its parent company UniCredit, into four divisions: retail, corporate, wealth management and markets and investment banking.

HypoVereinsbank AG (HVB) has been a member of the UniCredit Group since 2005. According to UniCredit, it is the first banking institution in Europe to truly deserve the title of "European bank." As a result of the Unicredit move, in January 2006, HypoVereinsbank began offering free cashpoint withdrawals from UniCredit Banca cashpoints in Italy and from all Bank Austria Creditanstalt cashpoints in Austria, perhaps as a way of uniting UniCredit users in different countries. HypoVereinsbank now has approximately 11,000 cashpoints available for use free of charge, knocking out the regular surcharge of at least 3.95 euros.

To its credit

As part of its consolidation manoeuvres, UniCredit Group adopted a "master brand strategy" for its brands. Under this strategy, the "UniCredit Group" master brand was leveraged as an umbrella brand across all the group's business divisions and the countries in which it operates. Most banks under its aegis changed their names to UniCredit Bank, but those with highly recognised brands of their own such as its German banks kept their existing local names, just adopting Unicredit's visual identity.

Buying and selling

In July 2006, HypoVereinsbank (HVB) announced that it was to sell its three Activest firms to Pioneer Global Asset Management, a UniCredit subsidiary, for 600 million euros. HVB maintained a partnership with the transferred Activest firms. Pioneer also agreed to buy investment fund NORDINVEST Norddeutsche Investment-Gesellschaft from HypoVereinsbank in January 2007.

Alhough it sold off the Activest businesses, HypoVereinsbank continued investing. In June 2006, in an acquisition for the UniCredit Group, HypoVereinsbank entered into an agreement with Nordea Bank Finland plc to purchase an additional 20 percent stake in ZAO International Moscow Bank (IMB) for roughly 395 million US dollars. Acquiring Nordea's stake increased HVB's participation from 52.9 percent to 79.3

percent of IMB's voting capital, thereby solidifying HVB's controlling position in the bank. In May 2006, HVB and IMB jointly tendered a structured export finance loan of 77 million euros to OAO Ural Steel to fund the construction of a new steel mill. This allowed Ural Steel to finally tap into the international export market.

HypoVereinsbank (HVB) has other interests in Eastern Europe. In June 2006, the bank announced it would be advising the Croatian government on the restructuring and privatisation of its shipyards. Shipping is the Balkan state's second-highest grossing industry and Croatia is hoping to make its shipyards internationally competitive. HVB's global shipping branch in Hamburg is one of the world's leading ship financiers, with a portfolio of over 5.5 billion euros. HVB bought a 26.44 percent stake in International Moscow Bank from Nordea Bank in October 2006 for 395 million dollars, boosting the 50 percent stake it already held. IMB is Russia's first joint-venture bank, formed in 1989 with Nordea, a financial services group in the Nordic and Baltic regions.

In January 2007, HVB transferred its 77.53 percent stake in Bank Austria Creditansalt (BA-CA) to its parent UniCredit for about 12.5 billion euros. HVB also sold its 100 percent stake in HVB Latvia to BA-CA for 35 million euros plus 40 million euros of capital it invested in August 2006. The deal also included selling a 70 percent stake in International Moscow Bank for one million euros, with the option to buy five percent more. HVB also unloaded HVB Bank Ukraine to UniCredit for 83 million euros.

Shedding some real estate

HVB sold a real estate portfolio with 86 properties to Varde Partners in December 2006 to shed its non-core holdings. Most of the buildings were office space that weren't being used by HVB. The bank said at the time of the deal that it didn't want to hold real estate used by third parties, and that the buildings were non-strategic holdings. The same month the bank sold a 960 million euro real estate loan portfolio to Goldman Sachs after an auction. The deal includes loans to 1,100 HypoVereinsbank / UniCredit Group borrowers.

GETTING HIRED

Something for everyone

HypoVereinsbank / UniCredit Group run a series of one-year graduate programmes to provide you with the theoretical knowledge and hands-on experience to kit you out for the banking world. The programmes are available in all of its business segments, from private to corporate banking. Your career will most likely kick off in one of HVB's German offices, so you'll need a strong command of German from the outset. If you're a non-German speaker, you should look into the Markets & Investment Banking graduate programme which is conducted in English. The kick-off for the MIB Graduate programme could be in several locations, such as Munich, London, Milan, Vienna, Warsaw or Moscow. The programmes are explained in detail on www.hvb.de/jobs.

Been there, done that

If you're an experienced hire, you can find HVB's vacancy listings by clicking "jobbörse." Once again, you'll need to be fluent in German. If you have your heart set on a job in Italy, Austria or Central and Eastern Europe, take a look at www.unicreditgroup.eu or www.ba-ca.com.

Moving up from the inside

Getting in the door initially might be your biggest hurdle at HVB. The bank recruits internally as well as "at the universities in Germany and Italy." But insiders say landing a position is "neither very easy nor nearly impossible," although current candidates have the best shot at filling open slots-one insider says that "for the hiring of many jobs, we promote juniors to the intermediate level." To apply for a position, click on the jobs link on the main site at www.hypovereinsbank.de. Past the "initial interviews," you can expect a "full round of six to eight interviews in one day," says one source.

ICAP

2 Broadgate
London
EC2M 7UR
United Kingdom
Tel: + 44 (0) 20 7000 5000
www.icap.com

The Stats

Employer Type: Public Company
Ticker Symbol: IAP (LSE)
Chief Executive: Michael Spencer
2007 Revenue: £1.3bn
2007 Profit: £330m
2006 Revenue: £1.1bn
2006 Profit: £252m
No. of Employees: 3,900
No. of Offices: 31

Departments

Electronic Broking • Information
Services • Voice Broking

European Locations

London (HQ)
Denmark • Germany • The
Netherlands • Norway • Poland •
Spain • United Kingdom

Employment Contact

General recruitment:
recruitment@icap.com

Graduates and students:
ukgraduates@icap.com

Tel: +44 20 70 005000
www.icap.com/careers

THE BUZZ
WHAT EMPLOYEES AT OTHER FIRMS ARE SAYING

• "Growing fast"
• "Unknown"

THE SCOOP

CAP is the world's premier voice and electronic inter-dealer broker and source of global market information and commentary for professionals in the international financial markets. ICAP provides a specialist broking service to trading professionals in the global wholesale financial markets. Its customers include investment and commercial banks. ICAP covers a broad range of OTC financial products and services in commodities, FX, interest rates, credit and equity markets. The electronic networks deliver global connectivity to customers seeking unparalleled liquidity and flow in an orderly marketplace.

Working across Europe

ICAP's head office in London is home to 1,250 employees, including 740 brokers. The firm has six other offices in Europe, each providing unique services to its region. ICAP's Copenhagen office was established in 1968 and has expanded to include approximately 40 staffers that focus on money market products, foreign exchange and derivatives, with an emphasis on Scandinavian currencies.

In Spain, ICAP operates via a 25 percent shareholding in Grupo Corrataje e Informacion Monetaria y de Divisas — its office is in Madrid. In Amsterdam, ICAP is represented by ICAP Energy's Dutch arm is APB Energy, located in Amsterdam, which offers a full-service energy brokerage. It is a leading

> " ICAP's head office in London is home to 1,250 employees "

electricity and energy broker in natural gas, coal and weather derivatives in seven countries. Nordic operations, in Bergen, Norway, are also conducted through APB Energy.

In Germany, ICAP's business was built by a series of acquisitions, starting with Intercapital's 1998 takeover of Exco plc. ICAP's Frankfurt office focuses on money markets, fixed income and interbank deposits. Frankfurt works in close collaboration with London. It also offers execution in spot transactions, switches, spread trades and orders on the Frankfurt Stock Exchange. Finally, ICAP's Polish office, in Warsaw, traces its roots to 1998, when it was known as Harlow Butler Sp.zo.o. Now it covers the Polish government bond market, swaps, forward rate agreement, foreign exchange and money markets, and is active in both local currency and deposits in US dollars as well as major European currencies — and it is staffed by only 14 people.

A force to be reckoned with

ICAP was formed in 1999 when Garban plc and Intercapital plc merged. Garban's strength in government and corporate bonds, interest rate products and money market instruments was combined with Intercapital's expertise in interest rate swaps and options, commodity swaps, illiquid securities and foreign exchange options. Initially called Garban-Intercapital plc, the joint entity was renamed ICAP in 2001. Today, ICAP is led by Intercapital Founder Michael Spencer and employs more than 3,900 people in 30 offices around the world.

In April 2006, ICAP agreed to acquire the total share capital of EBS Group Limited, a leading provider of foreign exchange trading and market data solutions to the professional spot foreign exchange community. Since then, the EBS platform, one of the leading electronic broking platforms for spot FX, has formed an integral part of the expansion of ICAP's electronic broking business.

ICAP makes the list

ICAP joined the UK's FTSE 100 Index in June 2006, replacing BAA, the world's biggest airport owner, which had been on the index for almost 19 years. BAA was removed following its acquisition by Spain's Grupo Ferrovial SA. At the time of its indexing, ICAP reported a market value of 3.18 billion pounds.

Off to China

Not wanting to miss the boat of opportunity in the fast-growing Asian markets, in July 2006, ICAP announced a joint venture with the China Foreign Exchange Trade System and National Interbank Funding Center (CFETS). The new entity, Shanghai CFETS-ICAP International Money Broking Co. Ltd., will provide voice broking services to the money, bond and derivatives markets in both the Chinese currency and international markets. The move — and the opening of the CFETS-ICAP office in Shanghai in October 2007 — is part of ICAP's strategy to gain a foothold in Chinese inter-bank financial markets.

Scoping the market for an exchange

As rumours of a possible takeover of the London Stock Exchange swirled in 2006, ICAP's name emerged as a potential buyer. Although Nasdaq owns 25 percent of the London exchange, the LSE rejected Nasdaq's 4.2 billion dollar takeover offer in March 2006. In September, ICAP revealed it had held merger talks with the LSE, which had already turned down offers from Deutsche Borse, Euronext, Macquarie Bank and the New York Stock Exchange.

However, the initial round of ICAP-LSE talks didn't result in a deal because the LSE's 2.6 billion pound valuation was too pricey for ICAP. Since then, ICAP has announced that it is itself applying for exchange status as a Recognised Investment Exchange, in order to have the option to list new products in an exchange traded environment.

One day's work

ICAP holds an annual Charity Day — "a day on which all revenues and commissions are given away to just a few charities." In December 2007, the firm celebrated the 15th anniversary of Charity Day by raising a record 9.2 million pounds. On Charity Day, the proceeds from the firm's global broking activities go to approximately 80 selected charities worldwide. Since Charity Day began in 1992, ICAP has raised more than 42 million pounds for various good causes.

GETTING HIRED

Do your homework

ICAP runs full-time and internship programmes in its broking (voice, electronic, shipping) and accounting departments. You'll need a predicted or actual 2:1 in any discipline, and the company recommends that you learn all there is to know about ICAP to improve your chances of success. If you have a second language, you're already at a distinct advantage.

The full-time programmes last for at least one year, and their structure varies with the division you're working with. In general, you'll go through an orientation period, followed by classroom training to hone your technical skills, before being placed on several rotations in company offices.

A suppprtive structure

The summer internship programmes last for ten weeks, and could land you with a job before you've even finished university. With the assistance of a mentor, you'll receive technical training, followed by two five-week desk rotations, giving you a look inside the company and a selection of its product areas. On top of this you'll be given a group project to complete as part of your overall assessment. You'll find a link to apply at the bottom of each page on the careers site, and any queries can be directed to ukgraduates@icap.com.

ING

ING House
Amstelveenseweg 500
Amsterdam, 1081 KL
Netherlands
Tel: +31 (0) 20 54 15 411
www.ing.com

The Stats

Employer Type: Public
Ticker Symbol: ING (NYSE)
Chairman: Michel Tilmant
2007 Revenue: €76.5bn
2007 Profit: €9.5bn
2006 Revenue: €73.6bn
2006 Profit: €8.03bn
No. of Employees: 120,000
No. of Offices: Offices around the
world

Departments

Asset Management • ING Direct •
Insurance • Retail Banking • Wholesale
Banking

European Locations

Amsterdam (HQ)
Austria • Belgium • Bulgaria • Czech
Republic • France • Germany • Greece •
Hungary • Ireland • Italy • Luxembourg •
The Netherlands • Poland • Romania •
Russia • Slovakia • Spain • Sweden •
Switzerland • Ukraine • United
Kingdom

Employment Contact

www.ing.jobs
www.ingtalentprogramme

Key Competitors

AXA • Citi • Fortis

Pluses

• "Employee friendly" and "flexible"
• Good benefits

Minuses

• Little international mobility
• Few women in management roles

THE BUZZ
WHAT EMPLOYEES AT OTHER FIRMS ARE SAYING

• "Large commercial"
• "Getting bigger"
• "Mid-sized Dutch player"
• "Regional bank"

VAULT career library

THE SCOOP

n an era where banks and corporations often have tunnel-vision when it comes to developing markets like China and India, Dutch banking giants ING Group are comfortably not limiting their options. They're looking in their own backyard to pursue organic growth. Despite the fact Western Europe is a bit oversaturated when it comes to banking and financial services — particularly retail banking — ING seems rather undaunted about expanding from the ground up in a potentially lucrative market for the group, such as Germany.

However, in June 2008, ING quashed much existing public speculation that the global financial services group may be about to bid for Germany's Deutsche Postbank AG, citing the group's desire to strictly pursue "organic growth" as its main reason. The group's chief executive Michel Tilmant told media that growing in Germany was "The best way to conquer saturated markets via our direct banking unit ING."

Clearly ING is not willing to let the grim economic climate of summer 2008 (influenced by the global subprime crisis) influence the group's desire to expand … and conquer. It's all about adjusting strategy — and that is what ING seems to have done exceptionally well over the decades.

Building a name

While it holds a strong presence in the global arena, ING is the number one financial services company on its own turf: Belgium, The Netherlands and Luxembourg. Within its home market, ING provides its clients with banking, insurance and asset management services.

In the 2007 Forbes Global 2000, ING was the tenth-largest company in the world by assets. The Dutch bank provides banking, investments, life insurance and retirement services to more than 75 million customers in over 50 countries. Based on market capitalisation, ING ranks among the 20-largest financial institutions in the world, and among the top ten in Europe. Moreover, the Dutch giant is the world's largest direct bank with more than 20 million customers in nine large countries. As an asset management firm, ING manages around 635 billion euros in assets and in real estate, and has the world's biggest portfolio of real estate investments

The firm has managed to gain a strong foothold in today's largest markets such as North America, Western Europe, Japan and Australia, and a strong presence in the most attractive developing markets in Asia-Pacific, Central Europe and Latin America. In Asia Pacific, ING is the second-largest international life insurer and the second-largest regional investment manager. Its regional accomplishments don't stop there — ING is also the number one pension provider and number two life insurer in Central and Eastern Europe (CEE). The firm is also the number two pension provider in Latin America and maintains retail banking positions in Poland, Turkey and Romania. Thomson Financial ranked ING 23rd for announced mergers and acquisitions activity in France in 2007, up from 34th place in 2006. The eight deals announced in 2007 amounted to a rank value of 5.1 billion US dollars and a market share of 1.6 percent.

A six-armed giant

ING Group has six main business areas and divisions. In terms of banking, the main divisions are: wholesale banking, retail banking and ING Direct, which is a direct savings bank. ING's retail banking market encompasses the Netherlands, Belgium, Poland, Romania and India. Additionally, private banking is offered in The Netherlands, Belgium, Switzerland, Luxembourg and selected countries in Asia.

ING Direct is the virtual retail-banking brand for the bank, and provides ATM, telephone and online banking services to private clients in Australia, Canada, France, Germany, Austria, Italy, Spain, the UK, the US and Japan. The ING Card division falls under the ING Direct umbrella and manages a credit card portfolio within the Benelux region.

Wholesale banking operations are divided into five key segments — clients, network, products, corporate finance and equity markets, and financial markets. Within the Benelux countries, ING provides a full range of products to corporations and institutions. Elsewhere, ING Wholesale Banking offers selected products. At the beginning of 2008, ING Wholesale Banking launched it's fitter, focused strategy to become the number one bank in The Netherlands and Belgium as well as the top five bank in CEE, a top five player in payments and cash management and lease in Europe and a top-ten player in structured finance globally.

> ❝ The Dutch giant is the world's largest direct bank with more than 20 million customers in nine countries ❞

Making sure everyone is covered

In addition, the group has three major insurance divisions, for markets in Europe, the Americas and Asia-Pacific. The three insurance divisions are divided by geography, with variations in products offered across each group. Insurance Europe covers all of the company's insurance activities for The Netherlands, Belgium, Spain, Greece and Central Europe.

In Europe, insurance represents approximately 23 percent of ING's total profit, mostly through sales of life insurance. Insurance Europe also offers non-life insurance to clients in The Netherlands and Belgium. Insurance Americas handles all insurance and asset management in the Americas, particularly in the US where it offers retirement services, annuities and life insurance. This business provides roughly 20 percent of ING's total profit. ING's Insurance Americas business operates in Canada, Mexico, Chile, Brazil and Peru. The group's Insurance Asia-Pacific business operates in the fast-growing markets of China, India and Thailand, and mainly offers life insurance and asset and wealth management services.

The shores of America

During 2007, ING Insurance Americas continued to hone its strategy, focusing resources on higher-growth markets including those for investment products, life insurance and retirement services in the US and Latin America. In 2008, ING continued looking into Latin America's rapidly growing pensions and life insurance markets, with a view to becoming the top operator in the region in the next few years. Focusing on acquisitions and organic growth to build its presence, ING began eyeing up pension companies, asset managers, life insurance and distribution networks in the region, and steering clear of the already consolidated retail banking sector.

"I think you will probably see us being very active over the next 12 to 24 months," Carlos Muriel, ING's regional head in Latin America, stated in *The Financial Times*. "What we foresee is a development similar to what the US had in the 1950s with the baby boomers," he said, with reference to the young populations, rapidly developing middle classes and macroeconomic stability now present in most Latin American countries.

In 2007, ING announced the acquisitions of pension business in Argentina, Chile, Colombia, Mexico and Uruguay and became the second-largest pension fund manager in Latin-America with 40 billion euros in pension assets under management in the region. That same year, ING's Latin American operations contributed 237 million euros to the group's pre-tax profit — 12 percent of ING's Americas Insurance business. The intention is to have the region generating 25 percent within three to five years.

Seriously Dutch history

ING can boast more than a century of history behind it, beginning with Dutch bank De Nederlanden and Nationale Levensverzekering-Bank. Founded in 1845 and 1863 respectively, the two companies came together 100 years later to form Nationale-Nederlanden, which became the largest insurer in The Netherlands. NMB Postbank Groep came about in 1986 after the merger of NMB and Postbank. The latter arose from the earlier merger between Rijkspostspaarbank (founded in 1881) and Postcheque-en Girodienst (founded 1918).

Today's ING was formed through the 1991 merger of prominent Dutch banks Nationale-Nederlanden and NMB Postbank Group. Out of this union arose the first Dutch banking and insurance giant the world had seen. Since then, the group has expanded to become an international financial services provider. At the time of the merger, the company was known as Internationale Nederlanden Groep, this was swiftly abbreviated to "ING" by market commentators. The new company took the cue, re-branded straight away and changed its legal name to ING, and currently offers banking, investments, life insurance and retirement services to more than 75 million customers in over 50 countries.

East is east

Recognising the importance of China's economic growth and development, ING has been steadily building up a presence in the country since the turn of the millennium. ING is currently active in 12 cities in China, operating in life insurance, retail banking, corporate and investment banking, asset management and properties development.

In March 2005, ING purchased a 19.9 percent stake in Bank of Beijing, one of China's largest city banks. According to ING, the deal, worth 166 million euros, was part of a broader strategic alliance. Founded in 1996, Bank of Beijing, which was renamed from Beijing City Commercial Bank, is now China's second-largest city commercial bank. The bank employs more than 3,600 people in 120 branches and at the time of purchase had total assets of 18.9 billion euros. In December 2006, ING received approval from China's Insurance Regulatory Commission to set up life insurance branch operations in the Henan Province in China, the largest in terms of population. ING Capital Life will partner with Beijing Capital Group to offer products to approximately 100 million people.

Bidding on brokers

ING's online banking arm, ING Direct, made a bid for German direct mortgage broker InterHyp in May 2008, offering 64 euros a share, or 416 million euros of equity value. At a time when mortgage broking is a phrase that strikes fear into bankers' hearts, the move indicated confidence in the residential mortgage sector in Germany. The confidence was partly due to the face that, unlike the US, UK and Spanish markets, the German market has not experienced a major boom and so is unlikely to suffer a major bust.

ING Direct will maintain InterHyp's business model, brand and management structure, and will roll out its "open architecture" broking model, which involves working with multiple lenders, throughout Europe. The co-founders of InterHyp, Robert Haselsteiner and Marcus Wolsdorf, will sell their combined 32 percent stake, and will remain with the firm. ING currently has a mortgage book of 35 billion euros in Germany.

GETTING HIRED

If you're a Master

For graduates with a Master's degree and no more than two years of work experience, there is the possibility to start within ING as a trainee in one of the ING Talent Programmes, most of which have a duration of three years. To be eligible for the Talent Programme you need to have a good command of English and show that you have developed extra curricuae besides your studies.

Applications are made online at www.ingtalentprogramme.com. Your application, consisting of a curriculum vitae and a motivation letter, will be assessed by the recruitment department. Once you're through the initial screening, you'll be invited to complete a 60-minute capacity test. If you complete the test successfully, a telephone or face-to-face interview will ensue. The fourth step in the selection procedure is an assessment by an external assessment agent. The last step is a panel interview with senior management, which will take place in The Netherlands.

Vacancies for experienced hires at ING are listed on the company's regional websites. Just click the world map on the main careers page and select the country you want to work in. There are multiple ways to join ING, from an internship and traineeships to lateral job entry. To learn more about jobs and internships, follow the links from the company careers page (www.ing.jobs) to the localised websites of its various regional operations.

Don't lose sleep over it

When asked about the firm's intervew process, one recent hire based in Amsterdam tells us "I had a three-day interview session, with three to four interviews, a panel interview and an external assessment". "The questions I was asked varied, although they were mostly general as I was going for a management trainee position." The three-day assessment process is the norm with this firm and the sorts of things involved include "a knowledge assessment, a motivation meeting, and a personal assessment."

As far as internships go it can be an advantage to have been in a summer job at the firm, "because you will know people from within," a manager tells us. But the consensus among respondents was that internships are "not that important when it comes to getting a job". One notes, "I don't think your chances of employment post-internship increase that much. But it does help."

OUR SURVEY SAYS

You can still live for the weekend

The majority of respondents describe an average 40-50 hour working week. A project manager praises the fact that working hours are, "understood in a very good way. It is not the number of hours that counts, but the work you can do during those hours." An investment analyst tells us, "They're really quite flexible, as long as you meet the objectives. I arrive before 9:30 am and usually leave at 7pm, with a one to two-hour break during the day." Weekend work is a rare occurrence, he says, although one contact in Belgium points out, "My branch is open at the weekend, so I need to be there from time-to-time on Saturdays." He assures us that for doing that, he is "compensated" by the firm.

"My contract is for 36 hours a week," a trainee tells us, "So I have a day off every other week. I work eight hours a day." He notes that he is allowed to work at home one day a week and with his "own targets and responsibilities", he's quite satisfied. "How I manage to achieve them is up to me and that gives me some freedom, which I believe is very important for engaging employees."

Life in a performance culture

There is a never-ending effort to bring people to a higher level of knowledge and experience at ING, says a project manager, noting that ING's culture is focused on challenging people in their job and is still trying to find new and more frequent ways to identify those challenges. While the culture does "depend on your department and location," in general it's a "very informal, friendly environment" in which to develop your skills. An employee in Amsterdam tells us, "It's a performance culture — very open and egalitarian. A bit bureaucratic sometimes, but very employee-friendly."

Slow on the intake

In Amsterdam, a worker notes that it's a very international environment because the traineeships are open to foreign students. On male/female diversity, workers in

Amsterdam say, "We should do better in hiring and retaining women," while a Belgium based staffer says, "Like most other firms, the higher in the management ranks you look, the fewer women there are."

Time out with your managers

"Management takes time to listen and to give you opportunities in your job," a banker in Brussels tells us. "But from time to time they spend too much time on day-to-day work and ongoing projects to make time free to coach in a satisfying way" he adds. In Amsterdam, experienced hires assure us "There is a very respectful way of working together and managers often take time to help and coach you."

Sweetening the deal

One of the main work perks employees cite is the employability budget. Every employee receives money on a three-year basis to spend on personal development unrelated to their work says an employee in Amsterdam. It includes things like "taking classes to become a yoga teacher or photographer." Access to free tickets to the Royal Concertgebouw Orchestra (the most respected symphony orchestra in the Netherlands), the New Year Concert, the Christmas gift package and a discount on mortgage interest were also held in high esteem by workers.

Can it get any better?

ING staff commented on a few areas where the firm could improve, including more international moving and exposure, better talent management, more effort to challenge talents and to stretch people in their jobs, more responsibility and better compensation and appreciation. The issue of easier international assignment in particular, was raised several times. A banker in Amsterdam says, "there should be better alignment of compensation to individuals' skills and training," while in Brussels, one worker wants to see "more transparent promotion policies".

Overall, employees are happy working for ING, citing "great work experience with challenging projects and a lot of exposure to senior management," as some of their reasons. While a project leader tells us "the money is not so good" he concedes, "the work is challenging and the work/life balance is good."

INTESA SANPAOLO

Via Monte di Pieta, 8
Milan, 20121
Italy
Tel: +39 (0) 2 879 11
www.intesasanpaolo.com

The Stats

Employer Type: Public Company
Ticker Symbol: ISP (Milan)
Chairman: Giovanni Bazoli
Chief Executive: Corrado Passera
2007 Revenue: €18bn
2007 Profit: €7.2bn
2006 Revenue: €17.9bn*
2006 Profit: €4.7bn*
(*restated on a consistent basis,
considering the merger between
Banca Intesa Sanpaolo IMI and the
connected transactions with Crédit
Agricole and the changes in the
consolidation area)
No. of Offices: 7,329 offices and
branches

Departments

Corporate and Investment Banking •
Eurizon Financial Group • Foreign
Banks • Group's Finance • Public
Finance • Regional Banking

European Locations

Milan (HQ)
Italy • Offices across Europe and
worldwide

Key Competitors

Capitalia • Grupo Santander •
UniCredit

Employment Contact

www.bancaintesa.it/piu/jsp/editorial

Pluses

• Strong position in market
• Respected

Minuses

• Italian language skills are key
• Not considered progressive

THE BUZZ
WHAT EMPLOYEES AT OTHER FIRMS ARE SAYING

• "Increasingly significant Italian bank"
• "Regional"

THE SCOOP

B ased on market value, Italian super-bank Intesa Sanpaolo is ranked 12th on the list of the top-20 Global Financial Institutions as of March 31, 2008, with a market value of 52.9 billion euros. Not entirely surprising, considering the firm is the fruit of a mega-merger just a year earlier in January 2007, between Italy's No. 2 and No. 3 banks, Banca Intesa S.p.A. and Sanpaolo IMI.

The deal, which had been announced in late August 2006, closed quickly after earning approval from shareholders and Italian bank regulators alike. Milan-based Banca Intesa took over the smaller Turin-based Sanpaolo, offering 3.115 of its own shares for each Sanpaolo share. Citigroup advised on the 29.6 billion euro deal (38 billion US dollars), which created Italy's largest bank, surpassing UniCredit S.p.A. in size and assets. Impressively, Intesa Sanpaolo's share of the Italian retail market is now well over one-fifth of the total.

The new Intesa Sanpaolo is legally incorporated in Turin — Sanpaolo's original home — with operating headquarters in Milan. At the close of the January 2007 merger, Intesa Sanpaolo held 541 billion euros (690 billion dollars) in assets and represented 13 million customers in 30 countries, including Russia, China and India.

> ❝ Milan-based Banca Intesa took over the smaller Turin-based Sanpaolo, which created Italy's largest bank ❞

The combination of two Italian superpowers boosted the confidence of analysts in the Italian banking world — Fitch Ratings upgraded its rating of Intesa Sanpaolo from two to one.

Emerging a giant

Intesa Sanpaolo has six business units and 16 head-office departments. Its six business units are the Banca dei Territori (which includes retail and small business banking in Italy), corporate and investment banking, foreign banks, public finance (which combines the operations of two subsidiaries, BIIS and Banca OPI), Eurizon Financial Group and group's finance. The 16 head office departments include a number of corporate support operations, such as legal affairs, audit, IT and tax. Former Banca Intesa chief executive Corrado Passera was named chief executive of the new bank. Sanpaolo chairman Enrico Salza leads the management board, and Banca Intesa chairman Giovanni Bazoli now heads the supervisory board.

Catering to the market

The bank provides a range of services, including investment banking, public and infrastructure finance, factoring and trade financing services. The retail division serves individuals, small businesses, micro enterprises, SMEs and nonprofits. Intesa Sanpaolo also offers retail banking, wealth management, private banking and industrial credit via Banca Intesa Mediocredito, which has a leading position in Italy.

The corporate division serves mid-sized and large corporations, financial institutions and public administrations. Its main activities include mergers and acquisitions, structured finance services, merchant banking, capital markets (through Banca Caboto), global custody and an international network focused on corporate banking, which includes ZAO Banca Intesa, the only Italian banking subsidiary licensed to operate in Russia.

The specialised subsidiary, Banca Intesa Infrastrutture e Sviluppo, supports the public and infrastructure sectors. Its fields of activity range from public work lending to securitisations for public entities and project finance. The Italian subsidiary banks division includes regional banking subsidiaries Cariparma & Piacenza, Banca Popolare FriulAdria, Biverbanca, Banca di Trento e Bolzano and Intesa Casse del Centro. The international subsidiary banks division is composed of subsidiaries abroad, mainly in Central and Eastern Europe, that offer retail and commercial banking services.

Ukraine: second time lucky

In February 2008, Intesa agreed to pay 504 million euros for Pravex Bank in Ukraine, with a view to reaping the rewards of investment in the country's high-growth economy. Selective expansion into countries such as Central and South-Eastern Europe and the Mediterranean basin is an ongoing company strategy, and one seen in an increasing number of Western European banks. In the past three years, the presence of foreign banking groups in the Ukraine alone, in the form of net assets, has increased from ten percent to over 35 percent. In 2007, Intesa had already made a failed grab for Ukrsotsbank, one of Ukraine's top five banks. Approximately 94 percent of Ukrsotsbank was later purchased by Intesa rival UniCredit Group.

Giving the GAM away?

In March 2008, Intesa Sanpaolo entered into talks with Julius Baer about a possible acquisition by Intesa of a portion of Baer's asset management business. Of particular interest is the involvement of GAM in the discussions, the extremely profitable asset manager Baer bought from UBS in 2005. While Baer has been cagey with its comments and has emphasised GAM's status as a core asset, speculation has revolved around GAM's possible future operation as a joint venture. Baer has noted that is always looking to enhance GAM's distribution. A logical partner for this kind of operation would be a large retail bank, such as Intesa.

Intesa, seeking to grow its investment management operations beyond Italian borders as part of its expansion strategy, considers GAM to be among its possible targets. Banca Intesa had shied away from asset management operations in the past, but since the merger, it is looking into the matter with renewed vigour. While commentators close to Intesa and Baer have

> ❝ Selective expansion into [regions] such as Central and South-Eastern Europe is an ongoing strategy ❞

asserted that a deal is not imminent, Intesa's objective in this arena is clear. In 2007, Intesa chief executive Corrado Passera told *The Financial Times*, "We will be one of the big boys [in asset management]. In a couple of moves, if we are capable and lucky enough, we might be in the top ten in Europe."

GETTING HIRED

Apple of the Italian eye?

A top Italian media consultancy and research firm, Recent Graduate Survey, conducted their annual graduate survey, examining which firms Italian graduates want to work for. The 2007 survey results were fantastic for Intesa Sanpaolo, ranking the firm as "Best Employer of Choice 2007". This was determined by surveying 2,500 graduates in Italy, face-to-face, about their views, attitudes and preferences according to what course path they are studying at university, the labour market, their location and what media they are interested in.

To find out more about career opportunities at Intesa Sanpaolo, check out the company's site at http://group.intesasanpaolo.com, and click on "lavore con noi", which means "work with us". That said, most information is only available in Italian, so you'll need fluency in the language to pursue most opportunities at the firm.

A time to show off

Be prepared to demonstrate your impressive language skills and speak confidently. "The interview process was quite long," an associate in Milan tells us. "I had seven or eight different interviews. Most of the interviews were non-technical, but the atmosphere was quite tense — probably to see how I reacted. They also tested my languages."

OUR SURVEY SAYS

An office in the sun

"The workplace is nice," a Milan-based worker discloses. "The people are quite young on average, and relaxed. The corporate culture though is quite 'Italian' and therefore hierarchical." Another junior employee tells us, "Intesa Sanpaolo is now the second-biggest bank in Italy, so it's a good opportunity [to work there]." □

JEFFERIES INT'L LTD

Jefferies International Ltd.
Vintners Place
68 Upper Thames Street
London
EC4V 3BJ
United Kingdom
Tel: +44 (0) 207 029 8000
www.jefferies.com

The Stats

Employer Type: Public Company
Ticker Symbol: JEF (NYSE)
Chief Executive: Richard B. Handler
2007 Revenue: $2.7bn
2007 Profit: $144m
2006 Revenue: $1.96bn
2006 Profit: $205.7m
No. of Employees: 2,400
No. of Offices: 25

Departments

Asset Management • Investment
Banking • Private Client Services •
Research • Sales and Trading

European Locations

London (European HQ)
Frankfurt • Paris • United Kingdom •
Zurich

Employment Contact

www.jefferies.com/careers

Pluses

• Strong entrepreneurial culture
• Excellent European presence

Minuses

• Demanding hours
• Small firm may not suit all types

THE BUZZ
WHAT EMPLOYEES AT OTHER FIRMS ARE SAYING

• "Nice player, good house"
• "Not that high profile"

THE SCOOP

A s far as mid-market firms go, Jefferies International Limited is really where it's at. The London-based firm has been making heads turn for some time now, with an emerging reputation as a popular investment bank choice for mid-market companies in the US, Europe and Asia. Jefferies' focus in Europe is on aerospace, defence, energy, health care, media, technology and maritime. The bank's European equity research encompasses consumer, energy, gaming, healthcare, media, telecommunications and technology and France country coverage. The London office is also home to a UK sales team dedicated to providing US securities and research information to European clients.

Business at Jefferies is broken into five divisions: investment banking (including specialised industry groups), sales and trading, research, asset management and private client services. As of 2008, Jefferies employed more than 2,400 people in its 25 offices around the world.

A fresh face

While Jefferies International Ltd (JIL) has been operating in the UK for more than 25 years, it is a relative newcomer on the investment banking scene, with a fast-growing presence and client base. The firm recently acquired "Sponsor" and "NOMAD" status on the Alternative Investment Market (AIM) and the UKLA, both on the London Stock Exchange. In 2007, Jefferies nabbed former Deutsche Bank star David Weaver to drive its activities in Europe, Asia and the Middle East and further bolstered its expertise by acquiring a further handful of key industry veterans. Since 2006, the firm has established offices in Frankfurt, Dubai, Singapore, New Delhi and Shanghai. In November 2007, it consolidated its various London offices into one centralized location on Vinter's Place in the City, overlooking the Thames and St. Paul's Cathedral.

All around the world

Jefferies International Limited (JIL) and US-based Jefferies & Company are the primary operating subsidiaries of Jefferies Group, Inc. (NYSE: JEF). Together, they comprise a global investment bank and institutional securities firm focused on bringing multi-product expertise to growing companies and their investors.

Jefferies' European presence is strong. In Zurich, Jefferies (Switzerland) Limited conduct sales, trading and investment management of global convertibles. It is one of the world's largest providers of asset management services for global convertible bonds for institutional investors. JIL has approximately two billion US dollars (1.55

billion euros) of investment assets under management. Jefferies' Paris office is home to a sales and research team that conducts French and European equity research for domestic and international clients. Finally, Jefferies' new Frankfurt team covers all major industry sectors in German-speaking Europe, initiating and executing transactions. The Frankfurt team covers private equity, venture capital and other financial sponsors in the region.

In 2007, the firm made several key additions to its investment banking platform in the media and financial services sectors. It acquired LongAcre Partners, a leading UK-based, European media and internet M&A advisory firm, as well as the investment banking division of Putnam Lovell, a leading advisor to the financial services sector with offices in San Francisco, New York and London. In 2007, partly as a result of the LongAcre acquisition, Jefferies completed more digital media transactions under a billion dollars than any other investment bank in North America and Western Europe, and ranked second amongst media M&A advisors in Western Europe in 2007 according to Thomson Financial.

This was far from the only accolade Jefferies scooped in 2007. The firm also ranked "Top M&A Advisor" in the technology and defense sectors and No. 2 in the energy industry in North America and Western Europe, according to Thomson Financial. Adding to the plaudits was *Buyouts* Magazine, naming Jefferies "Middle Market Investment Bank of the Year" in 2006. As a follow-up to 2007's wins for Madagascar, Norway and Greece, the firm also captured three 2008 Deal of the Year awards from *The Banker* magazine for energy-related transactions involving companies in Bangladesh, Gabon and Mauritania. Outside of banking, Jefferies' equity investment banking effort earned a total of 17 analyst honours from *The Wall Street Journal*'s "2008 Best on the Street" and Starmine's 2008 Analyst Survey, including three country coverage awards for France. As if all this wasn't enough, the firm is doing well when it comes to green business too. At the *Euromoney* and Ernst & Young 2007 Annual Global Renewable Energy Awards, one of its transactions was named "Equity Deal of the Year".

Familiar with the Far East

Jefferies is hardly a stranger to the Middle East and Asia — the firm established a Tokyo office in 1992. It has grown as an underwriter in the region and has worked on several cross-border M&A transactions involving Asian companies. Since 2004, Jefferies has raised almost three billion dollars in equity and debt transactions for Asia-based companies, and its M&A advisory fees in the region totalled 2.5 billion dollars, and the firm helped raise more than 850 million dollars for China-based companies during 2007.

Jefferies International Limited

The east-looking bank has also worked with several China-focused private equity and venture capital funds. In March 2007, the firm's Singapore office officially became licensed. In October, the firm opened an office in New Delhi, India. Outside India, its investment banking professionals have to date raised close to two billion dollars for Indian issuers, including more than 850 million in 2007 for clients in a range of sectors including media, industrials, technology, healthcare and textiles. In addition, Jefferies' Dubai office played a key role in the firm's execution of the high profile sale of Aston Martin to a consortium of international investors.

We're all friends here

Employees of Jefferies are not just employees — they are described as "employee-owners". This is probably because, in a fairly novel structure in the banking world, Jefferies employees and board members own approximately 50 percent of the firm's equity. In a contest sponsored by online financial news publication *Here Is The   City*, Jefferies' employee-owners turned out in record numbers to vote their firm ninth Best Place to Work in Global Financial Markets 2008.

More than 86 percent of Jefferies' global staff of 2,247 people voted for their employer. In response, chief executive Richard Handler thanked his fellow employee-owners, declaring that their dedication and passion were the firm's biggest assets. He added, "We still have much work to do in accomplishing our worldwide goals in the middle market, and [we] are continually looking for good partners. If you work at another financial services firm and want a career at a company where one person can still make a difference, please think of us."

GETTING HIRED

The brighter the better

Jefferies seeks applicants with strong analytical skills and an academic record with a specific emphasis on finance or accounting. As a graduate entering the analyst programme, or an MBA holder entering the associate programme, you can choose a number of different paths. The generalist track allows you to work on a number of project areas, such as equity, leveraged finance and M&A, exploring different disciplines before you settle on your specialism. Industry areas you'll work in include aerospace and defence, energy and healthcare amongst others. The industry track sees you begin in the aerospace and defence, energy or technology groups and receive exposure to a range of product areas within each group. Choosing this route will let you, as an analyst or associate, develop specialised skills in one industry of particular interest, while being exposed to other areas which could include M&A, recapitalisation and restructuring.

The traditional way in

Jefferies' hiring process is "pretty standard," says a senior analyst in London. After the initial selection process there are "numerical and group exercises which are done in advance of one-to-one interviews with members of the team." If you're successful at the first stage, he says, "That's when you have to bite the bullet and meet senior team and firm members." "I had four interviews with an associate, with the vice-president, the director and the managing director," another analyst says. The firm handpicks most of its staff from "top universities" in the UK. Jefferies recruits mainly from Oxbridge, the London School of Economics and Imperial, but also top universities in mainland Europe, such as Bocconi.

Doing an internship with Jefferies is a step in the right direction if you're looking for full-time employment with the firm. "Summer internships are key to the firm's selection process," a third-year analyst tells us, "as most of these candidates will be selected to move into the full-time analyst programme." Other respondents corroborate, "Most interns will receive an offer — it's very important."

One insider describes the firm as "very aggressive" albeit "fast-growing". An experienced hire admits that hours can sometimes be long when the firm is busy, but says, "although hours are still very normal for the industry". He reported that in some cases he worked an average of 80 to 90-hours per week, with weekend work "a frequent occurrence". That said, most respondents listed 60 hours as the weekly average, while one noted, "working hours are largely dependent on the team you're in, rather than your seniority."

How to meet the right people

Jefferies recruits through an exclusive recruiting agent: Oxbridge Life. After conducting a screening process and first round interviews, it puts together a shortlist of potential candidates. If you're on the list, you'll be invited to attend a "superday" meeting with five associates and vice-presidents from a range of investment banking divisions. The final stage involves a case study and meeting with senior vice-presidents and managing directors. Go to www.cornellpartners hip.com/jefferies for more information. First round interviews are most commonly held on campus in autumn.

If your school isn't on the list of those that Jefferies visits, just submit your CV online, and be happy that CVs are welcomed from both graduates and experienced professionals. The firm recruits from a long list of schools, but if you prefer the direct route, you can also submit a resume via www.jefferies.com/careers. If you are called in, expect two to three rounds of interviews.

One insider says applicants should anticipate "a series of interviews with an analyst/associate, a vice president and a managing director."However, be ready to prove yourself. Jefferies has a "strong entrepreneurial culture," he adds, "This is often the hardest criteria to meet and to demonstrate that you have these skills."

OUR SURVEY SAYS

Proving your worth

Jefferies' London-based employees talk of a strongly meritocratic firm, noting "this is key." At Jefferies, should you be efficient in your job, "you will get a fair treatment by superiors. An experienced hire says, "this is a place where hard work is encouraged and rewarded." "Our team is a very open one," an investment banker in London tells us, "people work to their ability and are given a large amount of responsibility early on." Even more encouragingly, "the culture is excellent and we all work as a team," a second year analyst concludes. Several employees tell us the firm's promotion policies show room for improvement. "They could fast track high-performers," a first year analyst says, while a second year notes: "fast track promotion would be better than rigidly sticking to years of service when you're a junior." An analyst in London raises the issue that the firm could "organise more events for interns, analysts and associates to get to know each other."

According to one London-based worker, Jefferies has a "very specific positioning, being a mid-size, fast-growing firm that focuses on the middle-market industry." The corporate culture is therefore very different to what you might find in a bulge bracket, says one insider, explaining that it's: "more informal, much more dynamic, less hierarchical, very entrepreneurial and highly challenging."

Analysts are expected to have much more direct exposure to senior people and clients than in a bulge bracket bank. A senior analyst reflects, "Jefferies is a great place to start a career," adding that "the firm is growing fast and offers a lot of opportunities in other groups."

More junior respondents agree that the company operates: "a flat corporate structure allowing juniors to take on responsibility and to have contact with senior bankers," while a first year analyst in London describes the environment as: "open, and full of entrepreneurial people. Expectations are high, but people are there to help you." □

KBC GROUP

Havenlaan 12
B-1080 Brussels
Belgium
Tel: +32 (0)78 152 153
www.kbc.com

The Stats

Employer Type: Public Company
Ticker Symbol: KBC (Luxembourg);
KBC (Euronext)
Chief Executive: André Bergen
2007 Revenue: €13.3bn
2007 Profit: €3.4bn
2006 Revenue: €12.6bn
2006 Profit: €3.6bn
No. of Employees: 57,000
No. of Offices: 2,146 (banking),
15,125 (insurance)

Departments

Brokerage • Collateral Management •
Corporate Banking • Corporate
Finance • Derivatives • Diamond
Industry • Factoring • Financial
Institutions • Financing • Private Equity •
Real Estate • Reinsurance • Securities
Services • Securitisation • Social Profit
and Public Finance • Stock Option
Plans • Structured Finance • Treasury •
Wealth Management

European Locations

Brussels (HQ)
Austria • Bulgaria • Belgium • Czech
Republic • Estonia • France • Germany •
Hungary • Ireland • Italy • Latvia •
Lithuania • Luxembourg • The
Netherlands • Poland • Romania •
Russia • Serbia • Slovenia • Spain •
Switzerland • Turkey • Ukraine •
United Kingdom

Employment Contact

KBC Recruitment and Selection
Department
Tel: +32 (0)2 429 97 34

Email: vacature@kbc.be

THE BUZZ
WHAT EMPLOYEES AT OTHER FIRMS ARE SAYING

• "Most solid of Belgian banks
• "Big locally, small globally"

THE SCOOP

K BC Bank is the main subsidiary of KBC Group, one of Europe's leading financial organisations and the second-largest financial institution in Belgium. KBC Group describes itself as an integrated multi-channel banking and insurance group which delivers services to customers, private banking clientele and small and medium-sized enterprises. Belgium, Central and Eastern Europe and Russia are its areas of focus for retail banking, insurance and asset management. The bank has a market capitalisation of 30 billion euros and 52 percent of its capital is controlled by a syndicate of core shareholders, while its free float in the stock markets represents 40.7 percent.

KBC Bank is one of the leading three banks in Belgium, where it holds a 20 to 25 percent market share. The up-and-coming bank operates across four business divisions: Belgium, Central and Eastern Europe, European private banking and merchant banking. The merchant banking division is extensive, sitting at the head of an array of subsidiaries which together have operations in more than 30 countries worldwide. Delivering services such as project finance, brokerage, financial products, private equity, custody clearing, re-insurance, real estate and leasing services, it even offers specialist services in the diamond industry.

> " In July 2007, KBC Bank completed its purchase of a 95 percent stake in Russia's Absolut Bank for €700m "

Key subsidiaries include KBC securities, KBC asset management, KBC private equity, KBC lease and KBC's integrated European investment firm. The latter focuses on corporate finance and securities services and boasts its own Western and Central European platform. In London, this division goes by the name KBC Peel Hunt. KBC financial products, purchased by KBC Bank in 1999, has offices in London, New York, Tokyo and Hong Kong. It delivers equities, high-yield bonds and structured credit products with a specific emphasis on technology.

The book of Belgian banking history

The group's roots can be traced back to the formation of Volksbank van Leuven in 1889, which in 1935, alongside Algemeene Bankvereeniging, merged with Bank voor Handel en Nijverheid to form Kredietbank. Following the Great Depression, Kredietbank was the sole bank in Belgium remaining under Flemish control. By the end of World War II, the bank's growth strategy focused on foreign expansion and moved into Luxembourg in 1949, establishing Kredietbank S.A. Luxembourgeoise.

During the 1960s, the bank expanded its network, establishing branches in New York, London, the Cayman Islands and a subsidiary in Geneva in 1966. In 1971, it formed the Inter-Alpha banking group along with six other banks. As of 2008, its members include Société Générale, Banco Santander, Commerzbank and the Royal Bank of Scotland Group.

The KBC Group came into being in 2005 through the merger of KBC Bank & Insurance Holding Company and Almanij, its parent. KBC Bank & Insurance Holding Company was itself created through the merger of the Belgian financial institutions CERA Bank, ABB Insurance and Kredietbank in 1998.

Its global positioning and corporate history is largely attributable to the firm's policy of expansion into Central and Eastern European countries, establishing operations in countries which became EU members in 2004 — Hungary, Poland, the Czech Republic and Slovakia.

Mixing it up

KBC Bank's strategy at the end of fiscal year 2006 was a process of consolidation of its market position through strategic acquisitions. KBC Financial Products increased its product offering by stepping into life insurance settlements, a process by which life insurance policies are purchased from their holders.

CEE market leader KBC Securities acquired the Romanian brokerage, confusingly named Swiss Capital (now KBC Securities Romania) and Hungarian online retail broker Equitas. These reinforced its already leading position in the region. As the only Belgian financial institution to offer private investors an online broking service to trade stocks on the Budapest, Warsaw and Prague stockmarkets, KBC enjoys a key role in share distribution in the region.

What's the Russia?

In July 2007, it was time for a high-profile move by the Belgian bank. KBC Bank completed its purchase of a 95 percent stake in Russia's Absolut Bank for 700 million euros — a record purchase for the Russian banking sector. The bank's new board included Absolut's chief executive Nikolai Sidorov along with representatives of the new owners.

With capital resources exceeding 400 million dollars thanks to a ten-year subordinated loan from KBC, Russia's 25th-largest bank is all set to expand its retail business further with the assistance of Belgium's bank and insurance market leader.

GETTING HIRED

A cornucopia of opportunity and support

Impressively, KBC has received a 'Lifelong Learning' award for the training programmes it offers and you'll find the bank is happy to enthuse endlessly about the coaching opportunities and career-long learning initiatives it offers on the job. Just a selection of the training programmes it operates are the KBC Academy for "young potentials", the KBC Master Plus for senior managers and an International Management Development programme for employees who show great potential. It should be noted that the "young graduates" section is only available in Dutch so a fluent command of this language is needed to apply for jobs in this section.

KBC's careers page colourfully depicts its business divisions as five continents that go together to comprise the "KBC World". These are retail, business and management support, ICT, products and merchant banking. At the bottom of the page you'll find links to current vacancies and a link to submit your CV online. You can also send your CV directly to vacature@kbc.be, referencing the vacancy you're interested in.

The firm describes its ideal candidates as possessing Masters degrees, advanced business degrees or PhD's in subjects such as economics, informatics, engineering, law, actuarial and other quantitative sciences. However, a quick look at some of KBC's vacancies will reveal that some positions require qualification at Masters level or above. Other vacancies are open to those with an undergraduate degree, or the equivalent level of work experience. Similarly, some positions will require you to have a thorough knowledge of English.

Have two bananas

KBC provides numerous employee benefits and an active social life. Working with the company for a full year will entitle you to a supplementary double holiday allowance at 92 percent of a regular monthly salary. Salaries are reviewed yearly and in addition to raises, good performance could see you step into a higher pay bracket entirely.

Profit-sharing bonuses and performance bonuses for teams and individuals are among the firm's golden carrots, as are hospital and personal assistance insurance, a pension plan and an extra allowance for home-to-work travel. □

LANDESBANK BERLIN

Landesbank Berlin AG
Alexanderplatz 2
D - 10178 Berlin
Germany
Tel: +49 30 869 801
www.lbb.de

The Stats

Employer Type: Public Company
Ticker Symbol: BEB2 (Frankfurt)
Chief Executive: Hans-Jörg Vetter
2007 Revenue: €291m
2007 Profit: €220m
2006 Revenue: €784m
2006 Profit: €687m
2006 Revenue: €1,949m
No. of Employees 2007: 6,670
No. of Employees 2006: 7,976
No. of Offices: n/a

Departments

Capital Markets • Real Estate Financing • Regional Corporate Banking • Retail Banking

German Locations

Berlin (HQ)
Düsseldorf • Frankfurt • Hamburg • Munich

European Locations

Czech Republic • The Netherlands • Luxembourg • Poland • United Kingdom

Employment Contact

www.lbb.de
(Click on "about us" then "careers")

THE BUZZ
WHAT EMPLOYEES AT OTHER FIRMS ARE SAYING

• "Lots of business with small caps in Germany/Austria"
• "Tiny German bank"

THE SCOOP

T racing its roots to the Berliner Sparkassen of 1818, one of the world's oldest companies still in existence, Landesbank Berlin (LBB) is the wholly owned subsidiary of Landesbank Berlin Holding. A global bank which bundles together many different activities, its four main divisions are: retail banking, regional corporate banking, capital markets and real estate financing.

The bank primarily offers regional corporate banking services in the Berlin-Brandenberg economic region, and counts public-sector companies, small and medium sized enterprises and local authorities amongst its clients. In a joint business with its subsidiary Berlin Hyp, it offers real estate finance services to companies throughout Europe. Through its Berliner Sparkasse retail banking centres it offers

> " Landesbank Berlin traces its roots back to the Berliner Sparkasser of 1818 "

pension systems, asset accumulation and consumer and real estate financing services, and boasts half the population of Berlin as account holders. Finally, its capital markets division concentrates on client trading and sales activities, offering capital market products for private investors, and an international banking focus on Central and Eastern Europe.

Fall of the wall

The end of the East-West divide in Berlin saw Landesbank Berlin Girozentrale founded as a bank subject to public law on October 1, 1990. The city's savings banks were simultaneously transferred to Landesbank Berlin and formed the joint Berliner Sparkasse, operated today as a branch of LBB. In 1994, holding company Bankgesellschaft Berlin was formed through the merger of the state-owned Landesbank Berlin Girozentrale and real estate firm Berliner Pfandbriefbank und Hypothekenbank (Berlin Hyp for short), with the private Berliner Bank. As the primary state-owned financial entity in Berlin, Bankgesellschaft was tied up closely with the redevelopment of the city throughout the 1990s. Due partly to the creation of extremely risky property-backed funds, the bank announced the gigantic loss of 1.65 billion euros for the year 2000 in a high profile real estate scandal. At the brink of insolvency, but rebalanced by 23 billion euros in state aid, Bankgesellschaft Berlin underwent a fundamental restructuring. This included a simplification of its structure, a measure required by the EU (European Union) Commission as the first step in its call for the bank's sale by 2007.

Landesbank Berlin Holding AG

305

A European reality

After the restructuring in 2006, the bank was renamed Landesbank Berlin Holding and the primary banking business of the company was transferred to its subsidiary, Landesbank Berlin. Landesbank Berlin Holding is now the listed financial holding and the parent company of its wholly-owned subsidiary Landesbank Berlin.

In 2007, the sale of the bank offered the DSVG, the German Savings Bank Association, the chance to buy up the prized brand. Up until this point Germany's savings banks had remained public organisations; for the first time the chance for private ownership was a reality.

Shaking the pillars

When bidding closed, the DSVG acquired the state's shares of Landesbank Berlin Holding, having paid 5.3 billion euros in total. It took the city of Berlin's 81 percent stake in Landesbank Berlin for 4.6 billion euros, and 723 million euros worth of reserves held by Berlin, effective from January 1, 2008.

Political price-tag

Commerzbank, the closest private bidder, claimed it just couldn't compete with LBB's political price-tag. Many who believed the sale would pave the way for a long-needed modernisation of Germany's banking system were disappointed at the continuation of public control, together with LBB's shareholders, who looked to double their share prices if LBB had gone to IPO, or been sold to a private sector consortium. One Berlin-based banker speaking in *Financial News Online* said the flotation of the company had faced fierce opposition from politicians and the unions, noting, "these things are always very political."

Go plastic

As well as a market share in retail banking of 39 percent in the Berlin area, LBB is Germany's market leader in the credit card business, with 1.8 million cards issued throughout the country. Making particular use of cross-branding, working alongside companies such as Amazon and Microsoft, the company has channelled considerable resources into marketing its cards to younger Germans by offering prepaid varieties to those with a low credit score, or who are forbidden by law to have credit. This is now the company's fastest growing segment. In January 2008 LBB Holding bought the sales financing division of Deutsche Postbank subsidiary BHW Bank, adding 179,000 customers, a credit portfolio of around 485 million euros and 125,000 credit cards.

GETTING HIRED

Choose the right path

The bank runs several different graduate training schemes, each specialising in a different area of the business. The degree required is dependent on the scheme; some require a specific degree, such as economics, while others are open to graduates in all disciplines. Each scheme lasts 18 months and requires good German and English language skills. Applications should be made in writing; selected applicants will be invited for interview. The descriptions of each scheme on the website (www.lbb.de/ karriere, then go to "Die LBB als Arbeitgeber", then "Hochschulabsolventen > Bewerbung als Trainee") also give the names of the relevant contact person.

There are also opportunities for school leavers to train as bank personnel. The majority of Landesbank's jobs are, unsurprisingly, in Berlin, a city which offers cheap rent and high standards of living. ⬚

MEDIOBANCA S.P.A

Piazzetta E. Cuccia, 1
20121 Milan
Italy
Tel: + 39 (0) 2 882 91
www.mediobanca.it

European Locations

Milan (HQ)
France · Germany · Italy · Spain ·
United Kingdom

The Stats

Employer Type: Public Company
Ticker Symbol: MD (Milan)
Chairman of the Supervisory Board:
Cesare Geronzi
Chief Executive: Alberto Nagel
2007 Revenue: €1.3bn
2007 Profit: €966m
2006 Revenue: €1.2bn
2006 Profit: €867m
No. of Employees: 516
No. of Offices: 10

Employment Contact

www.mediobanca.it

Human Resources: Andrea Ventura
Tel: +39 (0)2 8829.282
Fax: +39 (0)2 8829.267

THE BUZZ
WHAT EMPLOYEES AT OTHER FIRMS ARE SAYING

· "Impressive firepower in Italy"
· "More of a local bank"

Departments

Equity Investment
Private Equity
Retail Financial Services
Trust Businesses

THE SCOOP

A s part of Italy's reconstruction in the wake of World War II, Mediobanca was first created by a joint initiative organised by Banca Commerciale Italiana, Credito Italiano and Banco di Roma. Their goal was to provide medium-term financing for Italian manufacturers and to create a link between investors and Italian industries struggling to recover from the war. From its birth in 1944, until 1973, Mediobanca was limited to medium-term credit. Then, in October 1973, the bank changed its mission to include financing on terms of up to 20 years.

Mediobanca joined the Italian stock market in 1956, and overhauled its ownership structure in 1988, dividing its shares between the public and private sectors. The shares held by its founding banks, BCI, Credito Italiano and Banco di Roma, were reduced as a combined holding from 56.9 percent

> ❝ Politically, a position on Mediobanca's board has carried weight in Italy since the bank was founded ❞

of the share capital to 25 percent. In 2000, BCI sold its interest in Mediobanca to other members of a block shareholders' syndicate, which currently includes such major Italian finance houses as Capitalia and UniCredit.

Today Mediobanca offers underwriting, M&A advisory, wholesale banking and financial advisory to its corporate clients while providing loans, credit and retail banking services to individual clients. In addition to its main office in Milan, Mediobanca has offices in Frankfurt, Paris, Madrid and London.

Bulking up

Mediobanca launched a three-year business plan in 2006, involving the expansion of its retail financial services and private banking sectors by acquiring other firms. The plan was to be concentrated in France, while keeping an eye out for lucrative opportunities in Spain and Germany. Corporate and investment banking would be expanded into France, Spain, Germany and the UK.

In June 2008, the bank took another step in its plan with the acquisition of an 100 percent share in Italian firm Linea, picking up the consumer credit company from Banco Popolare and Banca Popolare di Vicenza and other banks for 388.5 million euros.

Also in 2008, the bank unveiled its business plan for 2009-2011. This revolves around growth driven by specific initiatives, including: European positioning in corporate and investment banking; the structuring of new principal investing activity; leadership in consumer credit with the brand Compass and the launch of an innovative retail platform, with the new brand CheBanca! By 2011, the bank is looking to push its total income up by a cool billion, from 2.1 to 3.1 billion euros.

Time to reform

In 2007, Mediobanca announced its move to a single chief executive and dual-board structure, in an effort to embrace reform. The move also came in the same week as UniCredit's acquisition of Capitalia, which formed Europe's second largest bank. Both UniCredit and Capitalia are large shareholders in Mediobanca.

The bank, previously run by a shareholder pact built up of the country's biggest banks, had stronger management autonomy and the reduction of conflicts of interest with its competitors as its objectives.

Politically, a position on Mediobanca's board has carried weight in Italy since the bank was founded, and the bank has been at the heart of power broking and negotiations for 61 years. Managers and shareholders however, were eager to have distinct roles so as to act more effectively. The new dual board will consist of a supervisory board comprised of pact representatives and a management board comprised of executives. Only the management board now has the right to propose major change at the bank to the supervisory board.

Are you in the running?

Each year, Mediobanca offers the Mediobanca Prize, awarded to medium-sized Italian companies with the best growth rates. According to the bank, the prize is meant to identify and reward Italy's most dynamic mid-sized companies, especially those with the potential to become larger corporations. Applications for the prize are reviewed by Mediobanca's research department, which makes recommendations to an independent committee.

Of course, Mediobanca isn't just trying to reward others — its commitment to Italy's mid-sized companies underscores its plan to boost its own growth in the mid-corporate segment. Mediobanca says it plans to build an integrated, dedicated platform of services for mid-sized businesses, offering specialised expertise from its headquarters in Milan.

GETTING HIRED

The Italian job (s)

Mediobanca notes the bulk of its new employees are taken from Italian universities, so you might want to bear this in mind if you're an overseas graduate. It also notes that it prefers people who have graduated in economics-related disciplines. For the junior analyst role, which is the graduate entry position, the firm wants economics graduates with fluent spoken and written English and Italian.

You can submit your CV speculatively on the company careers page, and Mediobanca requests you also submit a covering letter in the same document, stating what kind of work you're particularly interested in.

Mediobanca S.p.A.

MIZUHO CORPORATE BANK

Bracken House,
One Friday Street,
London
EC4M 9JA
United Kingdom
Tel: +44 (0) 20 7012 4000
www.mizuhocbk.co.jp/english

The Stats

Employer Type: Public Company
Ticker Symbol: 8411 (Tokyo), MFG
(NYSE)
Chief Executive: Hiroshi Saito
2007 Revenue: ¥4.5tr
2007 Profit: ¥311bn
2006 Revenue: ¥4.34tr (FYE 03/07)
2006 Profit: ¥620bn (FYE 03/07)
No. of Employees: 47,000 (Mizuho
Financial Group)
No. of Offices: 770 (Mizuho Financial
Group)

Departments

Acquisition Finance • Custody
Services • Deposit and Lending •
Financial Products • Investment
Banking and Custodial Services •
Project Finance • Real Estate Finance •
Securitisation of Client Assets •
Syndication

Financial Services: Asset Management •
Asset Management Business • CMS •
Investment Trust-Related Business •

Next-Generation Supply Chain
Management • Settlement and Foreign
Exchange • Trust-Related Business •
Various EB Services • Yen Clearing
Service • Yen Custody Services

Market Products: Sales and Trading •
Various Derivative-Related Services

European Locations

London (European HQ)
Austria • Belgium • France • Germany •
Italy • The Netherlands • Russia •
Switzerland • United Kingdom

Employment Contacts

London, Human Resources
Fax: +44 (0) 207 253 8971

Contact details for other European
branches:
www.mizuhocbk.co.jp/english/global_
branch/index.html

THE BUZZ
WHAT EMPLOYEES AT OTHER FIRMS ARE SAYING

• "Good in leveraged finance"
• "Not strong in Europe/US"

THE SCOOP

M izuho is Japanese for "a fresh harvest of rice," and "mizuho country," or bountiful country, is commonly used poetic shorthand in Japan. Emerging from the wreckage of Japan's lost decade under this moniker of plenty, the Mizuho group was born on September 29, 2000. Dai-Ichi Kangyo Bank, the Fuji Bank and the Industrial Bank of Japan were brought under a single holding company: Mizuho Holdings. The group entities increased in number in October 2000 with the merger of the banks' respective subsidiaries. The securities subsidiaries became Mizuho Securities, while the trust bank subsidiaries merged to form Mizuho Trust & Banking.

In April 2002, the group's three banks came together to form a wholesale banking subsidiary. Fuji Bank's retail branches were transferred to Dai-Ichi Kangyo Bank, which was then renamed Mizuho Bank. Fuji Bank's corporate division was then consolidated with the Industrial Bank of Japan and called Mizuho

> ❝ Emerging from the wreckage of Japan's lost decade under this moniker of plenty, the Mizuho Group was born ❞

Corporate Bank. Mizuho Financial Group was established at the beginning of 2003 as a corporation under Japanese law, and took over from Mizuho Holdings as holding company of the Mizuho group.

As of 2008, Mizuho Financial Group as a whole is one of the largest financial institutions in the world. Through its companies, the Mizuho group provides financial services that range from retail banking to securities, trust and asset management, credit cards, private banking and venture capital services.

Like it or slump it

Following Japan's economic slump in the 1990s, the bank pulled off a significant corporate revitalisation project in July 2003, primarily in order to segregate borrowers going through restructuring from those using the bank's normal credit function. After achieving good results in 2004, the group set out a business strategy named "Channel to Discovery." This was primarily to mark its shift from an "emergency reaction phase," suited to making the best of difficult economic times in Japan and winning the trust of consumers, to a phase focused on organisation and growth into a globally competitive financial group. In practical terms, the new organisation divided the bank into three groups: global corporate, global retail and global asset and wealth management.

The global corporate group comprised Mizuho Corporate Bank and Mizuho Securities, and was given the task of providing specialised products through cooperation between the global corporate banking sector and the wholesale securities sector. The union is part of a wider trend for closer alliances between banks and brokerage houses, primarily as a measure to tackle a predicted intensity in competition worldwide. The global corporate division focuses on finance and business strategies services for global corporations and national governmental public sector entities.

Fine China

In the summer of 2007, Mizuho Corporate Bank's chief executive, Hiroshi Saito, put the finishing touches to transfer the bank's five China-based branches — located in Shanghai, Beijing, Shenzhen, Dalian and Wuxi — to its new, wholly owned banking subsidiary in China. The imaginatively named "Mizuho Corporate Bank (China) Ltd" is the very first Japanese financial institution to have begun operations through a local subsidiary in China.

By the end of July of 2007, MHCB (China) set up its first new branch, in the Binhai New Area of Tianjin, or "BNAT". This region, a designated national development priority as part of China's 11th Five-Year Plan, is set for major economic development. The acceleration of investment in the region is augmented by a business cooperation agreement that MHCB signed with the Tianjin Economic and Technological Development Area (TEDA), which promotes and offers support to Japanese companies investing in the region. The establishment of a branch in Tianjin comes as an extension to this encouraged investment. Support for the ever greater number of Japanese companies establishing operations in the area will be enhanced and transactions will be reinforced.

Added to the Mizuho Financial Group's four representative offices in China — Guangzhou, Wuhan, Nanjing and, Xiamen — the addition of the Tianjin branch takes the group to a network of ten offices across the country.

In January 2008, MHCB (China) received approval to replace its representative office in Guangzhou with a full-scale branch, establishing a firmer foothold in the Southern Chinese city. Thanks to the presence of three leading Japanese automobile manufacturers, the region is known to be a hub for auto-related industry in China.

GETTING HIRED

European footprint

Among some of the characteristics Mizuho Corporate Bank considers sought-after are self-motivation, the ability to manage complex relationships and to work autonomously whilst being part of a team. At the same time you should have a creative approach, relevant experience and enjoy being challenged.

The firm's English website provides links to its European branch network, though this essentially comes down to a phone number for each office. The English branch recruits through the mainstream financial press and welcomes speculative applications by post or fax.

People in different places

Mizuho Corporate Bank says it is determined to be the "first-call global financial institution for all its customers." The firm offers "hands-on training" with experienced professionals "to further develop your existing expertise and establish new skill sets to act in today's demanding and fast-paced business environment.

The firm also offers a Global Mobility Program providing its employees with opportunities to work across various Mizuho Corporate Bank's branches and subsidiaries around the world, including the global headquarters in Tokyo. Interested applicants should fax or write to the firm's HR dept. ☐

315

NATIXIS

45, rue Saint-Dominique
Paris, 75007
France
Tel: +33 (1) 58 32 30 00
www.natixis.fr

The Stats

Employer Type: Public Company
Ticker Symbol: KN (Euronext)
Chief Executive: Dominique Ferrero
2007 Revenue: €6.0bn
2007 Profit: €1.2bn
2006 Revenue: €4.2bn
2006 Profit: €999m
No. of Employees: 23,000
No. of Offices: 157 offices in 68
countries

Departments

Asset Management • Corporate and
Investment Banking • Private Equity
and Private Banking • Services •
Receivables Management • Retail
Banking

European Locations

Paris (HQ)
Austria • Belgium • Bulgaria • Croatia •
Czech Republic • Denmark • Estonia •
France • Germany • Hungary • Ireland •
Italy • Latvia • Lithuania • Luxembourg •
Netherlands • Poland • Portugal •
Romania • Russia • Slovakia • Slovenia •
Spain • Sweden • Switzerland • Turkey •
Ukraine

Key Competitors

BNP Paribas • HSBC Finance • Société
Générale

Employment Contact

www.natixis.com

(click on the Human Resources link)

THE BUZZ
WHAT EMPLOYEES AT OTHER FIRMS ARE SAYING

• "Small, nice, friendly"
• "Mid-size French bank"

THE SCOOP

D o not be misled by this banking firm's Greek-sounding name, because it's as French as they come. Formed through a deal between Groupe Banque Populaire, one of France's largest retail banking networks, and Groupe Caisse d'Epargne in November 2006, the resulting joint subsidiary is controlled by the banks' two holding companies (each with 34.4 percent). Natixis combines Natexis Banques Populaires, a leader in the French property leasing market and a bookrunner for both syndicated loans and acquisition financing in France, and various Caisse Nationale des Caisses d'Epargne subsidiaries in finance and investment banking, specialist banking services and private asset management sectors.

In addition to retail banking, Natixis, through its several constituent entities provides services to mid-and large-sized European companies. As an example, the company's wholly owned subsidiary Natixis Interépargne provides employee savings plan management services to French companies, while Coface, another subsidiary, is one of the world's leading providers of credit insurance and credit

> ‶ Natixis, through its constituent entities, provides services to mid- and large-sized European companies ″

management services. In this way, the bank and its various subordinate companies operate in 68 countries throughout the Americas, Africa, Asia and Oceania.

In addition to their equal share in Natixis, Groupe Banque Populaire and Groupe Caisse d'Epargne have equal presence on a supervisory board. Chairmanship of Natixis alternates between executives from each company; the first chairman of the supervisory board is Caisse d'Epargne's chairman, Charles Milhaud, while Banque Populaire's chairman, Philippe Dupont, is the first chairman of the management board.

Planes, planes and cocoa beans

Natixis participated in several major airline financing deals in 2006. Natixis Transport Finance, a wholly owned Natixis subsidiary, joined with Calyon to finance the 400 million dollar down payment of seven Airbus A321 aircraft for the Russian national airline Aeroflot in April 2006. Natixis Transport Finance is no stranger to dealing with aircraft — it was also a joint arranger with HSH Nordbank for the 250 million US dollar loan to EasyJet to finance Airbus planes and in October 2006, it participated in the 96 million dollar financing of Boeings for Alaska Airlines as well as a 120 million dollar financing for China Southern Airlines. The bank also makes more down-to-earth investments, such as taking the lead with Standard Chartered Bank in the 810 million dollar funding of the

Ghana Cocoa Board in September 2006, in the largest structured soft commodity (in this case cocoa beans) deal in Africa.

The wind beneath their wings

Sustainable development has been a part of Natixis' corporate and institutional banking and markets processes since the times of its creators. Its parent, Natexis Banques Populaires, had created a team responsible for buying and selling European carbon dioxide quotas on the Amsterdam Stock Exchange and also increased its financing of environmentally-friendly wind energy parks at home and abroad.

Continuing this trend, Natixis's subsidiary in charge of the financial management of the European Carbon Fund (ECF), Natixis Environnement and Infrastructures, is serving as lead arranger with Caja Madrid to finance the construction of two thermo-electric solar plants developed by Abengoa that will be built near Seville. The project will have a 302MW capacity, making it one of the largest European solar platforms.

The bank also served as lead financer with Caixa BI, funding the construction of two wind farm portfolios in France in September 2006, and in 2008, it finalised two major carbon credit purchasing deals in China and in Egypt. The bank also practises what it funds, promoting waste reduction programmes for its offices, researching carpooling systems for its workers and focusing on purchasing eco-friendly products.

Fraud prevention

In early 2006, Natixis signed a one million euro deal with Norkom Technologies to implement Norkom financial crime and compliance software, thus strengthening bank security against money laundering and scams. The bank has been rolling out the software throughout its French branch offices and will rely on behavioural analysis, customer profiling and case management to prevent fraud.

The Norkom technology will instantly detect suspicious banking activity and send alerts to a special team of bank investigators. Implementing the software is part of Natixis' overall strategy to comply with tough European anti-money laundering rules and will allow it to streamline its compliance systems.

Market meltdown

Panic and fear spread around the world during the summer of 2007 — not as a result of a natural disaster or a terrorism plot, but as a consequence of a potential market crash. The subprime mortgage financial crisis, which began with a sharp rise in home foreclosures in the US in 2006, reached global proportions in July of the following year. The effects of the meltdown spread beyond housing and disrupted global financial markets, banking in France included. As a result, in November 2007, *Les Echos* reported that Natixis may have to inject 1.5 billion euros to recapitalise its credit enhancement subsidiary, CIFG, following the damage it incurred during the subprime crisis.

According to the newspaper, a recapitalisation would require controlling shareholders Banque Populaire and Caisse d'Epargne to agree on how much of the costs to bear, while a decision not to recapitalise could lead to CIFG losing its excellent credit rating.

In Autumn 2007, reports in papers like *La Tribune* claimed that Société Générale may take over Natixis from Caisse d'Epargne and Banque Populaire, offering them in return a 20 percent stake in Natixis. Thomson Financial reported in November 2007 that Caisse d'Epargne and Banque Populaire denied that they are considering any change in the capital structure of their jointly owned unit Natixis.

The repercussions of the subprime credit crisis echoed further, and in summer of 2008 Reuters reported that Natixis was readying to eliminate some 1,650 jobs. The redundancies would affect mainly support staff, including IT personnel and banking and investment personnel. The layoffs are part of Natixis' strategy of lowering fixed costs by ten percent or 400 million euros by 2009.

The French banking giant seems to be on the road to recovery already, having posted positive revenues where losses where predicted for the first trimester of 2008.

GETTING HIRED

Specific backgrounds are welcome

Natixis offers internships, lasting an average of six months, to business or engineering school students, in areas such as corporate business management or structured financing, trading, selling, structuring or engineering in quantitative research, portfolio management, research project management and IT analysis, among others.

To learn about careers at Natixis, go to www.natixis.com and click on the "human resources" link. Here you can find information on career development and training opportunities, current vacancies, internships and work placements as well as entry-level positions for students and recent graduates, applications, information about events where prospective applicants can meet employees and recruiters of the firm, as well as valuable information on Natixis' business area and its diversified lines of work.

Volunteer your way in the door

Natixis offers international voluntary placements (V.I.E's) for applicants under 29 who are interested in being assigned to work abroad for six- to 24-month periods. In 2006, Natixis offered 87 international voluntary placements in areas such as structured or corporate financing, commodities financing, capital market activities, and asset management. Roughly three quarters of participants were directly recruited into the company upon completion.

You can view and apply for the various programmes and job offers online and can also contact the HR department by submitting an unsolicited job application through the website or by sending your CV accompanied by a cover letter to Natixis' postal address, available on its website. ☐

NOMURA INTERNATIONAL PLC

Nomura House
1 St Martin's-le-Grand
London
EC1A 4NP
United Kingdom
Tel: +44 (0) 20 7521 2000
www.nomura.com

The Stats

Employer Type: Public Company
Ticker Symbol: NMR (NYSE)
Chief Executive: Kenichi Watanabe
2007 Revenue: ¥2.04tr
2007 Profit: ¥176bn
2006 Revenue: ¥1.79tr
2006 Profit: ¥304bn
No. of Employees: 18,000
No. of Offices: 190

Departments

Asset Management • Global
Investment Banking • Global Markets •
Global Merchant Banking

European Locations

London (European HQ)
Austria • France • Germany • Hungary •
Ireland • Italy • Luxembourg • The
Netherlands • Poland • Russia • Spain •
Switzerland • United Kingdom

Key Competitors

Bank of America Securities • Lehman
Brothers • Merrill Lynch

Employment Contact

www.nomura.com/europe/careers

THE BUZZ
WHAT EMPLOYEES AT OTHER FIRMS ARE SAYING

- "Making an effort to grow in Europe"
- "Underrated"
- "Asian flavour"
- "Seems messy and unorganised"

VAULT CAREER LIBRARY

THE SCOOP

N omura, a veritable powerhouse in Japanese banking, offers a full range of securities and investment banking services by way of more than 18,000 dedicated employees in more than 30 countries and 180 offices worldwide. The firm's four main departments are asset management, global markets (equities, fixed income and foreign exchange, derivates and portfolio trading), global investment banking and global merchant banking. Financial and advisory services and products are primarily dispensed to individual, institutional, corporate and government clients. Nomura also has a domestic retail business in Japan.

Osaka's giant

Established as Nomura Securities in 1925 in Osaka, Japan, the Nomura Holdings brand as we know it resulted as a spin-off from Osaka Nomura Bank. Nomura Holdings stands proud as Japan's largest global investment banking and securities firm. In 1946, the head office of Nomura Securities was moved from Osaka to Tokyo. Nomura began managing investments in 1951 and continued growing throughout the late 20th century, opening up consulting practices and branching out internationally.

Change at the top

There were changes to be made at Nomura in spring 2006, when the firm's structure was revitalised. After a re-shuffle, Nomura now manages group firms as a holding company and only has 14 executive officers. With the exception of a few people, executive officers no longer serve concurrently in positions at Nomura Securities and Nomura Holdings. The firm also reappointed all current business-line heads as division chief executives under the new structure. The final flourish to this re-organisation was the formation of an operating board consisting mainly of newly appointed divisional chief executives.

That's a good boss

More changes at the top went down in recent years. In April 2005, Yugo Ishida was named president and chief executive of Nomura International (the Europe, Middle East and Africa arm of Nomura Holdings). Deputy chief executive for the year prior, Ishida replaced Hiromi Yamaji, who returned to the company's headquarters in Tokyo after three years in London. Ishida joined Nomura in 1979 and during his career has worked in Nomura's offices in Bahrain, Hong Kong and Italy as well as Tokyo. In 2000, he moved from Milan to London to become managing director of European equity before becoming deputy chief executive in July 2004. Ishida appears to be making quite an impression; in December 2006, he was ranked No. 3 on *Here Is The City* 2006 "Boss of the Year" Poll.

Bound for the Americas

New York City was unsurprisingly the first American city to have a branch of Nomura located in it. The company has spread its wings since, officially operating under the Nomura Holding America Inc. brand and working out of offices in New York, Chicago, San Francisco, Los Angeles and São Paulo. The latest statistics according to Nomura are that its American wing has more than one billion dollars in capital and over 1,200 employees. Nomura Securities International (NSI) is the official name of the firm's American broker/dealer unit. Through its four main divisions, the firm offers capital raising, corporate advisory, sales and trading, foreign exchange, derivatives, research, asset management and online services in the Americas.

Nomura has invested time in bringing on board new talent, developing current employees and giving back to the community — and the Americas is no exception. In June 2005, financial whiz Jack Leventhal joined Nomura as managing director as its head of US financial institutions. Leventhal, former managing director and head of multinational financial institutions at UBS, is responsible for developing Nomura's

>   Yugo Ishida, chief executive of Nomura, was voted No.3 on *Here is the City's* Boss of the Year Poll

financial advisory business to multinational financial institutions based in the US. His role also takes in the creation of a middle-market investment banking business to US financial institutions.

In June 2007, Shigesuke Kashiwagi was nominated as senior managing director and head of regional management in the Americas. Kashiwagi, who is based in New York, joined Nomura Holding America, Inc. as the firm's chief operating officer in April 2006. Prior to that, he was senior managing director and head of global fixed income at Nomura Group.

Gold from a Silver Lake?

In February 2007, Nomura Holdings paid 1.2 billion US dollars to buy electronic stockbroker Instinet Inc. At the time, *The Associated Press* reported the move to be "the latest sign of its revived ambitions to expand overseas." Nomura bought the New York-based company, which took approximately half of its 400 million dollars in revenue from outside the US, from majority owner Silver Lake Partners, making Instinet a unit within Nomura. The deal, initially announced in late 2006, enabled

Nomura to trade on more than 50 securities markets around the world. The acquisition came as Nomura began to expand overseas again, significantly aided by a recovery in Japan's stock market at the time. Nomura, once a major player in financial markets in New York and London, pulled back from overseas operations in the 1990s, as it was hurt in part by the slump in the Japanese economy and markets. As its earnings and stock price improved, Nomura started to build back its business outside its home turf.

Nomura's interest in beefing up its already extensive foreign business is clear. In late 2005, the bank bought Code Securities, a "boutique investment bank" in the UK. Not long after, in February 2006, Nomura acquired a stake in Taishin Financial Holding Co., a large Taiwan bank, for 125 million US dollars. American business newspaper *The Wall Street Journal* reported: "Nomura, with revenue more than double its nearest domestic competitor, typically has relied on executing trades to generate the bulk of its revenue. Market liberalisation and the growth of electronic trading have eroded commissions, forcing Nomura to look for new business." Frustratingly, this foreign expansion was not to pay off, thanks in part to the subprime debacle which reared its ugly head in 2007.

So long Koga

Nomura chief executive Noboyuki Koga stood aside in March 2008 as former consumer operations head Kenichi Watanabe took the reins. The bank explained that Koga stepped down because it is common in Japanese companies to refresh management every three to four years. Koga stepped down in order for Nomura to seize the opportunity to introduce a younger management team with a fresh perspective, with the hope that it would take the company in a new direction. Since taking over, Watanabe has set out his vision to internationalise the company, with a global strategy to expand in emerging markets such as Asia and the Middle East. London has been decided as the firm's international product development hub.

The end of Koga's tenure was seen out with the withdrawal of Nomura from the residential mortgage-backed securities market in the US in 2007 and the dismantling of its US fixed income operations. The bank reported a 1.4 billion dollar loss on residential mortgage-backed securities-related investments in the nine months leading up to September 2007. Nomura is currently reviewing its operations and reconsidering where to focus its considerable resources.

A moral consciousness

In 1992, Nomura demonstrated what *The New York Times* called "a rare public admission of irregular sales practices" and paid 200 million dollars in compensation to customers for losses suffered on bonds they had been assured would never depreciate. Backed by buildings in the US, when the real estate market declined, the bonds' value suffered. This occurrence was seen as a fallout from the improper sales practices of Japan's 1980s boom years and the payout was considered a surprisingly candid admission.

As of 2008, Nomura remains on the up and up, at least as far as employees are concerned. In 2008, the bank came top in a poll of the "Best places to work in London" carried out by the capital's financial markets website *Here is the City* and was included in *The Times* 2007 Top 50 Places Where Women Want to Work listings.

GETTING HIRED

Ambition is key

If you're an undergraduate in your penultimate year and fancy getting a taste of working at Nomura, you should consider Nomura's ten-week internship programme for investment banking, global markets, finance and risk. Perform well and you're likely to be offered a job when you graduate. Click "apply now" on the company careers page to be taken to an online application form.

To begin your career at Nomura, your best bet is to apply for one of its graduate programmes. The bank operates them in a range of areas, including: global markets, finance and controllers, investment banking, technology and operations. You'll receive extensive training and hands-on experience in the area you choose.

Be warned, though, each programme is different, so make sure you check out the ins and outs on the company website's "graduate programmes" section. The common requirement across the board for all programmes is that you graduate with a 2:1 or equivalent. You'll be asked to fill in an online application form and sit a numerical reasoning test online. If you succeed, you'll undergo a telephone screening interview, before being invited to attend an assessment day.

See the world

If you're a more adventurous type, look into Nomura's international programme. Since most of its business areas are looking to staff their operations in Hong Kong or Singapore with new talent, joining this scheme trains you with a view to this end. While you'll start in London with classroom training and six months work experience, you will then transfer to an Asia-based role to continue your career.

Been busy?

If you hold an MBA and want to be a banker, the bank has great opportunities for you in investment banking and debt capital markets in its full-time or summer associate programmes. You will be in a client-facing role from the outset. You'll also receive excellent training and the hands-on experience you need to get the most out of beginning your career at Nomura.

If you're an experienced professional, you can view Nomura's vacancies by clicking "Vacancy Search" on the company careers page. ☐

BANCO PASTOR S.A.

Cantón Pequeño, I
15003 A Coruña
Spain
Tel: +34 981127600
www.bancopastor.es

The Stats

Employer Type: Public Company
Ticker Symbol: PAS (Madrid)
Chairman: Jose María Arias Mosquera
2007 Revenue: €740bn
2007 Profit: €202m
2006 Revenue: €637bn
2006 Profit: €156m
No of Employees: n/a
No of Offices: 643

Departments

Accounts and Deposits • Business
Banking • Distance Banking •
Insurance • Inversions Relations •
Loans and inversions • Private Banking •
Products and Services

European Locations

A Coruña (HQ)
Belgium • France • Germany •
Holland • Spain • Switzerland • United
Kingdom

Key Competitors

Banco Sabadell • Grupo Banco
Popular • Grupo Santander

Employment Contact

www.bancopastor.es
(Link "Bolsa de trabajo")

THE BUZZ
WHAT EMPLOYEES AT OTHER FIRMS ARE SAYING

• "Domestic retail bank"
• "Small regional player"

VAULT career library

THE SCOOP

B anco Pastor is the second-oldest bank in Spain — even older than Spain's central bank, Banco de España. The Galician bank was founded in the city of A Coruña in 1776, by Jaime Dalmau who aptly named it Jaime Dalmau y Cía (Jaime Dalmau and Company). Prior to founding the bank, Dalmau had a shipping company operating between the port of A Coruña and several American ports in order to service Galician emigrants, who used to send their savings back to their homeland using his services. This fact created the need to manage capital, so Dalmau created what at that time was known as Casa de banca, or the "Bank House".

In 1819, José Pastor Taxonera became a partner in the company and immediately gained full control of the business. He bought it out completely in 1845 and changed the firm's name to simply José Pastor. The business was handed down through generations, changing its name as it went, to Pastor Hermanos, José Pastor y Cía and Sobrinos de José Pastor. It was only in 1925 that the name was shortened to Banco Pastor and became incorporated.

In 1939, the bank came under the chairmanship of Pedro Barrié de la Maza who transformed the bank into a major supporter of the Galician business network. At the national level, it acquired stakes in different companies such as Astano, Renfe and Fenosa — a company also founded by Barrié in 1943. When he died in 1971, his wife Carmela Arias y Díaz de Rábago was appointed executive president of the bank — the first woman in Spain to hold such a position.

> " Carmela Arias y Diaz de Rabago was appointed executive president — the first woman in Spain to hold such a position "

In the late 1980s, Banco Pastor's plans were focused on the modernisation of the traditional banking business. It carried out a major restructuring of its organisation and modernised its corporate image. Following the line that her husband had begun, Díaz de Rábago strengthened the bank's development plan, which included opening new representative offices in countries where Galician people had emigrated and maintaining the bank's leadership position in Galicia.

Domestic growth

When the president stepped down in September 2001, the then chairman José María Arias Mosquera continued the strategy that his predecessor had begun. So, the bank increased its activity at its offices in other countries with a high number of Galician immigrants and

329

opened new ones where it saw a need. Arias launched a three year strategic plan in 2002, completed well in advance, and a new one in 2006 that will end in 2008. These ambitious plans have made Banco Pastor a domestic bank rather than a regional bank.

Because of that and Banco Pastor's financial strength and profitability, quality of its assets and good trajectory of its traditional bank business, the company has received good ratings from Moody's and Standard & Poor's.

Not too big, not too small

By 2007, Banco Pastor had become a jewel among medium-sized banks. The Galician born entity, controlled by the Fundación Barrie de la Maza, shot up in value to 4.6 billion euros in April 2007. The bank had renovated its shareholder base to include some of the biggest names in the Spanish economy such as Inditex's owner, Amancio Ortega, Ferrovial's controlling shareholders, the Del Pino family, and Caixanova.

According to the prominent Spanish financial newspaper *Cinco Días*, the bank experienced an amazing investment boost in the Spanish Stock Exchange in just one year. The 2005 involvement of Galician fashion entrepreneur Amancio Ortega, founder of ZARA and chief executive of retail fashion conglomerate Inditex, kick-started the good times for Banco Pastor. With new shareholders, Banco Pastor has doubled its value in the stock market in less than a year-and-a-half.

A giving banker

Concern for the socio-cultural development of Galicia led Barrié de la Maza, to create the Fundación Pedro Barrié de la Maza in 1966. The foundation's main purpose was primarily to encourage cultural, economic and social development of the region. The foundation has the biggest share of the bank, with more than 40 percent of the capital.

The foundation is a non-profit organisation with a global outlook. Its headquarters are in Spain, but it carries a distinctly Galician perspective with an international reach in education, research, culture and social services fields. It has a fund of around 1.8 billion euros and since its creation, has contributed 268 million euros to its chosen causes.

GETTING HIRED

What are they looking for?

Banco Pastor's Human Resources department looks for dynamic people with business skills and a good education to be part of its workforce. Around 58 percent of its workers have at least a graduate certificate, but this percentage is becoming bigger — of the 500 people hired in the spring of 2006, 87 percent had at least one degree. The company also offers different courses to its employees. In 2005, around 75 percent of its workforce attended 730 courses — an average of 41 training-hours per person.

Browse vacancies on its website under the link "bolsa de trabajo", where you can also fill in an online CV and where you can select which Spanish regions you would like to work in. It should be noted that its website is only available in Spanish and Galician.

Balancing work and life

In 2006, Banco Pastor incorporated a plan to combine the professional and personal life of its workers. Because of that, its employees can ask for a sabbatical year to work in a NGO or similar organization without losing their jobs. It also provides a number of measures in reference to the employees' families, such as unpaid leave of up to three years because of family's needs and childcare vouchers of 60 euros a month for nursing hours.

PETERCAM

Place Sainte-Gudule 19
Brussels, 1000
Belgium
Tel: + 32 2229 6311
www.petercam.be

The Stats

Employer Type: Private Company
Ticker Symbol: n/a
Chairman: Jean Peterbroeck
2007 Revenue: €252m
2007 Profit: €120
2006 Revenue: €197m
2006 Profit: €98m
No. of Employees 2007: 414
No. of Employees 2006: 381
No. of Offices: 10

Departments

Corporate Finance • Institutional
Asset Management • Institutional
Sales and Research • Private Banking

European Locations

Brussels (HQ)
Belgium • France • Luxembourg • The
Netherlands • Switzerland • United
Kingdom

Employment Contact

www.petercam.com (See "Jobs" link)

Key Competitors

AMB AMRO Belgium • Banque
Nationale de Belgique • Citibank
Belgium

THE BUZZ
WHAT EMPLOYEES AT OTHER FIRMS ARE SAYING

• "Small and specialised"
• "A smaller version of Rothschild"

THE SCOOP

P etercam is one of the leading banks in the Benelux region. The firm comprises four sectors: institutional sales and research, asset management, corporate finance and private banking. Petercam acts as an institutional sales and markets advisor for both Belgian and international clients, handling trading, execution and settlement of orders in stocks, bonds and derivatives products.

While its main strength is firmly centred in the Benelux region, Petercam — which is owned by 17 active partners — has branches throughout Europe, as well as an office in New York on the swanky Madison Avenue. In 2006, the bank extended and expanded its product range, launching PAM Equities, Energy and Resources — a fund focused exclusively on the ongoing energy investment revolution. The same year also witnessed the creation of a new division — Petercam Private Projects, or 3P, which offers products with non-traditional asset classes.

The institutional sales team boasts an extensive client base drawn from the UK, France, Germany, Luxembourg, Switzerland, Italy, Scandinavia, US and Canada. This impressively wide-ranging spread of clients allows Petercam the strongest placing capacity for Belgian equities. The asset management department does portfolio

> 6 6 Petercam acquired a majority interest in Concerto Capital Ltd, a company based in both London and New York 9 9

management for private and institutional clients, as well as creation and management of investment funds. The bank's corporate finance sector deals with stock exchange acquisitions, mergers and acquisitions and advisory services.

Those swinging sixties

The Petercam Group was formed by the merger of two foreign exchange brokers, Peterbroeck and van Campenhout, which in 1968 became the firm S.C.S. Peterbroeck, van Campenhout and CIE. The merged firm focused on stock broking and fund management, with a secondary interest in running foreign currency exchange outlets set up in several Belgian railway stations.

In 1990, one year after the firm entered the US market with the opening of a New York office, S.C.S. Peterbroeck, van Campenhout and CIE decided to transfer its stock market and foreign currency activities to two new and distinct limited liability companies called Petercam and Camrail. In 1994, the group took majority control of stockbrokers Pitti and Co. s.a., which gained it a presence in the Belgian city of Liège. In 1995, after the takeover of activities of the stockbrokers Beeckmans Van Gaver, Petercam opened an office in Antwerp. In 1999, the firm sold its participation in KBC Petercam Derivatives to KBC, opening two new offices — one in Ghent and one in Hasselt. The same year, Petercam extended its activities to the Netherlands by setting up Petercam Nederland N.V. — an institutional sales, research and corporate finance firm.

In 2000, Petercam took full control of CEPA in Geneva, which became Petercam Banque Privée Suisse in 2002. Also that year, Petercam acquired a majority interest in Concerto Capital Ltd, a company based in both London and New York that specialises in hedge fund management and consultancy. The firm also opened an office in Paris that year. By 2003, Petercam Nederland had acquired a bank status in The Netherlands. That same year, the asset-hungry firm took over Petercam Securities.

Talk about Respect

The bank's performance in mutual funds has won numerous accolades, including the Super Tijd Award for the best overall performance over five years and Standard & Poor's Ten-Year Internationally Marketed Funds (Smaller Group) for best overall performance over ten years. Petercam's other honours include the De Tijd Award for Best Fixed Income Manager over five years, Most Improved Benelux mid/small cap firm, first place in the Thomson Extel survey of Benelux mid/small caps sales, a second place ranking in the Thomson Extel survey of Benelux mid/small cap trading and a second place ranking for Benelux mid/small caps research.

Petercam Partner Guy Lerminiaux believes that on its own turf, Petercam has that special "savoir faire." In an interview with *De Standaard*, Lerminiaux explained that few investment banks focus on Belgium, preferring to take their business to big banking centres like London and Paris — and that's why Petercam comprises the vast majority of the Belgian banking market.

The Belgian equity funds that Petercam offers are definitely "European," as the euro has become universal and European stock markets have fused to form Euronext, but its mutual funds comprise anywhere from 30 to 75 percent Belgian companies. Lerminiaux explained that, while the EU makes for a universal European banking scene, banking in Belgium is "what we know." He adds, "It's the benchmark by which we measure our success."

Taking its own approach

Acknowledging that industries such as energy, mining, and the production of certain luxury goods does not exist in Belgium, Petercam invests beyond Belgium's borders. Nevertheless, where it can, Petercam stays local. As

Lerminiaux puts it, "Why invest in an Italian giant when Belgium has a small, similar enterprise that performs better?"

Despite fluctuations in the European stock markets and a slowdown in the US economy, as of June 2007, Petercam saw no need to change its strategy. According to an interview with *Boursorama*, Jan Leroy, upper manager with Petercam Equity Management, said, "Au contraire. If we do that, it would cost us in terms of performance." The firm prides itself on paying close attention to business cycles and industries that have global implications, such as energy. As for investments in agriculture and telecom, Petercam tempers its involvement, claiming that those industries are no longer "riding high" in Europe.

Well-rounded M&A shop

Petercam prides itself on offering comprehensive M&A advisory. From the evaluation of strategic alternatives to negotiating the final terms of a deal, the firm counsels clients in all kinds of transactions: trade sales, leveraged buyouts, acquisitions or disposals of minority or majority shareholdings and public takeover bids. In addition to sell-side and buy-side assignments, Petercam's M&A advisory services include advice on shareholders structure and assistance in the structuring and execution of public bids.

GETTING HIRED

Languages are key

Petercam posts its current vacancies on its website where you can browse and apply online. It should be noted that far more jobs are advertised on the company's French and Dutch language pages, for staffing offices in The Netherlands and Belgium. Those jobs advertised in English require fluency in French or Dutch in addition to English, and in some cases require you to be fluent in all three languages.

If you just want to make yourself known with a speculative application, this is welcomed by Petercam. Just click the "spontaneous application" link and submit your CV and letter. If you're a graduate looking for an internship, these are advertised along with jobs for experienced professionals, so keep your eyes open for opportunities among the company's vacancies.

BANCO POPULAR S.A.

Calle Velázquez, 34
28001 Madrid
Spain
Tel: +34 91 520 70 00
www.bancopopular.es

The Stats

Employer Type: Public Company
Ticker Symbol: POP (Madrid)
Chairman: Ángel Ron
2007 Revenue: €3.4bn
2007 Profit: €1.3bn
2006 Revenue: €3.1bn
2006 Profit: €1.1bn
No. of Employees: 15,038
No. of Offices: 2,531 locations in
seven countries

Departments

Administration • Asset Management •
Commercial and Retail Banking •
Human Resources • Life Insurance •
Pension and Mutual Fund
Administration • Private Banking •
Technology and IT Systems

European Locations

Madrid (HQ)
Belgium • France • Germany •
The Netherlands • Portugal • Spain •
Switzerland • United Kingdom

Employment Contact

www.bancopopular.es (Click on
"Trabaja con nosotros")

Key Competitors

Banco Sabadell • Grupo Santander •
Banco Pastor

THE BUZZ
WHAT EMPLOYEES AT OTHER FIRMS ARE SAYING

• "Significant role in Europe"
• "An old fashioned place to work"

THE SCOOP

I f there were a race between Spanish banks, Banco Popular would win the bronze medal, as it is the third-largest bank in Spain behind Santander Central Hispano and Banco Bilbao Vizcaya Argentaria (BBVA). The bank offers commercial and retail banking services through more than 2,500 branches. Ranked number 429 on *The Financial Times'* annual FT Global 500 list, Banco Popular is focused on its home market with an emphasis on commercial loans to small and mid-sized businesses. It also administers mutual funds and offers asset management, consumer credit, life insurance, factoring and securities trading.

The firm is made up of a national bank, Banco Popular Español, five regional banks (Banco de Andalucía, Banco de Castilla, Banco de Crédito Balear, Banco de Vasconia, Banco de Galicia) and a mortgage bank, Banco Popular Hipotecario. Banco Popular also has a French subsidiary, Banco Popular France, and a Portuguese subsidiary, Banco Popular Portugal.

Besides the Iberian Peninsula, Banco Popular also has a presence in Portugal, through Banco Popular Portugal, and in Germany and Switzerland. Moreover, it operates in the US through its subsidiary Totalbank, as well as in Hong Kong, Shanghai and Chile.

The monetary megalith was founded in 1926 and opened its first foreign branch office in Paris in 1968. By 1991, Banco Popular Español operated 14 branches in France. In 1992, the firm converted its French subsidiary into a joint venture with Banco Comercial Portugues under the name Banco Popular Comercial. In 2000, Banco

> " Banco Popular is the only bank in Spain that has remained independent throughoutconsolidation in the banking sector "

Popular established a network of Portuguese branches and then, two years later, Banco Popular Comercial became a wholly owned subsidiary of Banco Popular and changed its name to Banco Popular France. In Portugal, Banco Popular bought Banco Nacional de Crédito Inmobiliario and renamed it Banco Popular Portugal in 2005. Two years later, Banco Popular bought Totalbank, based in Florida.

An Angel named Ron

After 47 years on the board (32 as chairman), 78-year-old Luís Valls retired in October 2004 to resolve the succession issue at an "opportune moment." Although Valls stepped down as executive chairman, he remains chairman of the general shareholders' meeting. The board named the bank's current managing director, Ángel Ron, as chairman to replace Valls, making him the youngest chairman in Spanish banking at the tender age of 42. Ron shares chairmanship with Luis' brother Javier, who is co-chairman but has no executive responsibilities. Fernández Dopico, who had been with the bank for 34 years, was named chief executive.

Luís Valls passed away after a long illness at the age of 79 on February 25, 2006 in his house in Madrid. In June 2006, As a tribute to Valls, Ángel Ron decided to use his first shareholders meeting as the new chairman to remember Luís Valls. At the same time, Ángel Ron announced that Banco Popular would maintain the same strategy that it had followed for the past 50 years. He declared Banco Popular would preserve and promote its identity, strengthening its criterion of independency, transparency, discretion, prudence and strength.

Perhaps Ron made this statement to end rumours that were circulating about a possible merger with Banco Sabadell. At the meeting, Ron reminded the shareholders that Banco Popular was, and still is, the only banking entity in Spain that has remained independent throughout the consolidation in the banking sector over the past 20 years.

Growing with technology

Technology has always played an important part in the bank's growth. Since 1997, when Banco Popular created the telephone and internet banking service, the Spanish firm has tried to adapt the newest technologies to the needs of its customers. The internet spurred on the company's development in areas with good growth potential, such as real estate administration and private banking. As a result, in the year 2000, the firm created Bancopopular-e.com, the group's online banking service.

It wins more after reducing its exposure

Banco Popular suffered a 21 percent rise in bad loans in the 12 months leading up to September 2007, a trend likely to be repeated throughout the banking sector as funding costs rise and the Spanish economy slows down, dragged down by a troubled real estate sector.

After publishing its third-quarter results, Banco Popular's chief executive, José María Lucía declared Banco Popular was to reduce its exposure to the real estate sector by being more prudent and selective in their financing. Lending was still growing at double digits — up 17.6 percent year on year, although Lucía said that Popular was rebalancing its portfolio in favour of corporate loans to small and medium-sized businesses. According to Reuters, the portfolio may be worth as much as one billion euros.

GETTING HIRED

What the others say...

Banco Popular was selected one of the 2007 "Top Companies to Work For" by the international editorial company CRF and the consulting firm Accenture, which took into account the corporate culture, human resources management, innovation, corporate social responsibility and professional perspectives of a wide range of companies.

How to get in

The company does not have any graduate recruitment programme and the bank's human resources department does not follow the usual selection process of a test followed by an interview. In Banco Popular the process takes six months — it doesn't offer temporary contracts, so it wants to make sure it hires the right people. Although it can feel like a long process, if you pass you will be offered an indefinite contract and a personal plan which comprises a personal mentor, different courses, an evaluation plan and other formative activities according to your needs. Moreover, you will have other benefits, such as private health insurance, gym membership and financial help.

Applying the people filter

Banco Popular's career site declares that they're ready to "make dreams happen" for "our people, our communities, and for our financial performance." Quite a lofty assertion, but you can apply and decide for yourself at www.bancopopularcareers.com, where the firm's "people filter" lets you sift through a list of positions based on category and keyword. After selecting a position, you can apply online, where you'll be asked the standard questions along with ones such as your preferred "maximum commute."

Alternatively, if your Spanish written skills are good, you can log on to www.bancopopular.es and click on the "trabaja con nosotros" link, which offers more information about Banco Popular's corporate culture and has a link to create an online CV. □

RABOBANK INTERNATIONAL

Croeselaan 18
3521 CB Utrecht
The Netherlands
Tel: + 31 30 216 0000

The Stats (Rabobank Group)

Employer Type: Private Company
(Co-operative)
Ticker Symbol: n/a
Chief Executive: Bert Heemskerk
2007 Revenue: €11.4bn
2007 Profit: €2.6bn
2006 Revenue: €10.04bn
2006 Profit: €2.3bn
No. of Employees: 60,000+
No. of Offices (Rabobank Int'l):
14 in Europe

Divisions

Corporate Banking:
Agri Commodities • Corporate Advisory •
Corporate Clients in the Netherlands •
Corporate Finance • Corporate Finance
Regional Teams • Energy • Equities•
Equity Research • Export Finance •
Financial Logistics • Food&Agri • Large
Corporates • Leveraged Finance • Meta •
Mid-Caps Division • Project Finance:
Trade and Commodity Finance • Rabo
Securities • Structured Finance

Global Financial Markets:
Advisory • Benelux Sales • Corporate
Risk and Treasury • Debt Capital
Markets • Financial Institutions •
Member Bank Corporates • Member
Bank Desk • Risk Advisory

European Locations

Utrecht (Global HQ)
Belgium • France • Germany • Ireland •
Italy • The Netherlands • Poland •
Russia • Spain • Turkey • United
Kingdom

Employment Contact

www.rabobank.com/careers
Rabobank International
Recruitment, UC-Z 5026
P.O. Box 17100
3500 HG Utrecht
The Netherlands

Key Competitors

ABN AMRO • BNP Paribas • ING

Pluses

• "Very diverse"
• Great third world banking
 opportunities

Minuses

• "Hours can be long"
• "Not too well-known outside
 Benelux"

THE BUZZ
WHAT EMPLOYEES AT OTHER FIRMS ARE SAYING

• "Good in Benelux"
• "Big and Dutch"
• "Agriculture focused"
• "Regional bank"

THE SCOOP

W ith origins in a 19th century banking cooperative formed by Dutch farmers, Rabobank is today the largest provider of financial services in the Netherlands, although it retains some of its rural roots. Having built up its reputation for its leading role in the financing of food and agricultural matters, Rabobank still describes food and agribusiness as its "international prime focus". Its client base for these matters is primarily private individuals and small to medium-sized enterprises.

The group consists of its central pillar, Rabobank Nederland, 174 independent local cooperative Dutch Rabobanks and a worldwide network of offices. In total, the bank boasts nine million private customers, representation in 41 countries worldwide and an impressive AAA credit rating from both Standard & Poor's and Moody's.

Rabobank's core co-operative business is formed by the local Rabobanks. These in turn are members and shareholders of Rabobank Nederland, which offers both advice and support to the local banks' services whilst supervising their solvency, liquidity and organisation. Beyond this, Rabobank Nederland is a wholesale bank and the holding company for a range of specialised subsidiaries.

Plowshares to market shares

The creation of Dutch cooperatives was partly inspired by German mayor Friedrich Wilhelm Raffeisen's co-operative projects in Germany in the mid-19th century, established in an attempt to abate rural poverty and give farmers financial self-sufficiency. In 1898, two co-operative banks were founded in The Netherlands by the rural community, the Coöperatieve Centrale Raiffeisen-Bank in Utrecht, and the Coöperatieve Centrale Boerenleenbank in Eindhoven. The central principles of these banks included the unlimited liability of their members and locally limited operations.

While the two banks existed side by side and were almost identical in their operations, a mix of religious and legal differences kept them from uniting. In 1972 however, the banks merged, taking on the name Rabobank Nederland in 1980. Meanwhile, an increasing number of local banks were merging their operations to form Rabobanks, while benefiting from the centralised Rabobank Nederland's support and regulation. Significantly, when it comes to Rabobank's organisational structure, Rabobank Nederland is the subsidiary of the local banks which remain at the head of an inverted organisational pyramid.

As customer needs diversified, new government policy at the end of the 20th century enabled Rabobank to become an Allfinanz group, offering banking, investment and insurance products. Today the bank is a leader in a range of sectors, including small and medium-sized businesses and private customers. However, Rabobank's largest market share remains in the agricultural sector, where it holds around 80 percent of the market.

Spreading seeds

Rabobank International was formally established in 1996, although foreign acquisitions had begun earlier with the 1994 purchase of the Primary Industry Bank of Australia (PIBA). Rabobank International's manifold objectives were to better serve Rabobank's larger business customers with global operations, whilst establishing a European network of local banks and affiliated cooperative banks from abroad to amalgamate specialised subsidiaries. In 2002, the bank acquired Ireland's ACC Bank, along with the Valley Independence Bank in the US and Poland. More recently, in 2007, Rabobank acquired California's Mid-State Bank & Trust, spreading its tendrils deeper into California's strong agricultural market.

> “ Rabobank's largest market share remains the agricultural sector, where it holds around 80 percent of the market ”

Green fingers

In late 2007 Rabobank announced the launch of a carbon credits scheme. Hoping to encourage the replanting of areas subject to illegal deforestation in the Brazilian Amazon, particularly in the Xingu region in Mato Grosso state, the sustainability-aware bank presented 56,000 euros to eight soy farms and cattle ranches. Using this money in a pilot scheme to encourage replanting, the objective is to produce carbon credits which Rabobank can then use to cancel out its own carbon emissions. If the pilot is successful, the amount of funding will increase to several million dollars in successive years and the credits produced will be sold on a voluntary carbon credit market.

GETTING HIRED

Learning the business

Rabobank offers several opportunities to recent graduates, the shortest of these being the annual two-day Business Course, held in November. This is your chance to demonstrate your aptitude for the banking world by working on real-life cases, at commercial, organizational and analytical levels, as well as meeting the Corporate Management Traineeship recruiters. This will be your next step if the business course whets your banking appetite.

The Business Course first requires you to assist in bringing about a finance deal, "Rabo Real Deal," and in doing so it will test your ability in client handling, the acquisition of the deal itself, the development of the deal's financing structure and arranging the financing. You will get to grips with real life customer contact and be expected to behave as a qualified banker in order to issue clients with informative and useful professional advice. Coaching by senior managers is available on both days of the course.

To apply for the course, check the Rabobank website periodically for information on when the next registration period will open. A glance at the firm's recruitment calendar, which details the particular visits it makes to university campuses on recruitment drives, shows the majority of this activity takes place in March and April.

On the job

For students completing the final year of a Bachelor's or Master's university course, three types of internship are available to give you an extended glimpse of the banking world. The Work Experience Internship lets you work as part of the Rabobank team for around six months. The three to six-month Research Internship gives you the chance to develop a particular research issue and produce a report on your findings. The Graduation Internship calls upon participants to produce a thesis — of value to Rabobank — that must be defended at your university once complete.

Applications for internships should be made through the "Internship Bank" link, found by clicking "Careers" on the company homepage, selecting "Vacancies Rabobank International" on the left of the page, "Students and Starters," and clicking the "Graduation iInternship" drop down link. The application form is in Dutch, however, so you might want to inquire about internships in different languages via the bank's "internship agency" by following the link on the right.

The selection process for internships consists of an initial screening based upon letters of application, CVs and listed grades, followed by an interview for successful applicants. If your interview results are good, you'll be invited to a selection session, where you'll be given various tests to complete. You should be notified as to your success or failure within a week and given an internship contract to sign if you're through.

Already know the ropes?

To apply for jobs in The Netherlands, click on "Vacancies Rabobank International," and "Vacancy Bank RI", from where you can fill in a job search form, and apply online directly. For applications to any of the bank's other locations, you can contact your location of choice directly by following the "Vacancies Worldwide" link, and clicking the "Service and Location Finder" to find the contact details you need.

Not rocket science

"It's quite a straightforward interview process," says a banker in The Netherlands. "I had two rounds of interviews, two with my current boss, and one with my current boss to discuss all the benefits. After that they made me an offer."

Banking in the third world

Rabobank offers a system by which financial services are offered to some of the world's poorest people, through alliances made with regional banks in developing countries. By investing capital in these banks, Rabobank is aiming to modernise and improve them. Deployments vary from long-term missions of between one and three years, to short-term involvements of a few weeks to several months at the most. Under "Vacancies Worldwide" click "Rabo development program" followed by "Apply Here."

OUR SURVEY SAYS

Good banking vibes

The firm's culture is "open", "entrepreneurial" and "aimed at collaboration" say staffers. A manager tells us that there is "little bureaucracy and plenty of room for initiative", adding that employee morale is "very high". An experienced insider tells us, "People are loyal and committed and employees with many years of service are numerous." Other workers are happy the firm is "very diverse". One content employee in Amsterdam tells us, "There are all kinds of nationalities and we even have our own gay club."

The hours are "not bad" says an experienced insider in Amsterdam, explaining that hours range from "46 to 65 hours per week — depending on workload." Another insider says, "If you're performing well, there are opportunities for advancement. The group is big enough to give you an interesting career in banking." □

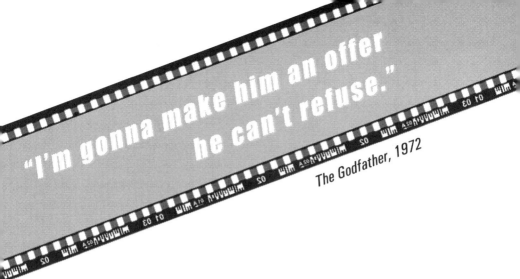

"I'm gonna make him an offer he can't refuse."

The Godfather, 1972

Find a job. Ace the interview.
Get a job you can't refuse.

Search the Vault job board.

Browse thousands of vacancies by industry, function or location.

Sign up for Vault's weekly Job Newsletter and receive jobs directly to your inbox.

www.vault.com/europe

RBC CAPITAL MARKETS

One Queenhithe
Thames Court
London EC4V 4DE
United Kingdom
Tel: +44 (0) 207 653 4000

71 Queen Victoria Street
London EC4V 4DE
United Kingdom
Tel: + 44 (0) 207 489 1188

www.rbccm.com

The Stats

Employer Type: Public Company
Ticker Symbol: RY (Toronto)
Chief Executive: Charles Winograd
2007 Revenue: CAD $22.5bn
2007 Profit: CAD $5.5bn
2006 Revenue: CAD $20.6bn
2006 Profit: CAD $4.7bn
No. of Employees: 70,000
No. of Offices: 75

Departments

Global Credit • Global Investment •
Banking and Equity • Global Markets •
Global Research

European Locations

London (European HQ)
France • Spain • Switzerland • The
Netherlands • United Kingdom

Employment Contact

www.rbccm.com
(Click on "careers" link in "about us"
menu)

For summer placements info:
summerplacements@rbccm.com

Key Competitors

CIBC World Markets • Citi • HSBC

THE SCOOP

B orn in the Great White North, RBC Capital Markets is the corporate and investment banking arm of RBC, the largest financial institution in Canada and one of the top banks in North America.

RBC Capital Markets offers products and services through five key business divisions: global investment banking and equity markets (corporate finance, mergers and acquisitions, equity capital markets, leveraged finance, syndicated finance, equity private placements), global markets (debt markets, foreign exchange, structured products, commodities), global credit and global research.

RBC Capital Markets has 3,300 employees in 75 offices located around the world, in North America, the UK, Europe, Asia and Australia. RBC's employee numbers in the US have more than tripled since 2001, growing from 500 to more than 1,700.

R-E-S-P-E-C-T

In 2007, Bloomberg ranked RBC No. 1 in corporate debt financing, equity underwriting and M&A in Canada, as well as No. 12 of the Top-20 Global Investment Banks, No. 13 in global equity and debt and No. 15 in global M&A. In 2008, the firm was ranked among the 100 Most Sustainable Corporations in the World, and came fourth in Waterstone Human Capital's ranking of the Ten Most Admired Corporate Cultures of 2007.

In 2006, RBC Capital Markets became an approved nominated adviser (NOMAD) to the Alternative Investment Market (AIM), which is owned by the LSE and caters to junior mining, oil and gas companies. The firm quickly sprung into action closing its first AIM transaction in December, advising Australian-based uranium miner Berkeley Resources Ltd. on its new listing on the London exchange.

For the love of Europe

In Europe, RBC Capital Markets' infrastructure team is firing on all cylinders. In addition to landmark mandates such as the 2007 eight billion pound Thames Water acquisition in the UK, the team is focused on expanding into targeted European countries and developing its product platform. Its debt capital markets business is also quickly expanding and has become a significant originator of both US dollar and non-core dollar bonds for European SSAs and FIs, ranking in the top five for US dollar-SSA benchmark issues.

In the 2007/2008 year, the firm's US investment banking business has operated exceptionally well. RBC Capital Markets acted as exclusive financial advisor to

American organic grocery giant Whole Foods in its recent acquisition of Wild Oats Markets. This transaction is a huge win for RBC Capital Markets as it builds its US franchise and is a good indication of how far the firm has progressed in the eyes of the US mid-market.

The Financial Times reported in March 2008 that RBC would open a leveraged finance business in London, with Nick Atkinson, Warrick Booth, Paul Brady and John Williams appointed by RBC Capital Markets to establish the new venture. RBC said "We want to take the opportunity to build a core team now, so that by the time the markets pick up we will be well-placed to take advantage of it".

Revenue from RBC's UK and US operations exceed revenue from the firm's homeland Canadian operations. The firm has strong global capabilities in energy, mining, fixed income, structured products, infrastructure finance and alternative dollars. Overall, RBC says it has an active global US dollar investor base of more than 4,700 accounts.

GETTING HIRED

Develop all the right skills

RBC Capital Markets operate a 17-week Graduate Training Programme to give you good look at what it means to work in capital markets. You'll pick up experience in sales, trading, infrastructure, debt capital markets and structuring through hands-on work in the following departments: treasury management, derivatives and commodities, fixed income and currencies, financial products, debt capital markets and infrastructure finance.

Using a mix of on-the-job and classroom training, RBC emphasises the programme's usefulness in developing participants technical knowledge and soft skills. The bank will also support you towards passing the FSA regulatory exams in your first months. On completion you'll be given a permanent position suited to both your strengths and preferences.

While the firm doesn't fuss about your degree discipline, it does require at least a 2:1, along with strong numerical and analytical skills and an awareness of global economic issues. It should also be noted that the majority of the bank's graduates hold degrees in business, economics, maths, science or engineering — so while not prescribed, these subjects are certainly looked upon kindly.

The online application process opens in September and deadlines are in November — be sure to check the company website for specific dates.

Your application will consist of a numerical reasoning test, an interview with someone from human resources, and if your performance is up to scratch, an assessment centre visit. The assessment centre will see you interviewed by senior management, undertaking role plays and presentations, along with a chance to meet and chat to senior bankers more informally. Around a week after this, the bank will let you know if you've been successful.

Summer loving

If you're working towards a 2:1 degree (or equivalent) and possess good numerical, analytical and technological skills, RBC Capital Markets would be interested in your application for their summer internship. The bank offers hands-on experience in any of the following: foreign exchange, treasury management, derivatives & commodities, fixed income sales & trading, financial products, debt capital markets, infrastructure finance, private banking, middle office, back office, global financial institutions and investment banking. Depending on the department you're placed in, you may also receive some classroom training.

Online applications open in December and the deadline is in February — but be sure to check the company website for specific dates. If you're selected for interview, you'll undertake a numerical reasoning test, followed by an interview with a human resources department member. You'll then be interviewed by someone from the department you applied to, and if this goes well, you'll be offered a place on the internship. □

BANCO SABADELL

Plaza de Cataluña, 1
08201 Sabadell, Barcelona
Spain
Tel: +34 93 728 92 89
www.bancosabadell.com

European Locations

Barcelona (HQ)
France • Italy • Portugal • Spain •
Turkey • United Kingdom

The Stats

Employer Type: Public Company
Ticker Symbol: SAB (Madrid)
Chairman: José Oliu Creus
2007 Revenue: €2.1bn
2007 Profit: €782m
2006 Revenue: €1.8bn
2006 Profit: €908m
No. of Employees: 10,177
No. of Offices: 1,196 in Spain, 17 in
other countries

Employment Contact

Human Resources
Pl. Sant Roc, 20
08201 Sabadell
Barcelona, Spain
Tel: +34 902 323 555
Email: RRHH@bancosabadell.com

Key Competitors

BBVA • La Caixa • Santander

Departments

Asset Management • Banking •
Investment • Commercial Banking •
Corporate Banking • Financing •
Insurance and Benefits • International
Business • Liquid Assets • Private
Banking • Real Estate Business •
Treasury

THE BUZZ
WHAT EMPLOYEES AT OTHER FIRMS ARE SAYING

• "Relatively local"
• "Small bank, clever bankers"

THE SCOOP

B anco Sabadell boasts a major presence in corporate, commercial and private banking and offers the full range of modern banking services for a range of different client types, including insurance products, asset management, resource-planning and tax assessment. For corporate clients in particular, it offers services such as banking investment, real estate business, assets, financing, international business and insurance products among others.

A solid foundation

In 1881, a group of 127 businessmen and traders from Sabadell, in the province of Barcelona, founded Banco Sabadell to finance the local industry and provide it with raw materials such as coal and wool. Early attempts were made at international expansion, with a Buenos Aires, Argentina, branch opened in 1891, but it foundered and was closed

> 66 The bank's main client base is in Catalonia, where Sabadell's market share exceeds that in Madrid by 19.72 percent 99

in 1894. As a result, the company decided to change its business operations. By 1907 the bank's focus had shifted strictly to commercial banking and non-banking operations were ceased.

Onwards and upwards

The Spanish Civil War caused major upheaval to industry and business across Spain from 1936 to 1939 and fascist rule further inhibited development in the period following this. It wasn't until 1953 that Banco Sabadell's shareholders constituted a share syndication agreement to preserve the bank's independence. They began to expand from this bastion into nearby towns in 1965.

Hi-tech pioneer

Establishing its first branch beyond the borders of Catalonia in 1975 with an office in Madrid, the firm's international expansion began in 1978, when the company opened its first overseas branch in London. Keeping up its reputation for implementing the latest technology, Banco Sabadell implemented remote banking for clients with telephone and computers incorporated as channels for client services and communication in 1986. Growth continued throughout the 1980s with the creation of Sabadell MultiBanca (subsequently called Sabadell Banca Privada) in 1988 — a bank providing equity management and private banking services, and bringing about the formation of the Banco Sabadell group.

A place in the sun

British bank Natwest made its appearance in the Spanish market in the 1970s. Some years later, in 1996, Banco Sabadell purchased Natwest España, a subsidiary of the English bank, paying out around 23.7 billion euros to its European neighbours for an 80 percent stake of its Spanish arm. Natwest España was renamed Solbank, from the Spanish word for sun, "sol", due to its sunny locations along the Levante coast in Andalucía and the Canary and Balearic Islands.

Sabadell reaped the rewards of its purchase; a success it still enjoys in 2008. Solbank almost doubled its profits in the first months after the acquisition. The former Natwest España had a strong market position to begin with, as it owned part of other Spanish banks such as Banco de Asturias, Herrero, Atlántico and Urquijo.

A gilded bank

Banco Sabadell Investment Funds were classified among the best-ranked in the Standard & Poor Expansion 2007 Awards. But even more important for the bank's reputation and standing was the Sello de Oro a la Excelencia (The Golden Stamp of Excellence), from the Club Excelencia en Gestión, representatives in Spain of the European Foundation for Quality Management (EFQM), in 2006.

Banco Sabadell has also been a leader in the Objective Quality Rating of the Financial Sector for two consecutives years in Spain — in 2005 and 2006. These ratings are conducted by Stiga, an independent consultancy firm, and carried out by the eight main Spanish banks. The quality rating is based on five criteria: quality of customer services, presentation and explanation of the product/service, physical appearance of the premises, commercial focus of employees and speed of response to client queries. The judging panel was composed of five researchers who posed as clients gathering information and opinions by visiting branches of the bank.

Sabadell sets its sights abroad

Since opening its first branch in Madrid in 1975, the bank has expanded throughout Spain, the US, South America and parts of Asia. Moreover, Banco Sabadell launched a full-on conquest of Madrid in August 2007. The bank's main client base is in Catalonia, where Sabadell's market share exceeds that in Madrid by 19.72 percent. The group intends to open more branches in the capital of Spain however, as well as in the smaller surrounding cities, to establish a comparable presence in this region.

GETTING HIRED

A guidance placement

Banco Sabadell has been ranked by the international Corporate Research Foundation (CRF) as one of the companies offering the best and greatest number of opportunities to aspiring and talented young professionals in Spain. In fact, the bank offers skilled banking graduates the opportunity to participate in a real company project under the guidance of experienced tutors who are open to new ideas and approaches.

Each applicant has a first interview with a representative from the human resources department. If successful, a second interview is arranged with the tutor of the department the prospective employee would be joining. The conditions for the length of the placement and working hours are established according to the project on which the graduate will be working.

A monitoring programme is then set up by human resources during the practice period to ensure that the training conditions have been fulfilled, the project is valuable and constructive and the graduate's performance is satisfactory. At the end of the placement, the tutor prepares a report on the graduate's profile and possible permanent positions are offered.

Plenty of opportunity

New graduates wishing to participate in this programme should send their CVs directly to Banco Sabadell by clicking "people" on the company homepage and following the "join us" link. A full list of employment opportunities can also be found at www.bancsabadell.com, by clicking on the "join us" link in the "people" section of the site. Once there, scroll to the bottom of the page to reach links to either view current opportunities or simply submit your CV to the human resources department through an automated form. Alternatively, native Spanish students and graduates can go through their school's employment resources department, as Banco Sabadell has connections with most of the top universities in Catalonia, like Pompeu Fabra and La Salle.

The firm is growing every day but only within the Spanish frontiers. Therefore, non-Spanish speaking applicants are at a considerable disadvantage. While much of the website is available in English, browsing vacancies and uploading a CV requires knowledge of either Spanish or Catalan as there is no English option. So if you are thinking about a career with Banco Sabadell and are not fluent in any of these languages, you might want to consider brushing up on your language skills first. □

SAL. OPPENHEIM JR. & CIE. KGaG

4, rue Jean Monnet
L 2180 Luxembourg
Luxembourg
Tel: +352 221522-1
www.oppenheim.lu

The Stats

Employer Type: Private Company
Ticker Symbol: n/a
Spokesman of the Personally Liable
Partners: Matthias Graf von Krockow
Chairman of the Supervisory Board:
Georg Baron von Ullmann
First Deputy Chairman of the
Supervisory Board: Friedrich Carl
Freiherr von Oppenheim
2007 Revenue: €333m
2007 Profit: €255m
2006 Revenue: €309m
2006 Profit: €241m
No. of Employees: 3,800
No. of Offices: 21

Departments

Asset Management • Corporate
Finance • Financial Markets •
Investment Banking • Private Banking •
Wealth Management

European Locations

Luxembourg (HQ)
Austria • Czech Republic • France •
Germany • Hungary • Ireland • Italy •
Luxembourg • Poland • Switzerland •
United Kingdom

Employment Contact

www.sal-oppenheim.com
(Click on "Career" link)

Key Competitors

Metzler seel Sohn & Co. • UBS •
Berenberg

THE BUZZ
WHAT EMPLOYEES AT OTHER FIRMS ARE SAYING

• "Small German bank"
• "Exclusive"

THE SCOOP

A s the largest family-owned private bank in Europe, Sal. Oppenheim offers asset management and investment banking services to corporations and high-net-worth individuals. It operates more than 20 offices in Germany and other European countries. In 2005, the 200 year-old-company entered a period of enormous expansion, nearly doubling in size, both in terms of assets and employees, following its acquisition of the BHF-BANK earlier that year.

Founded in 1789, Sal. Oppenheim began as a Bonn, Germany-based commissions and exchange house, which extended credit, dealt in commodities and provided foreign currency exchange. Nine years later, Sal. Oppenheim relocated its headquarters to Cologne. The bank's enterprising founder, Salomon Oppenheim Jr., was only 17 years old when he began his banking career, and successfully managed operations for most of his life. Upon his death in 1828, a tight succession plan saw management responsibilities shift to his wife, Therese, and their two sons, Simon and Abraham.

In 1904, though the bank shifted in structure from a general partnership to a limited partnership, it nevertheless remained firmly within the family. Under the Nazi regime, the bank was forced to adopt a new identity due to the Jewish origins of the founding family, even though the family had converted to Christianity in the 1850s. The firm was renamed after Partner Robert Pfedmenges, a

> ❝ Sal. Oppenheim has been involved in many of the most significant economic developments in Germany ❞

trustee for the Oppenheims, who withdrew to the background while the ownership structure remained intact. In 1947, the original family name was restored. Christopher Freiherr von Oppenheim, a personally liable partner since January 2000, represents the seventh generation of Oppenheimsto serve as head of private banking.

Building (and rebuilding) Germany

Sal. Oppenheim has been involved in many of the most significant economic developments in Germany over the past 200 years. The firm has provided financing for many key infrastructural projects, including the construction of Germany's railway system and steam shipping on the Rhine, in addition to much of the country's 19th Century industrialisation.

The years after World War II were difficult for Germany's private bankers, whose numbers were reduced from more than 800 to a mere 225. Sal. Oppenheim, however, re-emerged successfully. Its post-war activities included financing the German Auto

Sal. Oppenheim Jr. & Cie. KGaG

Union, which later became Audi AG; the mining and steel industries of the Ruhr area; and the German insurance industry.

Sal. Oppenheim won a major deal in 1989 when it sold its majority holdings in the Colonia Insurance Company, the second-largest in Germany. Part of the proceeds flowed into its equity, which leapt from 180 million to one billion Deutschmarks. In 1999 the bank redefined its strategies, identifying investment banking and asset management as its core businesses. Due to the firm's international expansion in recent years, Sal. Oppenheim now boasts offices and subsidiaries in Luxembourg, Switzerland, Austria, the Czech Republic, the UK and Ireland.

Dutch treat

In early 2005, Sal. Oppenheim made what ranks as one of the most significant acquisitions in the history of German private banking. It purchased the core business of BHF-BANK from the Dutch ING group for 600 million euros, effectively doubling in size overnight. However, the bank was careful to emphasise that the combined firm would not lose any of the individual strengths that it had been built upon. To this end, Sal. Oppenheim announced the integration would be accompanied by the launch

> ““ Sal. Oppenheim generates one-third of its income outside Germany, a figure expected to increase to 50 percent ””

of a "two-bank strategy," whereby both banks would retain their identities, decision-making authority and employees, along with a distinct market presence.

This dynamic growth strategy continued in 2006. Key steps included the investment in the Prader Bank, Bolzano, which gave the bank access to clients in northern Italy. In the alternative investments segment, Sal. Oppenheim was able to boost its presence in London through the acquisition of the Attica Group and an investment in Integrated Assets Management (IAM).

In Paris, the bank opened an office to set up an equity sales services team, further boosting its presence in France with the 100 percent takeover of the asset management specialist Financière Atlas. In Belgium Sal. Oppenheim also formed a joint venture with a holding company of the Frère-Bourgeois Group.

With a ten percent stake in the US investment bank Miller Buckfire, based in New York, Sal. Oppenheim entered into an exclusive partnership that would open up further market potential for cross-border M&A transactions between the US and the German-speaking world.

219 years of success

In 2007 the bank posted record results across the board. In fact, Sal. Oppenheim announced that its 219th financial year was the bank's most successful year in history. Consolidated income before taxes was up by 8 percent to 333 million euros. The bank saw an increase in equity to 2,174 million euros, and a growth in assets under management to 152 billion euros.

Sal. Oppenheim generates around one-third of its income outside of Germany, with this figure expected to increase to approximately 50 percent in the medium term. As a result, the bank's growth strategy aims to create a balanced relationship between its German and international business. In order to be able to fully exploit international growth opportunities in the future, Sal. Oppenheim moved the group headquarters to Luxembourg in July 2007, and bundled all Group activities in the new group parent company Sal. Oppenheim jr. & Cie. S.C.A.

GETTING HIRED

A guidance placement

Opportunities are available for undergraduates, graduates, and experienced professionals at Sal. Oppenheim. The bank offers an internship programme for students still in the process of completing their degree. The programme provides the uninitiated with experience of project work and daily business working alongside qualified teams. As an intern you are given the chance to work on tasks in a specific project within a real banking environment. To apply, you'll need to click on "job openings," select "students/interns", and choose a vacancy from the list.

The bank accepts a limited number of graduates each year in its training programme. You'll need a degree in business, business engineering or a similar discipline, and an international-oriented programme of study is preferred by the bank. If you've undertaken an international internship, this will also set you in good stead. Fluency in German is a must, as is knowledge of English and, with any luck, some other languages and extra curricular interests too.

Clerks in training

Sal. Oppenheim offers a banking clerk traineeship to give participants greater insight into the banking world. It consists of three parts: on-the-job training, with exposure to the firm's asset management, investment banking and bank services divisions; a range of seminars and project work and a vocational colleague to hone your theoretical knowledge. The programme begins on August 1 of each year and lasts for two years, and you'll need to get your application in by April of the previous year. The practical training takes place in Cologne, but includes fixed practical assignments in Frankfurt. To apply, send your CV by email to personal@oppenheim.de, or by post to the address found at the top of this profile.

The bank recruits potential candidates everywhere from universities to "executive search" agencies, insiders report, but the company website emphasises that its vacancies target the German market.

BANCO SANTANDER S.A.

Ciudad Financiera Santander
Boadilla del Monte
28660 Madrid
Spain
Tel: +34 902 112211
www.santander.com

European Locations

Madrid (HQ)
Belgium • Czech Republic • France •
Germany • Holland • Hungary • Italy •
Luxembourg • Spain • Switzerland •
Poland • Portugal • United Kingdom

The Stats

Employer Type: Public Company
Ticker Symbol: SAN (Madrid Stock
Exchange), BNC (LSE), STD (NYSE)
Chairman: Emilio Botín
2007 Revenue: €27bn
2007 Profit: €9bn
2006 Revenue: €22.3bn
2006 Profit: €7.6bn
No. of Employees: 129,749
No. of Offices: 5,772 branches in
Europe

Employment Contact

www.santander.com
(Click on "Jobs at Santander" section)

Key Competitors

Banco Pastor • Grupo Banco Popular •
Banco Sabadell

THE BUZZ
WHAT EMPLOYEES AT OTHER FIRMS ARE SAYING

• "Great culture and track record"
• "Increasingly important Spanish
  bank"
• "Good local player"
• "Still inexperienced"

Divisions

Administration • Americas • Asset
Management • Cards •
Communications and Marketing •
Financial Management • Global
Banking and Markets • Human
Resources • Insurance • Private
Banking • Retail Banking

VAULT career library

THE SCOOP

I n 1857, a group of businessmen from the northern Cantabrian port city of Santander launched Banco Santander with the aim of financing the port's bustling trade with Latin America. The Botín family has played a major role in the bank since 1920, when Emilio Botín y López was named the first fixed chairman of the company. The current chairman, Emilio Botín-Sanz de Sautuola y García de los Ríos, took the reins in 1986 from his father, who had followed in his father's steps, having headed Santander for 36 years.

The Spanish bank weathered the Great Depression thanks in part to Spain's economic isolation, and in the 1950s and 1960s it expanded into Latin America. Through the late 1980s, Santander grew faster than its Spanish peers and in 1994 it emerged as Spain's largest bank after the acquisition of Banco Español de Crédito (Banesto), which was auctioned by the government following an intervention by the Bank of Spain. In the mid-1990s, Santander began a series of acquisitions that would make it the largest bank in Latin America.

In 1999, Santander and Banco Central Hispano merged, forging the eurozone's first major banking consolidation and reinforcing Santander's leadership position in Spain, although at the time, the merger resulted in the layoff of 10,000 employees and the closing of up to a fifth of the combined banks' branches. Since then, however, employment and the branch network in Spain have grown steadily.

Ruling Europe

In 2007 Banco Santander was the largest public company in Spain, the biggest bank in the Eurozone by market capitalisation and the second-largest bank in Europe. Born out of a series of mergers and acquisitions, the group is the market leader in Spain; it is the third-largest bank in Portugal through Santander Totta; and in the UK it is the country's sixth-largest bank through its subsidiary Abbey.

Through Santander Consumer Finance, the group is also a leading consumer finance franchise in Germany, Italy, Spain and ten other European countries. Santander focuses on commercial banking, investment and pension funds, investment banking, corporate banking, internet and telephone banking, and treasury and capital markets. The bank had a market cap of 92.5 billion euros at the end of 2007 and assets of 913 billion euros.

Planting its flag in the Americas

Through its subsidiaries, Santander offers a full range of asset management, private banking, corporate and investment banking, and insurance. The bank has over 67 million customers at more than 11,178 branches around the world. With operations in 40 countries, Santander has a truly international footprint.

The company is also the largest bank in Latin America, with a strong presence in Brazil, Mexico and Chile. In July 2007, the firm announced that it will invest a further two billion US dollars in technology and branches in its Latin American operations. The group stated its interest in opening a further 945 new retail branches and 5,000 new cash machines in the region, which means that Santander's network will reach up to 20,000 branches by 2009, creating more than 6,000 new job positions in the process.

> ❝ The company is the largest bank in Latin America, with a strong presence in Brazil, Mexico and Chile ❞

Santander entered the US market in 2006 by buying a 24.9 percent share in Sovereign Bancorp as well as acquiring 90 percent of Drive Financial Services — an American auto lender focused on the subprime market — for 651 million dollars.

Boosting profits with Abbey

In November 2004, after its 12.5 billion euro-acquisition of Britain's Abbey, Santander became the number one bank in the eurozone by market capitalisation, a position it maintained in 2007, according to *El Economista*. The deal was the biggest ever cross-border purchase of a European retail bank. Prior to the deal, Abbey was suffering from two years of heavy losses caused by bad debt at the company's wholesale banking unit. Following a Santander cost-cutting programme and revenue initiatives, Abbey reported net profit of 1.2 billion euros in 2007.

As part of a strategy to transform Abbey into a full-service bank, in June 2006 Santander announced the sale of Abbey's life insurance business wholesale to Resolution for 3.6 billion pounds, including Mutual, Scottish Provident and Abbey National Life. However, Abbey retained all of its branch-based investment and asset management businesses.

In 2007, Santander's net profits rose 19 percent to 9.06 billion euros, making the bank fifth-largest in the world by profit. The group share price rose by 4.6 percent to end the year at 14.79 euros, valuing the group at 92.5 billion euros.

Shrugging off the subprime crisis

When asked about the effect of the US subprime crisis on its results at the end of 2007, Santander replied "zero." The bank's 19 percent increase in net attributable profits at the end of 2007 was the result of a 21 percent increase in revenues, a 22 percent increase in net interest income, and a 14.5 percent increase in net income from fees and commissions.

In February 2008 the company chairman, Emilio Botín, predicted continued growth throughout 2008 and 2009. "Sound economic policies" had helped to maintain investor confidence, he noted, while Latin America had been unaffected by the liquity crisis in credit markets on the whole.

The concentration of the Spanish bank on retail banking, "minimal" exposure to hedge funds, asset-backed securities and monocline insurers, and the limited use of structured products had jept it safe from subprime crisis fall out. Botín added, speaking in *The Financial Times*, that despite the difficult climate "Santander is not limiting its lending in any markets." "What we need now to stop the jitters are a series of exercises in realism and transparancy by global financial groups," he added.

Signing records

In October 2007, Banco Santander, together with the Royal Bank of Scotland and Fortis, purchased Dutch bank ABN Amro in a highly publicised deal. As a result of the acquisition, Banco Real, ABN Amro's Brazilian unit, has become part of Santander, making it one of the top three banks in Brazil. In November 2007, the Spanish giant signed another record-making deal. Santander acquired Italian bank Antonveneta and sold it to fellow Italian bank Monte dei Paschi, earning 2.3 billion euros of profit in the deal, which wrapped up in May 2008.

Banco Santander used another Italian asset it had acquired in the ABN Amro deal to complete a business swap with GE Money. In June 2008 General Electric's commercial finance unit acquired Santander's Italian wholesale banking arm, Interbanca, valued at one billion euros. In return, Santander snapped up several GE operations worth the same sum, including GE Money's businesses in Austria, Finland and Germany; its British automobile financing division; and its credit card business in Britain and Ireland.

A sustainable new asset

Banco Real, Santander's freshly-acquired Brazilian prize, took top honours at the 2008 *Financial Times* Sustainable Banking awards, held in London in June 2008. This marked the first time a bank in an emerging market had won the prize. According to the judging panel, Banco Real has "pioneered sustainable banking in South America, putting social and environmental issues at the centre of all its business issues and involving its 32,000 staff in the strategy."

Banco Santander S.A.

Strongest at home

Santander was ranked the No. 18 advisor of completed global mergers and acquisitions in the first quarter of 2008, according to Thomson Financial. This was a big step up from Santander's rank at No. 33 in the first quarter of 2007. In European deals, Santander was No. 25 in announced M&A and No. 13 in completed, with three announced transactions and 26 wrapped up.

The Spanish bank placed even higher in the UK league tables, coming in at No. 15 and No. 9 in announced and completed deals, respectively. At home in Spain, Santander cracked the top five, placing No. 4 in announced M&A and No. 5 in completed deals. It made an appearance in the Benelux region, as well, completing six M&A assignments to rank No. 19.

10 billion or bust

At Santander's annual general meeting in June 2008, group chairman Emilio Botín had plenty to brag about: the bank's traditionally conservative approach to risk management helped it escape the dire losses faced by so many financial institutions in 2007 and early 2008. However, he indicated that Santander may continue to prioritise its growing retail arm – currently, retail banking contributes 84 percent of revenue, and Botín told investors that, "We base the growth of our results on recurrent business."

While profit attributable to shareholders has grown a healthy 25 percent, on average, over the past ten years, Botín declared an ambitious goal for fiscal year 2008. "We aim to exceed ten billion euros in total profit for the group in 2008," he said.

That's a lot of beer

Santander is part of an all-star line-up of European banks standing by to finance a potential merger between Belgian beverage giant InBev and American beer legend Anheuser-Busch. If completed, the deal would create the world's largest brewer, home to the Stella Artois, Beck's, Hoegarden, Bass and Budweiser brands. InBev's June 2008 offer of 46.3 billion US dollars (23 billion pounds) was made in hopes of "a friendly agreement," chief executive Carlos Brito said.

The banks, including Barclays, BNP Paribas, Deutsche Bank, Fortis, JPMorgan and the Royal Bank of Scotland, as well as Santander, are poised to put together a financing deal that combines debt, equity finance and non-core asset sales.

GETTING HIRED

Santander's hiring spree

Over the last few years this banking giant has been focused on hiring a considerable number of new graduates and on giving opportunities to students who are nearing the end of their university studies, with the aim of creating junior players who will be faithful to the firm and will want to develop their professional careers within the company. In 2006, the HR department hired a total of 18,000 new recruits, of which more than 1,600 were in Spain. However, with approximately 100 different nationalities represented among its staff, Santander has established itself as a diverse and international bank, not only as a business but also as an employer.

After hiring 700 graduates in 2006, Santander became Spain's biggest graduate employer in banking, followed by rival firm BBVA. Santander also offers students internships in locations outside of Spain, including the UK (through Abbey), Portugal, Brazil, Mexico and Chile, to be trained in retail banking, investment banking, financial markets, risk and auditing, among others.

To find out more about career opportunities at Santander, log on to www.santander.com and click on the "Work with us" link.

Four paths to Abbey

In the UK, despite being fully-owned by the Santander Group, Abbey has so far recruited independently from Santander and employs approximately 16,600 people. Since becoming part of the Santander group in 2004, Abbey has revived its graduate programmes which are available in internal audit, finance, retail and risk and last between one and three years. Generally the programmes consist of a series of work placements in the bank's departments, completing projects and tasks alongside employees.

On the internal audit programme you'll be involved in research and evaluation of Abbey's business, testing and evaluation of a range of processes, and suggesting improvements. For the finance programme, you'll undertake four six-month placements before   specialising in your final year whilst progressing towards professional accountancy qualifications. You'll collect and analyse data for modelling, investigate technical problems and test assumptions. Your remit will also include collating and interpreting data to conduct investigations into variances and trends.

The risk programme lasts two years, and consists of three six-month placements in three areas, from a choice of secured credit strategy, unsecured credit strategy, Santander analytics, risk measurement and customer risk. The last six months are spent on a series of shorter placements in the remaining PFS lending functions, and in other business areas.

The remaining six months will consist of a series of shorter placements — lasting two to four weeks each — across the remaining PFS Lending functions and some other key business areas, including: the underwriting operational team, collections, risk governance and control, fraud strategy and operations, the mortgage surveyors team, operational risk, sales, operations, finance and product marketing.

Where am I — and what am I doing here?

The locations you'll find yourself in for each programme differ. The risk programme takes place in Milton Keynes, while the finance programme placements can occur in either head office in London or Milton Keynes. For finance, you'll need to be willing to live and work in both locations.

While the audit team is based in London, audits take place all over the country. You can expect to find yourself spending time away on location if internal audit is your chosen programme. The retail programme takes place in the firm's nationwide branch network, so you'll need to be mobile for moving from branch to branch in the course of your training. This can be within a geographical region or nationwide. Experienced professionals can browse vacancies and find more information about career opportunities at Abbey on the company's careers site at: www.jobsatabbey.com. □

SBERBANK

19 Vavilova St.
117997
Moscow
Russia
Tel: (+7 495) 957 5862
Fax: (+7 495) 957 5731
(+7 495) 747 3731
Telex: 414733 SBRF RU
Teletype: 114569 SBRF RU
Email: sbrf@sbrf.ru

The Stats

Employer Type: Public Company
Ticker Symbol: SBER (Moscow)
Chief Executive: German Gref
2007 Revenue: RUB 335bn
2007 Profit: RUB 106bn
2006 Revenue: RUB 254bn
2006 Profit: RUB 82.8bn
No. of Employees: 243,620
No. of Offices: 20,101

Departments

Bank Cards • Capital Markets •
Construction Projects Finance •
Corporate Banking • Documentary
Operations and Trade Finance •
Financial Markets • Foreign Currency
and Non-Commercial Operations •
Main Settlement Centre • Operations
Project Finance • Retail Deposits and
Payments • Securities • Treasury and
Financial Markets

European Locations

Moscow (HQ)
Locations throughout Russia

Employment Contact

www.sbrf.ru/personal/personal.htm

recruting@sbrf.ru (sic)
Tel: +7495 505 8815

THE BUZZ
WHAT EMPLOYEES AT OTHER FIRMS ARE SAYING

• "Huge in Russia"
• "Unknown outside of Russia"

THE SCOOP

The Savings Bank of the Russian Federation, or Sberbank, is both the largest and oldest bank in Russia. Tracing its roots to 1841, today it dominates the individual savings account sector with 65 percent of nationwide household deposits, and is represented by a 20,000 strong branch network that reaches from the commercial hubs to the nation's more remote regions.

Although it was privatised in 1991, 60 percent of the company's equity is held by Russia's Central Bank. It still maintains close government ties and benefits from a government guarantee on deposits. Since the economic meltdown of the 1990s, Sberbank has evolved into a universal commercial bank, one of Russia's primary oil and natural resources financiers, and offers comprehensive savings, investment and lending services.

Sberbank was ranked 66th internationally in the 2007 *Banker* magazine list of Top 1,000 World Banks 2007 based on Tier 1 capital and achieved a No. 1 ranking in Russia. The Russian banking monolith also reached

> ❝ Sberbank reached the 103rd spot on *The Financial Times* list of the largest companies in the world ❞

the 103rd spot on *The Financial Times'* list of the largest companies in the world.

Weathering change

While the Tsar instituted the first Russian savings banks in 1841, and transferred them under the jurisdiction of the State Bank of Russia — or Gosbank — in 1860, it was only with the abolition of serfdom in 1861 that Gosbank really began to see widespread savings activity. Despite major shifts in organisation during the Russian Revolution and two World Wars, by 1963, savings banks were once again under the control of Gosbank, which now carried out the functions of both a central and a commercial bank.

Following a period of economic stagnation from 1970 to 1985, Gorbachev instituted an overhaul of the banking system in 1988 which turned Gosbank into a central regulatory institution, and created five separate banks with individual specialisations, including foreign trade, agriculture, and industrial loans. One of these newly born banks was Sberbank and its remit was the operation of a savings and loan system for workers and average citizens. It was also set up as an umbrella institution for the USSR's 15 savings banks.

Efforts to privatise the bank began with Yeltsin in 1991. While the bank became an independent entity, a large chunk of it was still government owned. Full privatisation was indefinitely postponed in 1995 to thwart a Russian tycoon with a history of banking failures who wished to take control of Sberbank. Coming through the 1998 financial crisis in Russia relatively unscathed, the bank began to shift its focus to investment in the private sector and made significant loans in oil, mining, and gas concerns. It reduced its branch network to around 20,000 in 2001 in an effort to increase its profitability, and in 2003, placed a one billion dollar eurobond, the first by a Russian company to receive an investment-grade rating.

Slurbank

In 2003 Sberbank got into a dispute with investment fund and asset management company Hermitage Capital Management, a minority investor in the bank, considered an "activist" business in Russia. At a presentation at the Adam Smith Institute's Russian banking conference in London, Vadim Kleiner, a Hermitage director and member of Sberbank's supervisory board, read a report which accused the banking major of making subsidised loans to oligarchs at the expense of ordinary Russian depositors. He also claimed that the bank was overstaffed, inefficient and inequitable.

Sberbank denied the charges, accusing Kleiner of denigrating the bank's reputation, and began legal proceedings. Kleiner asserted that as an independent director it was his job to be difficult, and that the bank had prevented him from including the points in its own board meetings. With the court eventually ruling against Sberbank, the debacle emphasised the need for increased transparency in its dealings, and in its accountability to its board members and the public.

Old bank, new tricks

In early 2007, Sberbank approved a reformation of its organisational structure to make it more competitive. The new structure will aim to actively develop the banking services market, facilitate expansion in the bank's key business areas, and develop new banking products. Many view the change as the bank's first step towards implementing standard international business approaches: embracing corporate governance, better transparency and assignment of responsibility, diminished concentration of authority and more efficient interaction between regional structures and the central head office.

The new organisational structure is seen as one of the primary moves to reform the Bank and to make it more competitive, resulting in active development of the banking services market, facilitating expansion in the key areas of the bank's business and launching new banking products. The new organisation is transitional and will continue in effect until the bank adopts a five-year strategy before the end of 2008.

The bank's plan is to create separate areas for retail and corporate matters, and to establish a separate structure for the development of its regional branch network. It will also set up a board of chairmen of regional head offices, reporting to the bank's chief executive, as well as setting up two committees for strategic and corporate development and IT.

GETTING HIRED

If you speak Russian ...

Unfortunately for the majority of European graduates, finding a position at Sberbank will be next to impossible. Russia's national bank only advertises jobs to Russian-speakers on its website (although knowledge of English is often listed as one of the requirements). When it comes to entry-level traineeships and internships, Sberbank fills those with students from local institutions, such as the Moscow University of Industry and Finance, with which it has a long tradition of co-operation.

That being said, if you happen to be a Western-educated finance graduate who has a native-like knowledge of Russian, your application will likely be welcome. You can check for job listings under www.sbrf.ru/personal/personal.htm, and CVs or queries can be addressed to recruting@sbrf.ru.

STANDARD CHARTERED BANK

1 Aldermanbury Square
London
EC2V 7SB
United Kingdom
Tel: +44 (0) 207 280 7500
www.standardchartered.com

European Locations

London (European HQ)
France • Jersey • Switzerland • United Kingdom

The Stats

Employer Type: Public Company
Ticker Symbol: STAN (LSE)
Chairman: Mervyn Davies
2007 Revenue: $11.1bn
2007 Profit: $2.9bn
2006 Revenue: $8.62bn
2006 Profit: $2.35bn
No. of Employees: 54,000
No. of Offices: 1,299

Employment Contact

careers.standardchartered.com

THE BUZZ
WHAT EMPLOYEES AT OTHER FIRMS ARE SAYING

• "Big in emerging markets"
• "Local, not an IB player"
• "Good presence in India"
• "Big, but unexciting"

Divisions

Consumer Banking • Corporate Real Estate Services • Finance • Human Resources • Legal and Compliance and Assurance • Technology and Operations • Wholesale Banking

THE SCOOP

S tandard Chartered (StanChart) was created in 1969 by the merger of the Standard Bank of British South Africa and the Chartered Bank of India, Australia and China. Both banks trace their roots to the 1800s, when British trade activities created a need for banking and financial institutions throughout the far reaches of the British Empire. A period of peaceful growth lasted into modern times — until 1986 — when Britain's Lloyds Bank attempted a hostile takeover.

As of 2008, StanChart focuses its operations on Asia, Africa and the Middle East, and more than 90 percent of its profits are derived from these regions. The bank's European operations serve as a bridge to emerging markets. Based in London, StanChart offers consumer, corporate and institutional banking, as well as treasury services. It has more than 1,700 branches in 70 countries and employs approximately 73,000 people.

On the Q12

Employees at StanChart are familiar with Q12, an annual survey unveiled in 2000. This in-depth report is more than a simple employee satisfaction survey. It's designed to measure employee engagement on a number of indices and thus make employee responses a central part of StanChart's agenda. Results of the Q12 survey are used by top bank officials to plan the next year's course of action. In 2005, the survey was distributed to every country in which StanChart operates and a whopping 96 percent of employees chose to participate.

Presence in Paris

In June 2008, Standard Chartered announced it was opening a branch office in Paris, thanks to growth in its global corporates and financial institutions business in France. The year marks the 150th anniversary of consistent trade between the bank and two of its focus markets — China and India. Taking up a position in France, the bank hopes, will open new doors for French businesses looking for trade and investment opportunities in the bank's other main markets: Asia, Africa and the Middle East.

Mike Rees, chief executive of Standard Chartered wholesale banking, said: "We are excited about the prospect of working with French clients more closely. Thanks to our recent acquisitions and our growing strategic capabilities, we are in a position to compete with the leading providers in the M&A sector — and the acquisition of American Express Bank further broadens the range of services we are able to provide clients."

God bless American Express

In February 2008, Standard Chartered completed its acquisition of American Express Bank (AEB) from the American Express Company for 823 million US dollars. The buy will show particularly in StanChart's financial institutions and private banking businesses and adds 19 more markets to the bank's roster whilst providing access to several new growth markets. On top of this, the acquisition has doubled StanChart's US dollar clearing business and pushes the bank to the number six US dollar clearing business in the world.

Performance rewarded

In 2007, Standard Chartered picked up several award for its performance, most notably Best Emerging Markets Bank, Best Bank in Africa and Best Bank in Ghana at the *Euromoney* Awards for Excellence. *FinanceAsia* Country Awards for Achievement 2007 awarded the bank the title of Best Foreign Bank in South Korea. At the *Global Finance* awards, the bank took home Best Trade Finance Bank in Singapore, Best Bank for Liquidity Management in Africa, Best Bank for Risk Management in Africa and Best Foreign Exchange Bank in Gambia.

Building the road to trade

In December 2006, StanChart launched the China-Africa Trade Corridor, an initiative designed to offer financial solutions to small- and medium-sized enterprises (SMEs) in China and Africa, making their first strides into international business. The initiative was kicked off with a two-day seminar in Shenzhen, China, giving SMEs from both regions an opportunity to exchange ideas and explore cooperation. The Trade Corridor initiative will offer capital management services and financing solutions to SMEs, and will assist them in their globalisation processes.

GETTING HIRED

Tailor your focus

At careers.standardchartered.com, you can search globally for open positions or learn about the firm's intern recruitment as well as graduate and MBA recruitment programmes. The bank also offers FAQs regarding the application process along with a list of "hints and tips." For graduates looking to launch their career with Standard Chartered, the firm offers a two-year development programme to get you in the mood for banking. It consists of four primary elements to set up participants with the skills they need: the core skills programme, business development plans, development conversations and the graduate support network.

The core skills programmes are three-week-long residential training programmes that focus on building personal and management skills. At the outset you'll embark on the induction programme, focusing on personal effectiveness, relationship building and an introduction to the bank. After your first year, you'll take the

> `` The acquisition of American Express Bank further broadened the range of services the bank provides clients ''

manager programme, which focuses on team building and the bank's values. The last programme focuses on leadership skills and strategic management.

Each of the bank's divisions — consumer banking, wholesale banking, technology and operations, finance, human resources, legal and compliance and assurance, and corporate real estate services — has its own self-designed business development plan. The plans aim to develop the specific skills necessary to succeed in that particular area. For detailed breakdowns of what each plan involves, take a look at the business plan you're interested in on the firm's careers page.

Throughout the two-year programme, a series of conversations with your sponsor will give you advice and information on your progress in key areas. The conversations are dubbed performance management and reward, learning and development, engagement review, strengths finder, and career development.

On top of these structures, you'll enjoy a large support network consisting of a graduate sponsor, a rotation manager, a buddy, the human resources relationship manager, the graduate programme manager and the group graduate team.

Calling all interns

Standard Chartered operate a number of internship programmes that last from eight-to-12-weeks each. Each programme aims to provide participants with an insight into the firm's activities, a full induction and development programme, a strong support network and exposure to new business networks. It looks great on a CV and also provides good opportunities for career development, not least automatic consideration for the bank's international graduate opportunities in the following year.

WESTLB

Herzogstra e 15
40217
Germany
Tel: +49 211 826 01
www.westlb.de

European Locations

Düsseldorf (HQ)
Czech Republic • France • Germany •
Hungary • Ireland • Italy • Luxembourg •
Poland • Russia • Serbia • Spain •
Turkey • Ukraine • United Kingdom

The Stats

Employer Type: Private Company
Ticker Symbol: n/a
Chairman: Heinz Hilgert
2007 Revenue: €1.09bn
2007 Profit (loss): (€1.5bn)
2006 Revenue: €1bn
2006 Profit: €799m
No. of Employees: 6,477
No. of Offices: 17

Departments

Asset Management • Corporate
Banking • Investment Banking • Private
Banking

Employment Contact

www.westlbcareers.com

THE BUZZ
WHAT EMPLOYEES AT OTHER FIRMS ARE SAYING

• "Decent German bank"
• "Unknown"

VAULT career library

THE SCOOP

W estLB is one of Germany's biggest financial services companies and serves as a central bank for the *Sparkassen*, or savings banks, in North Rhine-Westphalia and Brandenburg. It's also an international commercial bank that links its home turf to global financial markets. Among its wide range of offerings, WestLB provides lending, structured finance, capital market and private equity products, asset management, transaction services and real estate finance.

The bank has dual headquarters in Düsseldorf and Münster, in addition to German branch offices in Berlin, Cologne, Dortmund, Frankfurt am Main, Hamburg and Munich. Throughout the rest of Europe, WestLB maintains branches in Istanbul, London, Madrid, Milan and Paris. The German financial services leader also has a foothold in more far-flung locations, with branches in Asia, Australia and New York, as well as representative offices and subsidiaries around the world.

The firm was created in 1969 by the merger of Landesbank für Westfalen Girozentrale, a Münster institution founded in 1832, and Rheinische Girozentrale und Provinzialbank, a Düsseldorf firm founded all the way back in 1854. In 2002, WestLB became a joint stock company and in July 2005, government support for the bank's institutional liability and guarantor liability was abolished, forcing WestLB to operate without state guarantees. WestLB is still partially owned by the government of North Rhine-Westphalia, Germany's largest federal state.

Cutting back

Part of the heavily afflicted Landesbank system that was brought to its knees by the subprime crisis of 2007, WestLB was hit harder than expectations, to the tune of 1.6 billion euros. The bank's 2007 profits were engulfed by two billion euros worth of writedowns, to which the regional government and savings banks that own the company reacted by taking a 23 billion euro portfolio of investments off its balance sheet and underwriting five billion of losses. WestLB reassured its shareholders that these steps would cancel out practically all of its losses and shield it against further writedowns and capital injections.

In an effort to tackle the setback, the bank decided to rein in its global operations, focusing on "core competencies" in fewer locations and cutting jobs both in Germany and overseas. This added up to a total staff reduction of 20 percent.

Looking for safer means of income, the bank decided to set its sights on picking up more mid-sized German corporate clients in an effort to stabilise its volatile investment banking takings. London and New York, which generate more than half the firms non-German profits, will remain a top priority in the bank's activity. However, 50 jobs in London had already been cut by April 2008.

Germany's next top model

WestLB has increased its competitive edge by setting high profit targets and improving its market capitalisation. It also boosted its number of sparkassen transactions and restructured its investment banking activities to focus on client-driven and fee-based business — a wise move that has resulted in greater investment banking profits, with especially strong performances in the structured finance, syndicated lending, equity issues and structured trading divisions.

The bank was also among the German banks that, in November 2006, entered into talks to buy a significant stake in the aeronautical firm European Aeronautic Defense & Space (EADS). German automaker Daimler, who owns a major stake in EADS, had plans to reduce its holding. Other German banks named in the deal were Commerzbank, Deutsche Bank and KfW, and a German government spokesman said the transaction would likely go through sometime in 2007.

WestLB's international growth strategy for 2007 included an expansion into the US. In late 2006, it ventured into new territory in Asia, opening offices in China and India. In June 2007, the bank decided not to sell its Latin American operations, despite talks to the contrary that other banks were particularly interested in acquiring its Brazilian operations. Despite the bank's efforts to become a global competitor, North Rhine-Westphalia finance minister Helmut Linssen announced in January 2007 that his government was considering selling its 38 percent stake in WestLB. "But we are not in a hurry," he said, citing WestLB's strong performance — which, if it continues, will make the government's share of the bank even more valuable. As of early 2007, WestLB was valued at approximately seven to eight billion euros. In addition, Linssen went on to say that selling the state's share to another major European bank was a possibility.

> ❝ The bank has set its sights on picking up more mid-sized German operations to stabilise its takings ❞

Recognise this

That said, WestLB won the International Finance Corporation's (IFC) Chairman's Award for Leadership in Sustainable Project Finance in 2007. A year earlier, in 2006, the firm won an impressive slew of awards, including: Dealogic's No. 1 Global Project

Finance Provider, IFC's Sustainable Bankers of the Year 2006, and *Mining Journal's* Outstanding Achievement Award (2006).

GETTING HIRED

Make a real contribution

WestLB take on between 20–40 paid interns each year for its ten week internship, the majority of whom will have registered their intention to join the firm's graduate programme in the following year. As WestLB is a relatively small company, internship opportunities vary with its requirements at any given time. This also means that when it takes you on as an intern, it's because there is some real business that they need you to help them with. You'll be at the heart of a team from the outset, and quickly responsible for the completion of real work.

Where do I sign?

To be eligible for the firm's UK programme you'll need to be in the penultimate year of your degree, on a gap year between undergraduate and postgraduate studies or at the "industrial placement" stage of a sandwich course. You'll also need to hold the right to live and work in the UK, or study in the UK, and hold 300 UCAS points.

To apply, simply complete the application form which you'll find on the company's careers page, www.westlbcareers.com. The closing date is around the end of February but check the site for specific dates around the time of your application. If you're selected, you'll be called in for a competence-based interview with a human resources manager and a business manager, as well as a financial aptitude appraisal test. This interview process is doubly useful — if you perform well in your internship, the firm will fast track you to the second round of the graduate recruitment application process.

Perks of work

While you're interning, you'll receive a monthly payment and two days holiday for each month completed. You'll also have access to the bank's subsidised in-house restaurant and gym, along with its online learning platform.

Best in the West

Approximately 15–20 graduates are welcomed into WestLB each September on the bank's full-time graduate training scheme. The divisions which graduates can apply to varies year-to-year, but a diverse range is usually on offer. These would generally be: global markets, global origination, group treasury, investment management and market risk management. Bear in mind the high level of attention and responsibility you'll get as part of a group of only 20.

For experienced professionals, vacancies at WestLB can be found by clicking the "jobforum" link on the company home page. You can also submit a speculative application here. □

ABOUT THE AUTHOR

Vault Staff Writer Martin Dean received a degree in English from the University of Cambridge in 2005. In addition to working in publishing, he is a musician and published poet.

ABOUT THE EDITOR

Based in London, Saba Haider is the editor of Vault Europe. Prior to joining Vault she spent eight years working as a journalist and editor in Toronto, San Diego, New York, Dubai and Amsterdam. She has a degree in Political Science from the University of Guelph in Canada. She is a Masters candidate at the University of London.

About the Author / Editor